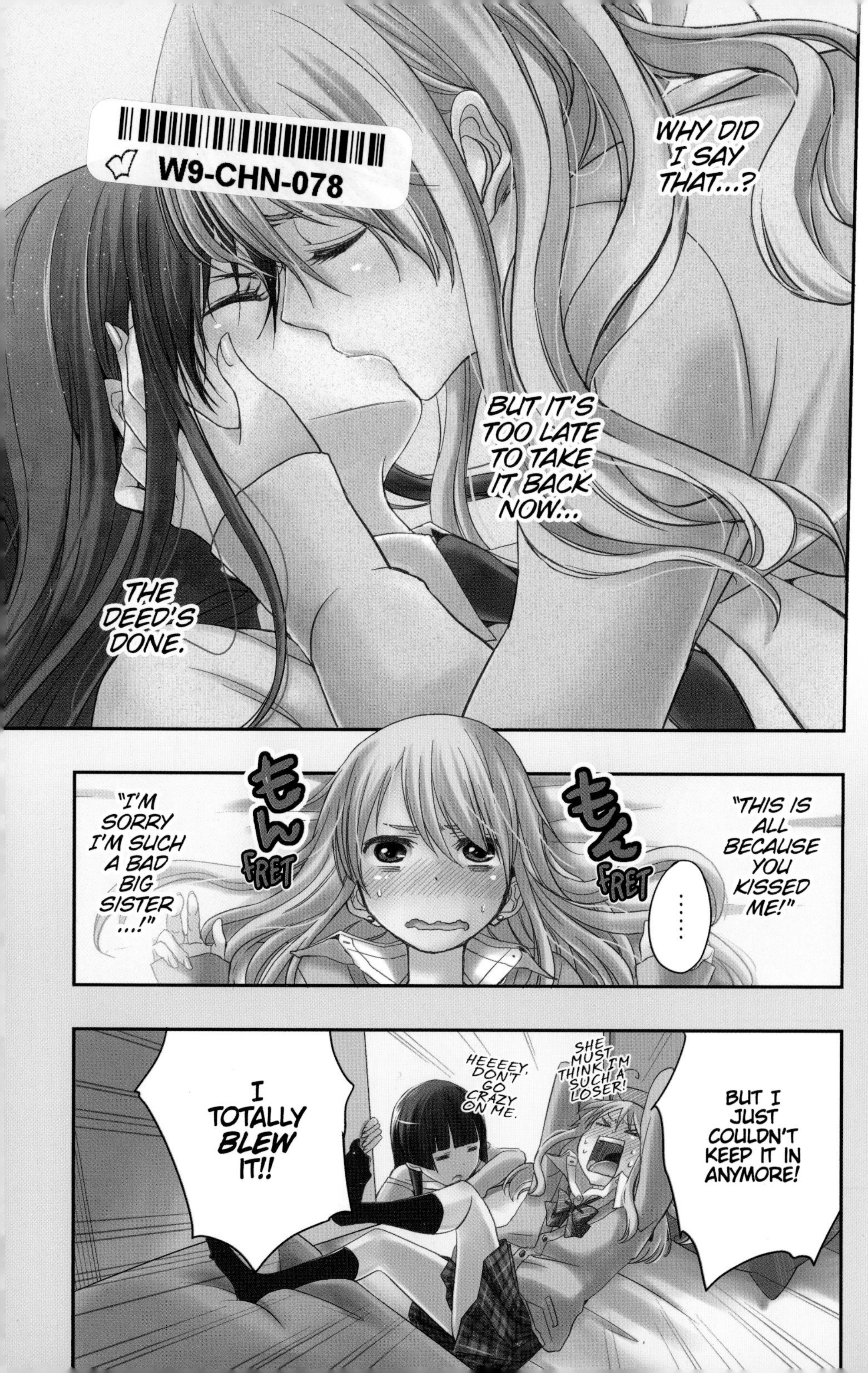
WHY DID I SAY THAT...?
BUT IT'S TOO LATE TO TAKE IT BACK NOW...
THE DEED'S DONE.
"THIS IS ALL BECAUSE YOU KISSED ME!"
もん FRET
......
もん FRET
"I'M SORRY I'M SUCH A BAD BIG SISTER ...!"
BUT I JUST COULDN'T KEEP IT IN ANYMORE!
SHE MUST THINK I'M SUCH A LOSER!
HEEEEY, DON'T GO CRAZY ON ME.
I TOTALLY *BLEW* IT!!

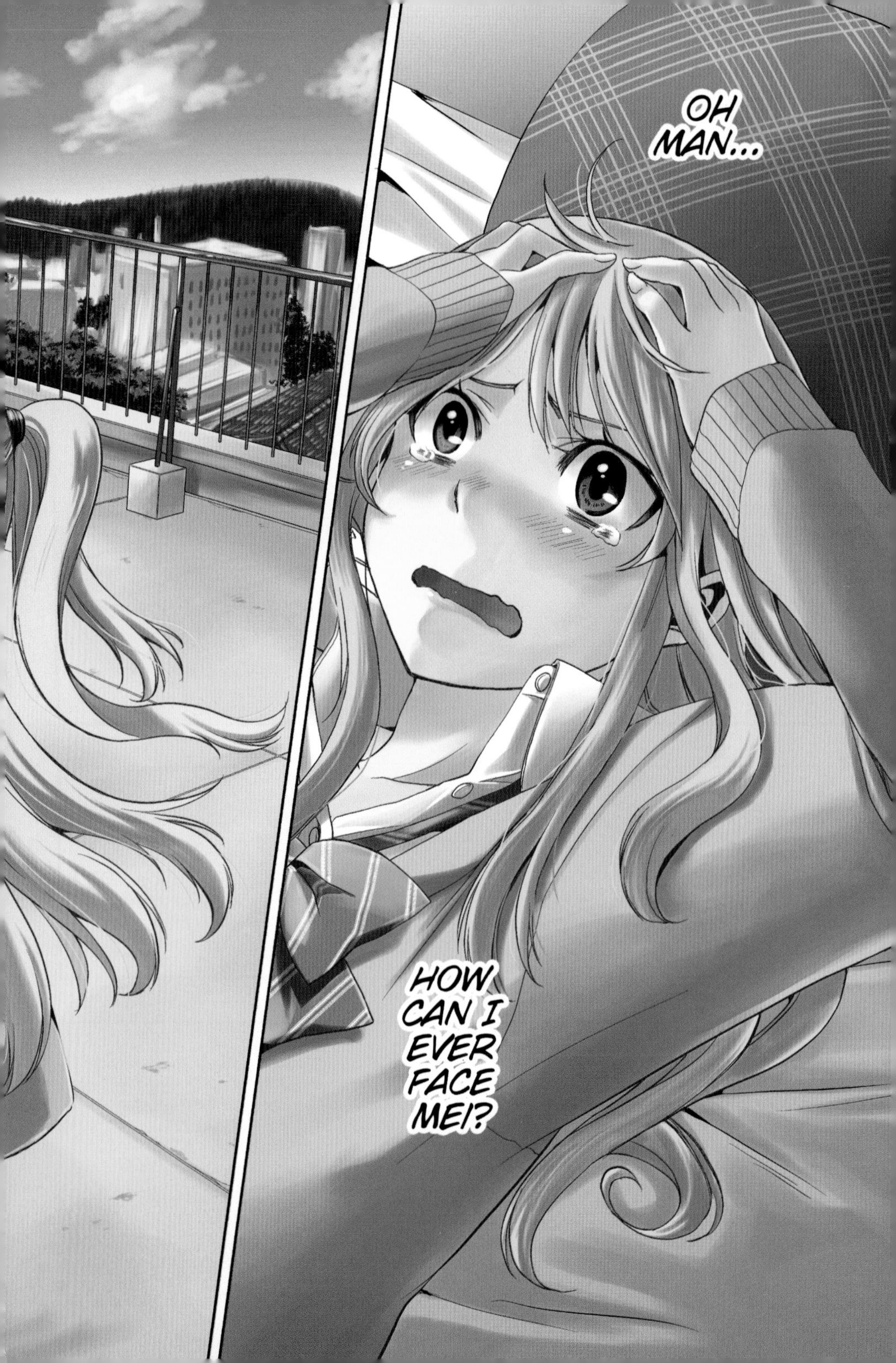
OH MAN...
HOW CAN I EVER FACE MEI!?

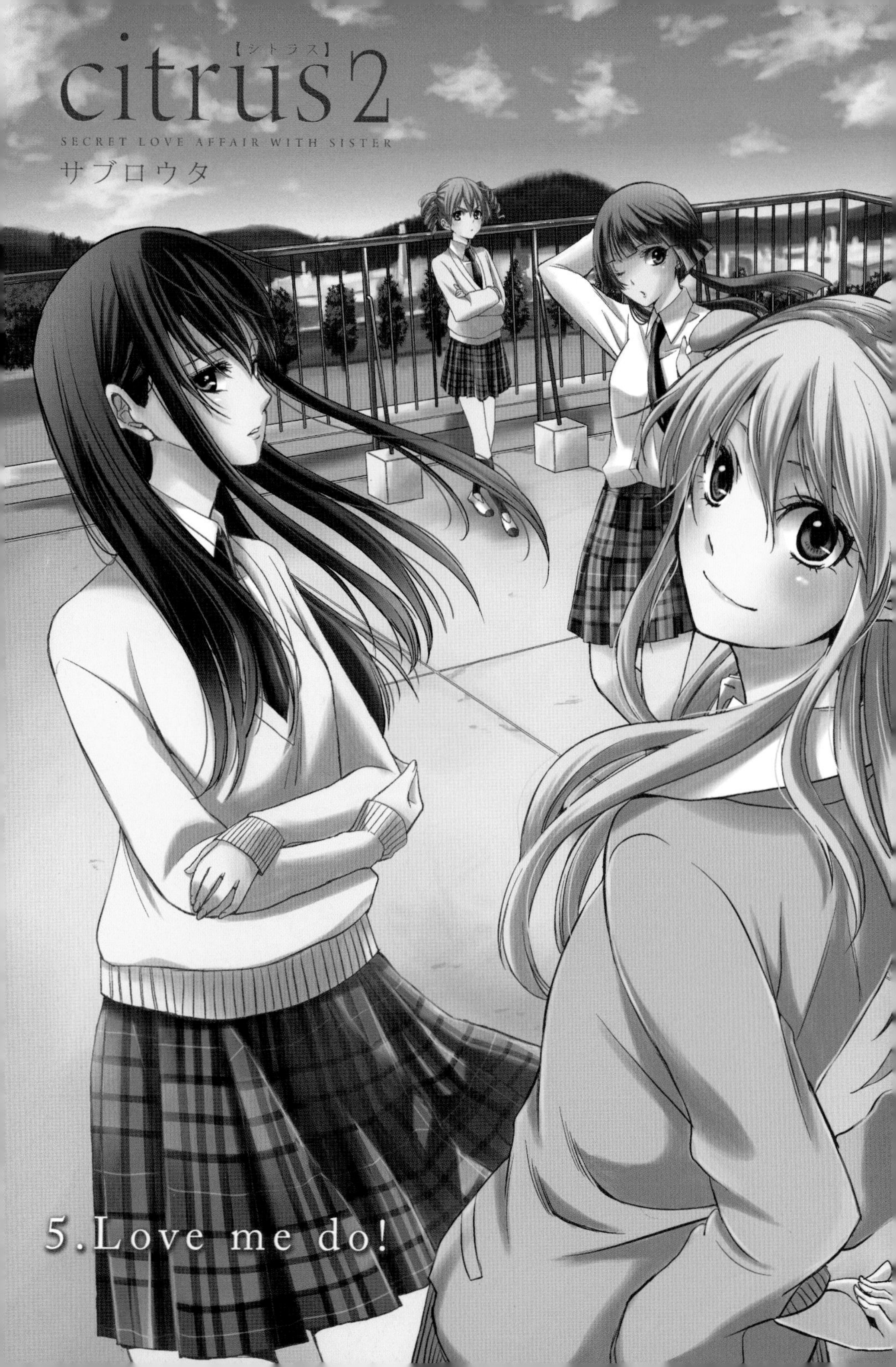
citrus 2
【シトラス】
SECRET LOVE AFFAIR WITH SISTER
サブロウタ
5. Love me do!

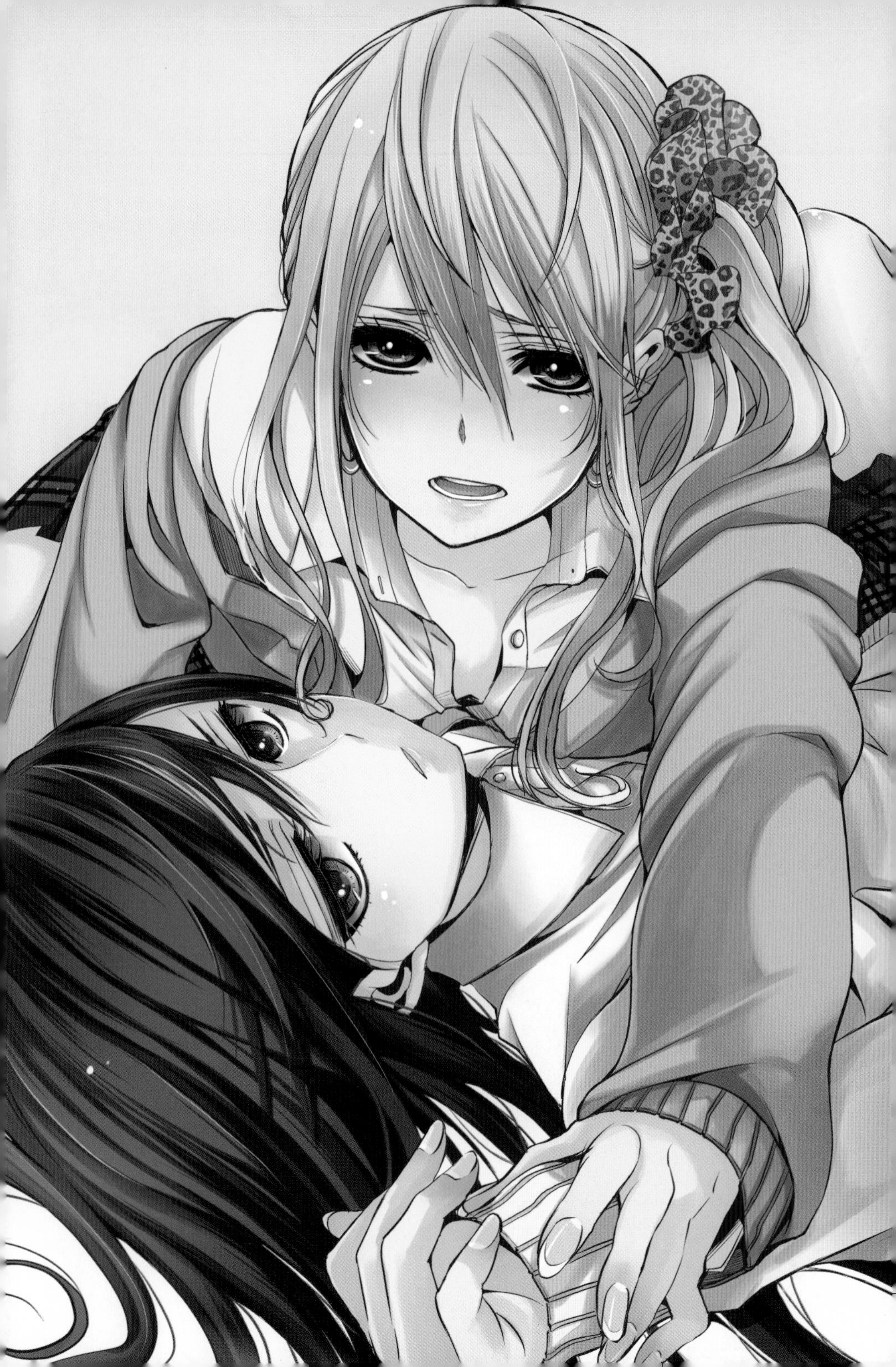

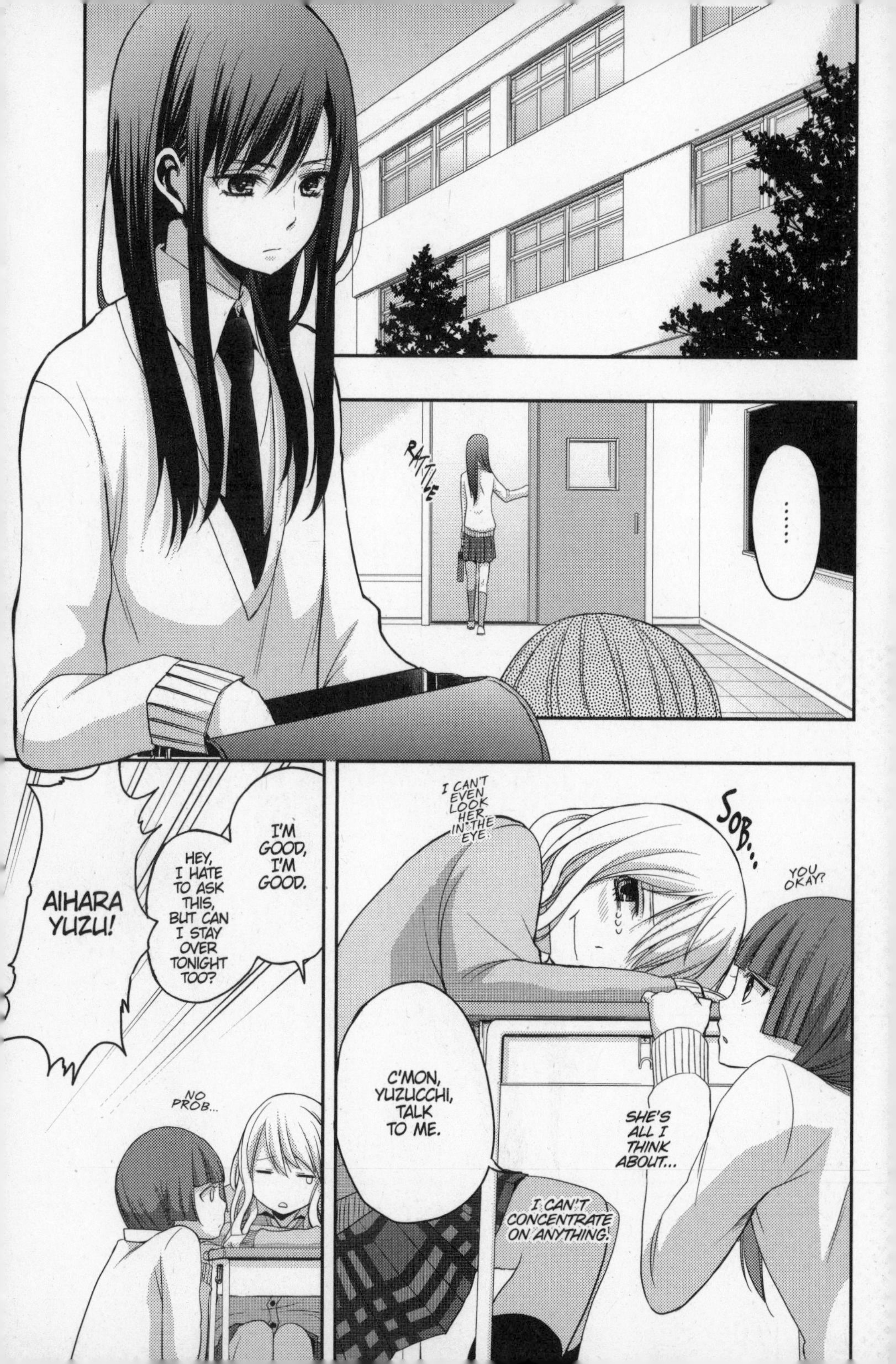
RATTLE
......
SOB...
YOU OKAY?
I CAN'T EVEN LOOK HER IN THE EYE.
C'MON, YUZUCCHI, TALK TO ME.
SHE'S ALL I THINK ABOUT...
I CAN'T CONCENTRATE ON ANYTHING.
I'M GOOD, I'M GOOD.
HEY, I HATE TO ASK THIS, BUT CAN I STAY OVER TONIGHT TOO?
AIHARA YUZU!
NO PROB...

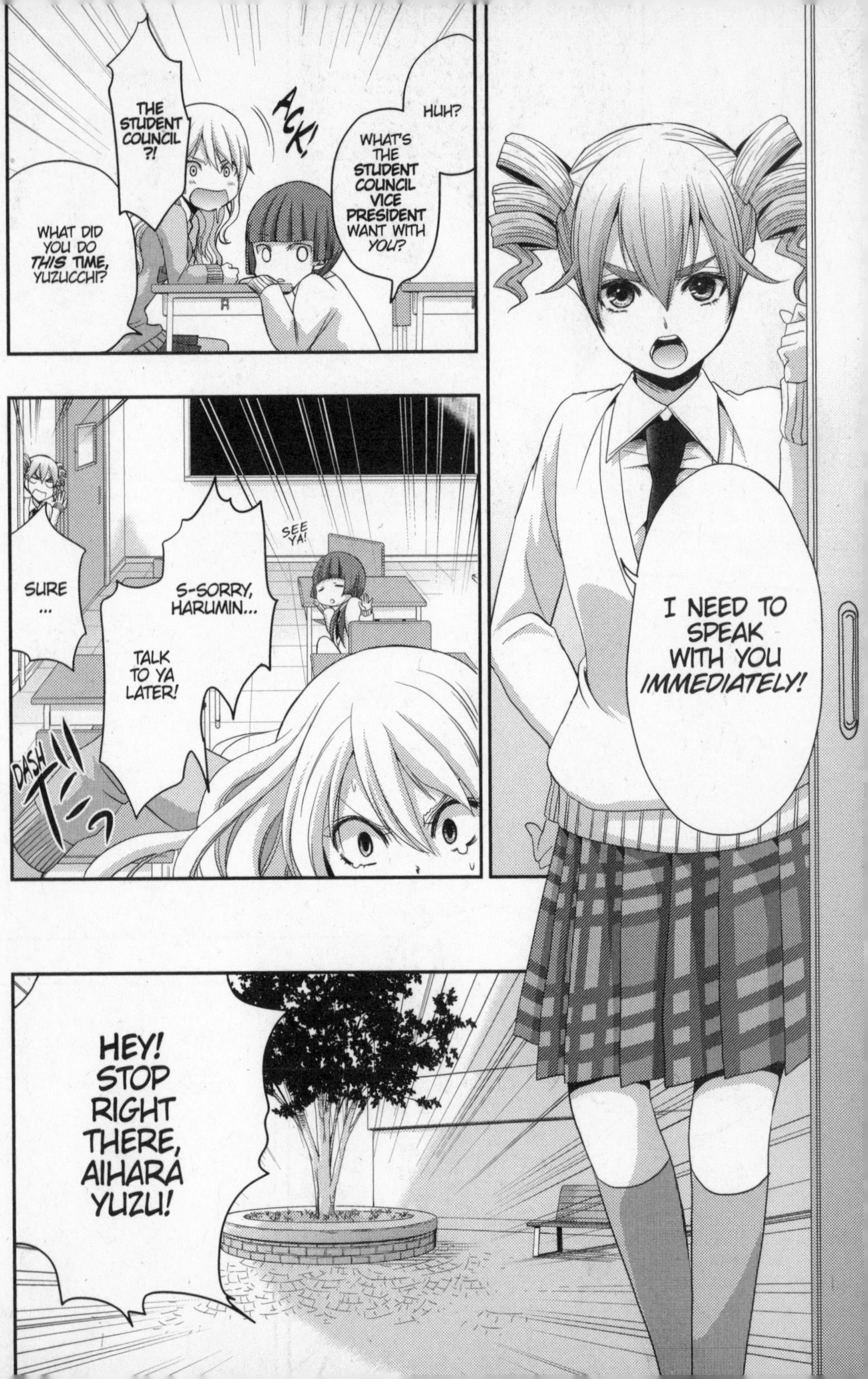
I NEED TO SPEAK WITH YOU IMMEDIATELY!
HUH?
WHAT'S THE STUDENT COUNCIL VICE PRESIDENT WANT WITH YOU?
ACK!
THE STUDENT COUNCIL ?!
WHAT DID YOU DO THIS TIME, YUZUCCHI?
SEE YA!
S-SORRY, HARUMIN...
TALK TO YA LATER!
SURE ...
DASH
HEY! STOP RIGHT THERE, AIHARA YUZU!

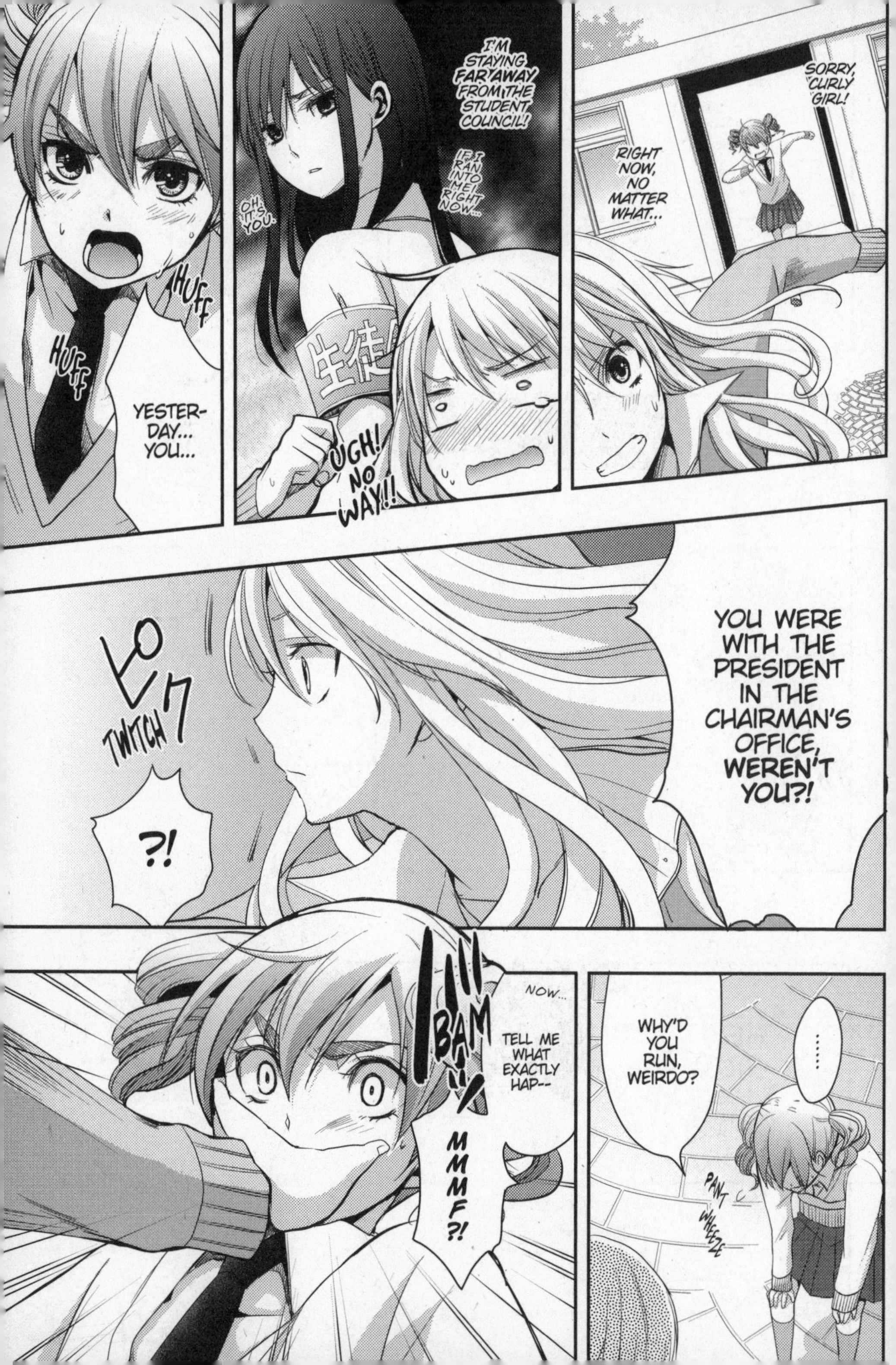
SORRY, CURLY GIRL!
RIGHT NOW, NO MATTER WHAT...
I'M STAYING FAR AWAY FROM THE STUDENT COUNCIL!
IF I RAN INTO MEI RIGHT NOW...
OH, IT'S YOU.
生徒
UGH! NO WAY!!
HUFF
HUFF
YESTER-DAY... YOU...
YOU WERE WITH THE PRESIDENT IN THE CHAIRMAN'S OFFICE, WEREN'T YOU?!
ピクッ
TWITCH
?!
WHY'D YOU RUN, WEIRDO?
......
PANT
WHEEZE
NOW...
TELL ME WHAT EXACTLY HAP--
BAM
MMMMF?!

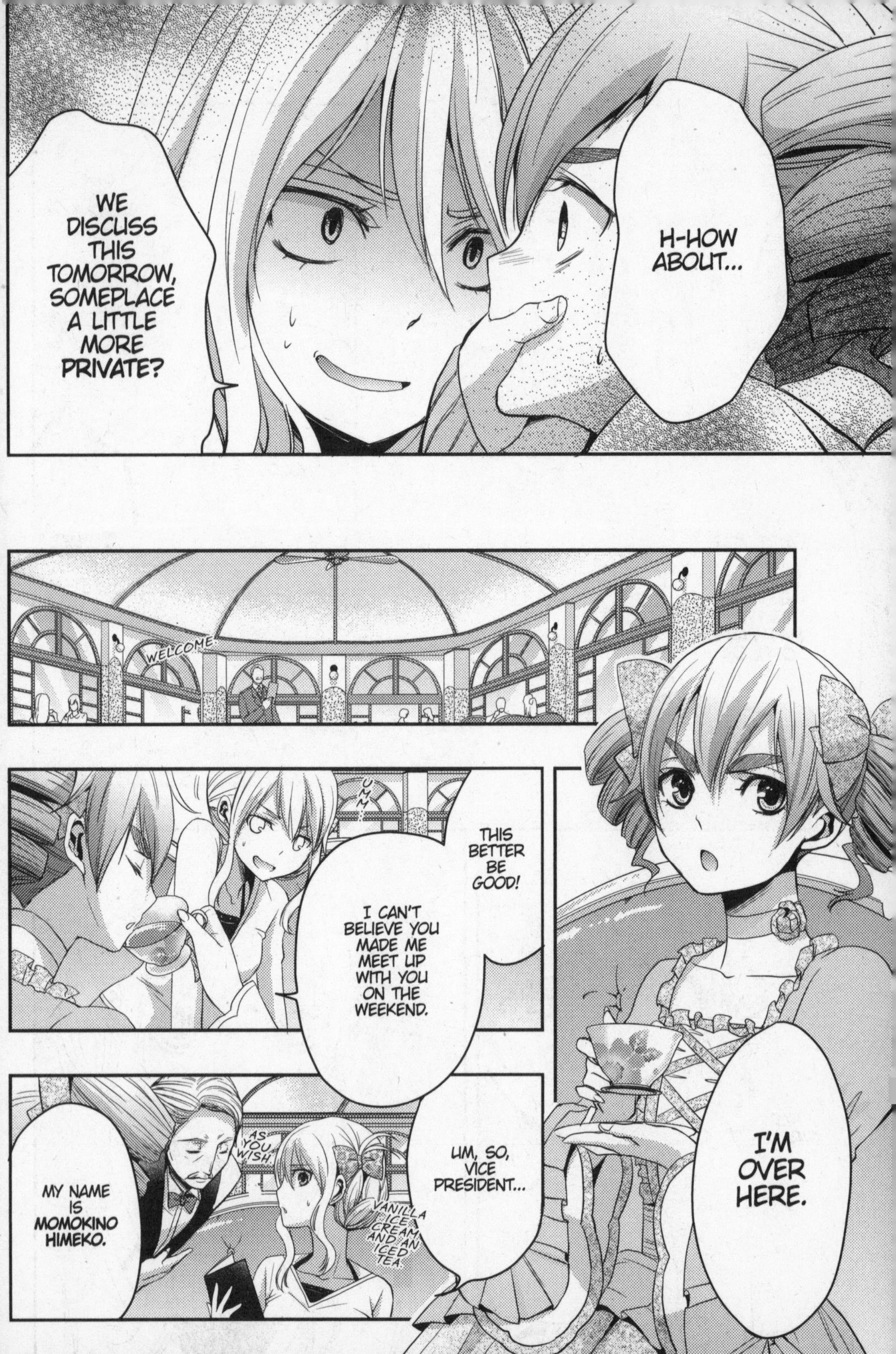
H-HOW ABOUT...
WE DISCUSS THIS TOMORROW, SOMEPLACE A LITTLE MORE PRIVATE?
WELCOME.
I'M OVER HERE.
UMM
THIS BETTER BE GOOD!
I CAN'T BELIEVE YOU MADE ME MEET UP WITH YOU ON THE WEEKEND.
VANILLA ICE CREAM AND AN ICED TEA
AS YOU WISH.
UM, SO, VICE PRESIDENT...
MY NAME IS MOMOKINO HIMEKO.

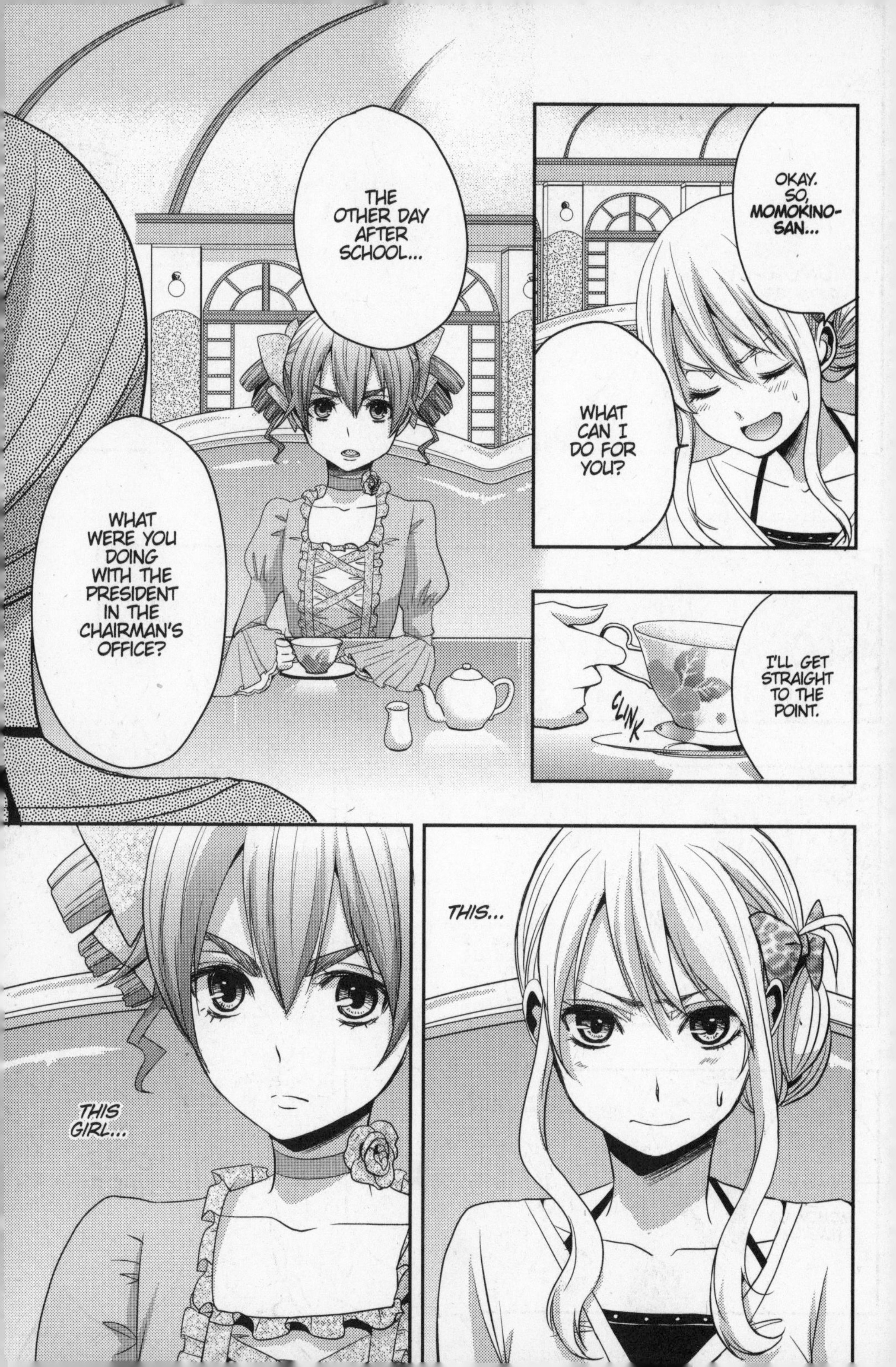
OKAY. SO, MOMOKINO-SAN...
WHAT CAN I DO FOR YOU?
I'LL GET STRAIGHT TO THE POINT.
CLINK
THE OTHER DAY AFTER SCHOOL...
WHAT WERE YOU DOING WITH THE PRESIDENT IN THE CHAIRMAN'S OFFICE?
THIS...
THIS GIRL...

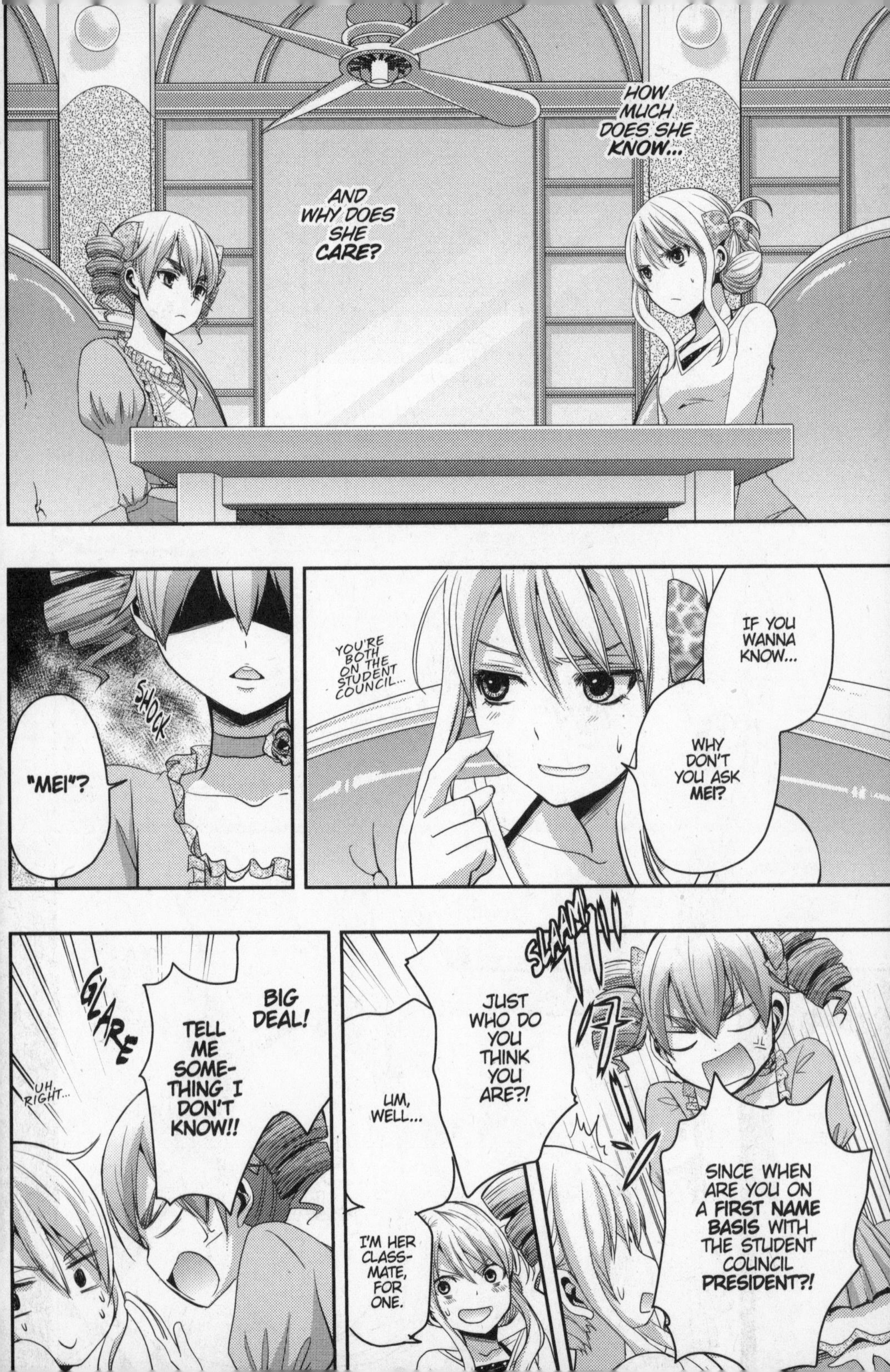
HOW MUCH DOES SHE KNOW...
AND WHY DOES SHE CARE?
IF YOU WANNA KNOW...
WHY DON'T YOU ASK MEI?
YOU'RE BOTH ON THE STUDENT COUNCIL...
SHOCK
"MEI"?
SLAAM!!
JUST WHO DO YOU THINK YOU ARE?!
UM, WELL...
SINCE WHEN ARE YOU ON A FIRST NAME BASIS WITH THE STUDENT COUNCIL PRESIDENT?!
I'M HER CLASSMATE, FOR ONE.
BIG DEAL!
TELL ME SOMETHING I DON'T KNOW!!
GLARE
UH, RIGHT...

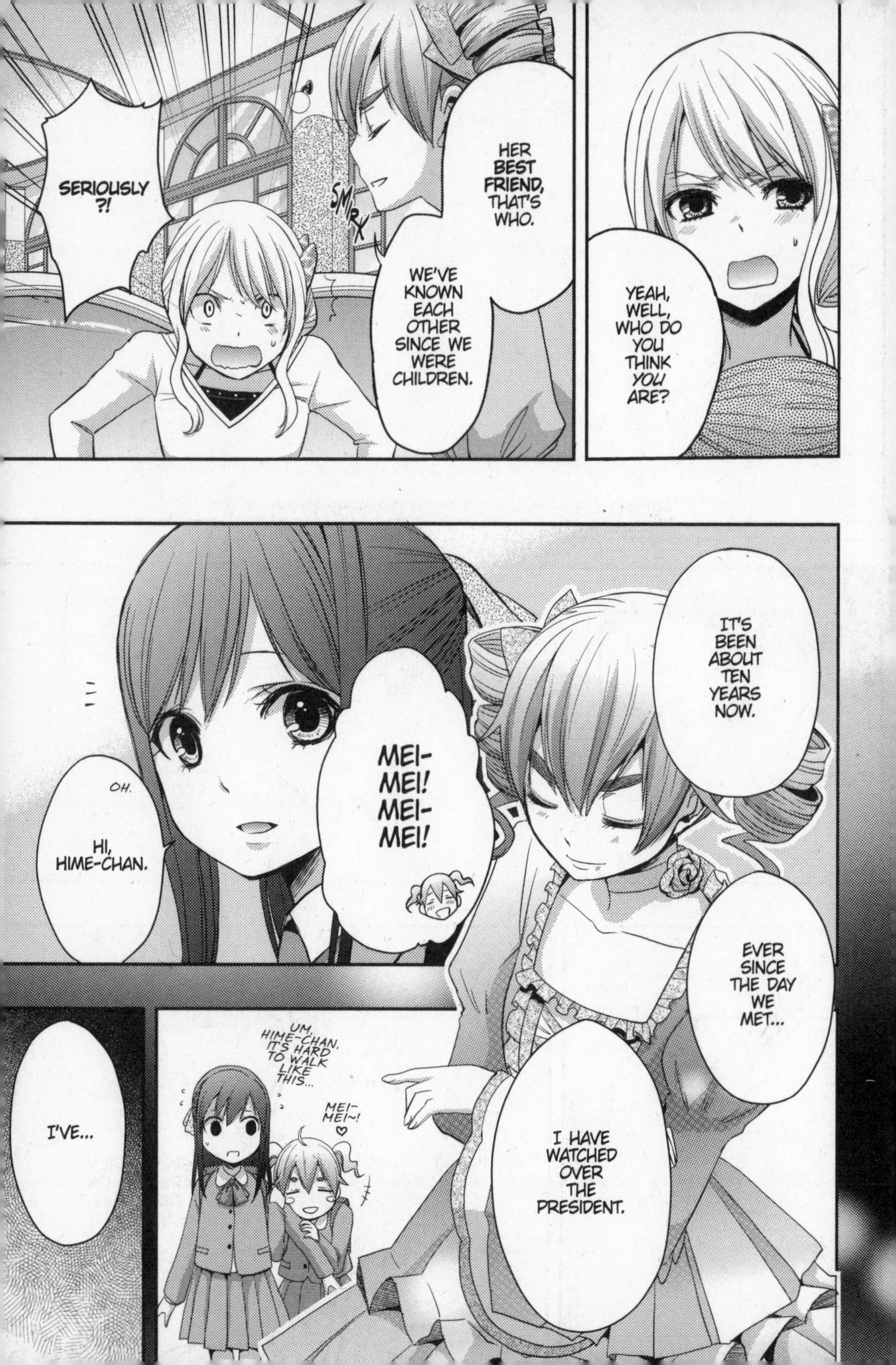
YEAH, WELL, WHO DO YOU THINK *YOU* ARE?
HER BEST FRIEND, THAT'S WHO.
WE'VE KNOWN EACH OTHER SINCE WE WERE CHILDREN.
SMIRK
SERIOUSLY?!
IT'S BEEN ABOUT TEN YEARS NOW.
MEI-MEI! MEI-MEI!
OH.
HI, HIME-CHAN.
EVER SINCE THE DAY WE MET...
I HAVE WATCHED OVER THE PRESIDENT.
UM, HIME-CHAN, IT'S HARD TO WALK LIKE THIS...
MEI-MEI~!
I'VE...

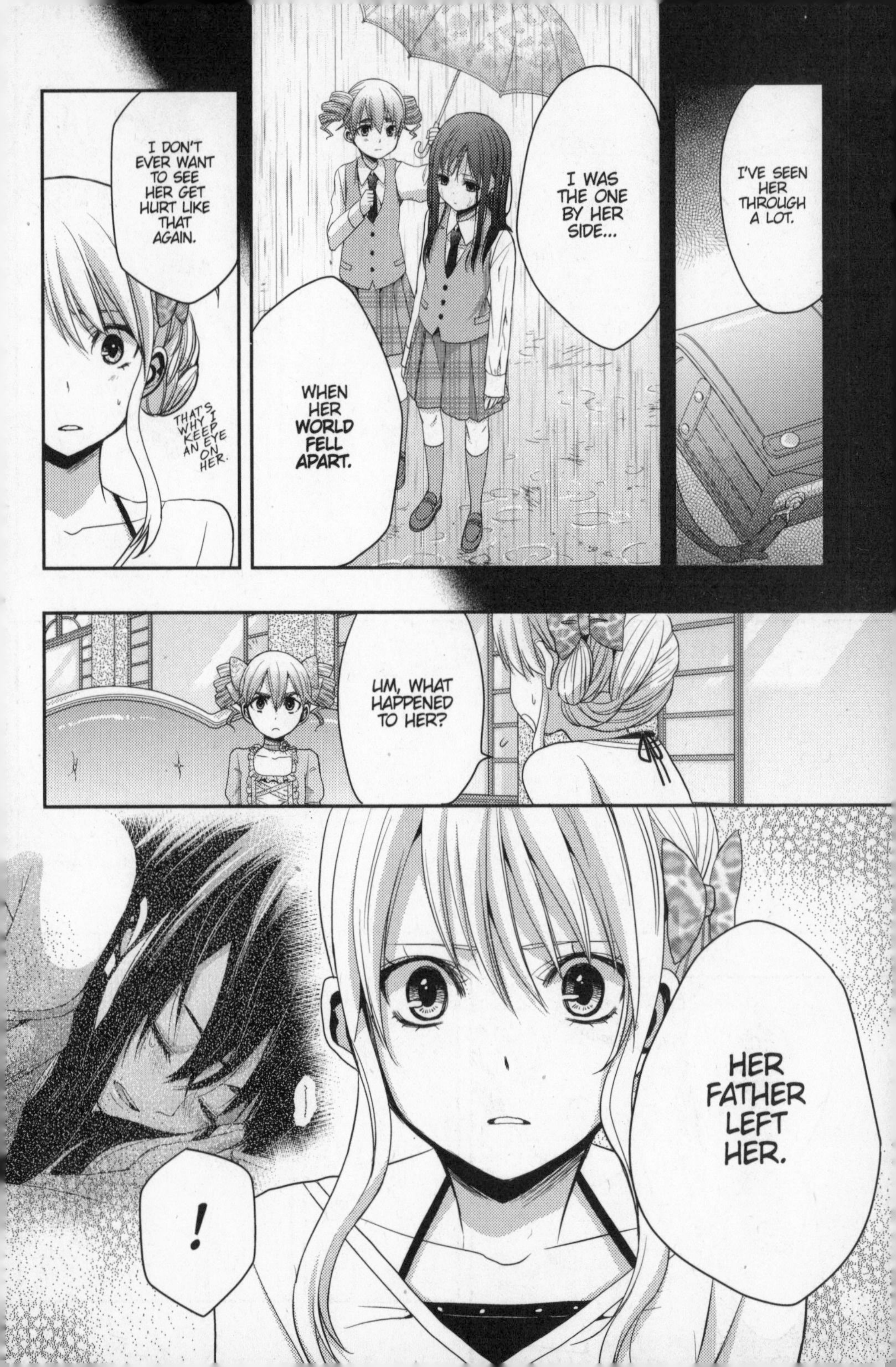
I'VE SEEN HER THROUGH A LOT.
I WAS THE ONE BY HER SIDE...
WHEN HER WORLD FELL APART.
I DON'T EVER WANT TO SEE HER GET HURT LIKE THAT AGAIN.
THAT'S WHY I KEEP AN EYE ON HER.
UM, WHAT HAPPENED TO HER?
HER FATHER LEFT HER.
!
!

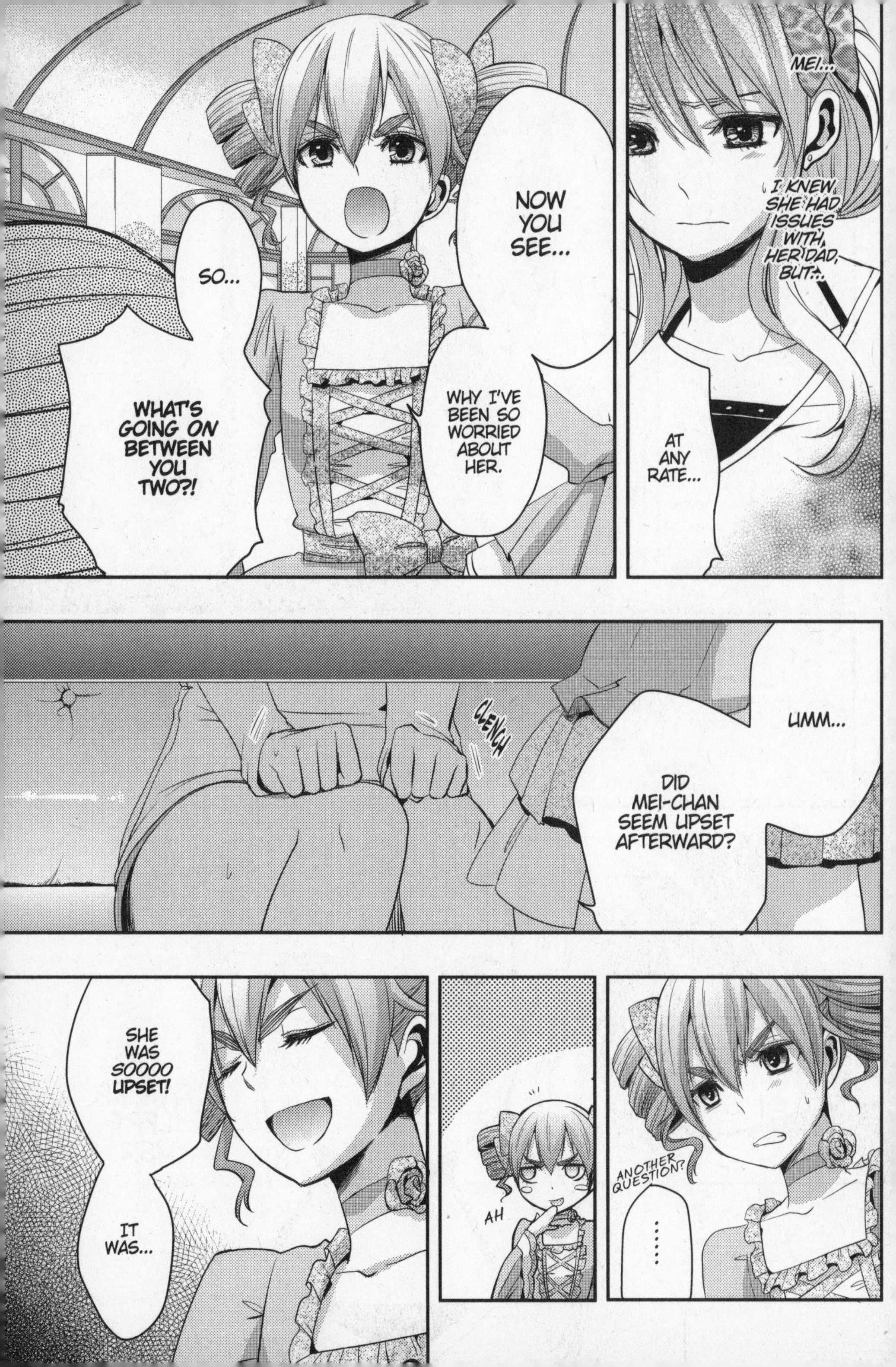
MEI...
I KNEW SHE HAD ISSUES WITH HER DAD, BUT...
AT ANY RATE...
NOW YOU SEE...
WHY I'VE BEEN SO WORRIED ABOUT HER.
SO...
WHAT'S GOING ON BETWEEN YOU TWO?!
UMM...
DID MEI-CHAN SEEM UPSET AFTERWARD?
CLENCH
ANOTHER QUESTION?
......
AH
SHE WAS SOOOO UPSET!
IT WAS...

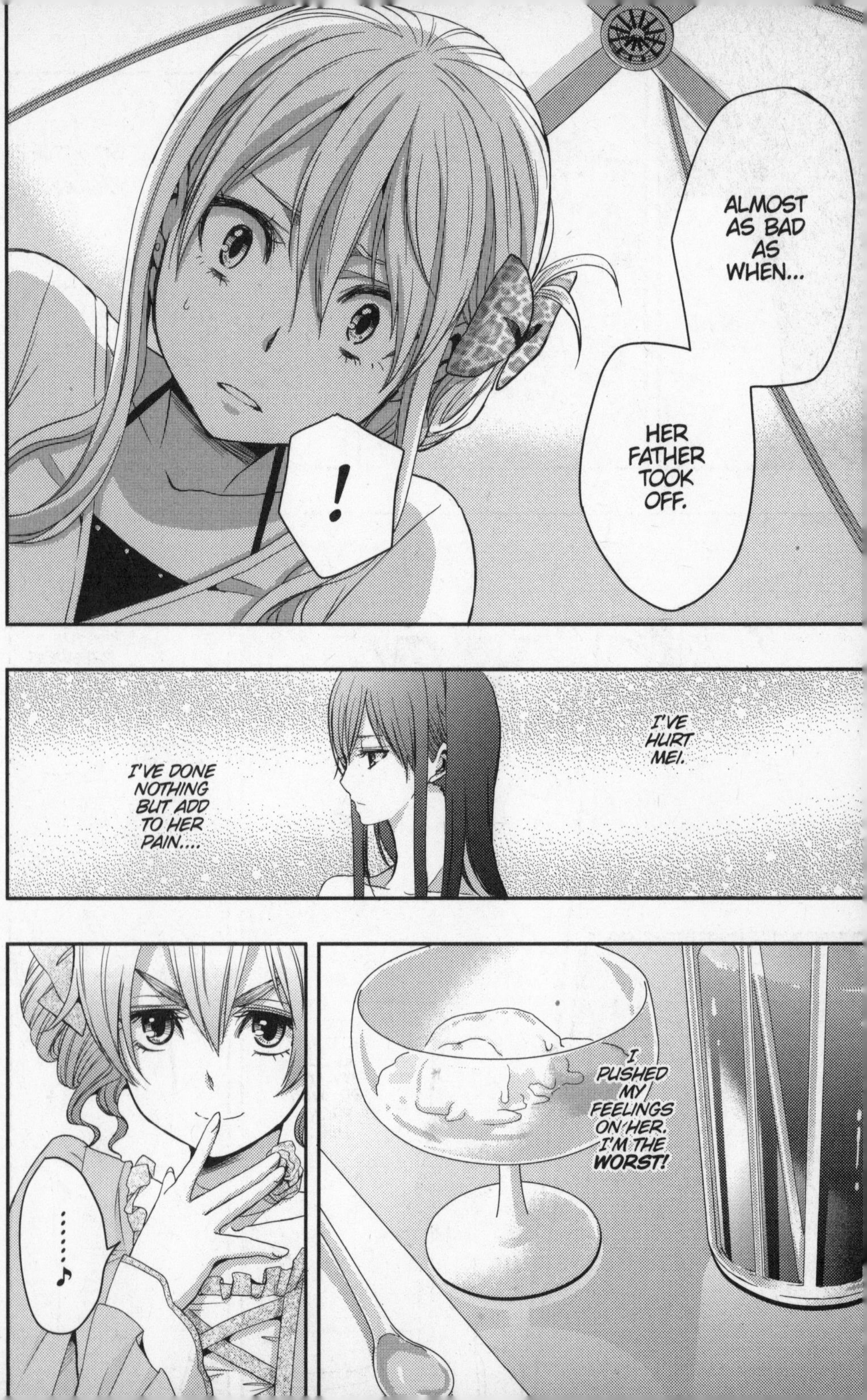
ALMOST AS BAD AS WHEN...
HER FATHER TOOK OFF.
!
I'VE HURT MEI.
I'VE DONE NOTHING BUT ADD TO HER PAIN....
I PUSHED MY FEELINGS ON HER. I'M THE WORST!
......♪

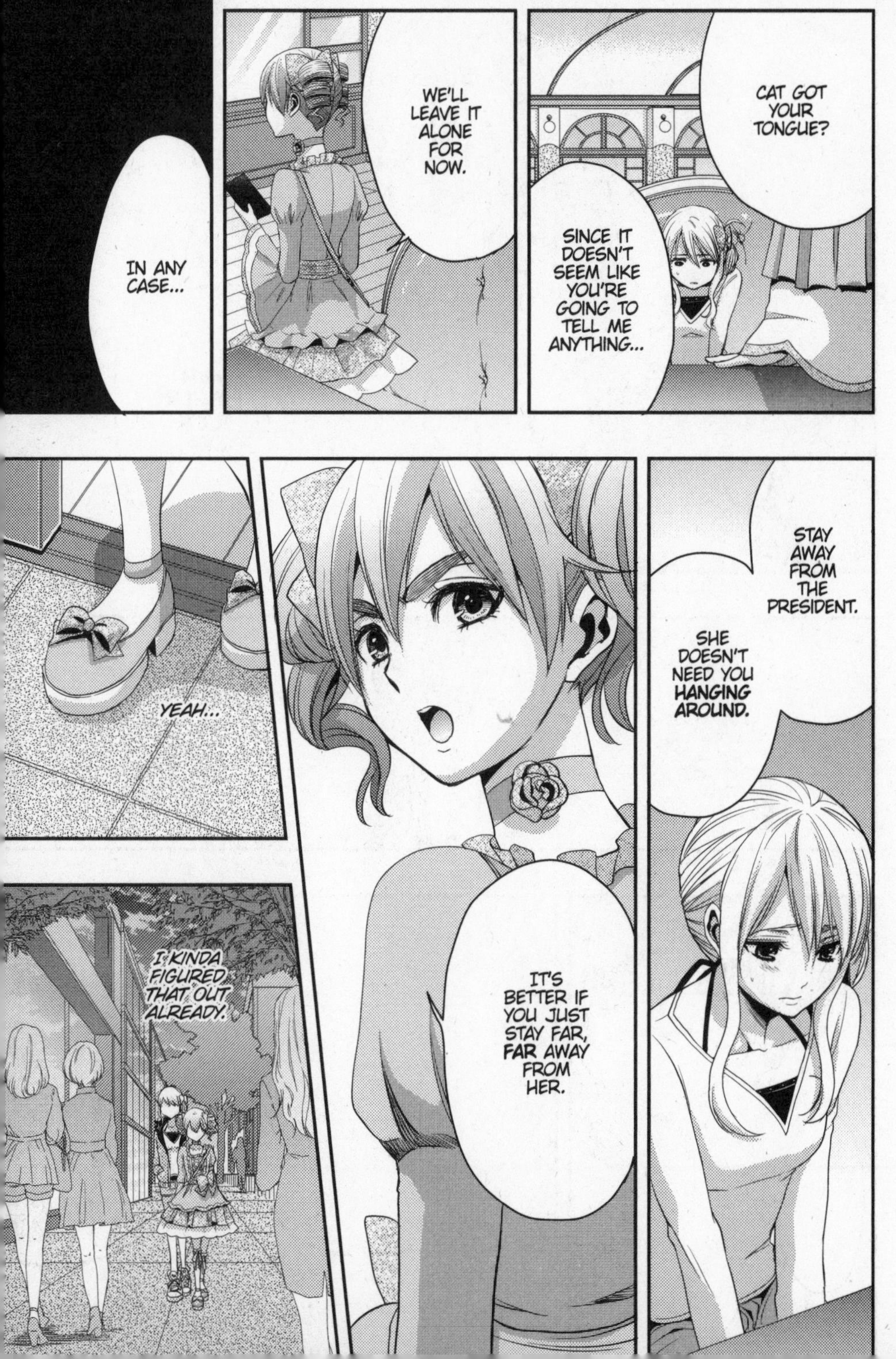
CAT GOT YOUR TONGUE?
SINCE IT DOESN'T SEEM LIKE YOU'RE GOING TO TELL ME ANYTHING...
WE'LL LEAVE IT ALONE FOR NOW.
IN ANY CASE...
STAY AWAY FROM THE PRESIDENT.
SHE DOESN'T NEED YOU HANGING AROUND.
IT'S BETTER IF YOU JUST STAY FAR, FAR AWAY FROM HER.
YEAH...
I KINDA FIGURED THAT OUT ALREADY.

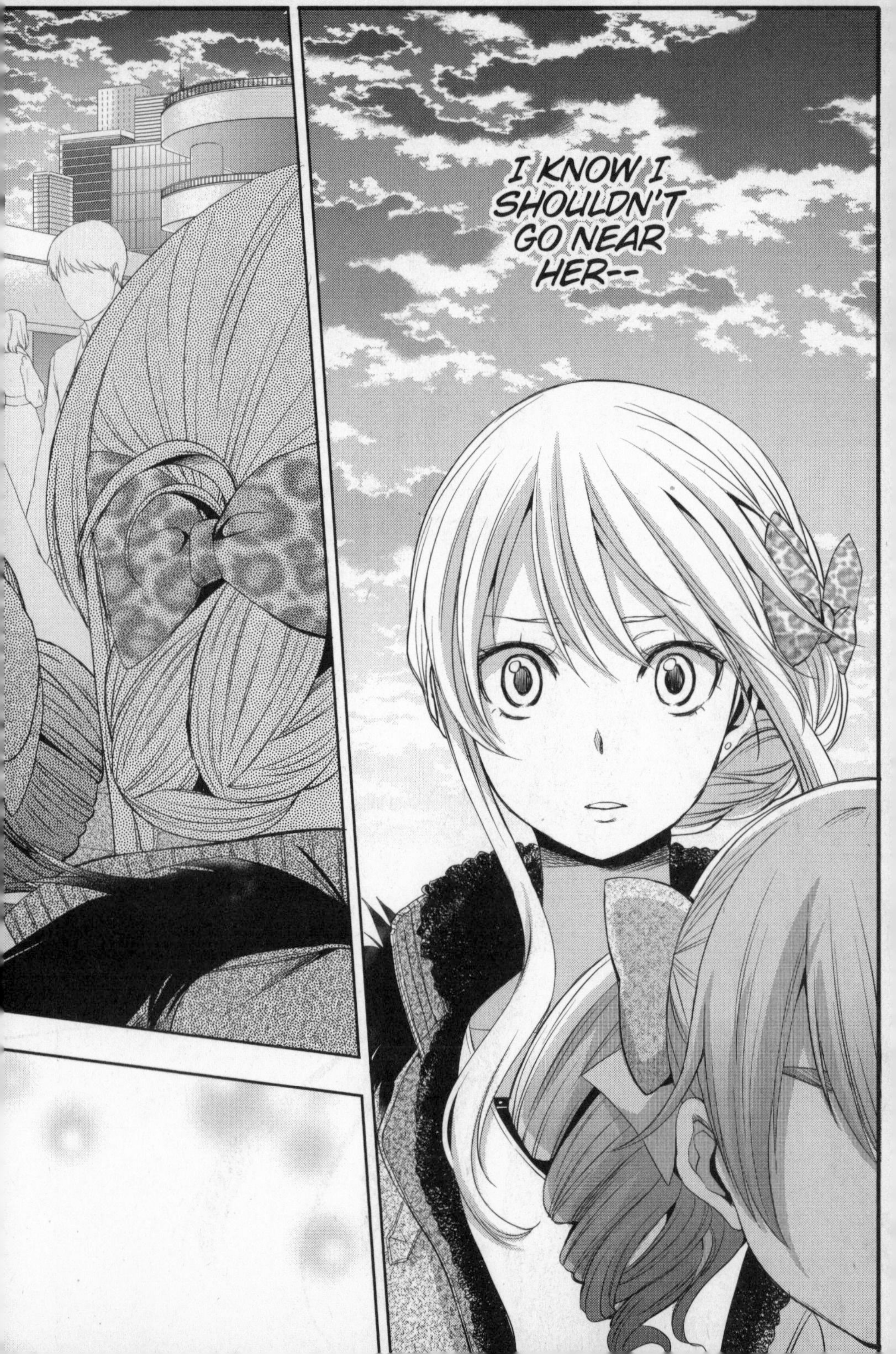
I KNOW I SHOULDN'T GO NEAR HER--

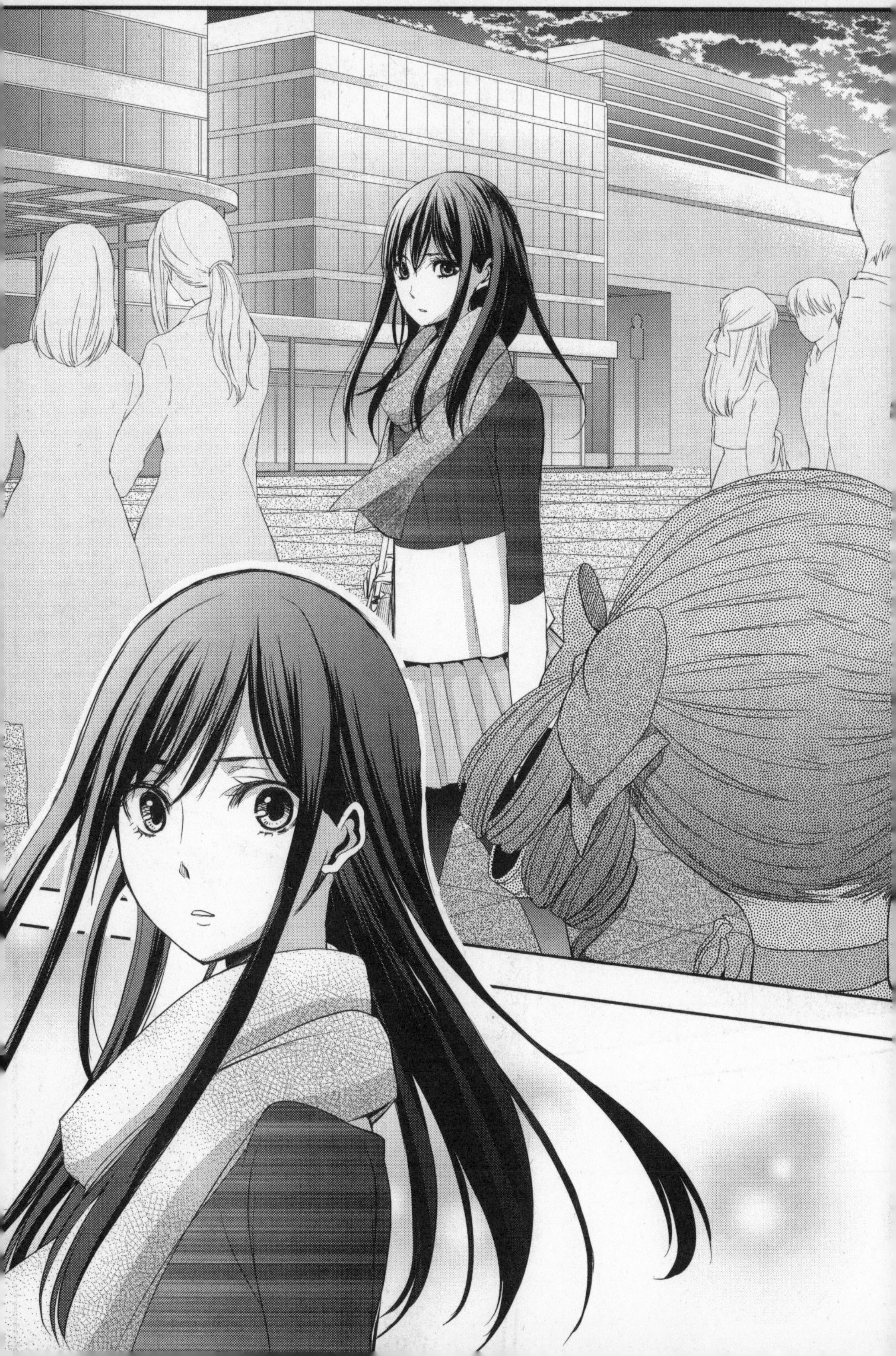

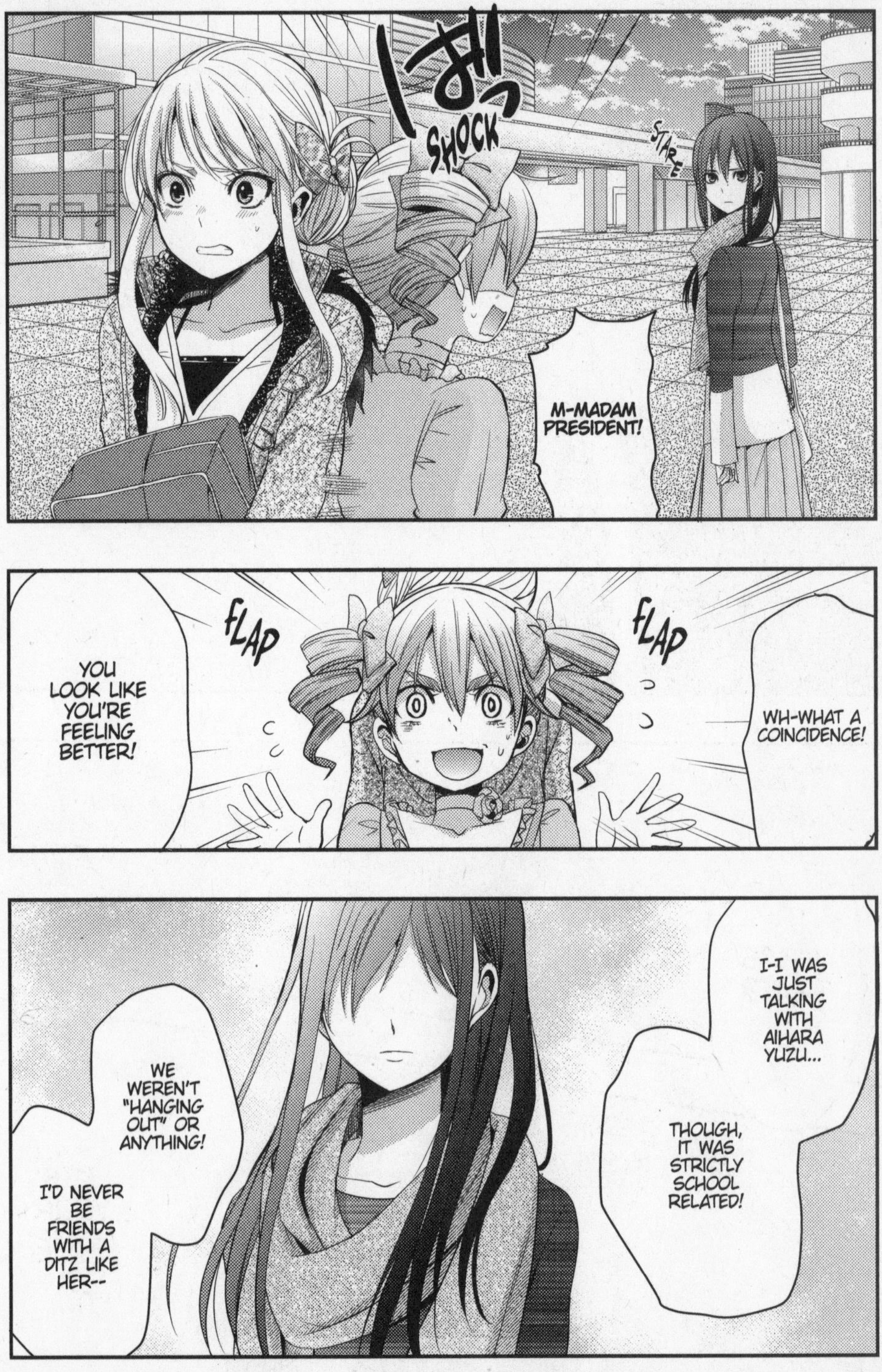
STARE
SHOCK
M-MADAM PRESIDENT!
FLAP
WH-WHAT A COINCIDENCE!
FLAP
YOU LOOK LIKE YOU'RE FEELING BETTER!
I-I WAS JUST TALKING WITH AIHARA YUZU...
THOUGH, IT WAS STRICTLY SCHOOL RELATED!
WE WEREN'T "HANGING OUT" OR ANYTHING!
I'D NEVER BE FRIENDS WITH A DITZ LIKE HER--

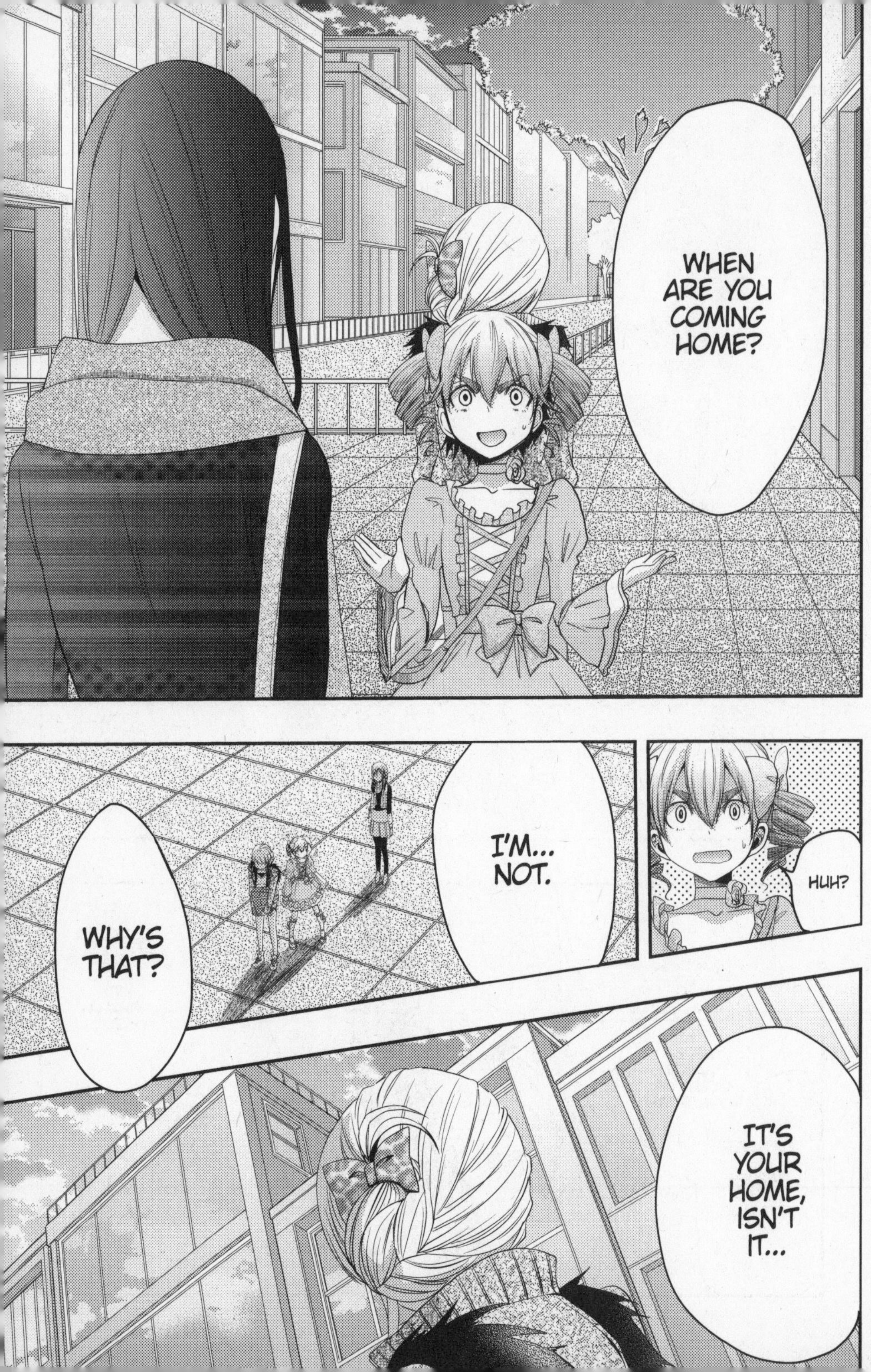
WHEN ARE YOU COMING HOME?
HUH?
I'M... NOT.
WHY'S THAT?
IT'S YOUR HOME, ISN'T IT...

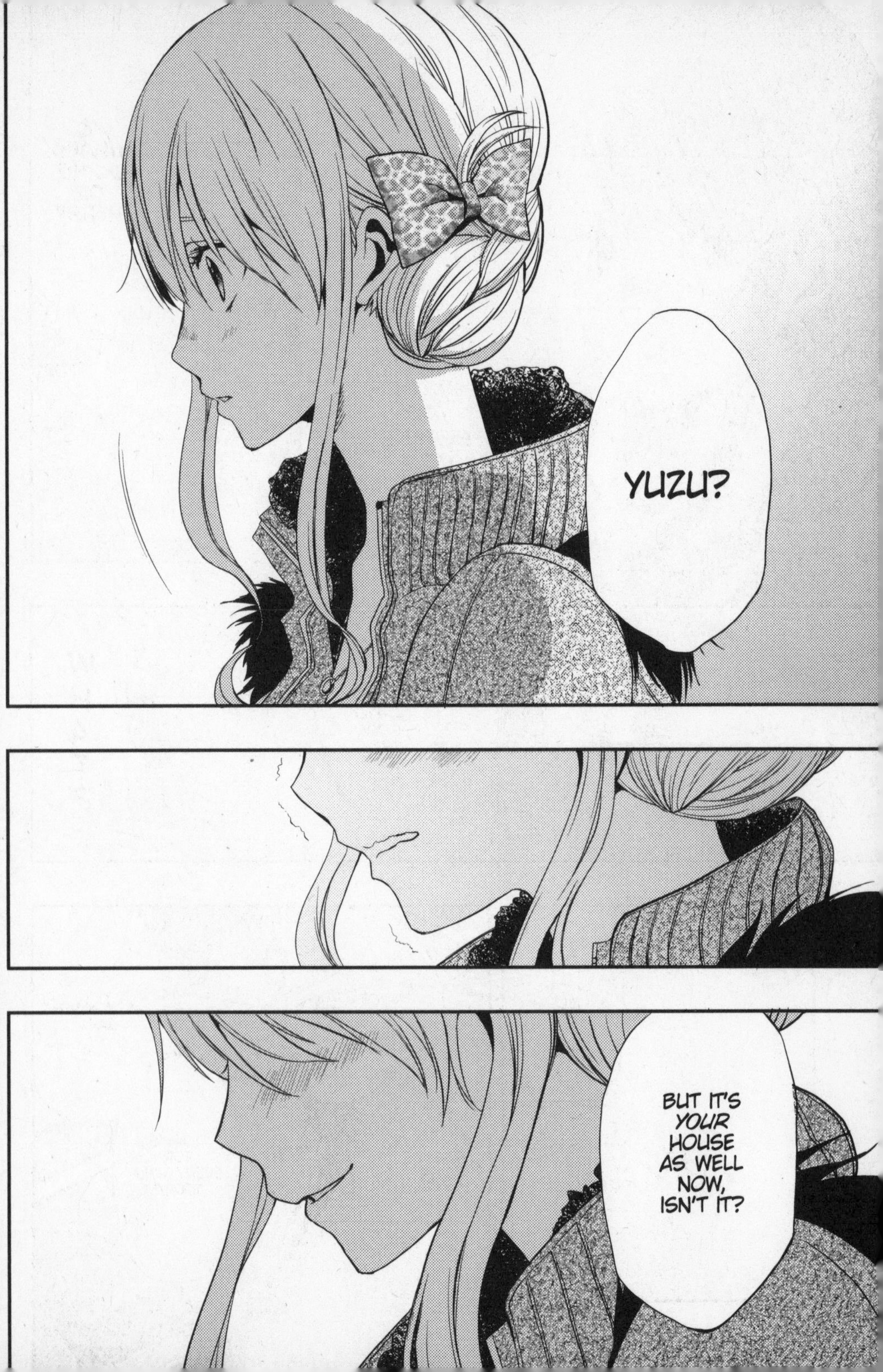
YUZU?
BUT IT'S *YOUR* HOUSE AS WELL NOW, ISN'T IT?

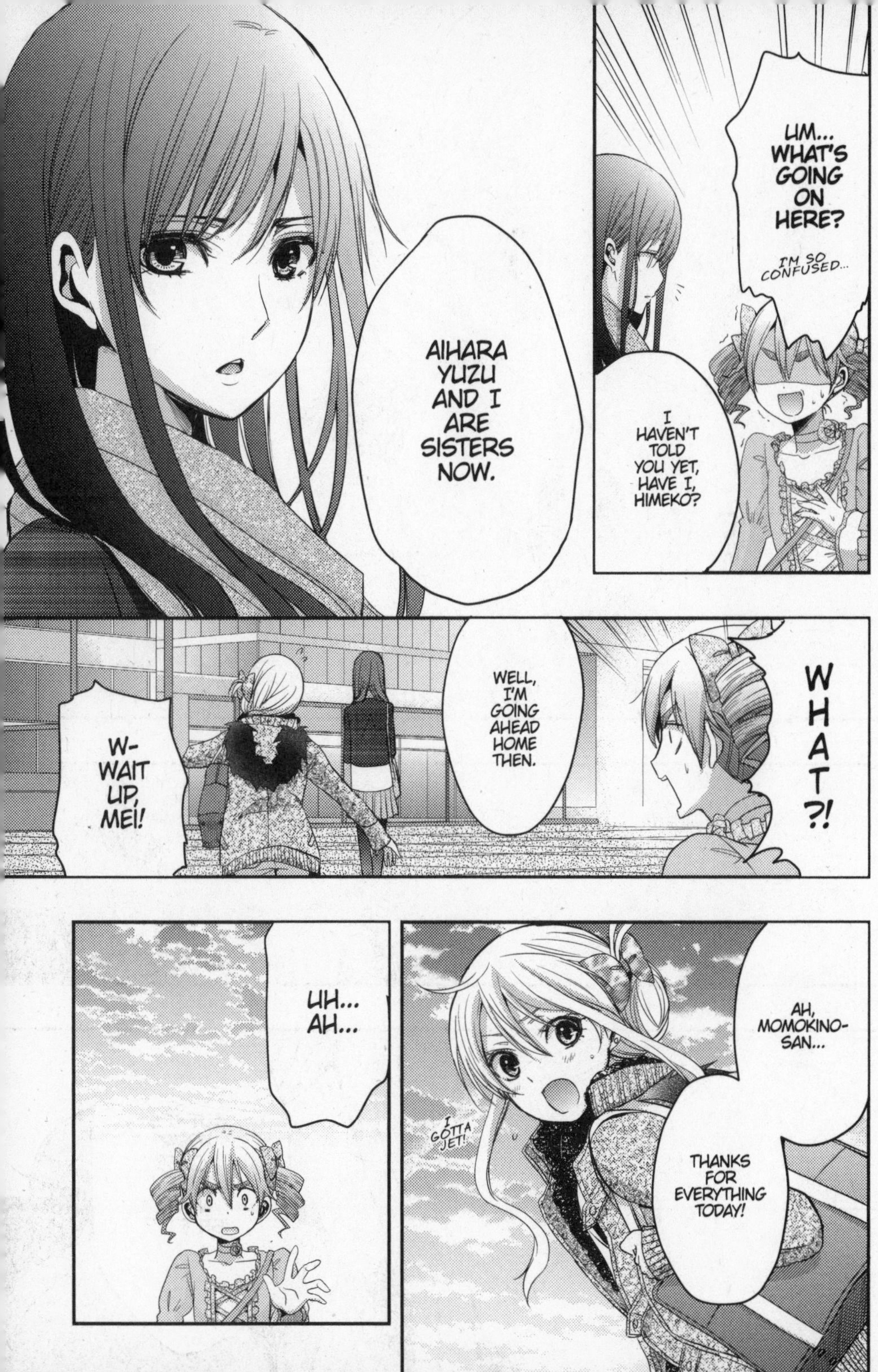
UM... WHAT'S GOING ON HERE?
I'M SO CONFUSED...
I HAVEN'T TOLD YOU YET, HAVE I, HIMEKO?
AIHARA YUZU AND I ARE SISTERS NOW.
WHAT?!
WELL, I'M GOING AHEAD HOME THEN.
W-WAIT UP, MEI!
AH, MOMOKINO-SAN...
THANKS FOR EVERYTHING TODAY!
I GOTTA JET!
UH... AH...

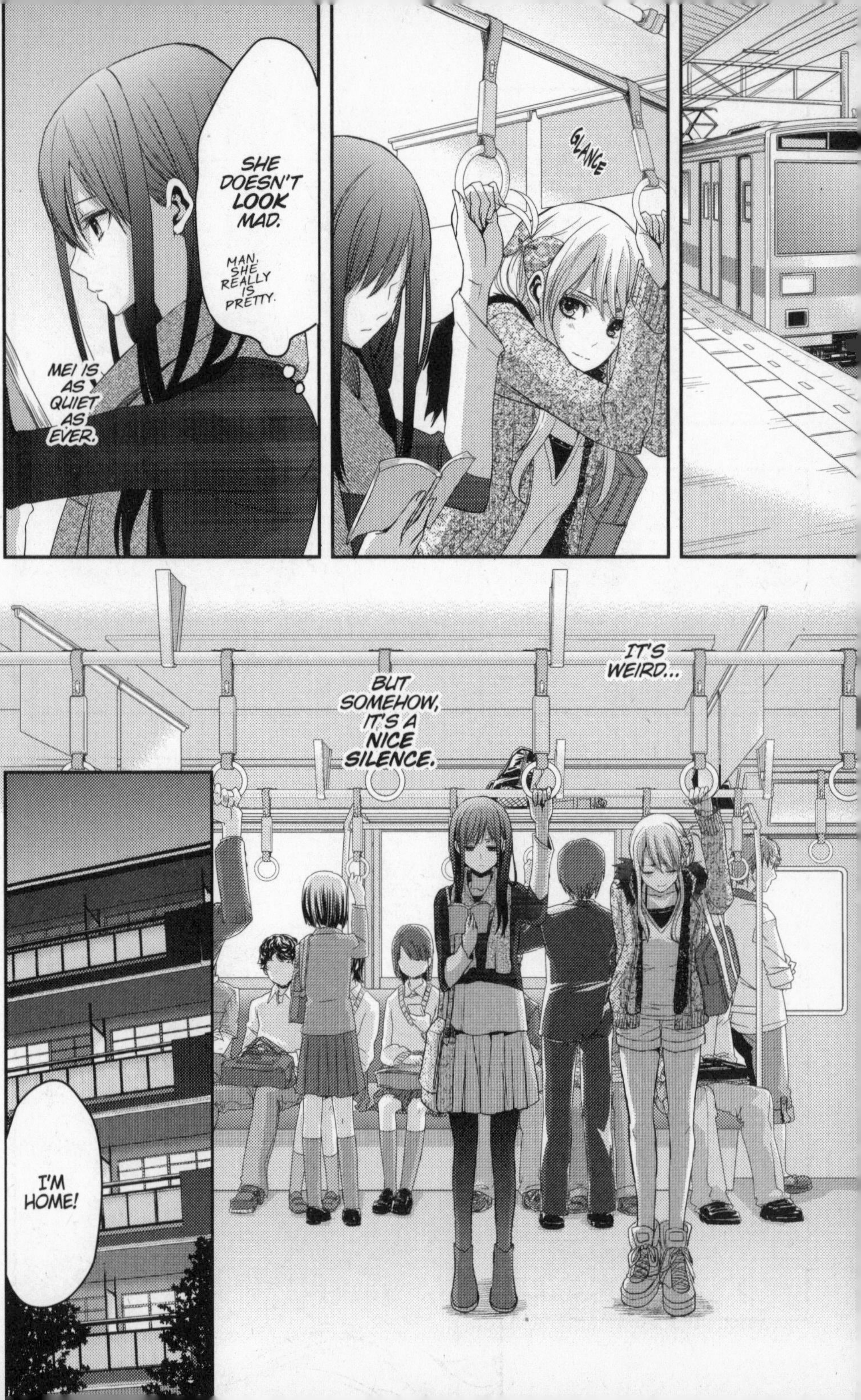
GLANCE
SHE DOESN'T LOOK MAD.
MAN, SHE REALLY IS PRETTY.
MEI IS AS QUIET AS EVER.
IT'S WEIRD...
BUT SOMEHOW, IT'S A NICE SILENCE.
I'M HOME!

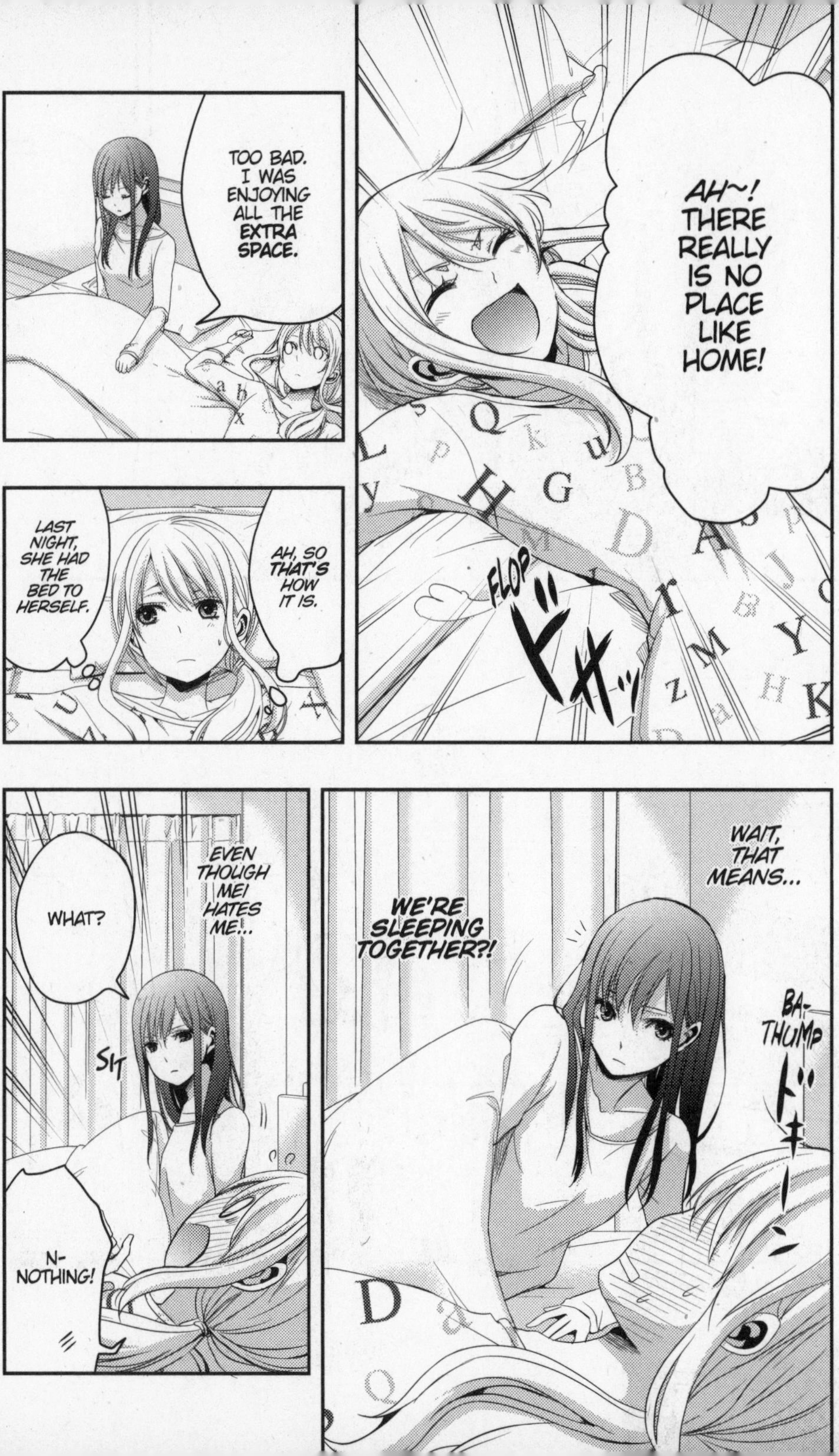
AH~! THERE REALLY IS NO PLACE LIKE HOME!
FLOP
ドサッ
TOO BAD. I WAS ENJOYING ALL THE EXTRA SPACE.
AH, SO THAT'S HOW IT IS.
LAST NIGHT, SHE HAD THE BED TO HERSELF.
WAIT, THAT MEANS...
BA-THUMP
ドキー
WE'RE SLEEPING TOGETHER?!
EVEN THOUGH MEI HATES ME...
WHAT?
SIT
N-NOTHING!

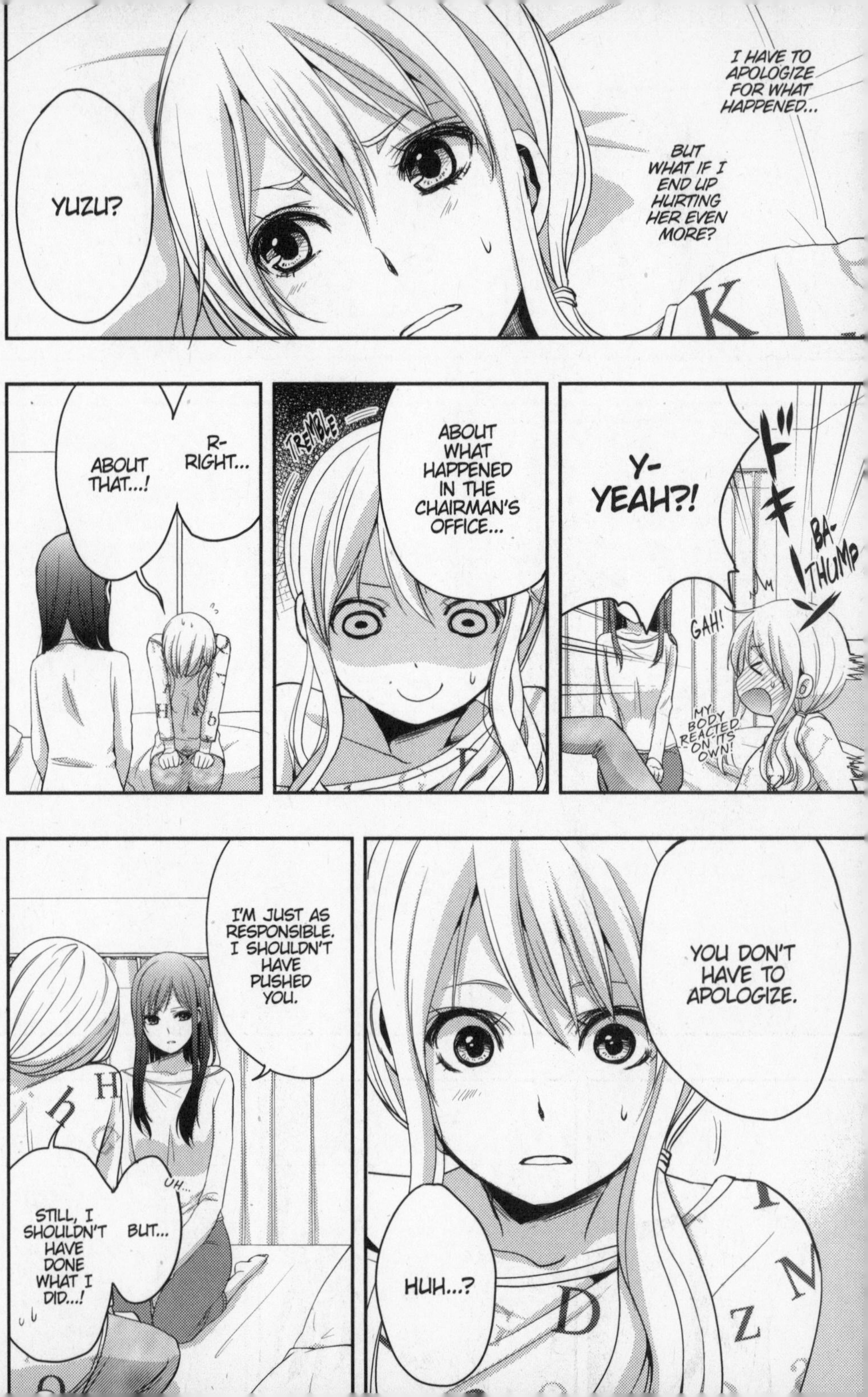
I HAVE TO APOLOGIZE FOR WHAT HAPPENED...
BUT WHAT IF I END UP HURTING HER EVEN MORE?
YUZU?
Y-YEAH?!
BA-THUMP
GAH!
MY BODY REACTED ON ITS OWN!
TREMBLE
ABOUT WHAT HAPPENED IN THE CHAIRMAN'S OFFICE...
R-RIGHT...
ABOUT THAT...!
YOU DON'T HAVE TO APOLOGIZE.
HUH...?
I'M JUST AS RESPONSIBLE. I SHOULDN'T HAVE PUSHED YOU.
UH...
BUT...
STILL, I SHOULDN'T HAVE DONE WHAT I DID...!

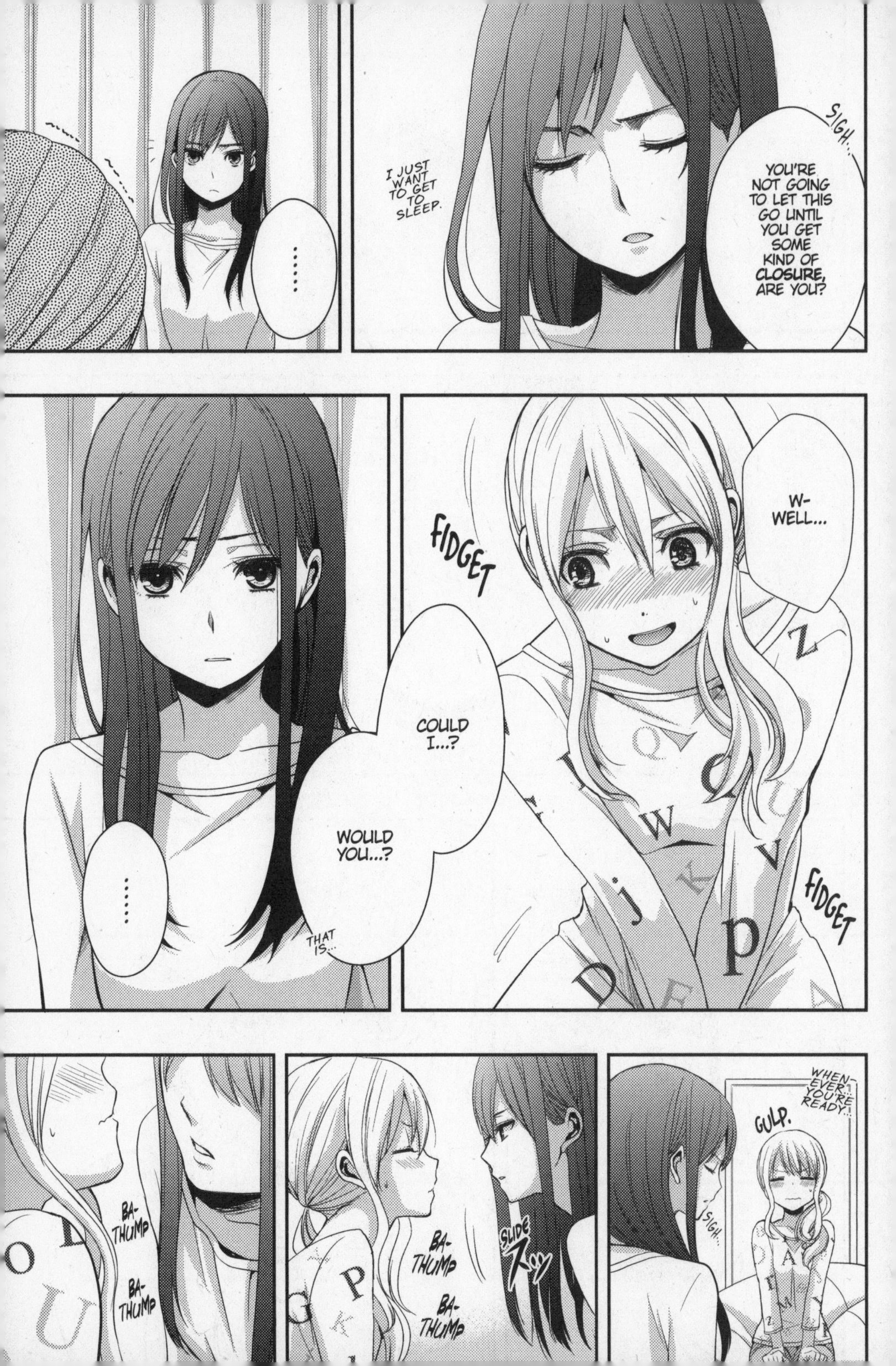
SIGH...
YOU'RE NOT GOING TO LET THIS GO UNTIL YOU GET SOME KIND OF CLOSURE, ARE YOU?
I JUST WANT TO GET TO SLEEP.
......
W-WELL...
FIDGET
COULD I...?
FIDGET
WOULD YOU...?
THAT IS...
......
WHENEVER YOU'RE READY...
GULP.
SIGH...
SLIDE
BA-THUMP
BA-THUMP
BA-THUMP
BA-THUMP

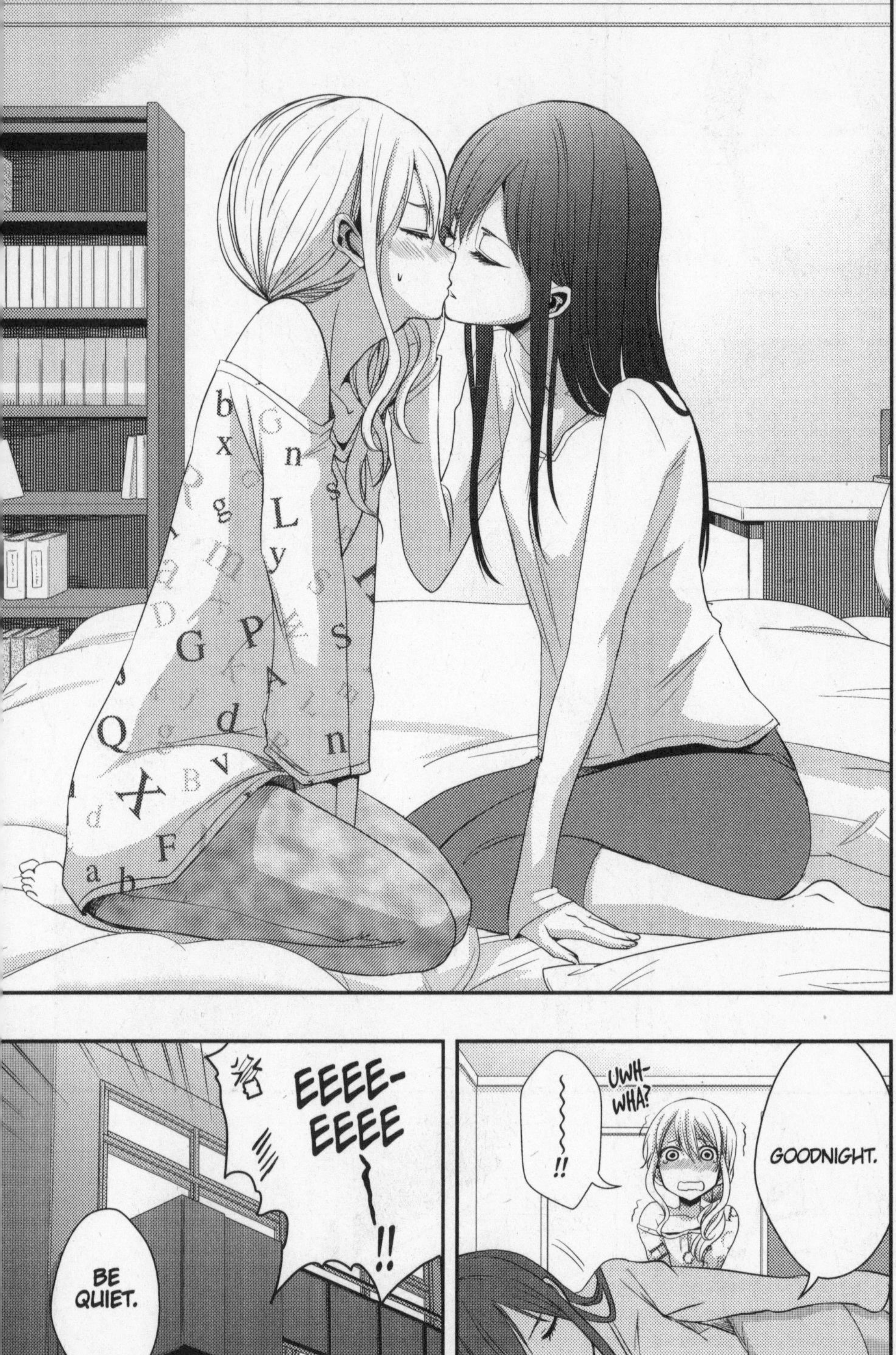
GOODNIGHT.
UWH-WHA?
~~~~!!
EEEE-EEEE~!!
BE QUIET.
~~~~

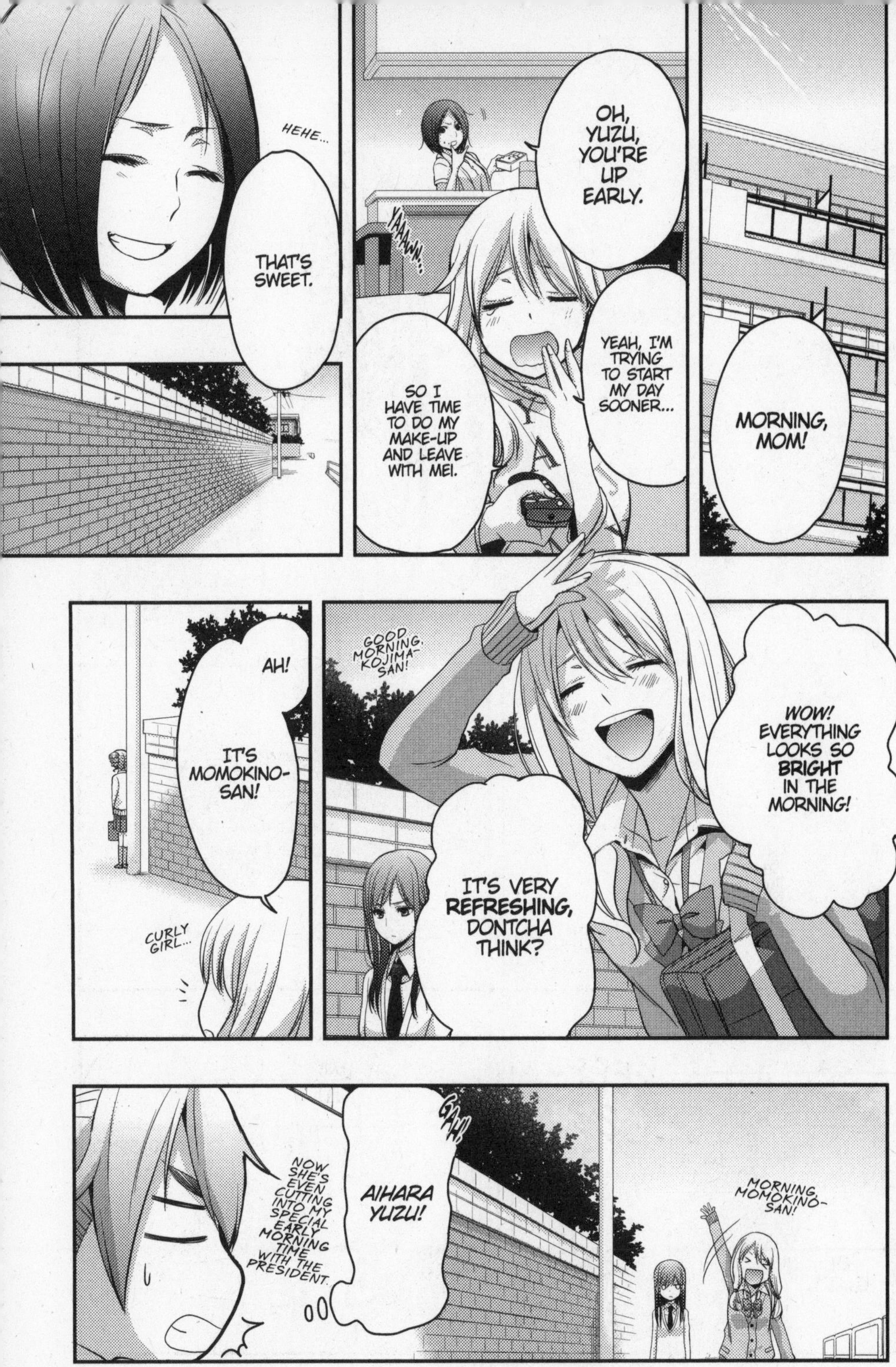
MORNING, MOM!
OH, YUZU, YOU'RE UP EARLY.
YAAAWN...
YEAH, I'M TRYING TO START MY DAY SOONER...
SO I HAVE TIME TO DO MY MAKE-UP AND LEAVE WITH MEI.
HEHE...
THAT'S SWEET.
GOOD MORNING, KOJIMA-SAN!
WOW! EVERYTHING LOOKS SO BRIGHT IN THE MORNING!
IT'S VERY REFRESHING, DONTCHA THINK?
AH!
IT'S MOMOKINO-SAN!
CURLY GIRL...
MORNING, MOMOKINO-SAN!
GAH!
AIHARA YUZU!
NOW SHE'S EVEN CUTTING INTO MY SPECIAL EARLY MORNING TIME WITH THE PRESIDENT.

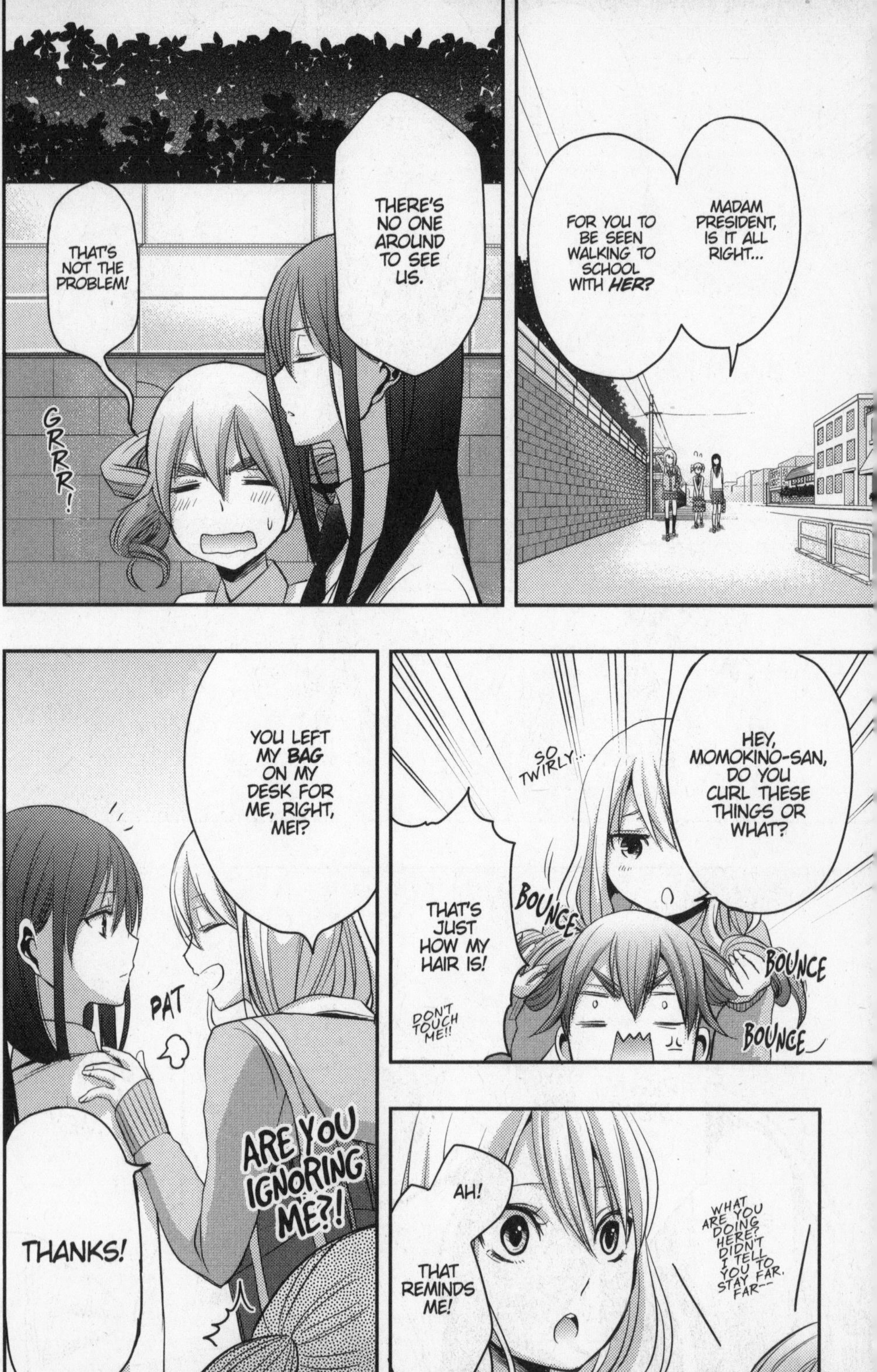
MADAM PRESIDENT, IS IT ALL RIGHT...
FOR YOU TO BE SEEN WALKING TO SCHOOL WITH HER?
THERE'S NO ONE AROUND TO SEE US.
THAT'S NOT THE PROBLEM!
GRRR!
HEY, MOMOKINO-SAN, DO YOU CURL THESE THINGS OR WHAT?
SO TWIRLY...
BOUNCE
BOUNCE
BOUNCE
THAT'S JUST HOW MY HAIR IS!
DON'T TOUCH ME!!
AH!
THAT REMINDS ME!
WHAT ARE YOU DOING HERE? DIDN'T I TELL YOU TO STAY FAR, FAR--
YOU LEFT MY BAG ON MY DESK FOR ME, RIGHT, MEI?
PAT
THANKS!
ARE YOU IGNORING ME?!

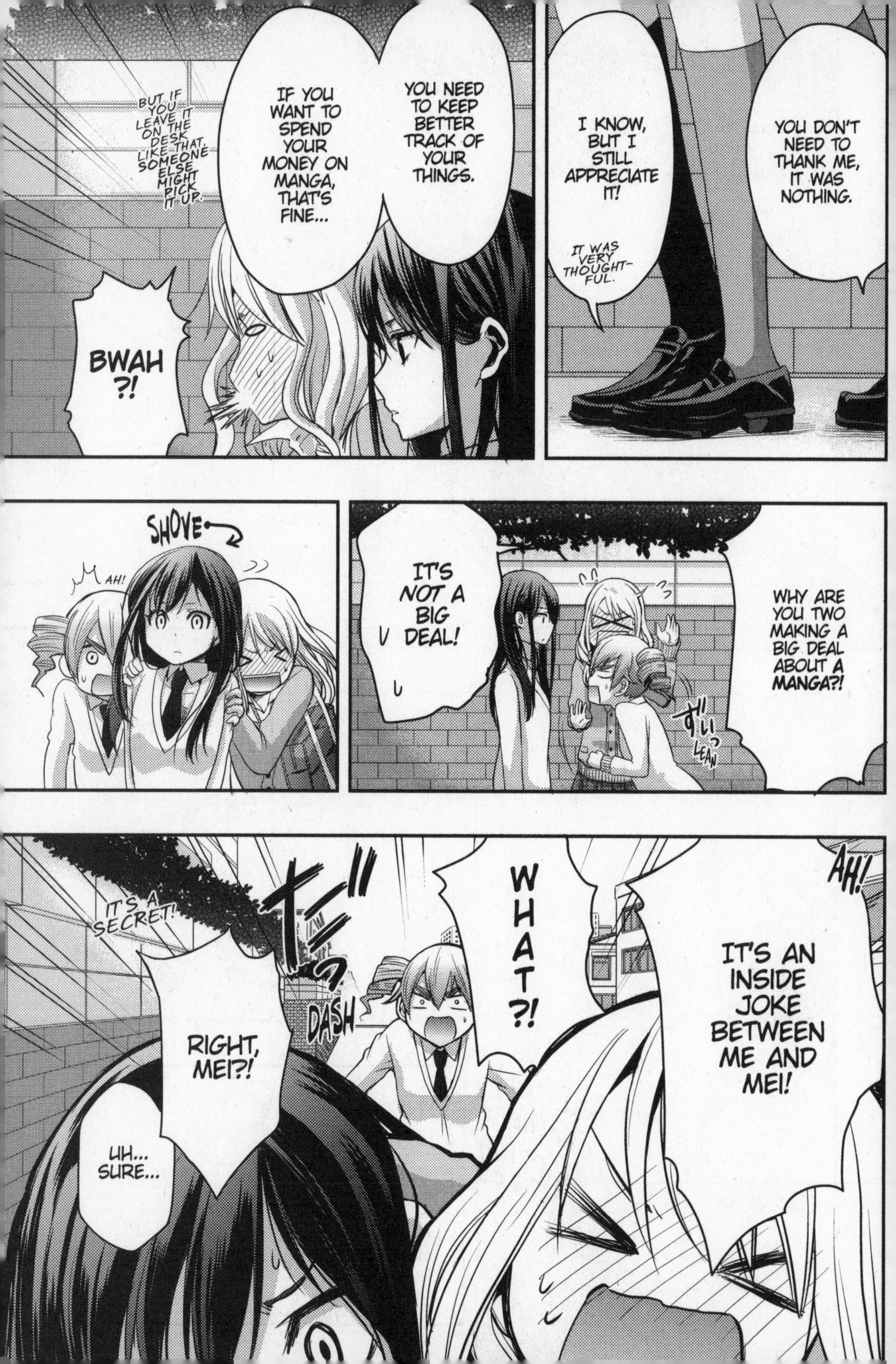
YOU DON'T NEED TO THANK ME, IT WAS NOTHING.
I KNOW, BUT I STILL APPRECIATE IT!
IT WAS VERY THOUGHT-FUL.
YOU NEED TO KEEP BETTER TRACK OF YOUR THINGS.
IF YOU WANT TO SPEND YOUR MONEY ON MANGA, THAT'S FINE...
BUT IF YOU LEAVE IT ON THE DESK LIKE THAT, SOMEONE ELSE MIGHT PICK IT UP.
BWAH ?!
WHY ARE YOU TWO MAKING A BIG DEAL ABOUT A MANGA?!
ずい LEAN
IT'S NOT A BIG DEAL!
SHOVE
AH!
AH!
IT'S AN INSIDE JOKE BETWEEN ME AND MEI!
WHAT?!
DASH
RIGHT, MEI?!
IT'S A SECRET!
UH... SURE...

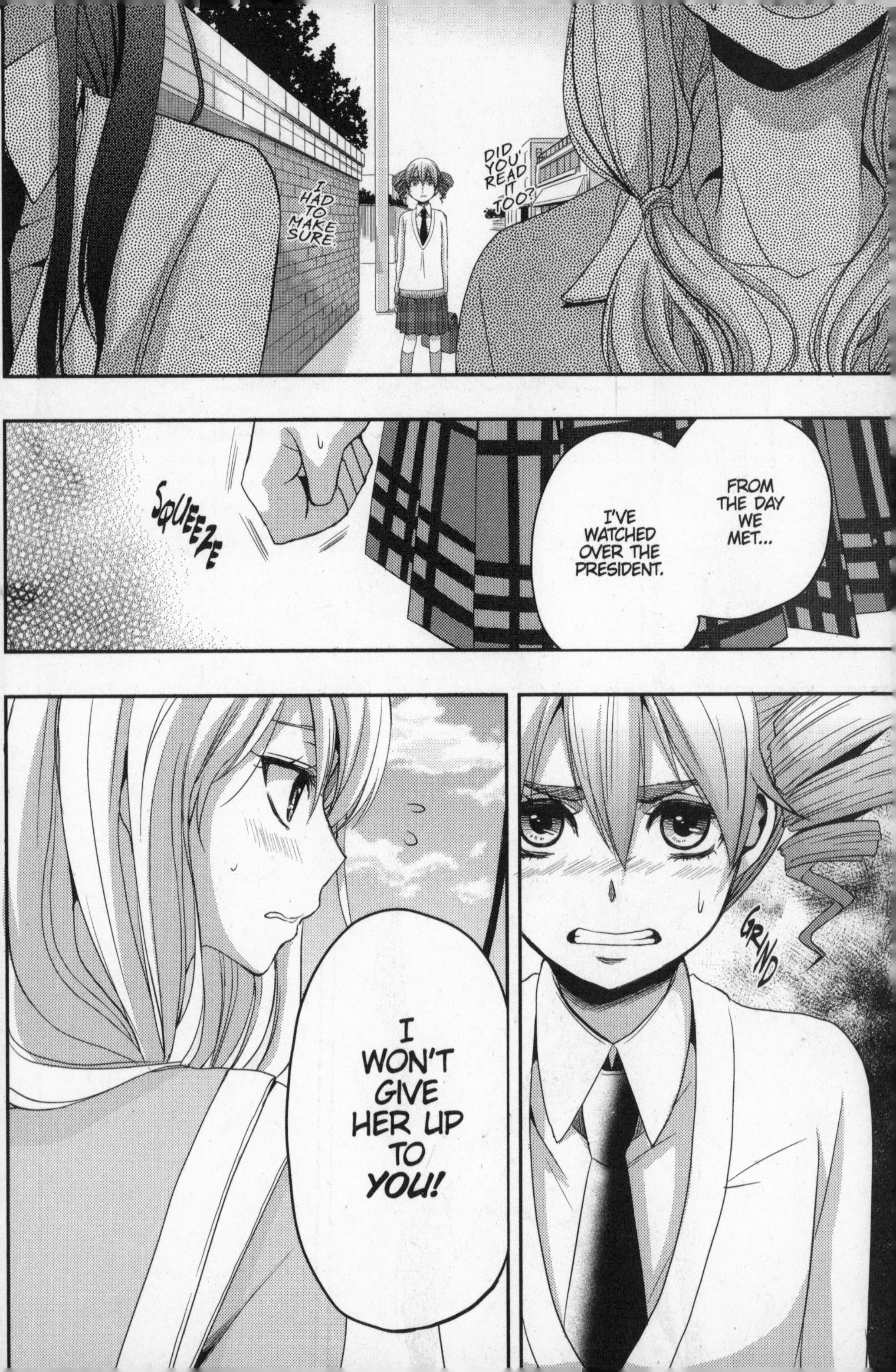
DID YOU READ IT TOO?
I HAD TO MAKE SURE.
FROM THE DAY WE MET... I'VE WATCHED OVER THE PRESIDENT.
SQUEEZE
GRIND
I WON'T GIVE HER UP TO *YOU!*

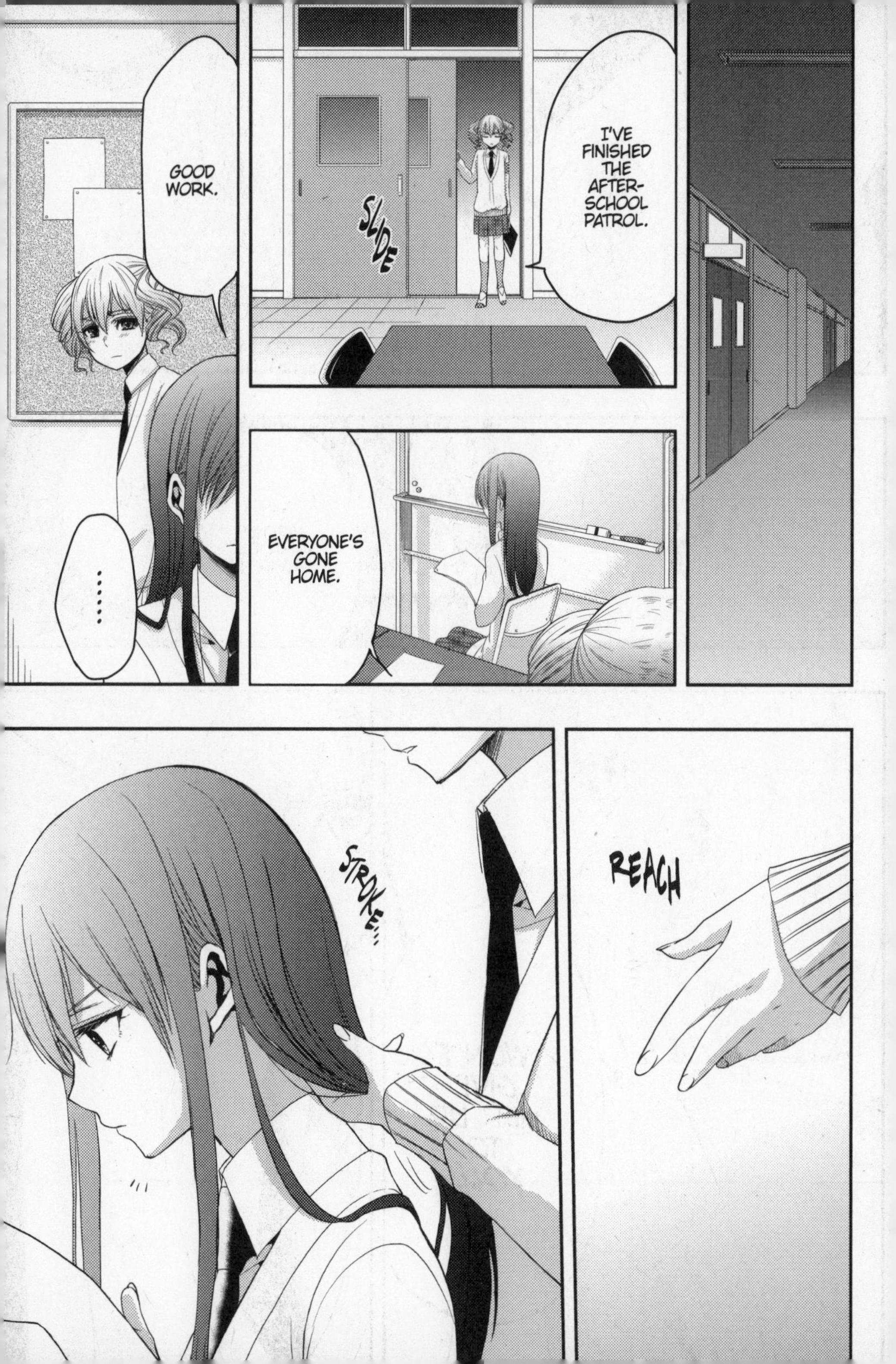
I'VE FINISHED THE AFTER-SCHOOL PATROL.
SLIDE
EVERYONE'S GONE HOME.
GOOD WORK.
......
REACH
STROKE...

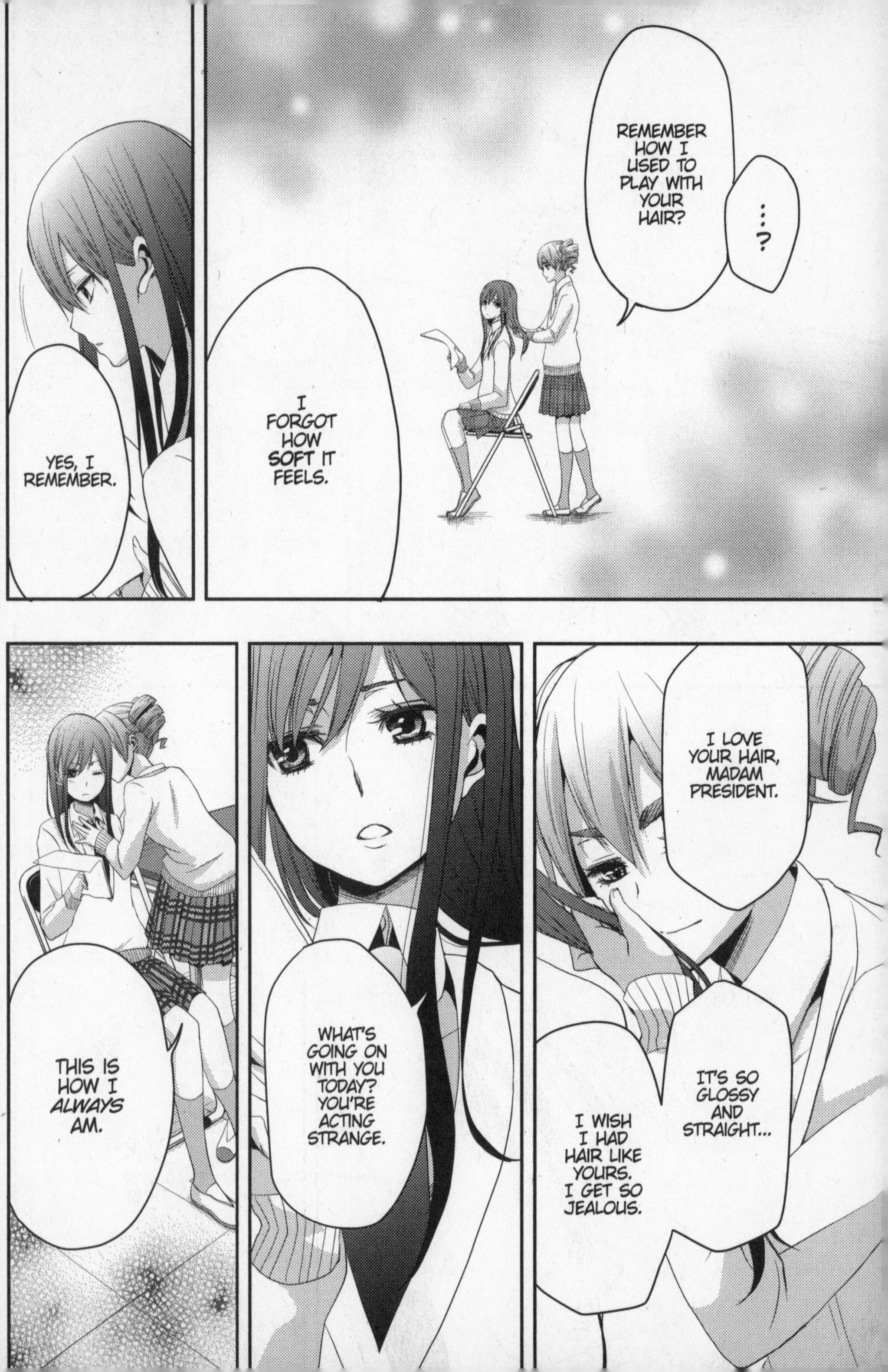
…?
REMEMBER HOW I USED TO PLAY WITH YOUR HAIR?
I FORGOT HOW SOFT IT FEELS.
YES, I REMEMBER.
I LOVE YOUR HAIR, MADAM PRESIDENT.
IT'S SO GLOSSY AND STRAIGHT...
I WISH I HAD HAIR LIKE YOURS. I GET SO JEALOUS.
WHAT'S GOING ON WITH YOU TODAY? YOU'RE ACTING STRANGE.
THIS IS HOW I *ALWAYS* AM.

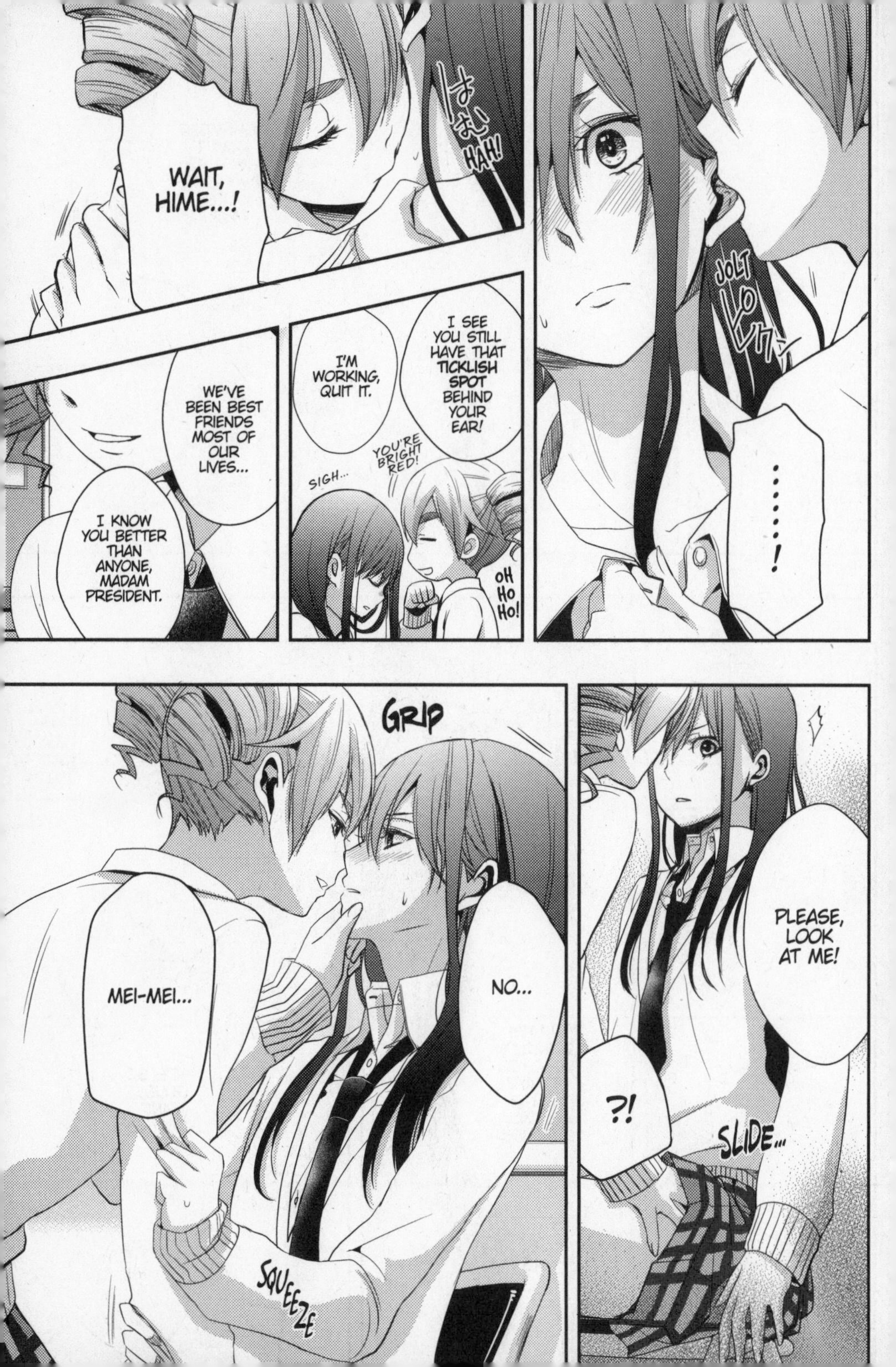

JOLT
ピクン
......!
はぁ
HAH!
WAIT, HIME...!
I SEE YOU STILL HAVE THAT TICKLISH SPOT BEHIND YOUR EAR!
I'M WORKING, QUIT IT.
YOU'RE BRIGHT RED!
OH HO HO!
SIGH...
WE'VE BEEN BEST FRIENDS MOST OF OUR LIVES...
I KNOW YOU BETTER THAN ANYONE, MADAM PRESIDENT.
PLEASE, LOOK AT ME!
?!
SLIDE...
GRIP
NO...
MEI-MEI...
SQUEEZE

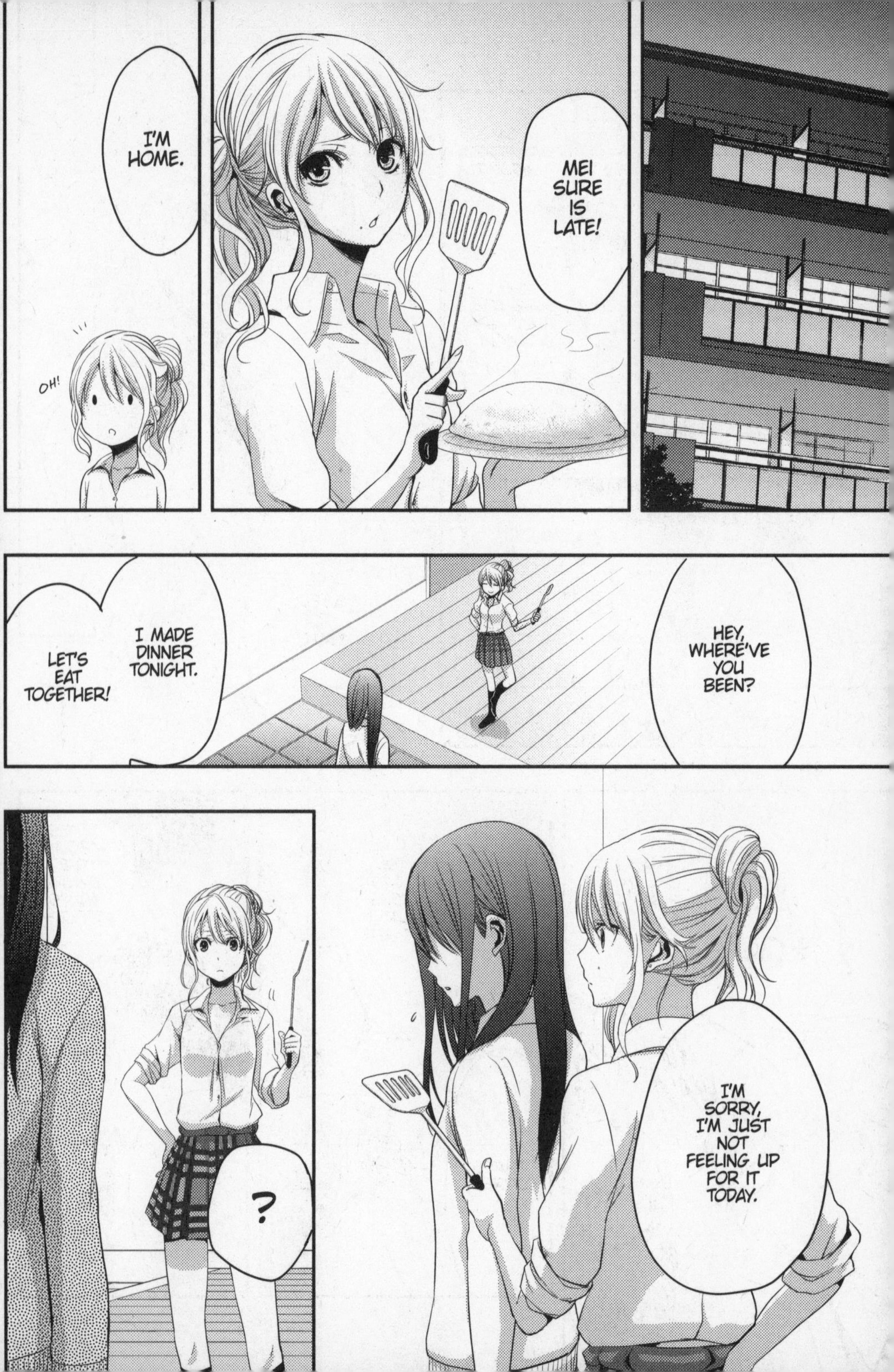
MEI SURE IS LATE!
I'M HOME.
OH!
HEY, WHERE'VE YOU BEEN?
I MADE DINNER TONIGHT.
LET'S EAT TOGETHER!
I'M SORRY, I'M JUST NOT FEELING UP FOR IT TODAY.
?

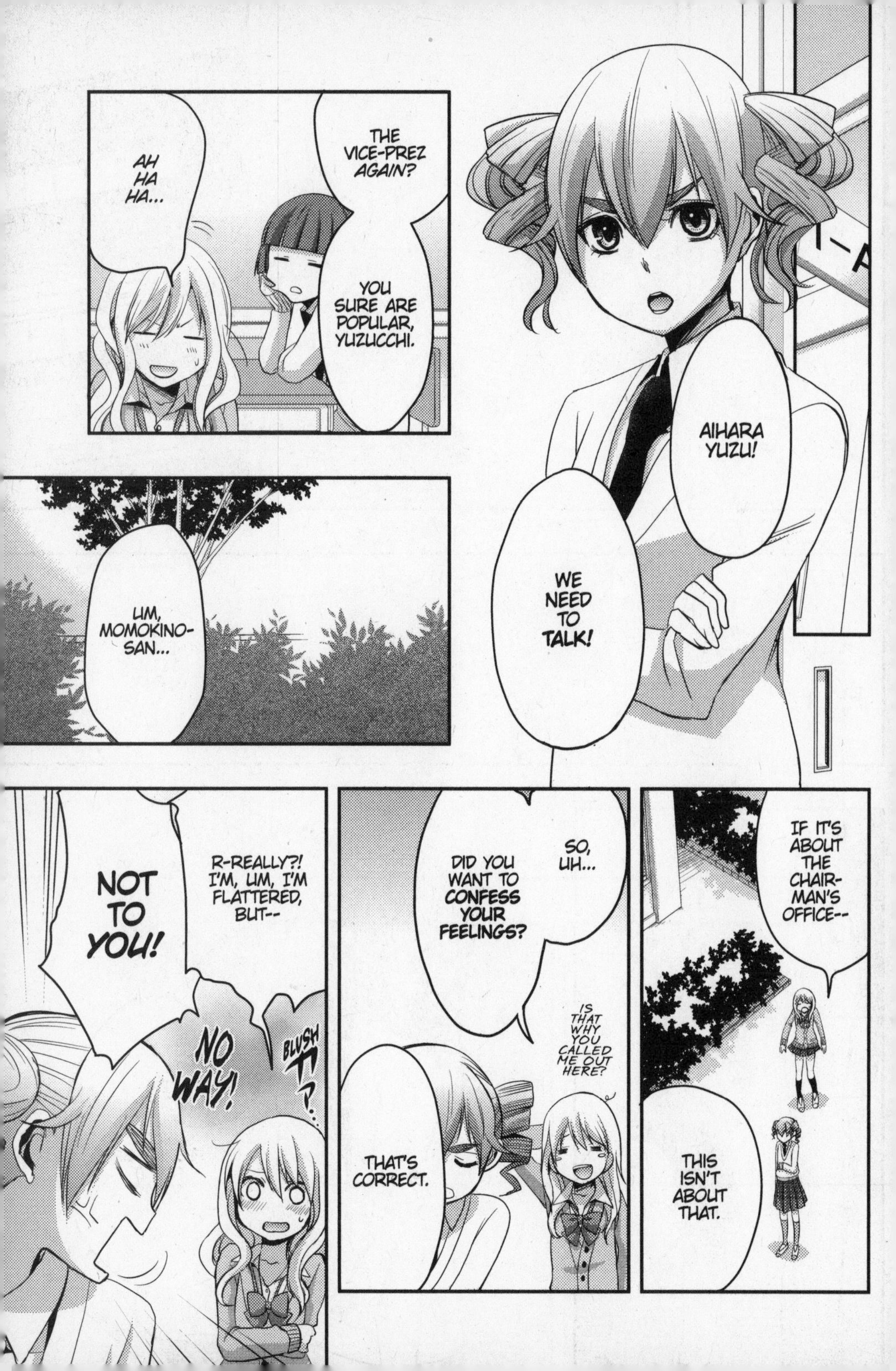
AIHARA YUZU!
WE NEED TO TALK!
THE VICE-PREZ AGAIN?
YOU SURE ARE POPULAR, YUZUCCHI.
AH HA HA...
UM, MOMOKINO-SAN...
IF IT'S ABOUT THE CHAIR-MAN'S OFFICE--
THIS ISN'T ABOUT THAT.
SO, UH...
DID YOU WANT TO CONFESS YOUR FEELINGS?
IS THAT WHY YOU CALLED ME OUT HERE?
THAT'S CORRECT.
R-REALLY?! I'M, UM, I'M FLATTERED, BUT--
NOT TO YOU!
NO WAY!
BLUSH

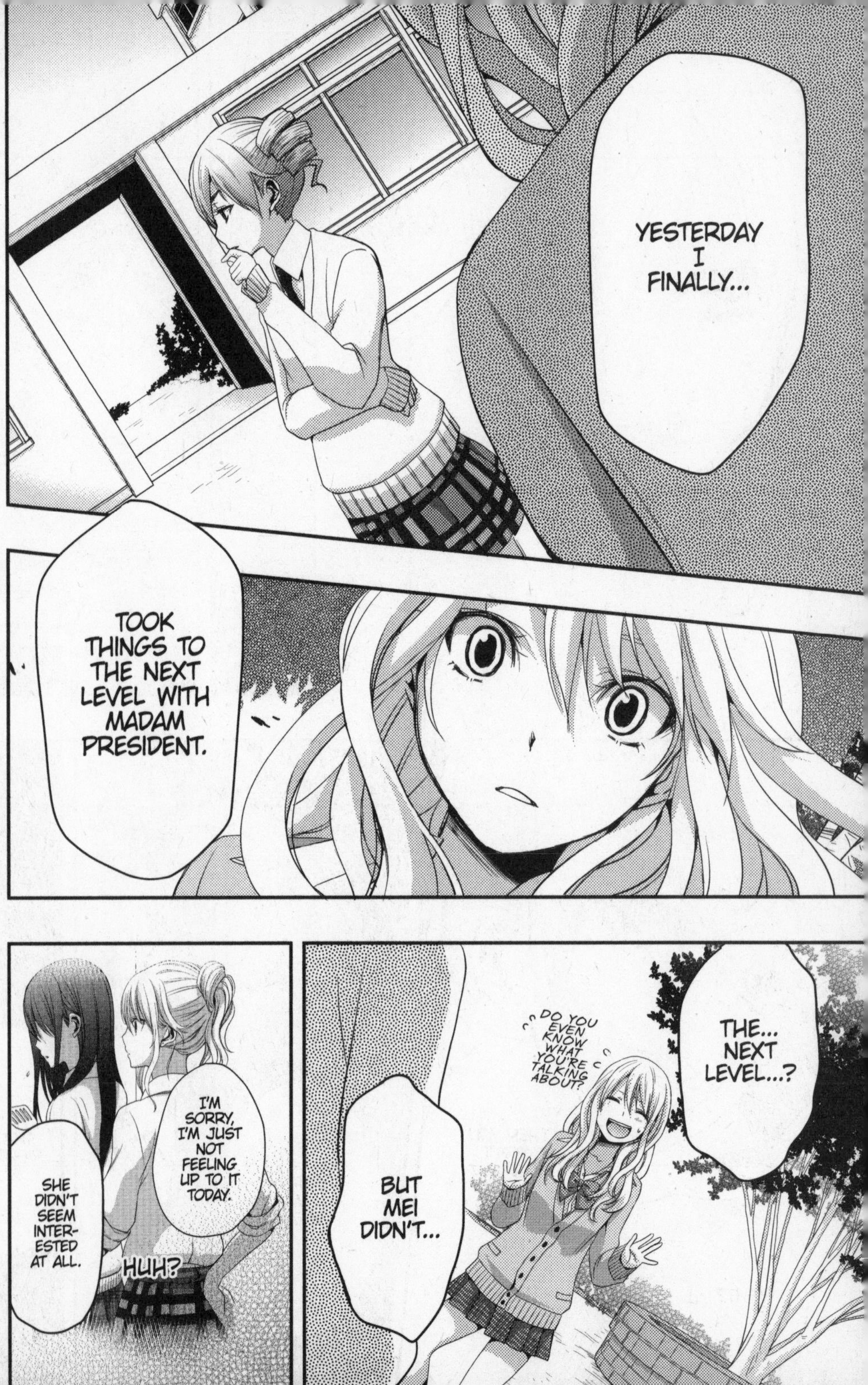
YESTERDAY I FINALLY...
TOOK THINGS TO THE NEXT LEVEL WITH MADAM PRESIDENT.
THE... NEXT LEVEL...?
DO YOU EVEN KNOW WHAT YOU'RE TALKING ABOUT?
BUT MEI DIDN'T...
I'M SORRY, I'M JUST NOT FEELING UP TO IT TODAY.
HUH?
SHE DIDN'T SEEM INTERESTED AT ALL.

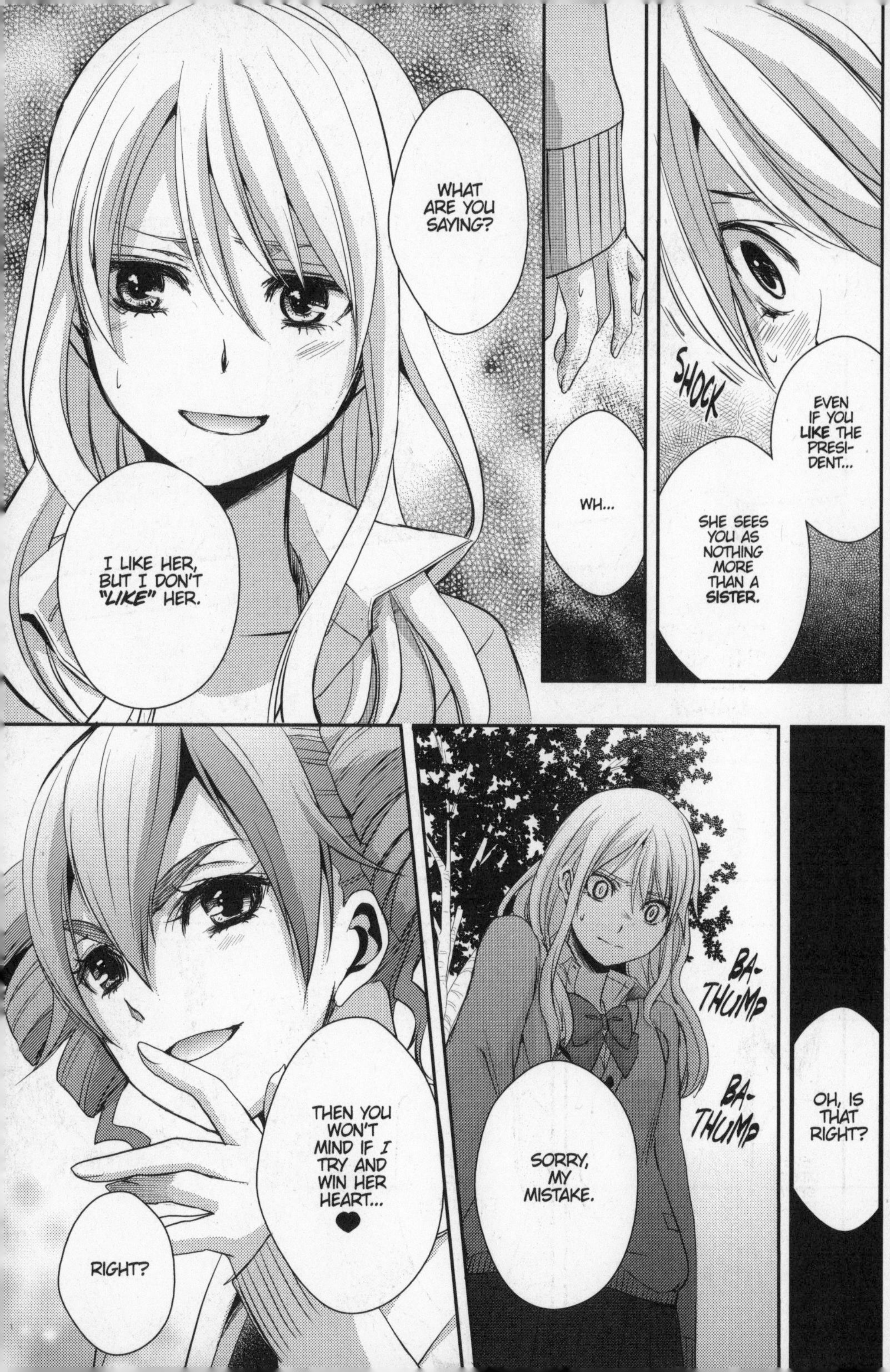
EVEN IF YOU *LIKE* THE PRESI-DENT...
SHE SEES YOU AS NOTHING MORE THAN A SISTER.
SHOCK
WH...
WHAT ARE YOU SAYING?
I LIKE HER, BUT I DON'T *"LIKE"* HER.
OH, IS THAT RIGHT?
BA-THUMP
BA-THUMP
SORRY, MY MISTAKE.
THEN YOU WON'T MIND IF *I* TRY AND WIN HER HEART... ♥
RIGHT?

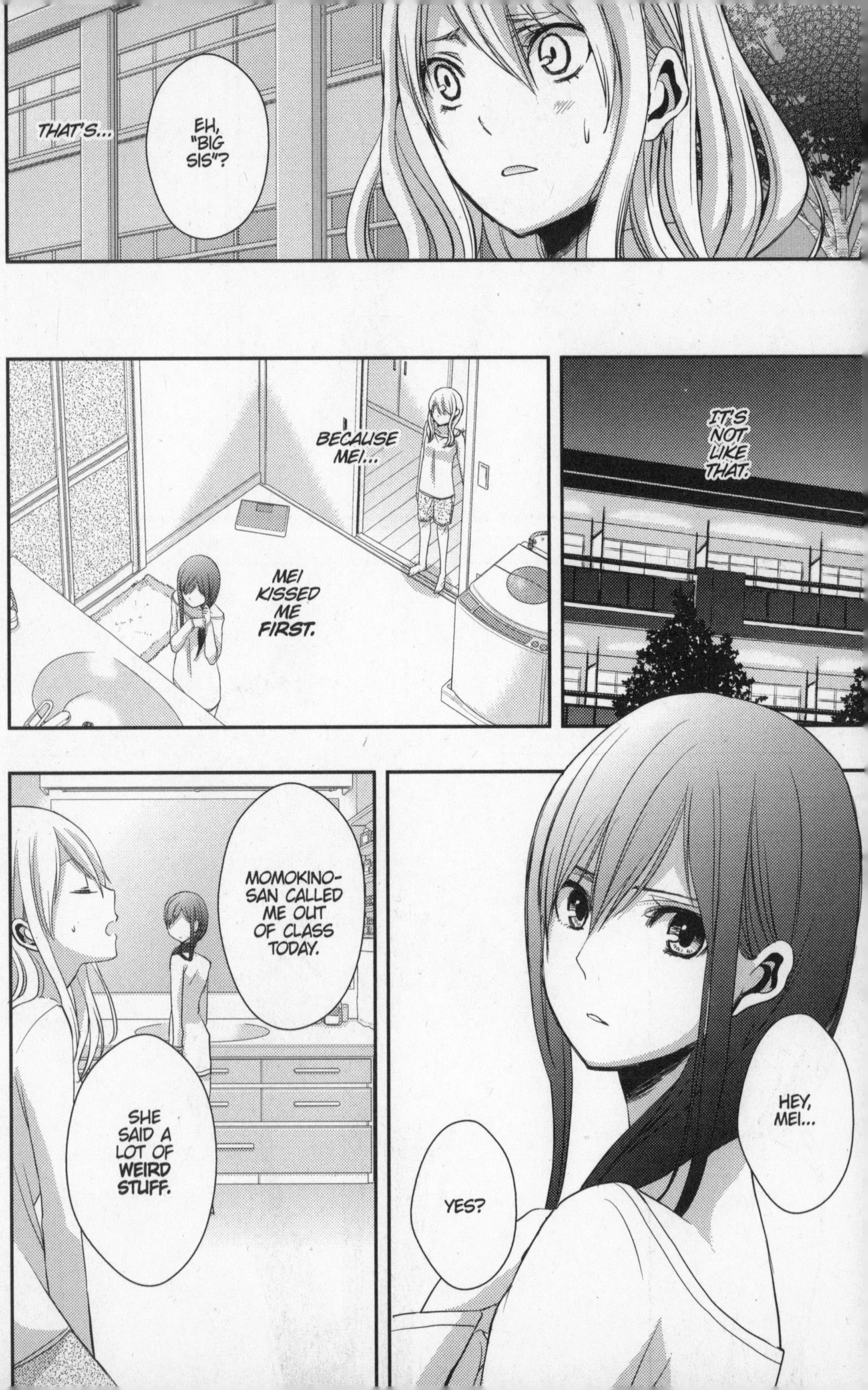
EH, "BIG SIS"?
THAT'S...
IT'S NOT LIKE THAT.
BECAUSE MEI...
MEI KISSED ME FIRST.
HEY, MEI...
YES?
MOMOKINO-SAN CALLED ME OUT OF CLASS TODAY.
SHE SAID A LOT OF WEIRD STUFF.

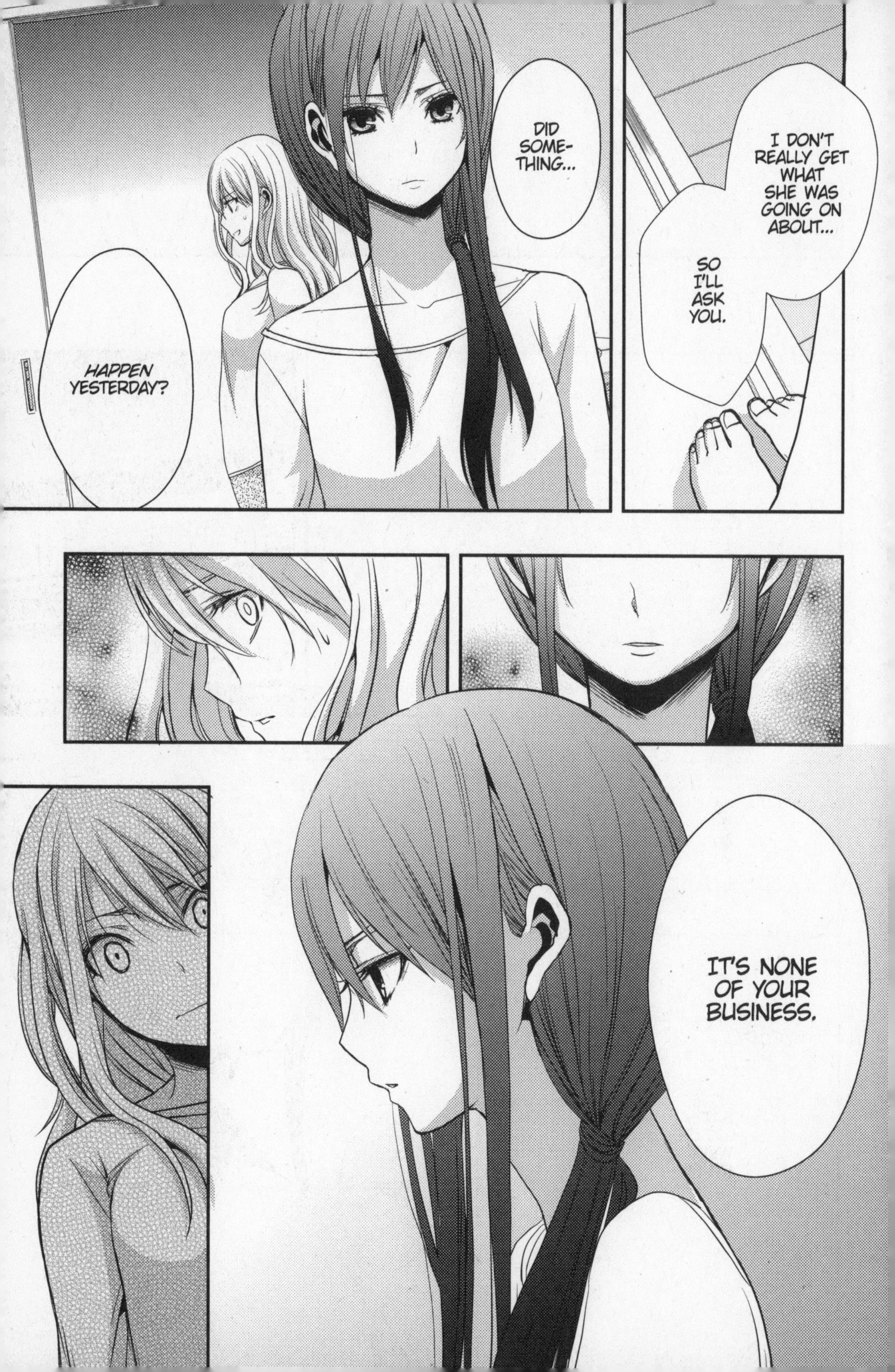
I DON'T REALLY GET WHAT SHE WAS GOING ON ABOUT...
SO I'LL ASK YOU.
DID SOME-THING...
HAPPEN YESTERDAY?
IT'S NONE OF YOUR BUSINESS.

RIGHT,
IT'S GOT
NOTHING
TO DO
WITH ME.

SORRY.

citrus

[シトラス]

SECRET LOVE AFFAIR WITH SISTER

citrus

SABUROUTA PRESENTS SECRET LOVE AFFAIR WITH SISTER

2

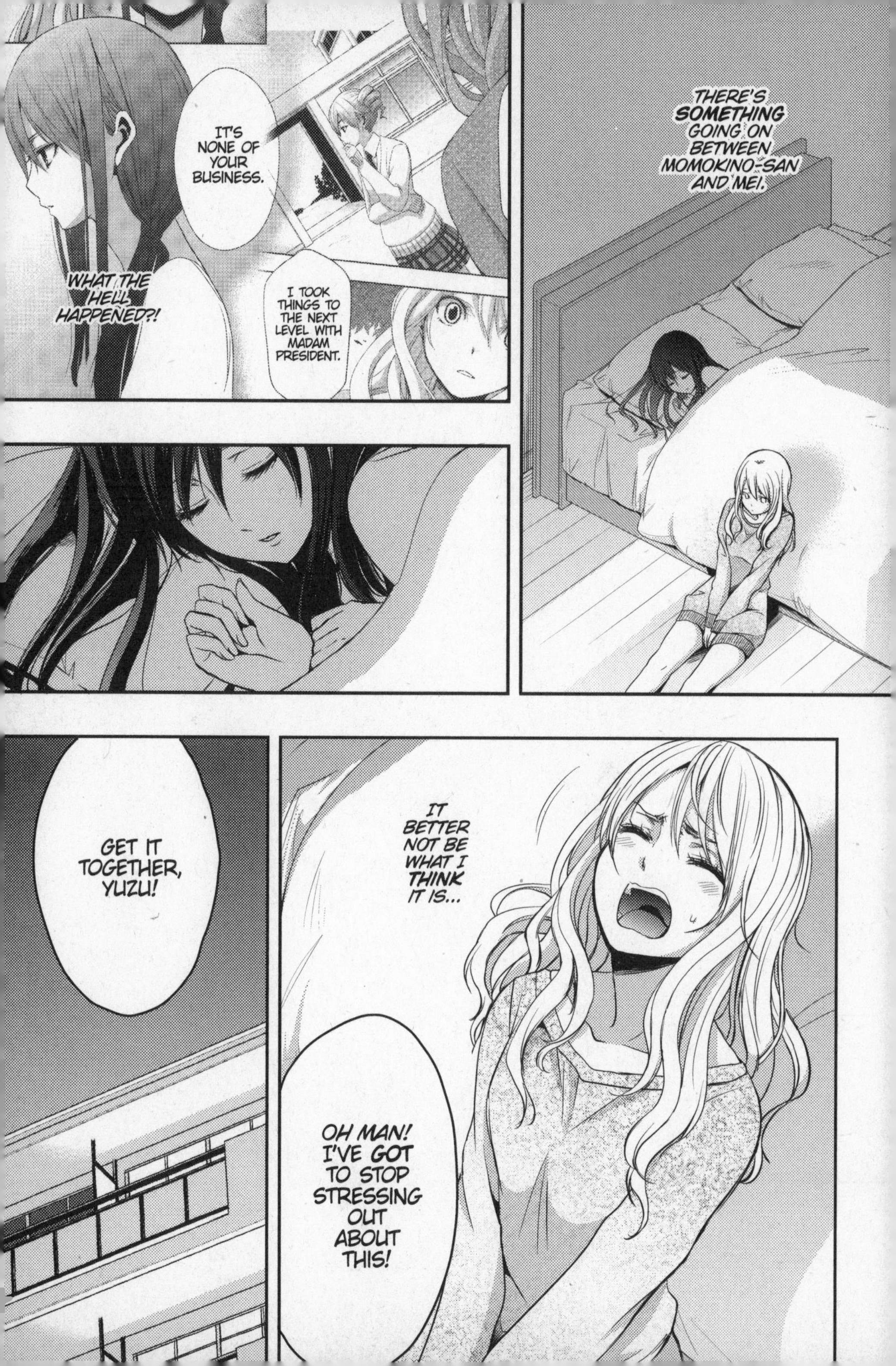
THERE'S SOMETHING GOING ON BETWEEN MOMOKINO-SAN AND MEI.
IT'S NONE OF YOUR BUSINESS.
I TOOK THINGS TO THE NEXT LEVEL WITH MADAM PRESIDENT.
WHAT THE HELL HAPPENED?!
IT BETTER NOT BE WHAT I THINK IT IS...
OH MAN! I'VE GOT TO STOP STRESSING OUT ABOUT THIS!
GET IT TOGETHER, YUZU!

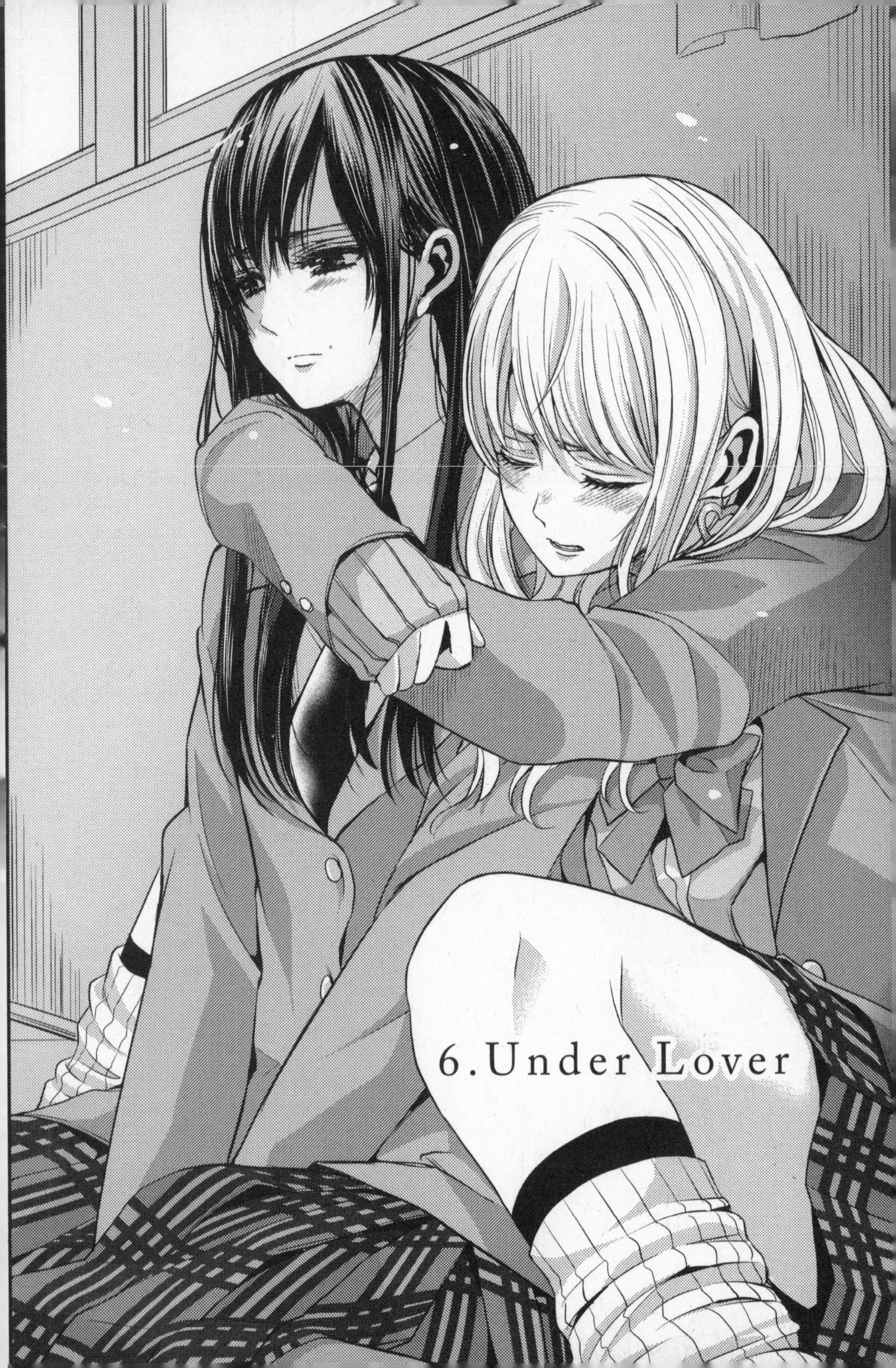
6.Under Lover

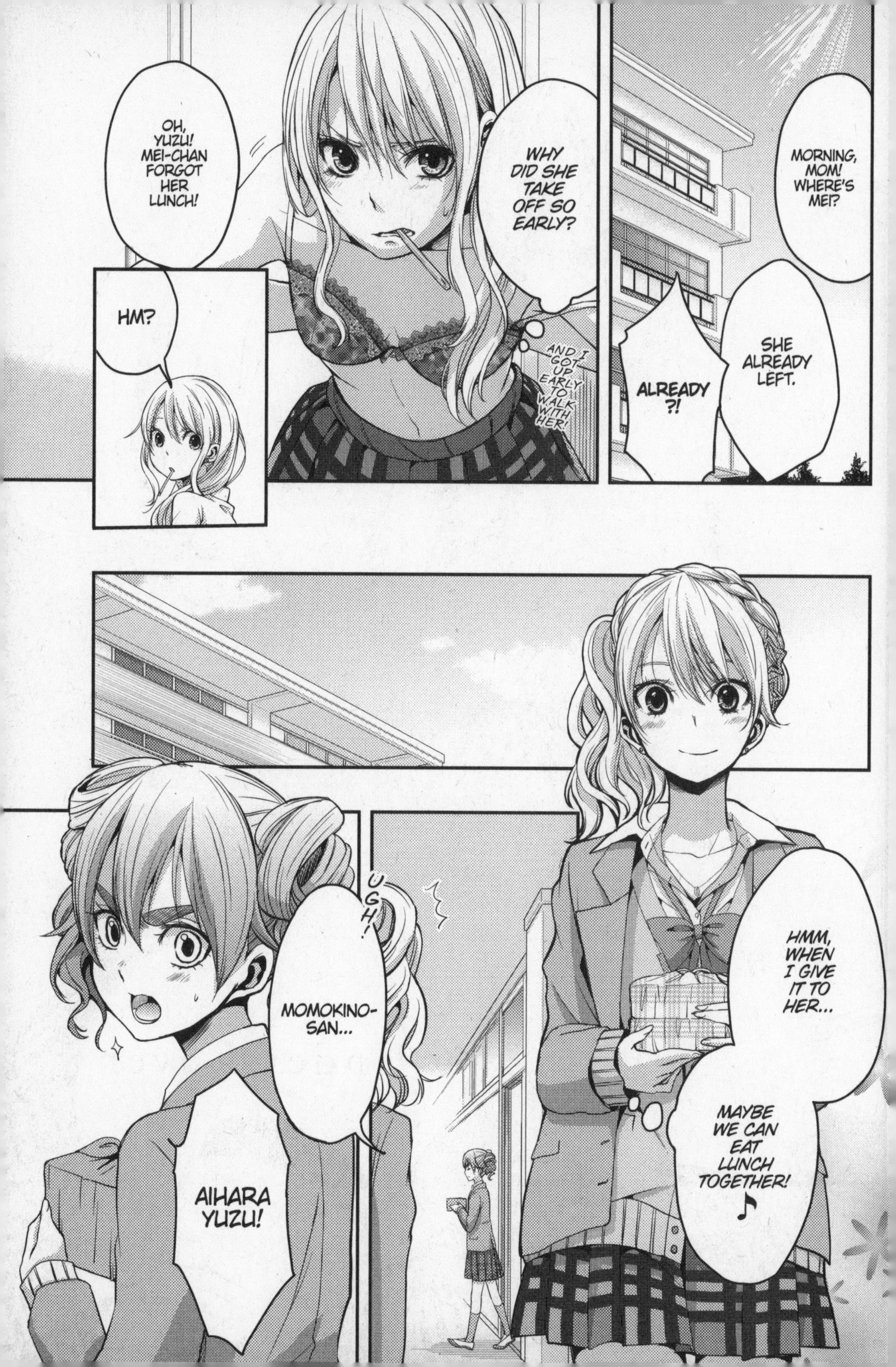
MORNING, MOM! WHERE'S MEI?
SHE ALREADY LEFT.
ALREADY?!
WHY DID SHE TAKE OFF SO EARLY?
AND I GOT UP EARLY TO WALK WITH HER!
OH, YUZU! MEI-CHAN FORGOT HER LUNCH!
HM?
HMM, WHEN I GIVE IT TO HER...
MAYBE WE CAN EAT LUNCH TOGETHER! ♪
UGH!
MOMOKINO-SAN...
AIHARA YUZU!

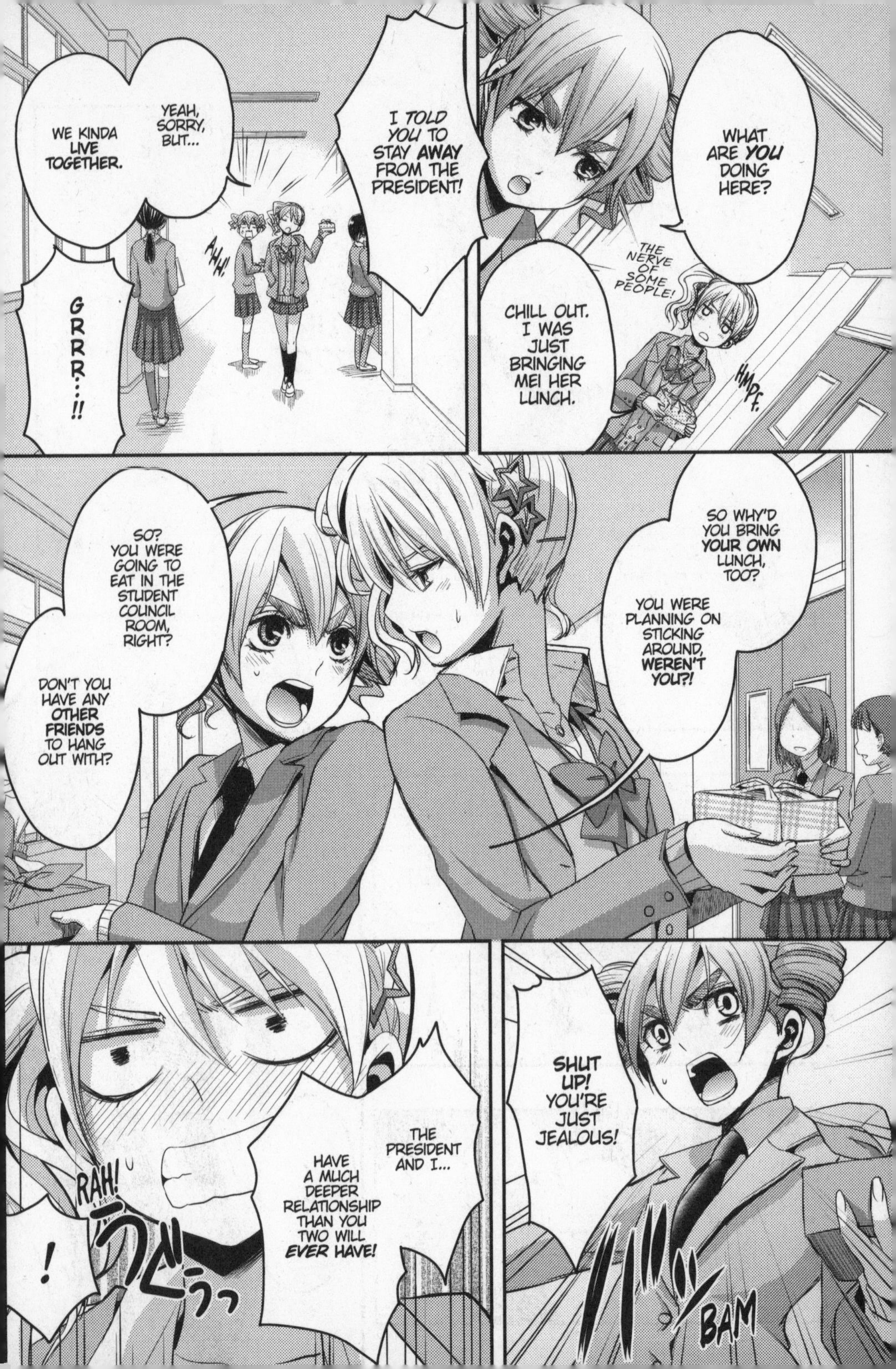
WHAT ARE YOU DOING HERE?
THE NERVE OF SOME PEOPLE!
CHILL OUT. I WAS JUST BRINGING MEI HER LUNCH.
HMPF.
I TOLD YOU TO STAY AWAY FROM THE PRESIDENT!
YEAH, SORRY, BUT...
WE KINDA LIVE TOGETHER.
AHH!
GRRR...!!
SO WHY'D YOU BRING YOUR OWN LUNCH, TOO?
YOU WERE PLANNING ON STICKING AROUND, WEREN'T YOU?!
SO? YOU WERE GOING TO EAT IN THE STUDENT COUNCIL ROOM, RIGHT?
DON'T YOU HAVE ANY OTHER FRIENDS TO HANG OUT WITH?
SHUT UP! YOU'RE JUST JEALOUS!
BAM
THE PRESIDENT AND I...
HAVE A MUCH DEEPER RELATIONSHIP THAN YOU TWO WILL EVER HAVE!
RAH!
!

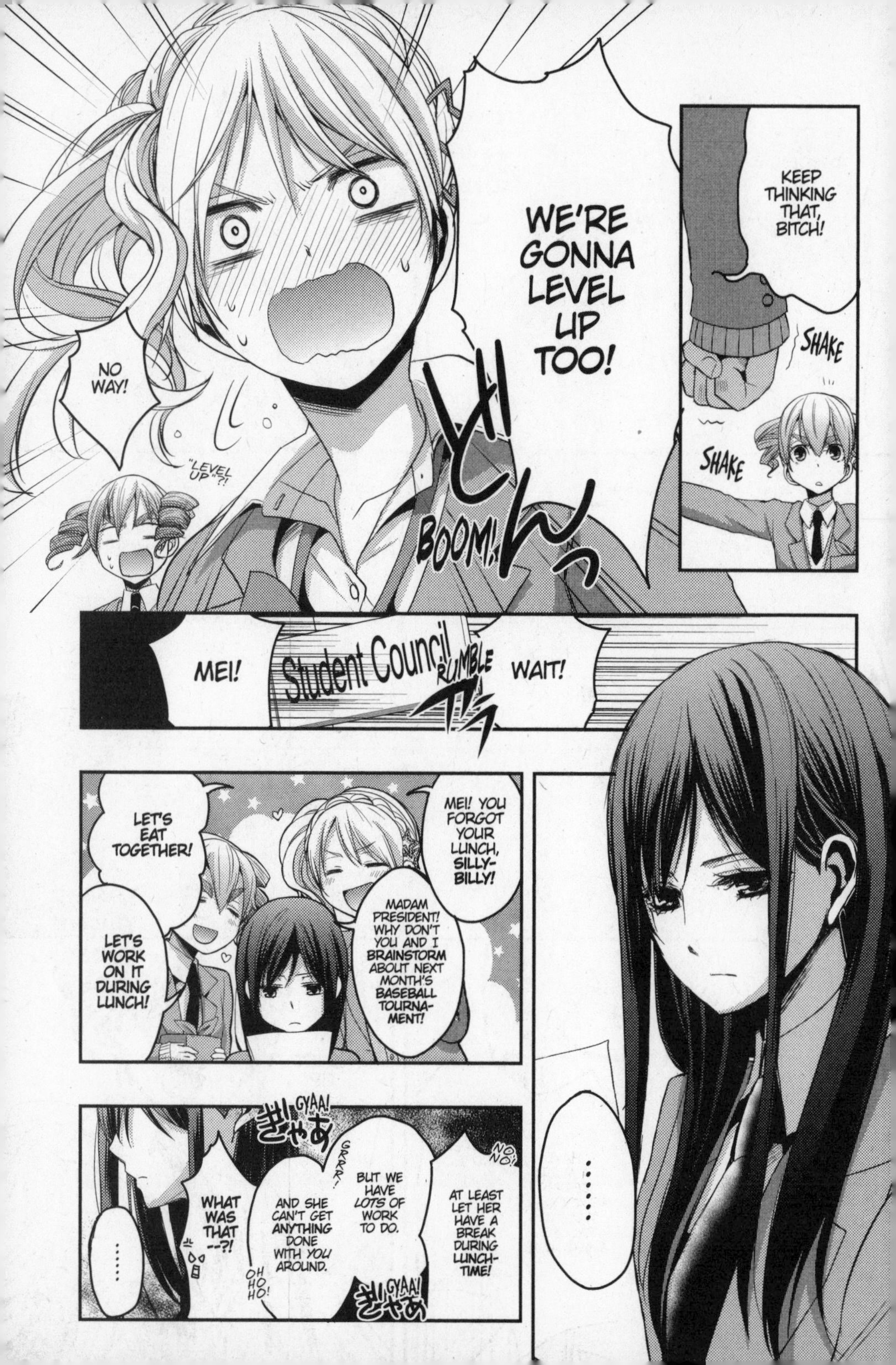
KEEP THINKING THAT, BITCH!
SHAKE
SHAKE
WE'RE GONNA LEVEL UP TOO!
BOOM!
NO WAY!
"LEVEL UP"?!
WAIT!
RUMBLE
Student Council
MEI!
......
MEI! YOU FORGOT YOUR LUNCH, SILLY-BILLY!
LET'S EAT TOGETHER!
MADAM PRESIDENT! WHY DON'T YOU AND I BRAINSTORM ABOUT NEXT MONTH'S BASEBALL TOURNAMENT!
LET'S WORK ON IT DURING LUNCH!
NO NO!
AT LEAST LET HER HAVE A BREAK DURING LUNCH-TIME!
GYAA!
GRRR!
BUT WE HAVE LOTS OF WORK TO DO.
AND SHE CAN'T GET ANYTHING DONE WITH YOU AROUND.
OH HO HO!
WHAT WAS THAT--?!
GYAA!
......

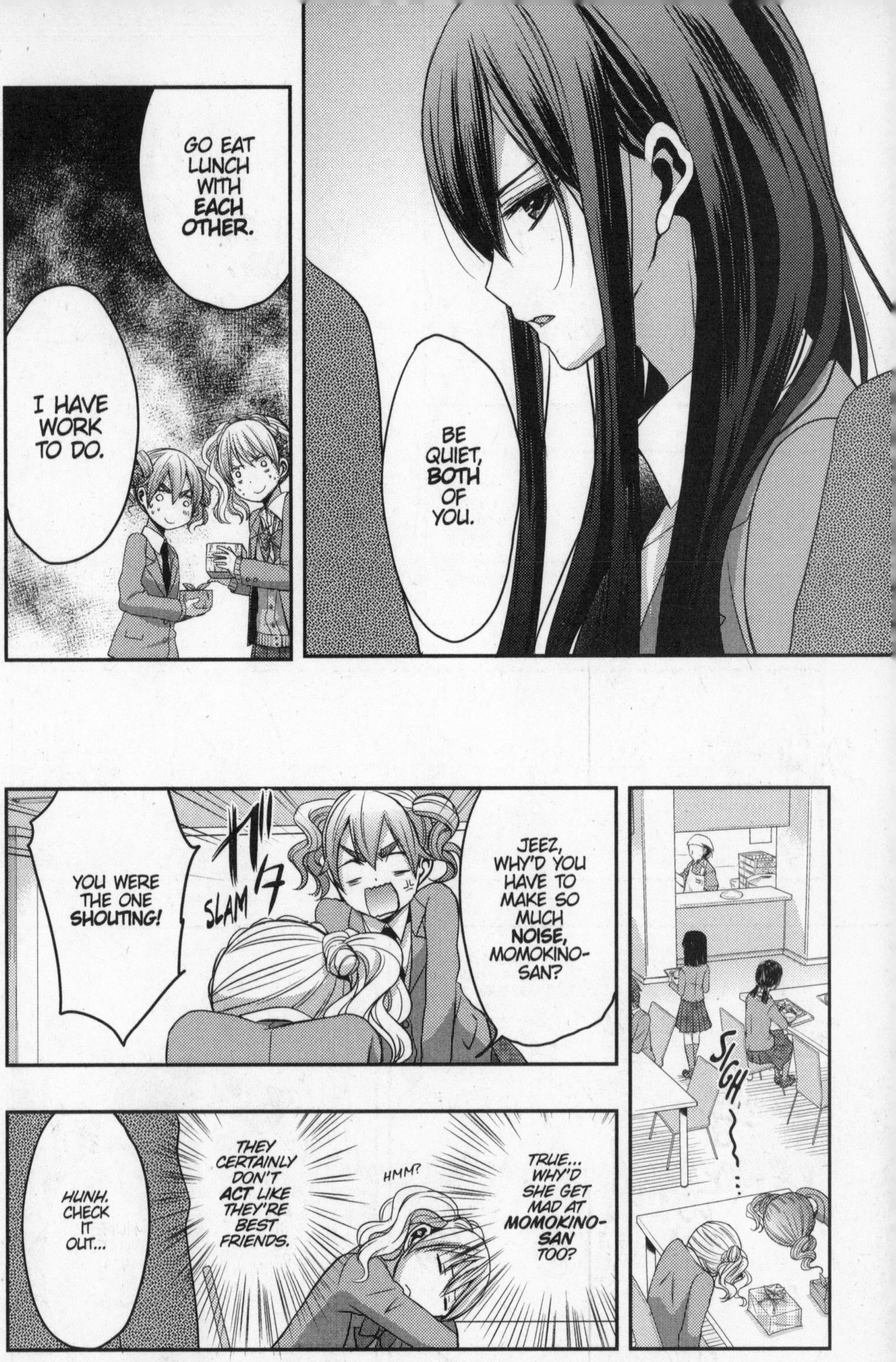
BE QUIET, BOTH OF YOU.
GO EAT LUNCH WITH EACH OTHER.
I HAVE WORK TO DO.
SIGH...
JEEZ, WHY'D YOU HAVE TO MAKE SO MUCH NOISE, MOMOKINO-SAN?
SLAM
YOU WERE THE ONE SHOUTING!
TRUE... WHY'D SHE GET MAD AT MOMOKINO-SAN TOO?
HMM?
THEY CERTAINLY DON'T ACT LIKE THEY'RE BEST FRIENDS.
HUNH. CHECK IT OUT...

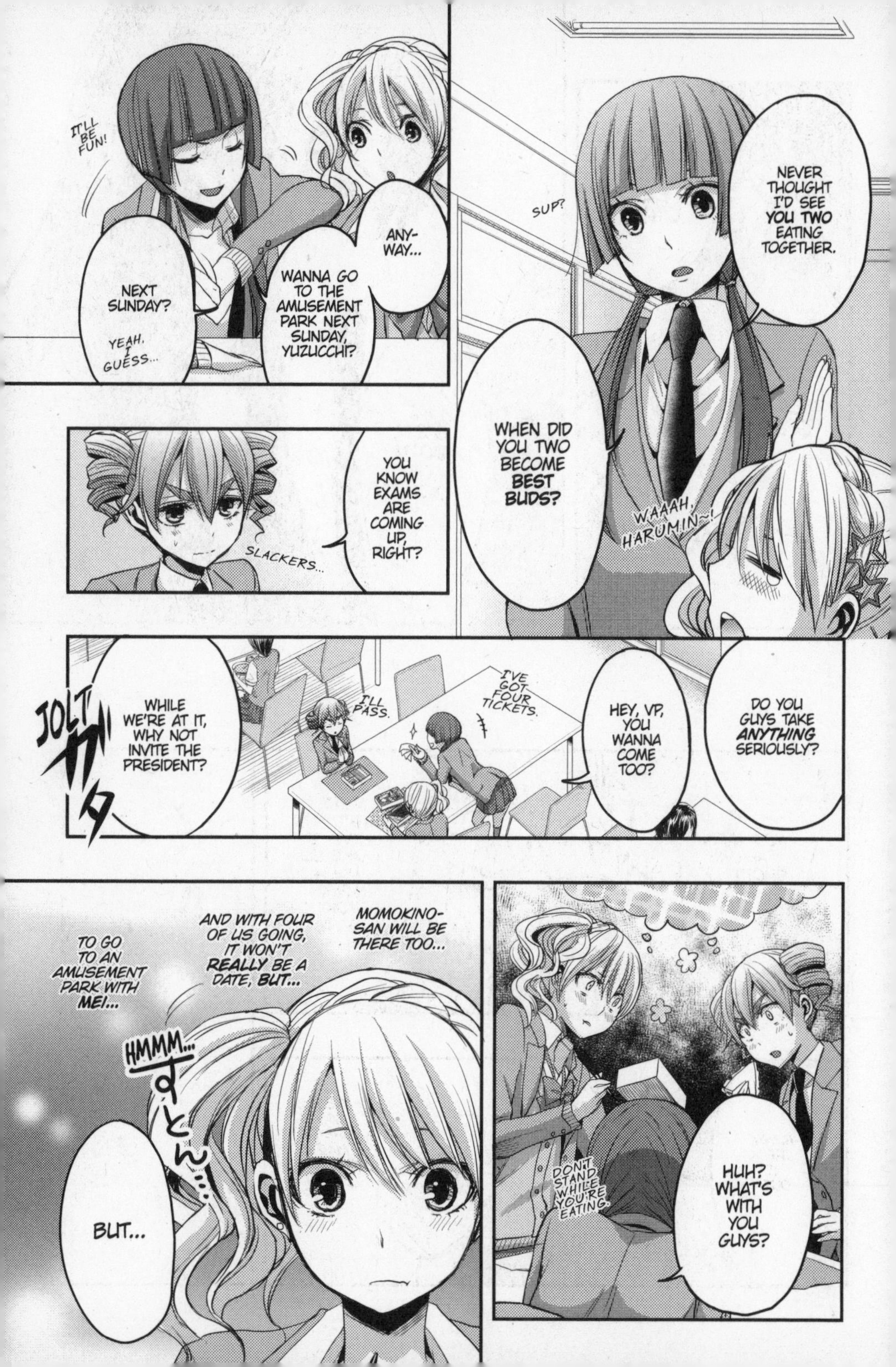
NEVER THOUGHT I'D SEE YOU TWO EATING TOGETHER.
SUP?
WHEN DID YOU TWO BECOME BEST BUDS?
WAAAH, HARUMIN~!
ANY-WAY...
WANNA GO TO THE AMUSEMENT PARK NEXT SUNDAY, YUZUCCHI?
IT'LL BE FUN!
NEXT SUNDAY?
YEAH, I GUESS...
YOU KNOW EXAMS ARE COMING UP, RIGHT?
SLACKERS...
DO YOU GUYS TAKE ANYTHING SERIOUSLY?
HEY, VP, YOU WANNA COME TOO?
I'VE GOT FOUR TICKETS.
I'LL PASS.
WHILE WE'RE AT IT, WHY NOT INVITE THE PRESIDENT?
JOLT
ガタ
HUH? WHAT'S WITH YOU GUYS?
DON'T STAND WHILE YOU'RE EATING.
MOMOKINO-SAN WILL BE THERE TOO...
AND WITH FOUR OF US GOING, IT WON'T REALLY BE A DATE, BUT...
TO GO TO AN AMUSEMENT PARK WITH MEI...
HMMM...
すとん...
BUT...

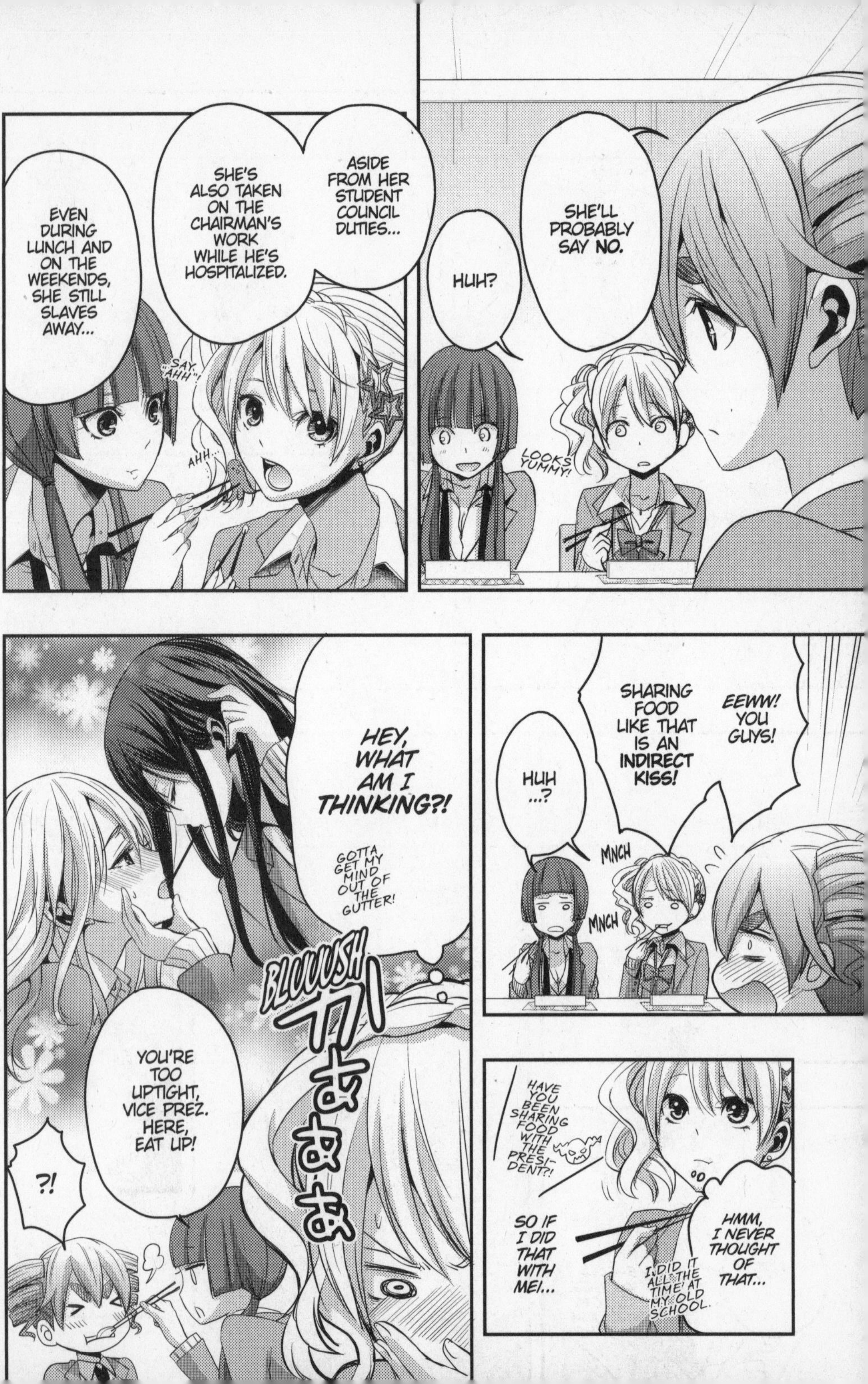
SHE'LL PROBABLY SAY NO.
HUH?
LOOKS YUMMY!
ASIDE FROM HER STUDENT COUNCIL DUTIES...
SHE'S ALSO TAKEN ON THE CHAIRMAN'S WORK WHILE HE'S HOSPITALIZED.
EVEN DURING LUNCH AND ON THE WEEKENDS, SHE STILL SLAVES AWAY...
"SAY, 'AHH'!"
AHH...
EEWW! YOU GUYS!
SHARING FOOD LIKE THAT IS AN INDIRECT KISS!
HUH ...?
MNCH
MNCH
HMM, I NEVER THOUGHT OF THAT...
I DID IT ALL THE TIME AT MY OLD SCHOOL.
SO IF I DID THAT WITH MEI...
HAVE YOU BEEN SHARING FOOD WITH THE PRESI-DENT?!
HEY, WHAT AM I THINKING?!
GOTTA GET MY MIND OUT OF THE GUTTER!
BLUUUSH
YOU'RE TOO UPTIGHT, VICE PREZ. HERE, EAT UP!
?!

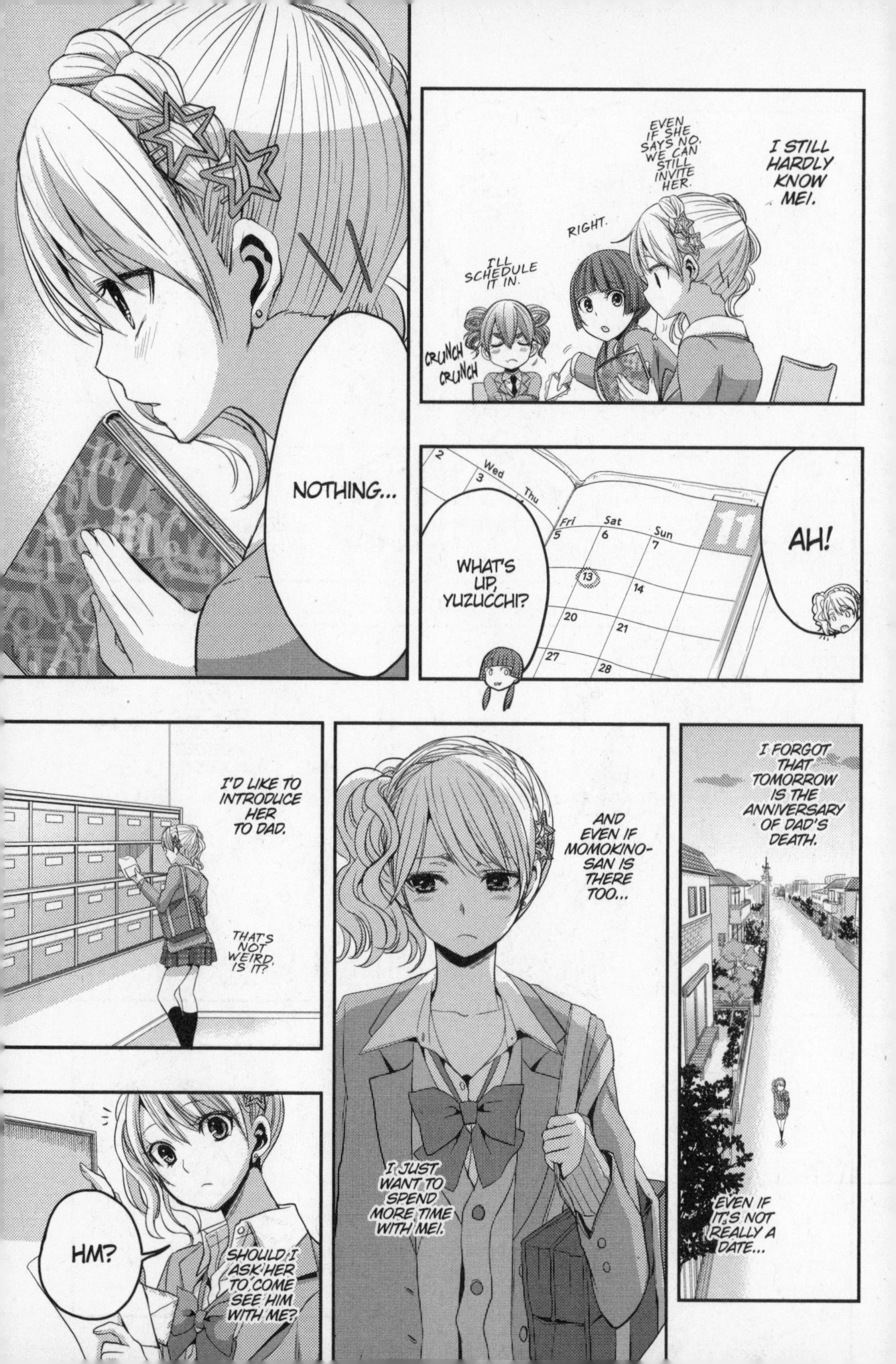
I STILL HARDLY KNOW MEI.
EVEN IF SHE SAYS NO, WE CAN STILL INVITE HER.
RIGHT.
I'LL SCHEDULE IT IN.
CRUNCH CRUNCH
AH!
11
2 Wed 3 Thu
Fri 5 Sat 6 Sun 7
13 14
20 21
27 28
WHAT'S UP, YUZUCCHI?
NOTHING...
I FORGOT THAT TOMORROW IS THE ANNIVERSARY OF DAD'S DEATH.
EVEN IF IT'S NOT REALLY A DATE...
AND EVEN IF MOMOKINO-SAN IS THERE TOO...
I JUST WANT TO SPEND MORE TIME WITH MEI.
I'D LIKE TO INTRODUCE HER TO DAD.
THAT'S NOT WEIRD, IS IT?
HM?
SHOULD I ASK HER TO COME SEE HIM WITH ME?

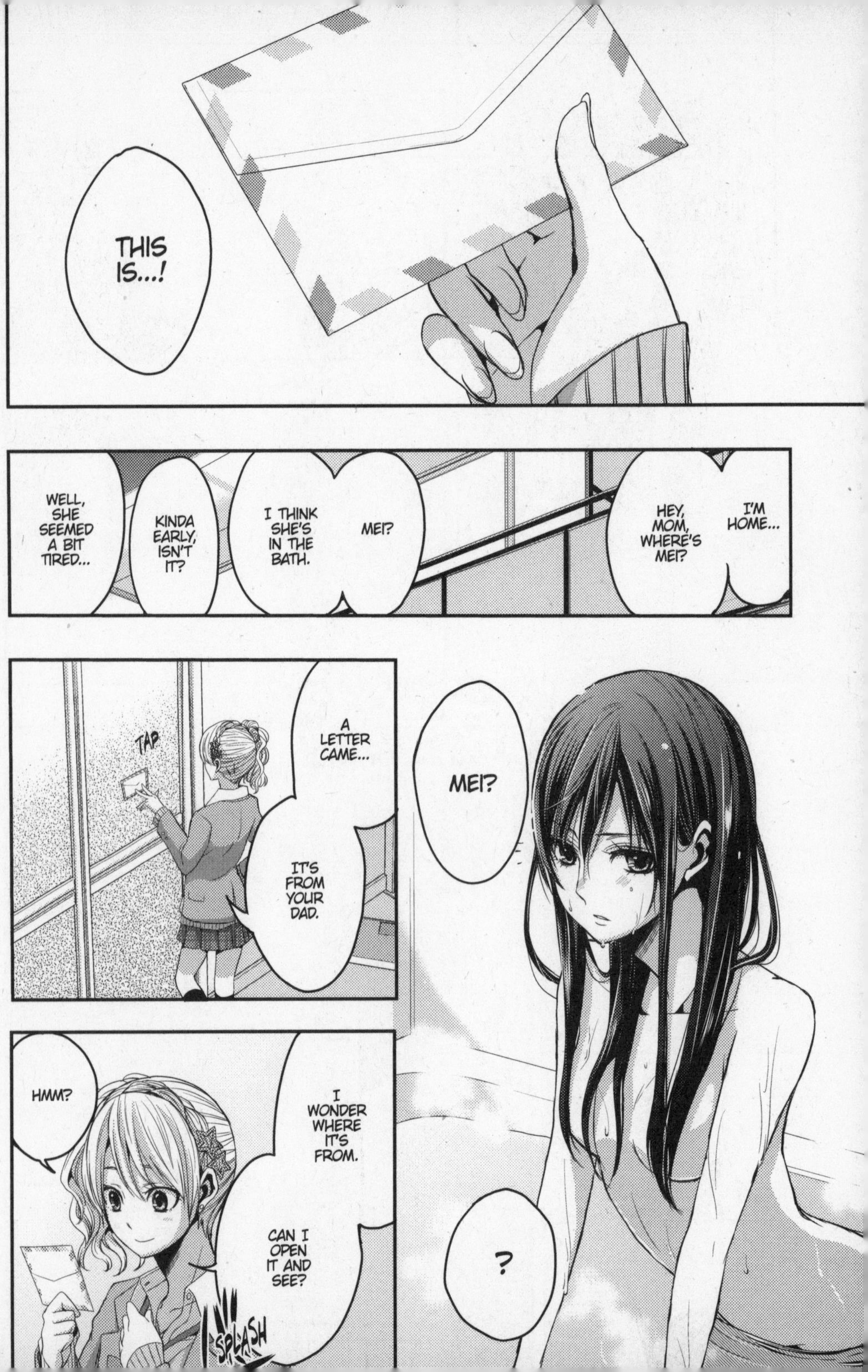
THIS IS...!
I'M HOME...
HEY, MOM, WHERE'S MEI?
MEI?
I THINK SHE'S IN THE BATH.
KINDA EARLY, ISN'T IT?
WELL, SHE SEEMED A BIT TIRED...
MEI?
?
TAP
A LETTER CAME...
IT'S FROM YOUR DAD.
I WONDER WHERE IT'S FROM.
HMM?
CAN I OPEN IT AND SEE?
SPLASH

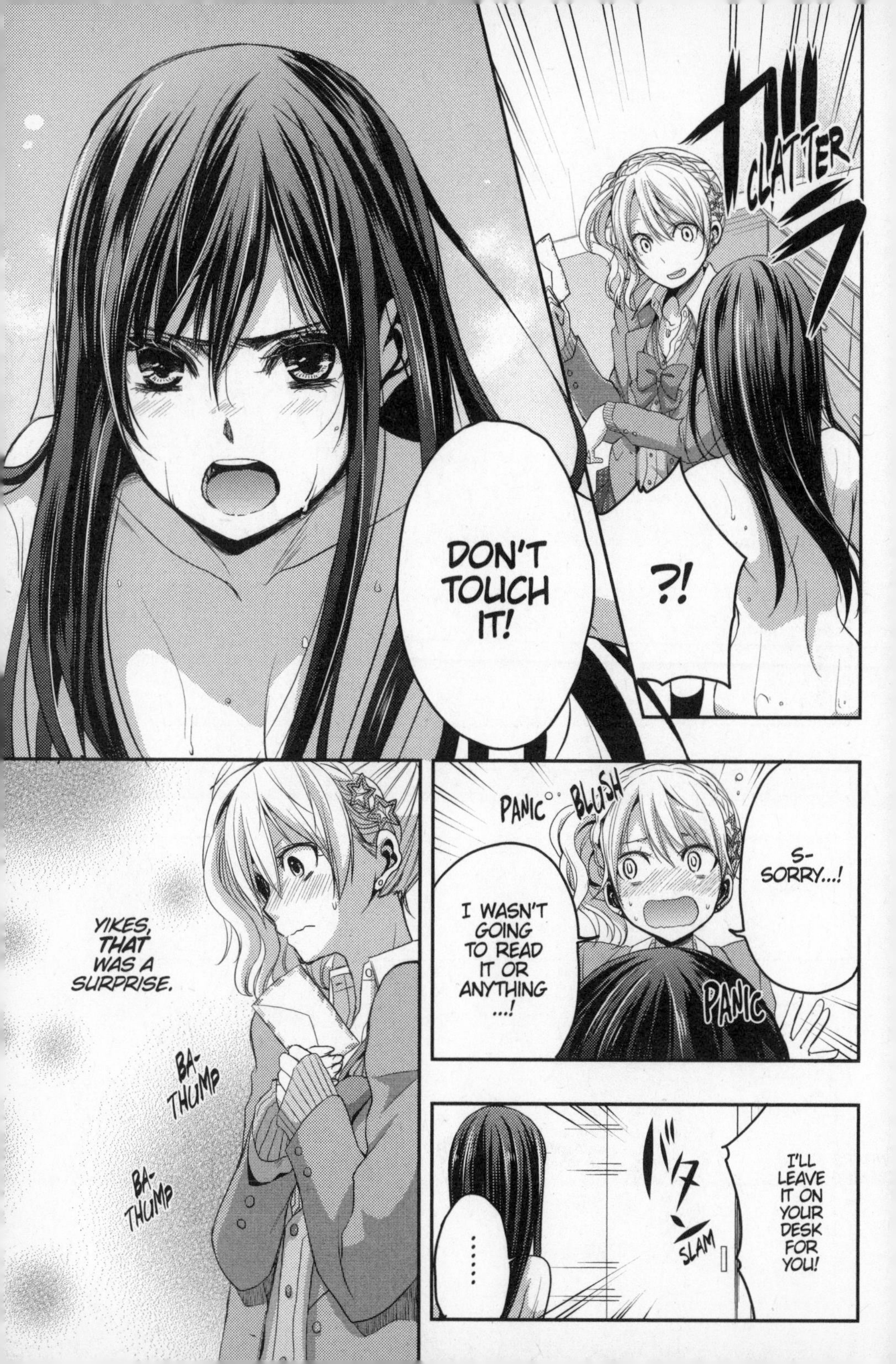
CLATTER
?!
DON'T TOUCH IT!
PANIC
BLUSH
S-SORRY...!
I WASN'T GOING TO READ IT OR ANYTHING ...!
PANIC
I'LL LEAVE IT ON YOUR DESK FOR YOU!
SLAM
......
YIKES, THAT WAS A SURPRISE.
BA-THUMP
BA-THUMP

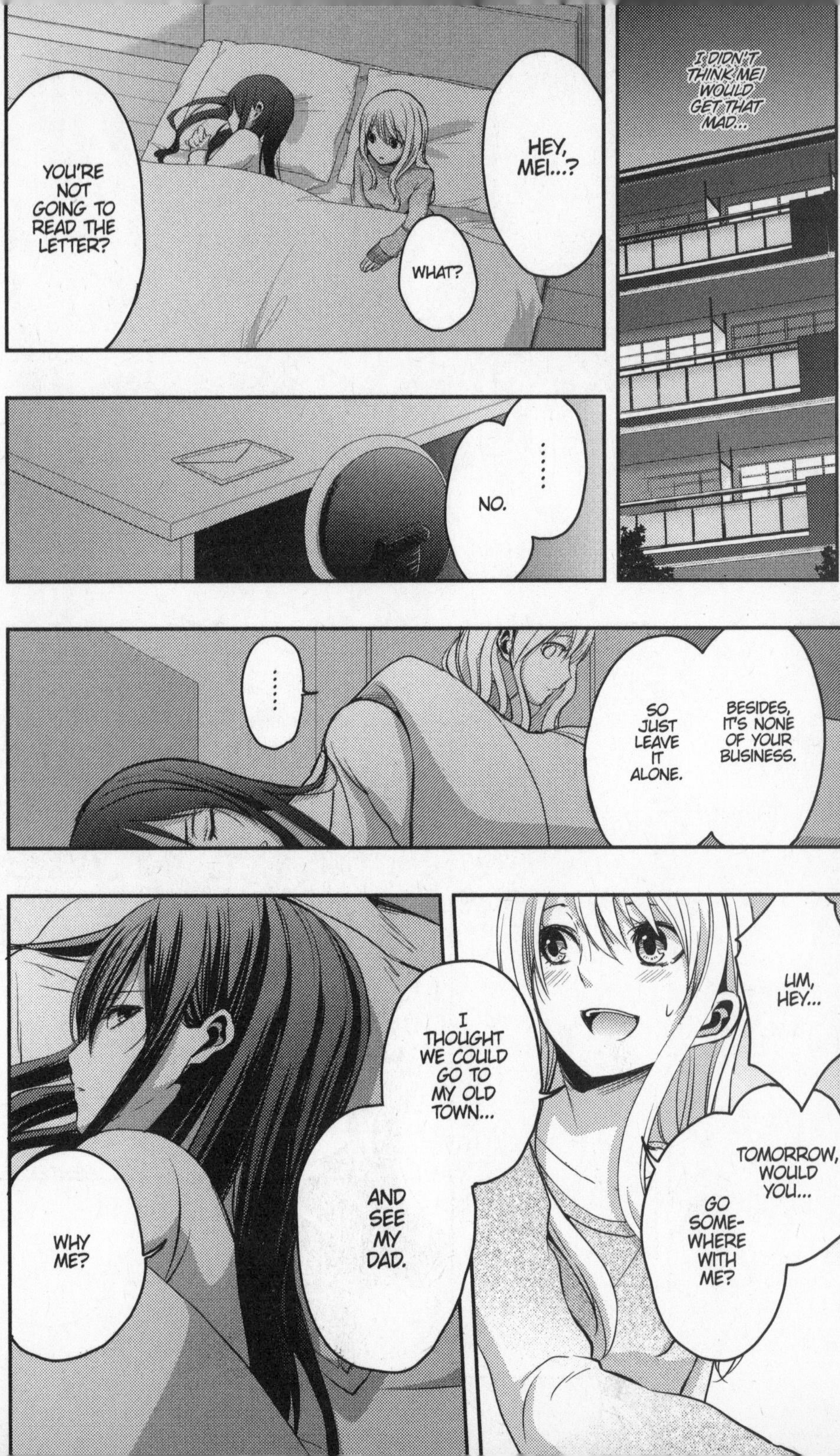
I DIDN'T THINK MEI WOULD GET THAT MAD...
HEY, MEI...?
WHAT?
YOU'RE NOT GOING TO READ THE LETTER?
......
NO.
BESIDES, IT'S NONE OF YOUR BUSINESS.
SO JUST LEAVE IT ALONE.
......
UM, HEY...
TOMORROW, WOULD YOU...
GO SOME-WHERE WITH ME?
I THOUGHT WE COULD GO TO MY OLD TOWN...
AND SEE MY DAD.
WHY ME?

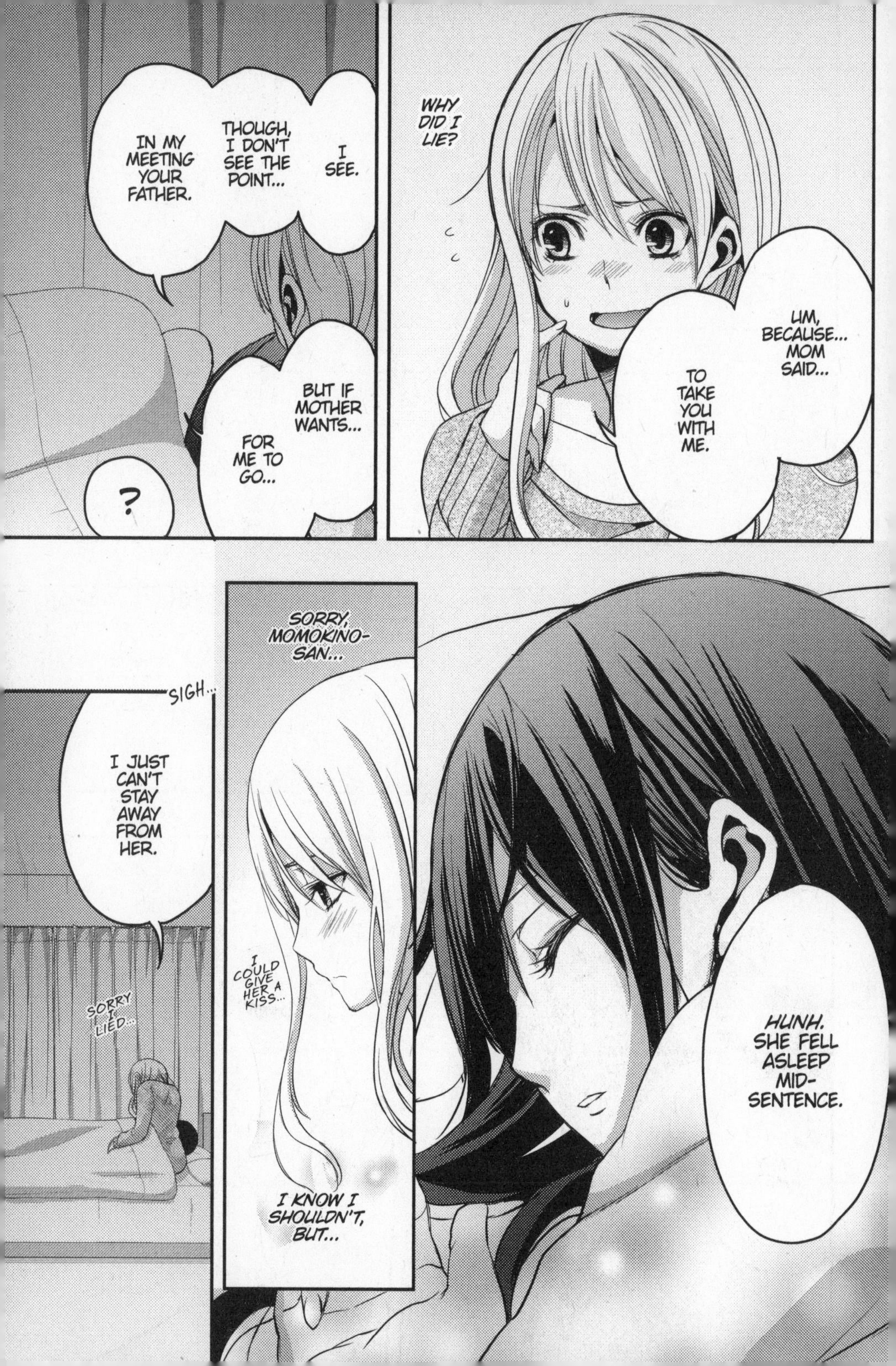
WHY DID I LIE?
UM, BECAUSE... MOM SAID...
TO TAKE YOU WITH ME.
I SEE.
THOUGH, I DON'T SEE THE POINT...
IN MY MEETING YOUR FATHER.
BUT IF MOTHER WANTS...
FOR ME TO GO...
?
HUNH. SHE FELL ASLEEP MID-SENTENCE.
SORRY, MOMOKINO-SAN...
I COULD GIVE HER A KISS...
I KNOW I SHOULDN'T, BUT...
SIGH...
I JUST CAN'T STAY AWAY FROM HER.
SORRY I LIED...

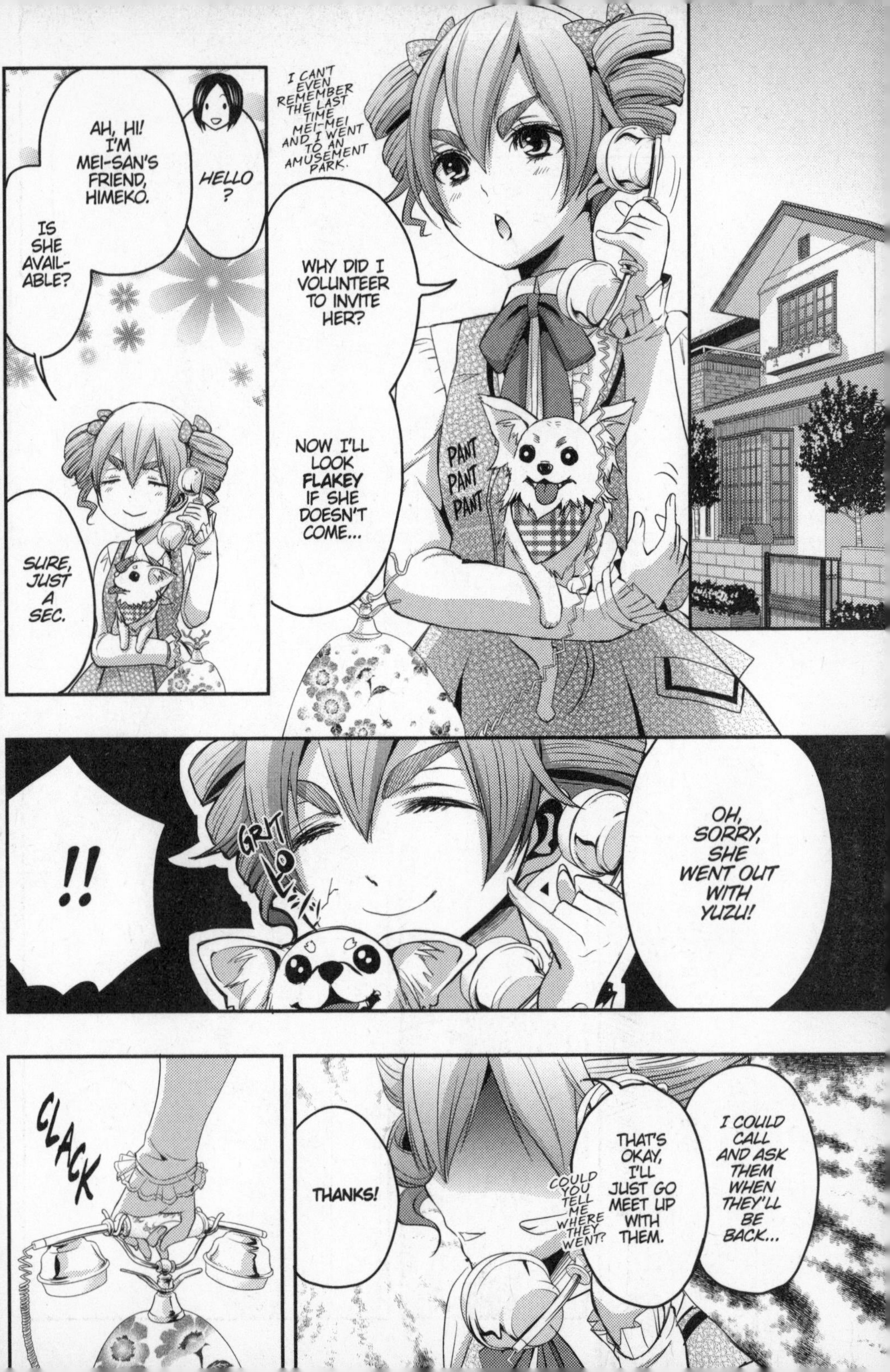
I CAN'T EVEN REMEMBER THE LAST TIME MEI-MEI AND I WENT TO AN AMUSEMENT PARK.
WHY DID I VOLUNTEER TO INVITE HER?
NOW I'LL LOOK FLAKEY IF SHE DOESN'T COME...
PANT PANT PANT
HELLO?
AH, HI! I'M MEI-SAN'S FRIEND, HIMEKO.
IS SHE AVAILABLE?
SURE, JUST A SEC.
OH, SORRY, SHE WENT OUT WITH YUZU!
GRIT
!!
I COULD CALL AND ASK THEM WHEN THEY'LL BE BACK...
THAT'S OKAY, I'LL JUST GO MEET UP WITH THEM.
COULD YOU TELL ME WHERE THEY WENT?
THANKS!
CLACK

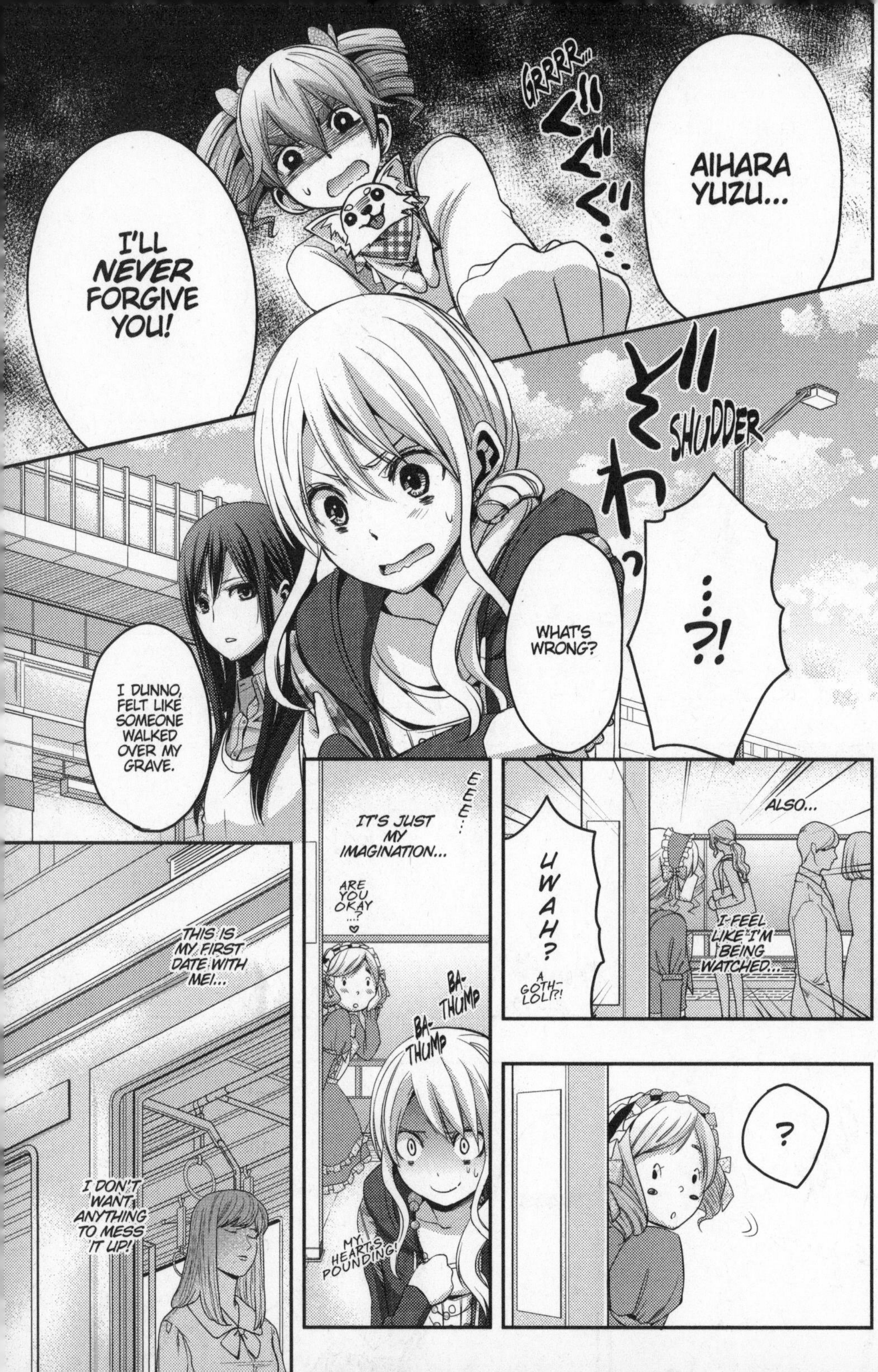
AIHARA YUZU...
GRRRR...
I'LL NEVER FORGIVE YOU!
SHUDDER
...?!
WHAT'S WRONG?
I DUNNO, FELT LIKE SOMEONE WALKED OVER MY GRAVE.
ALSO...
I FEEL LIKE I'M BEING WATCHED...
UWAH?
A GOTH-LOLI?!
EEE...
IT'S JUST MY IMAGINATION...
ARE YOU OKAY...?
BA-THUMP
BA-THUMP
MY HEART'S POUNDING!
?
THIS IS MY FIRST DATE WITH MEI...
I DON'T WANT ANYTHING TO MESS IT UP!

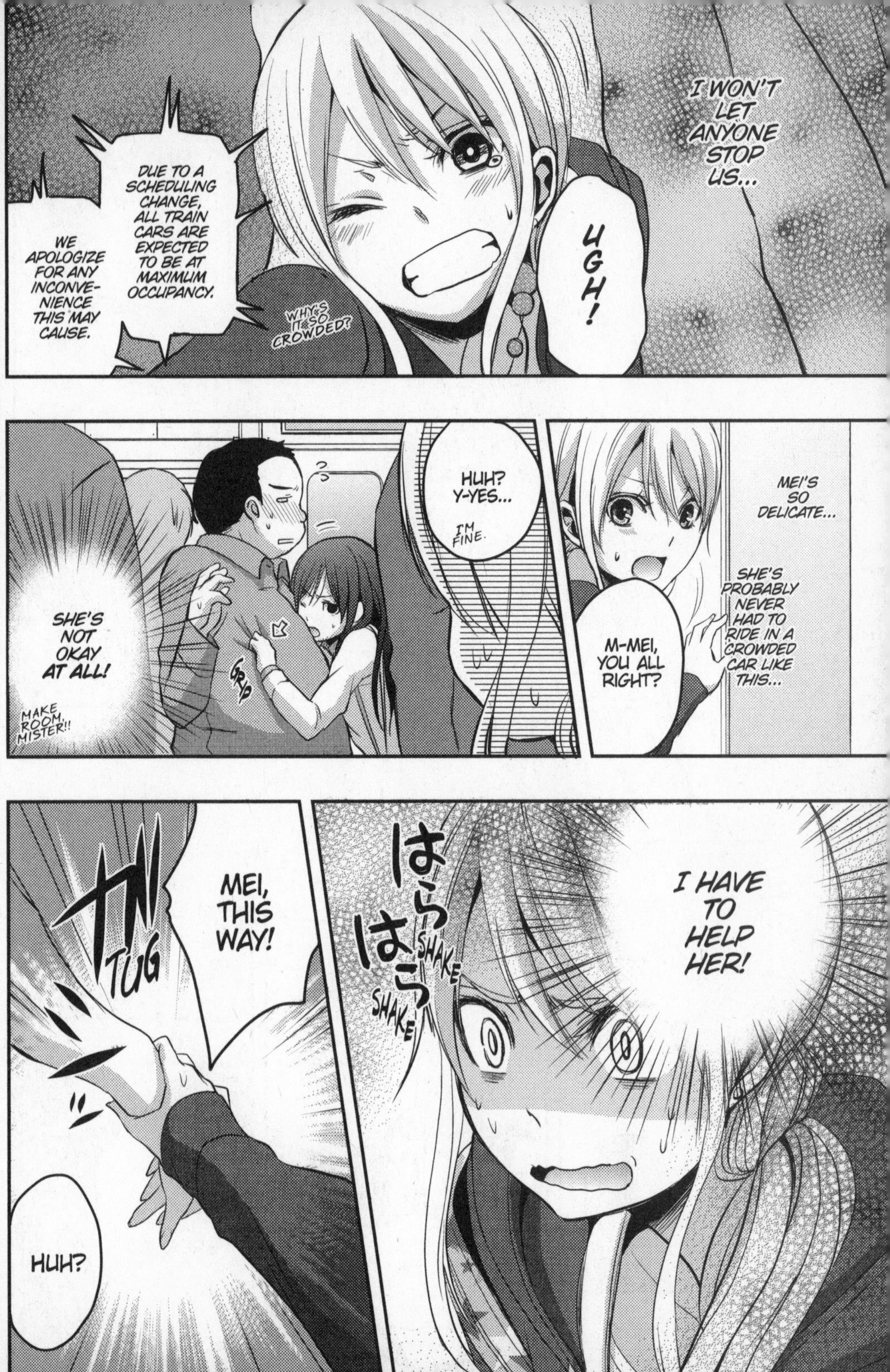
I WON'T LET ANYONE STOP US...
UGH!
WHY'S IT SO CROWDED?
DUE TO A SCHEDULING CHANGE, ALL TRAIN CARS ARE EXPECTED TO BE AT MAXIMUM OCCUPANCY.
WE APOLOGIZE FOR ANY INCONVENIENCE THIS MAY CAUSE.
MEI'S SO DELICATE...
SHE'S PROBABLY NEVER HAD TO RIDE IN A CROWDED CAR LIKE THIS...
M-MEI, YOU ALL RIGHT?
HUH? Y-YES...
I'M FINE.
GRIP
SHE'S NOT OKAY AT ALL!
MAKE ROOM, MISTER!!
I HAVE TO HELP HER!
はら はら
SHAKE SHAKE
MEI, THIS WAY!
TUG
HUH?

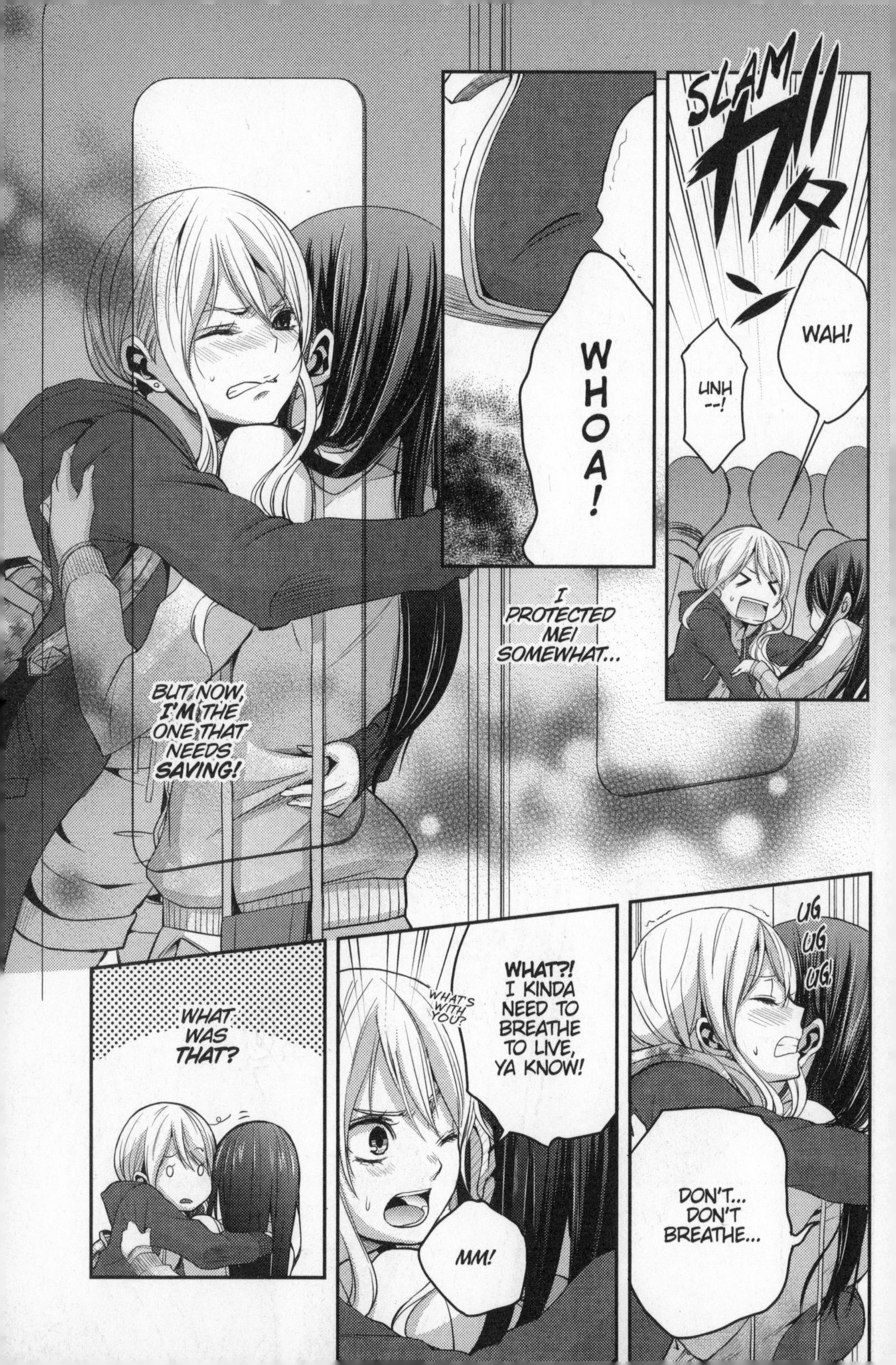
SLAM
ガタ
WAH!
UNH--!
WHOA!
I PROTECTED MEI SOMEWHAT...
BUT NOW, I'M THE ONE THAT NEEDS SAVING!
UG UG UG
DON'T... DON'T BREATHE...
WHAT?! I KINDA NEED TO BREATHE TO LIVE, YA KNOW!
WHAT'S WITH YOU?
MM!
WHAT WAS THAT?

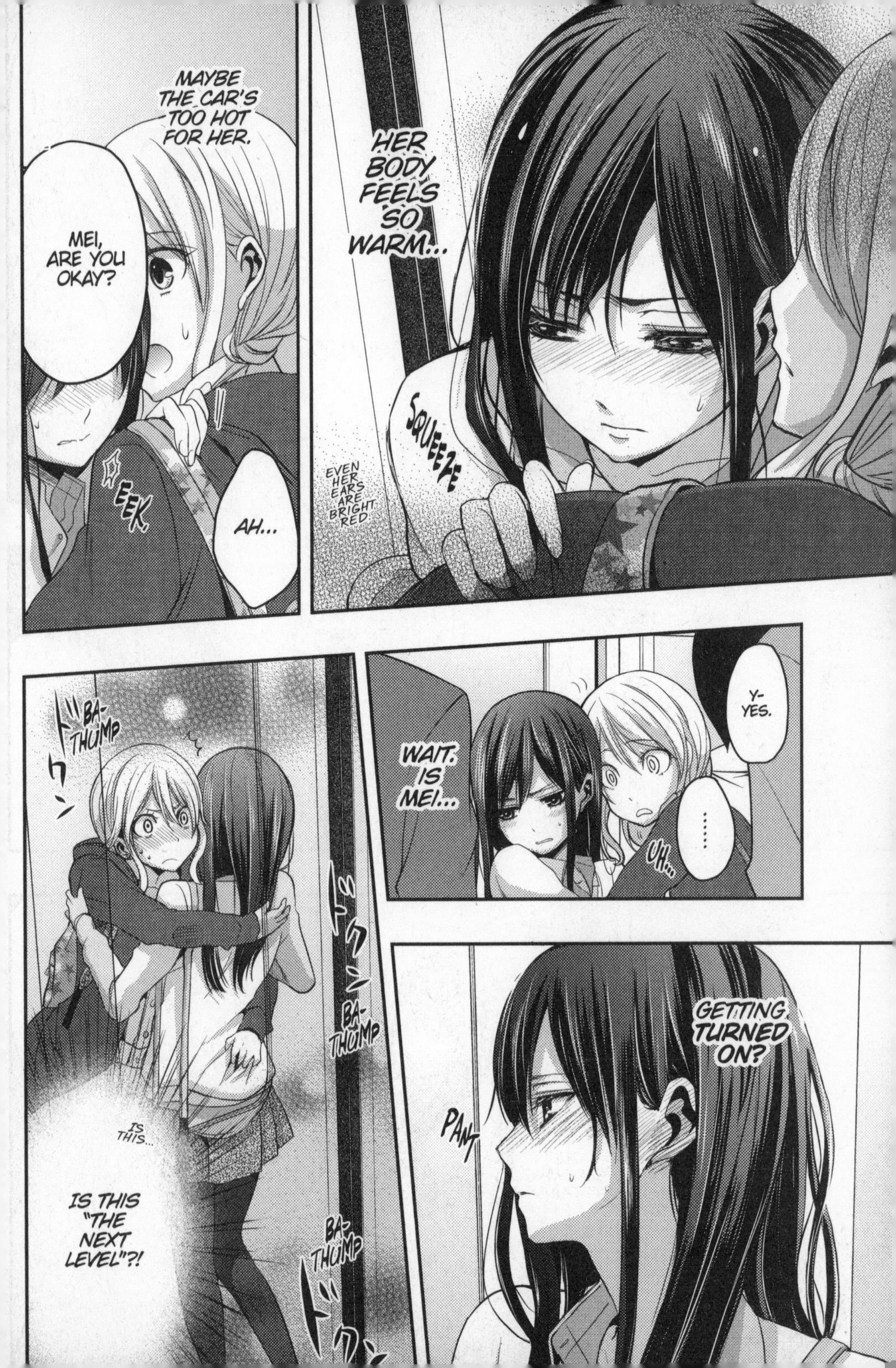
HER BODY FEELS SO WARM...
SQUEEZE
EVEN HER EARS ARE BRIGHT RED
MAYBE THE CAR'S TOO HOT FOR HER.
MEI, ARE YOU OKAY?
EEK
AH...
Y-YES.
WAIT. IS MEI...
......
UH...
GETTING TURNED ON?
PANT
BA-THUMP
BA-THUMP
IS THIS...
IS THIS "THE NEXT LEVEL"?!
BA-THUMP

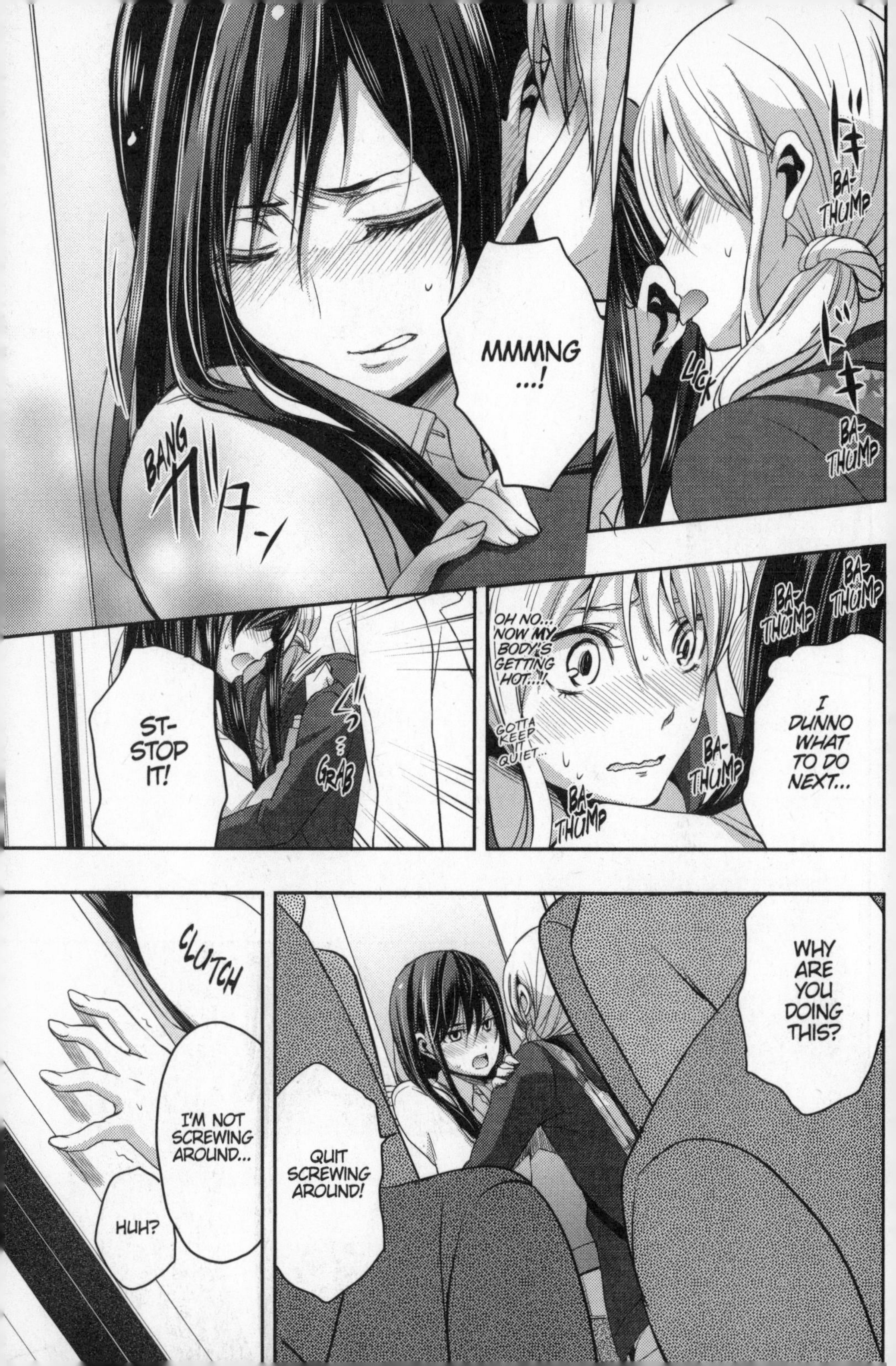

BA-THUMP
LICK
BA-THUMP
MMMNG ...!
BANG
BA-THUMP
BA-THUMP
OH NO... NOW MY BODY'S GETTING HOT...!!
I DUNNO WHAT TO DO NEXT...
GOTTA KEEP IT QUIET...
BA-THUMP
BA-THUMP
ST-STOP IT!
GRAB
WHY ARE YOU DOING THIS?
QUIT SCREWING AROUND!
CLUTCH
I'M NOT SCREWING AROUND...
HUH?

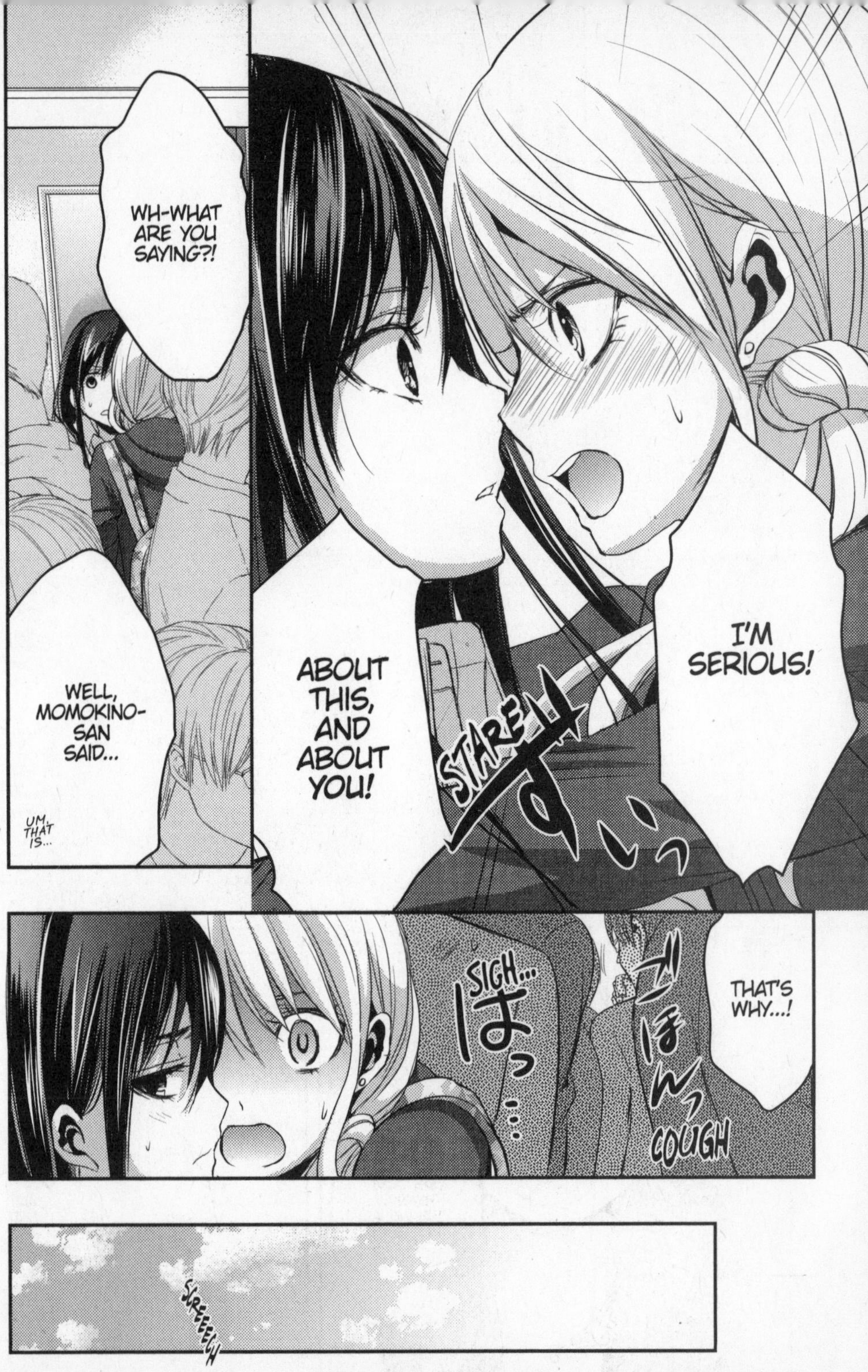
I'M SERIOUS!
STARE
ABOUT THIS, AND ABOUT YOU!
WH-WHAT ARE YOU SAYING?!
WELL, MOMOKINO-SAN SAID...
UM, THAT IS...
THAT'S WHY...!
COUGH
SIGH...
SCREEECH

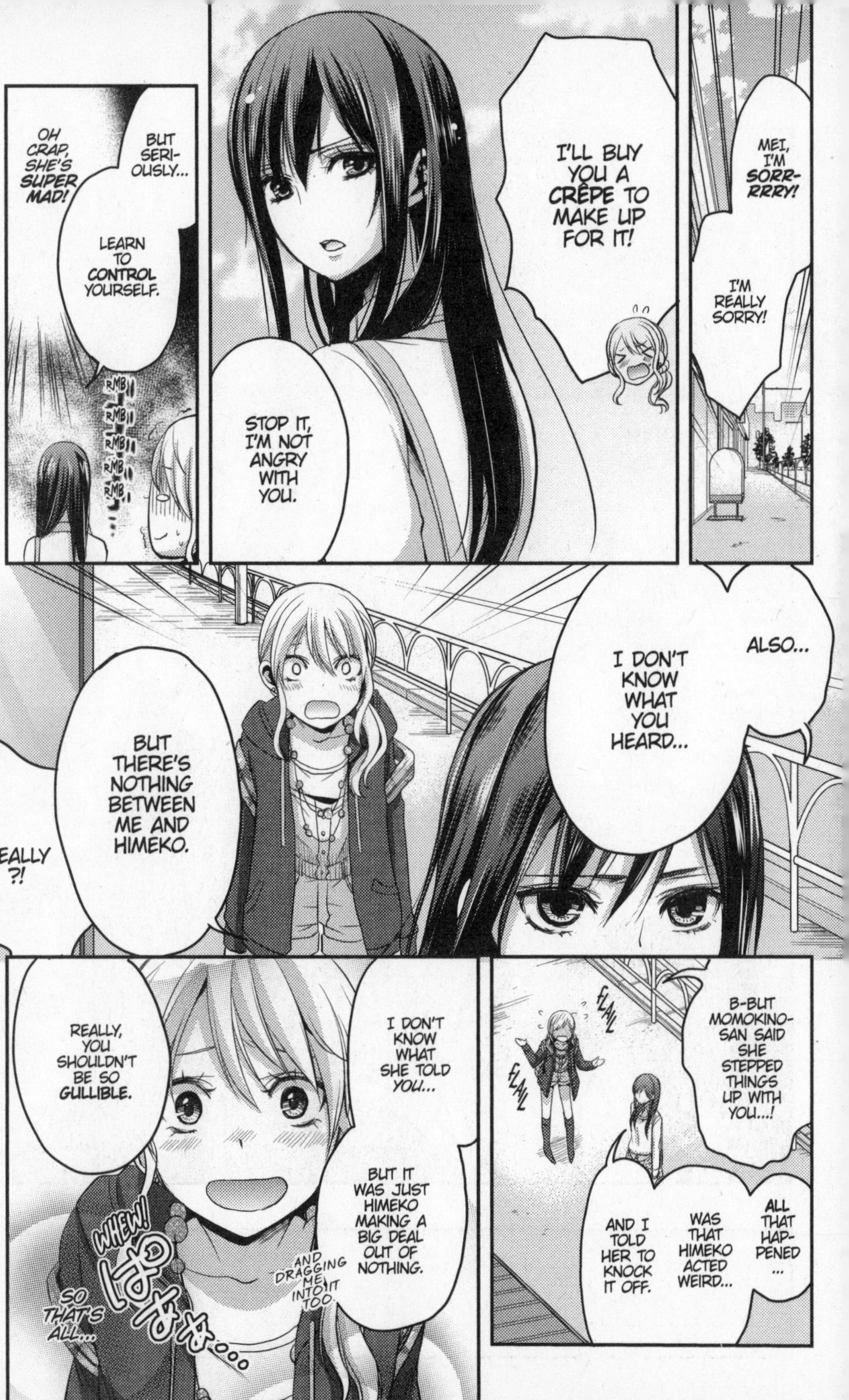
MEI, I'M SORRRRRY!
I'M REALLY SORRY!
I'LL BUY YOU A CRÊPE TO MAKE UP FOR IT!
STOP IT, I'M NOT ANGRY WITH YOU.
BUT SERIOUSLY...
LEARN TO CONTROL YOURSELF.
OH CRAP, SHE'S SUPER MAD!
RMB RMB RMB RMB RMB
ALSO...
I DON'T KNOW WHAT YOU HEARD...
BUT THERE'S NOTHING BETWEEN ME AND HIMEKO.
REALLY ?!
B-BUT MOMOKINO-SAN SAID SHE STEPPED THINGS UP WITH YOU...!
FLAIL FLAIL
ALL THAT HAPPENED...
WAS THAT HIMEKO ACTED WEIRD...
AND I TOLD HER TO KNOCK IT OFF.
I DON'T KNOW WHAT SHE TOLD YOU...
BUT IT WAS JUST HIMEKO MAKING A BIG DEAL OUT OF NOTHING.
AND DRAGGING ME INTO IT TOO.
REALLY, YOU SHOULDN'T BE SO GULLIBLE.
WHEW!
ぱぁぁ。。。
SO THAT'S ALL...

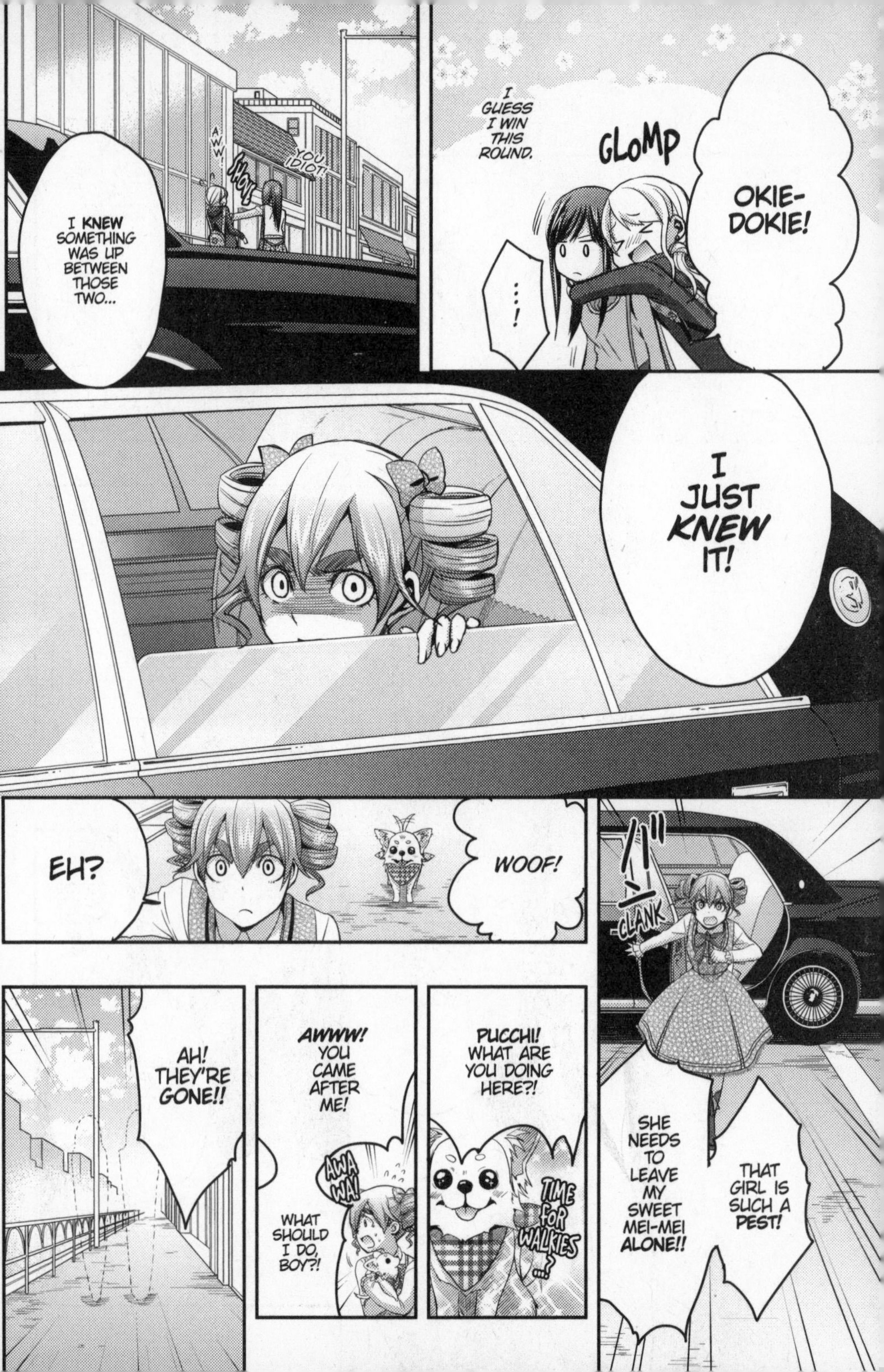
OKIE-DOKIE!
GLOMP
I GUESS I WIN THIS ROUND.
...!
YOU IDIOT!
HOY
AWW
I KNEW SOMETHING WAS UP BETWEEN THOSE TWO...
I JUST KNEW IT!
CLANK
THAT GIRL IS SUCH A PEST!
SHE NEEDS TO LEAVE MY SWEET MEI-MEI ALONE!!
WOOF!
EH?
PUCCHI! WHAT ARE YOU DOING HERE?!
TIME FOR WALKIES...?
AWWW! YOU CAME AFTER ME!
AWAWA!
WHAT SHOULD I DO, BOY?!
AH! THEY'RE GONE!!

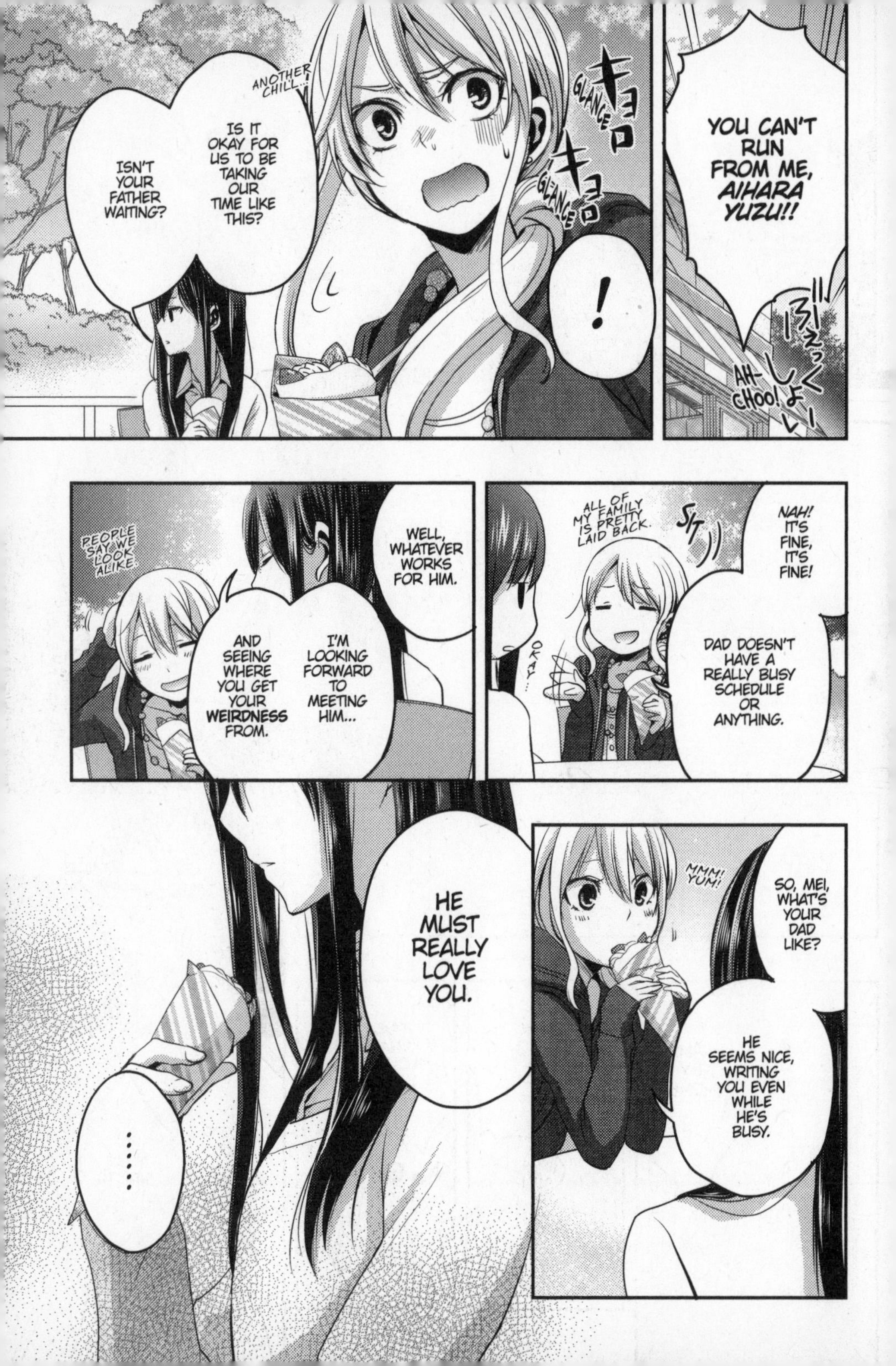
YOU CAN'T RUN FROM ME, AIHARA YUZU!!
AH-CHOO!
!
GLANCE
GLANCE
ANOTHER CHILL...
IS IT OKAY FOR US TO BE TAKING OUR TIME LIKE THIS?
ISN'T YOUR FATHER WAITING?
NAH! IT'S FINE, IT'S FINE!
DAD DOESN'T HAVE A REALLY BUSY SCHEDULE OR ANYTHING.
ALL OF MY FAMILY IS PRETTY LAID BACK.
SIT
OKAY...
WELL, WHATEVER WORKS FOR HIM.
I'M LOOKING FORWARD TO MEETING HIM...
AND SEEING WHERE YOU GET YOUR **WEIRDNESS** FROM.
PEOPLE SAY WE LOOK ALIKE.
MMM! YUM!
SO, MEI, WHAT'S YOUR DAD LIKE?
HE SEEMS NICE, WRITING YOU EVEN WHILE HE'S BUSY.
HE MUST REALLY LOVE YOU.
......

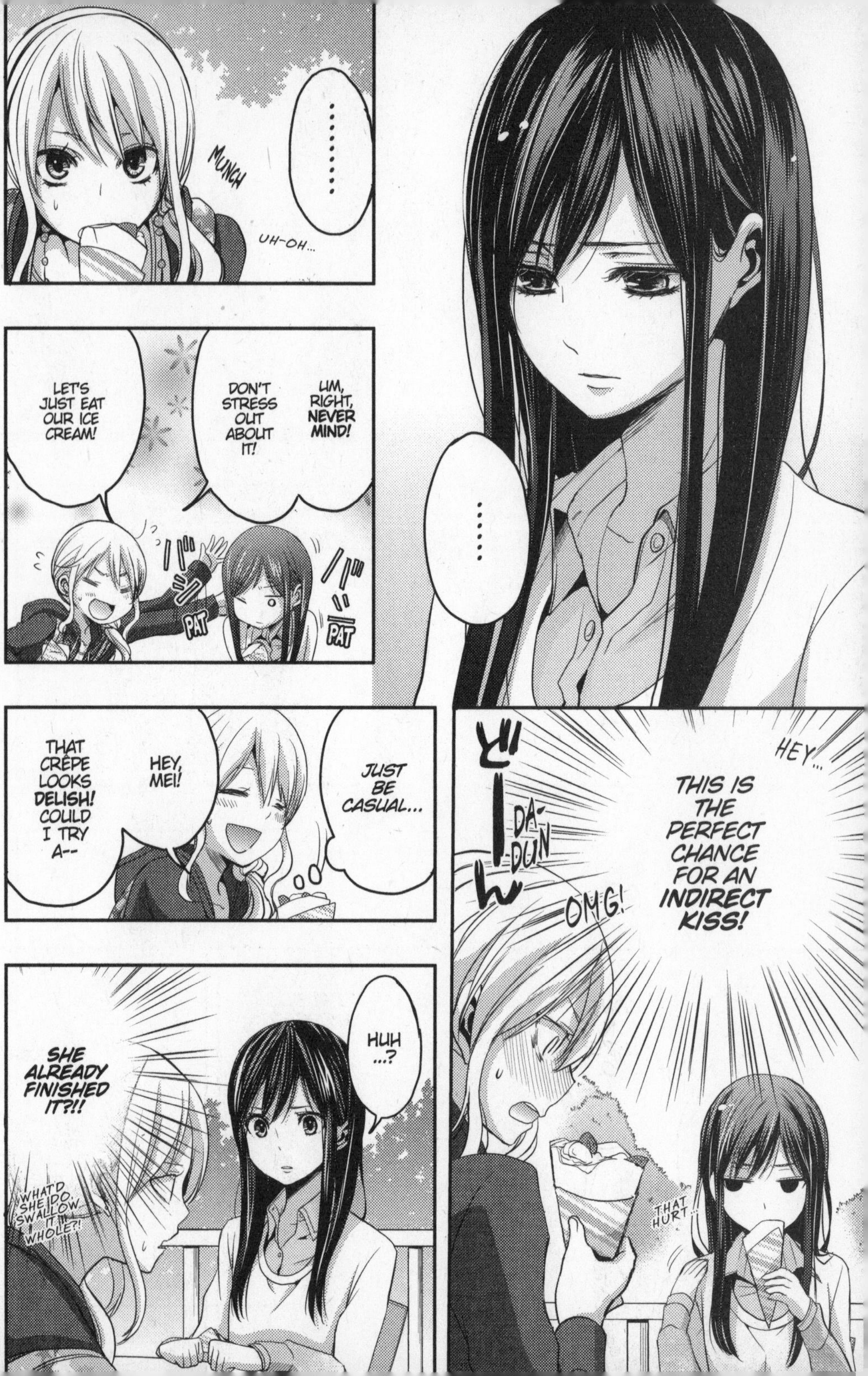
......
......
MUNCH
UH-OH...
UM, RIGHT, NEVER MIND!
DON'T STRESS OUT ABOUT IT!
LET'S JUST EAT OUR ICE CREAM!
PAT
PAT
HEY...
THIS IS THE PERFECT CHANCE FOR AN INDIRECT KISS!
OMG!
THAT HURT...
JUST BE CASUAL...
HEY, MEI!
THAT CRÊPE LOOKS DELISH! COULD I TRY A--
HUH ...?
SHE ALREADY FINISHED IT?!!
WHAT'D SHE DO, SWALLOW IT WHOLE?!

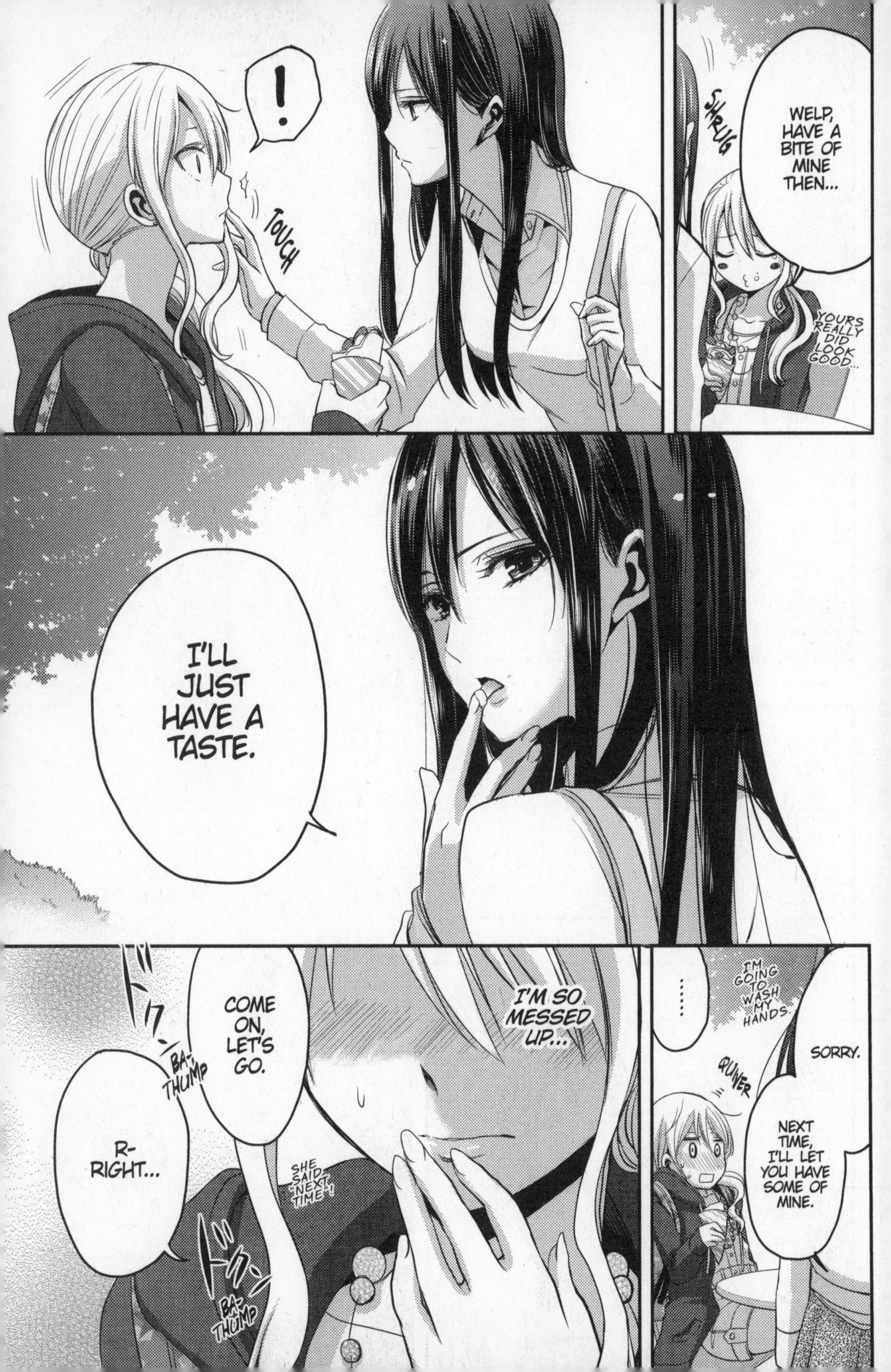
WELP, HAVE A BITE OF MINE THEN...
SHRUG
YOURS REALLY DID LOOK GOOD...
!
TOUCH
I'LL JUST HAVE A TASTE.
I'M GOING TO WASH MY HANDS.
......
SORRY.
QUIVER
NEXT TIME, I'LL LET YOU HAVE SOME OF MINE.
I'M SO MESSED UP...
COME ON, LET'S GO.
BA-THUMP
SHE SAID "NEXT TIME"!
R-RIGHT...
BA-THUMP

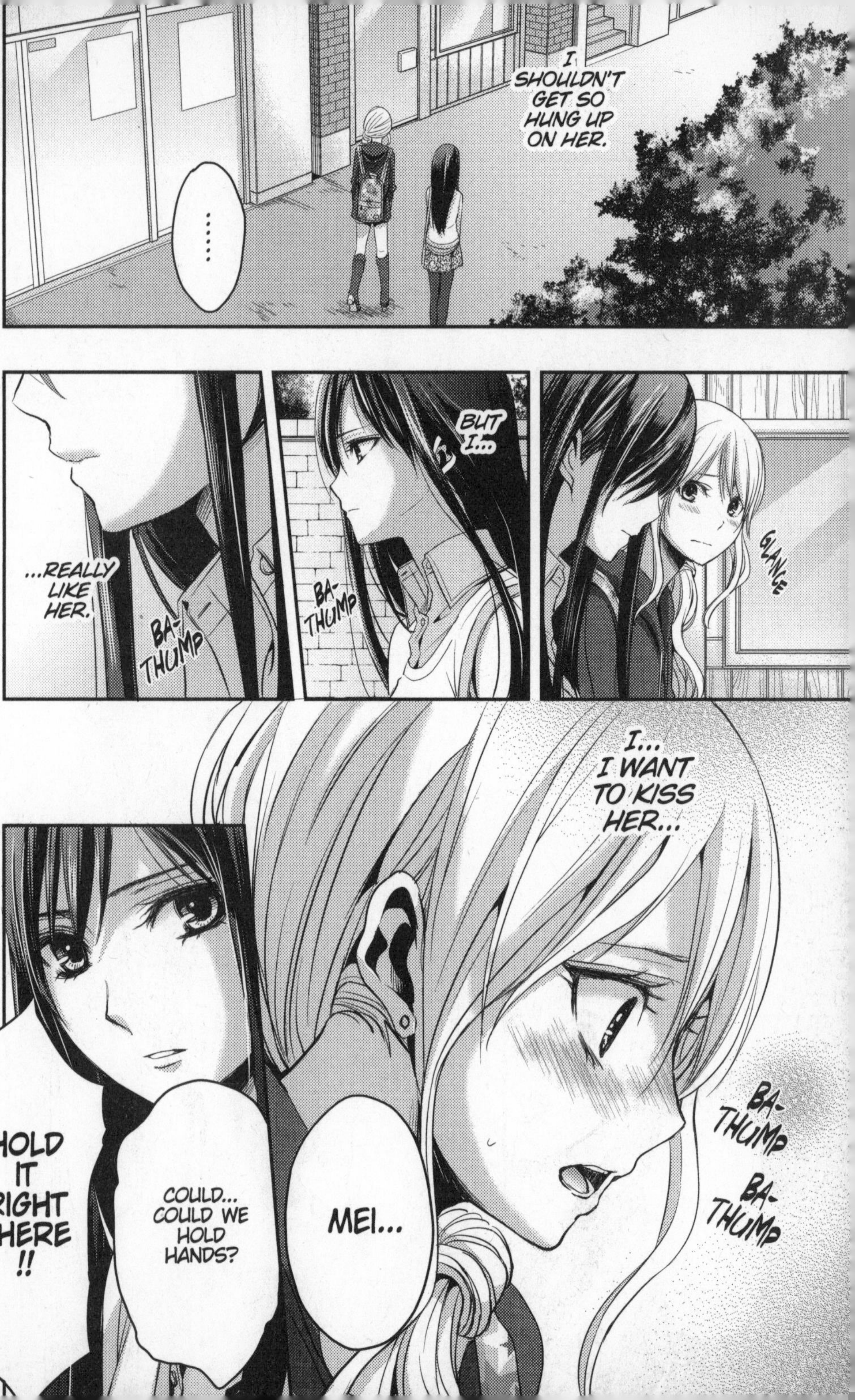
I SHOULDN'T GET SO HUNG UP ON HER.
......
GLANCE
BUT I...
BA-THUMP
...REALLY LIKE HER.
BA-THUMP
I... I WANT TO KISS HER...
BA-THUMP
BA-THUMP
MEI...
COULD... COULD WE HOLD HANDS?
HOLD IT RIGHT THERE !!

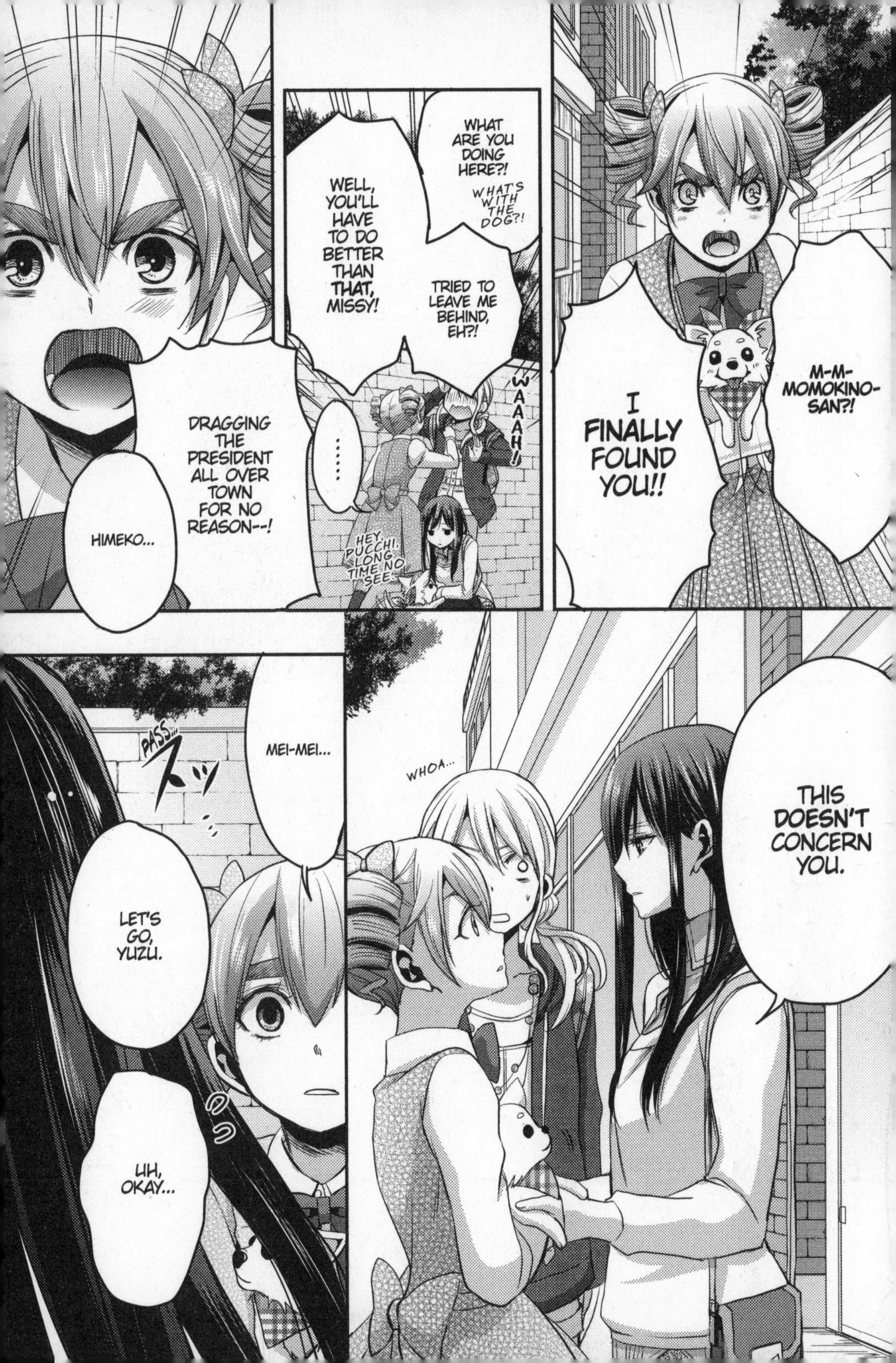
M-M-MOMOKINO-SAN?!
I FINALLY FOUND YOU!!
WHAT ARE YOU DOING HERE?!
WHAT'S WITH THE DOG?!
TRIED TO LEAVE ME BEHIND, EH?!
WELL, YOU'LL HAVE TO DO BETTER THAN THAT, MISSY!
WAAAAH!
......
HEY, PUCCHI. LONG TIME NO SEE.
DRAGGING THE PRESIDENT ALL OVER TOWN FOR NO REASON--!
HIMEKO...
THIS DOESN'T CONCERN YOU.
WHOA...
MEI-MEI...
PASS...
LET'S GO, YUZU.
UH, OKAY...

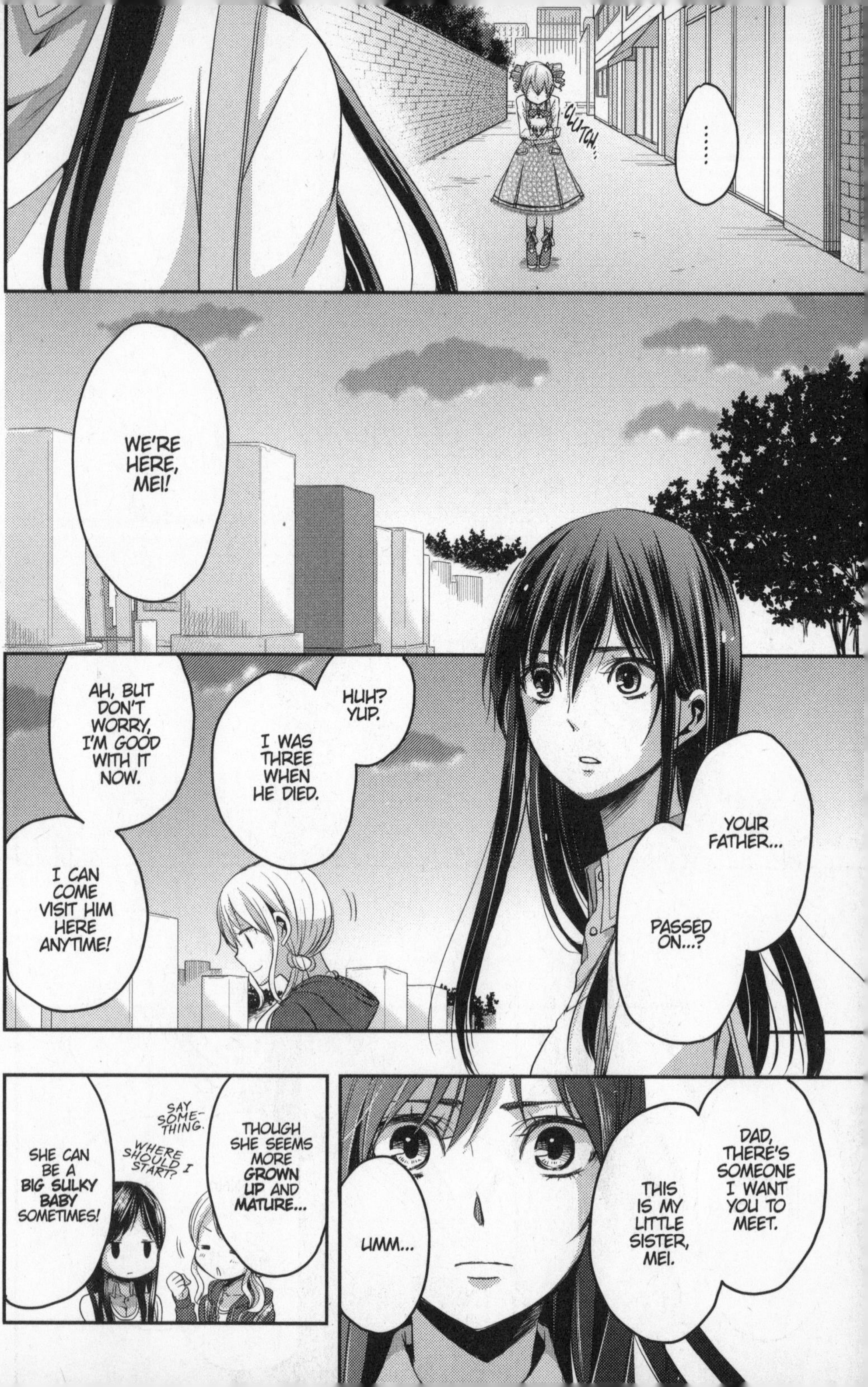
......
CLUTCH...
WE'RE HERE, MEI!
YOUR FATHER...
PASSED ON...?
HUH? YUP.
I WAS THREE WHEN HE DIED.
AH, BUT DON'T WORRY, I'M GOOD WITH IT NOW.
I CAN COME VISIT HIM HERE ANYTIME!
DAD, THERE'S SOMEONE I WANT YOU TO MEET.
THIS IS MY LITTLE SISTER, MEI.
UMM...
THOUGH SHE SEEMS MORE GROWN UP AND MATURE...
SAY SOME-THING.
WHERE SHOULD I START?
SHE CAN BE A BIG SULKY BABY SOMETIMES!

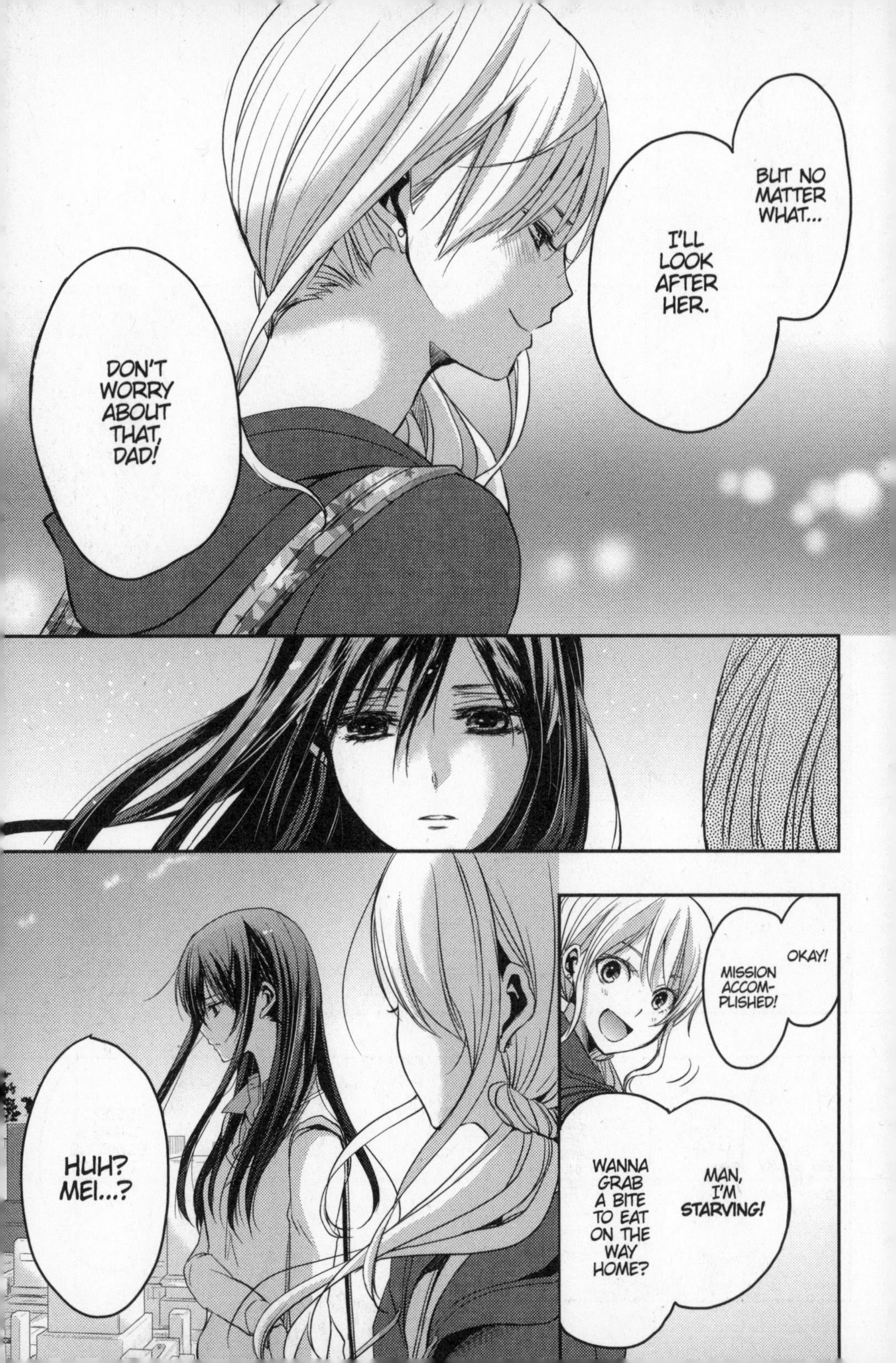
BUT NO MATTER WHAT...
I'LL LOOK AFTER HER.
DON'T WORRY ABOUT THAT, DAD!
OKAY! MISSION ACCOMPLISHED!
MAN, I'M STARVING!
WANNA GRAB A BITE TO EAT ON THE WAY HOME?
HUH? MEI...?

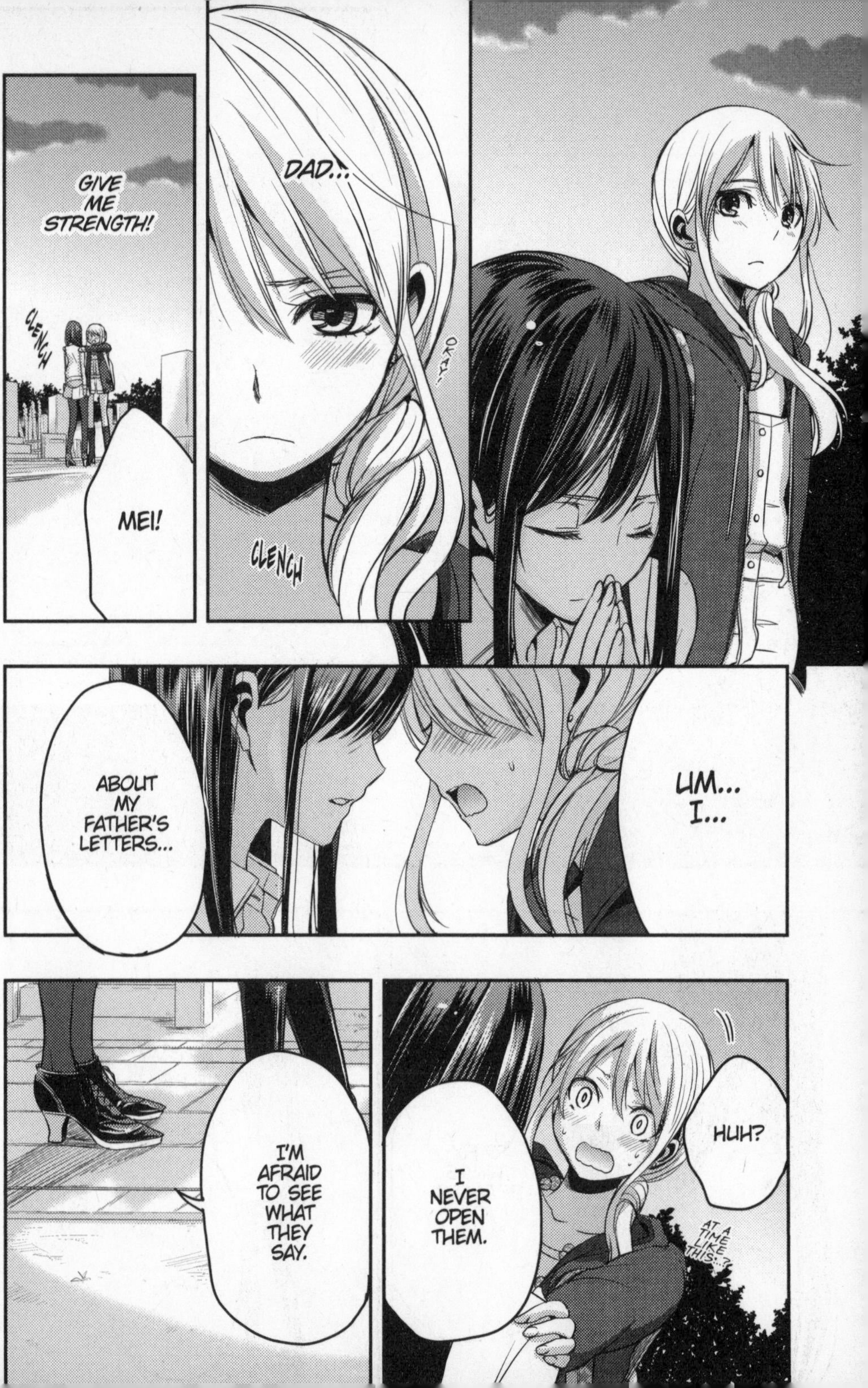
DAD...
OKAY...
CLENCH
GIVE ME STRENGTH!
CLENCH
MEI!
UM... I...
ABOUT MY FATHER'S LETTERS...
HUH?
AT A TIME LIKE THIS...?
I NEVER OPEN THEM.
I'M AFRAID TO SEE WHAT THEY SAY.

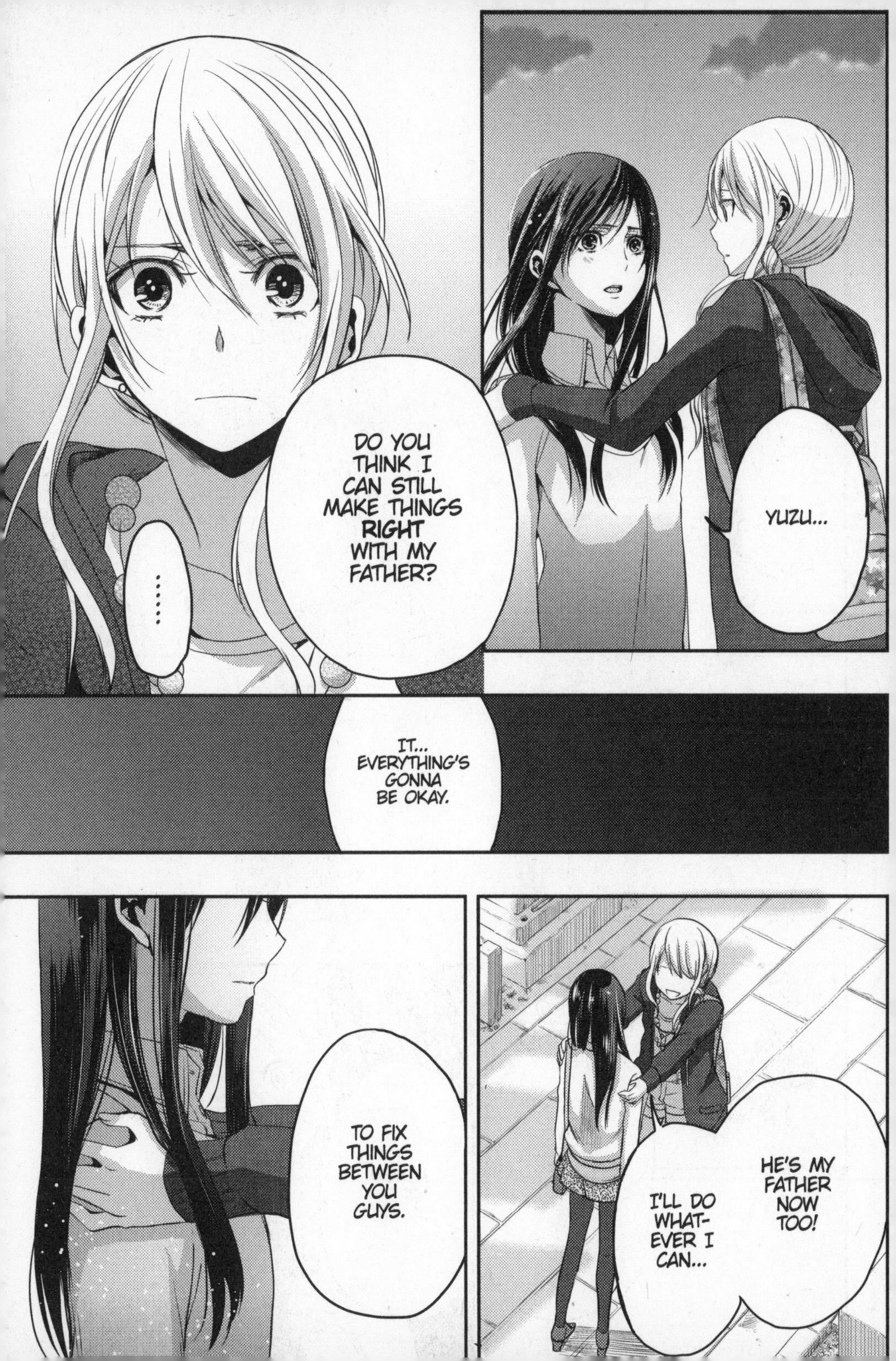
YUZU...
DO YOU THINK I CAN STILL MAKE THINGS RIGHT WITH MY FATHER?
......
IT... EVERYTHING'S GONNA BE OKAY.
HE'S MY FATHER NOW TOO!
I'LL DO WHAT-EVER I CAN...
TO FIX THINGS BETWEEN YOU GUYS.

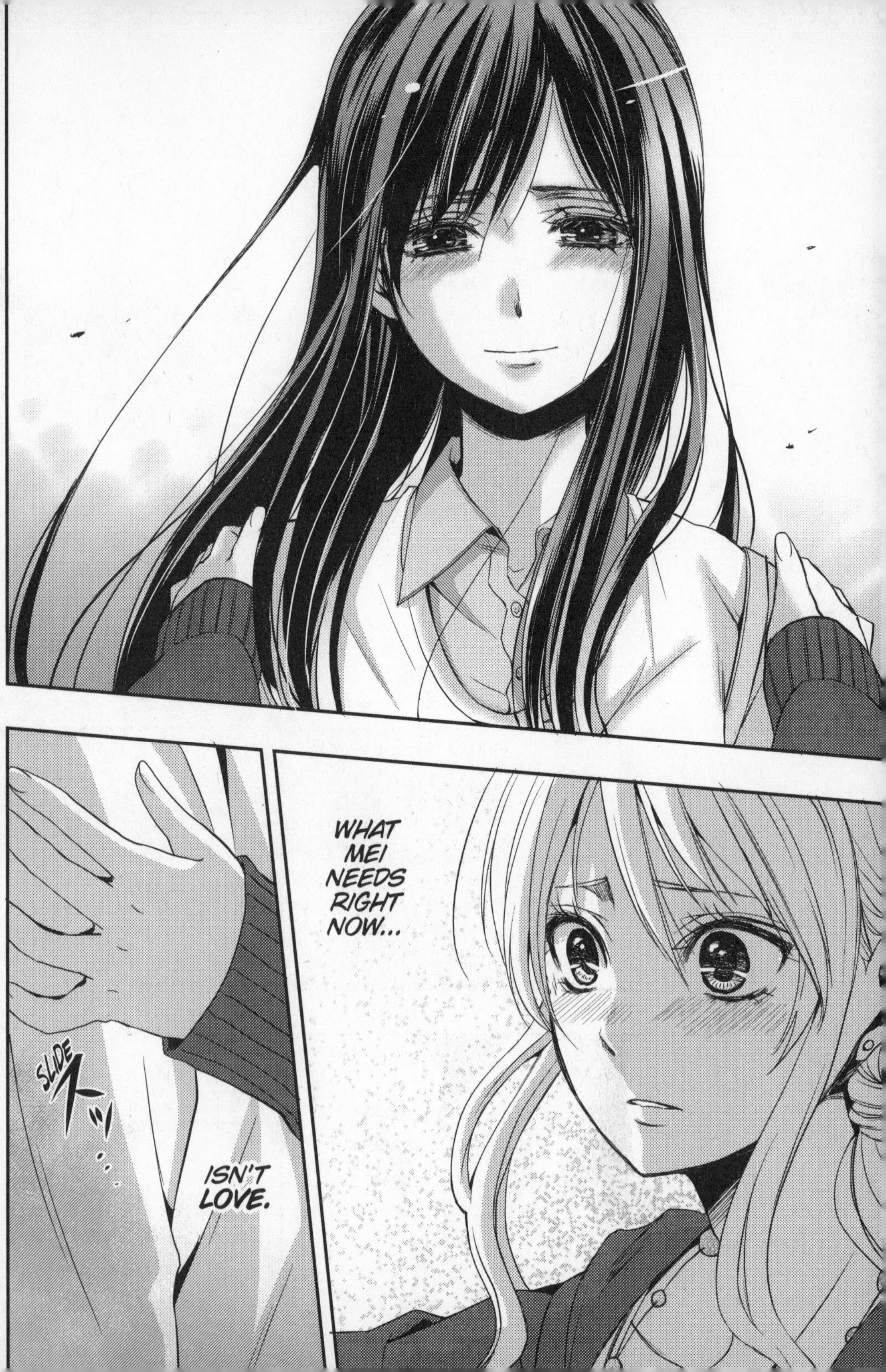
WHAT MEI NEEDS RIGHT NOW...
SLIDE
ISN'T LOVE.

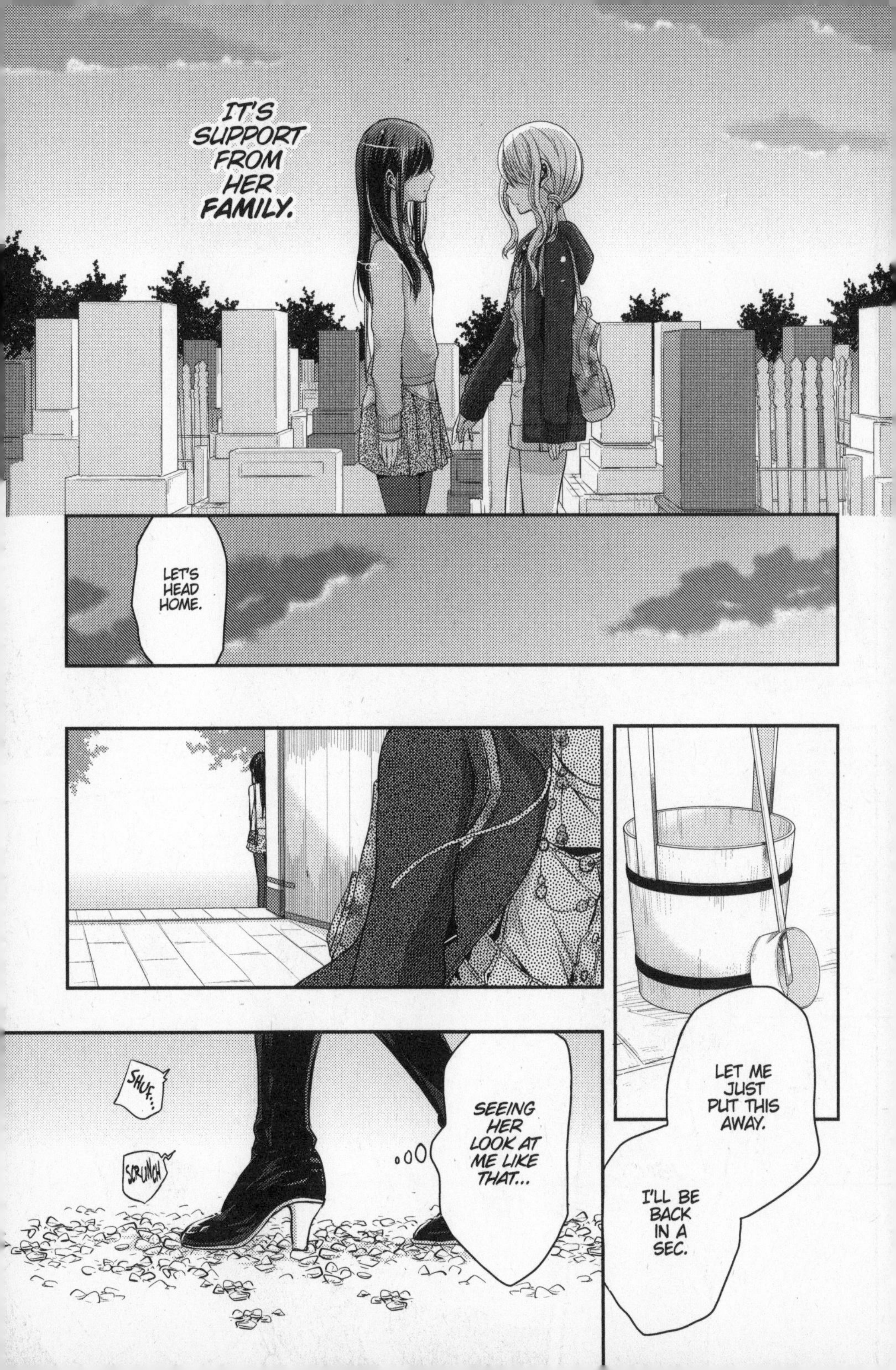
IT'S SUPPORT FROM HER FAMILY.
LET'S HEAD HOME.
LET ME JUST PUT THIS AWAY.
I'LL BE BACK IN A SEC.
SEEING HER LOOK AT ME LIKE THAT...
SHUF...
SCRUNCH

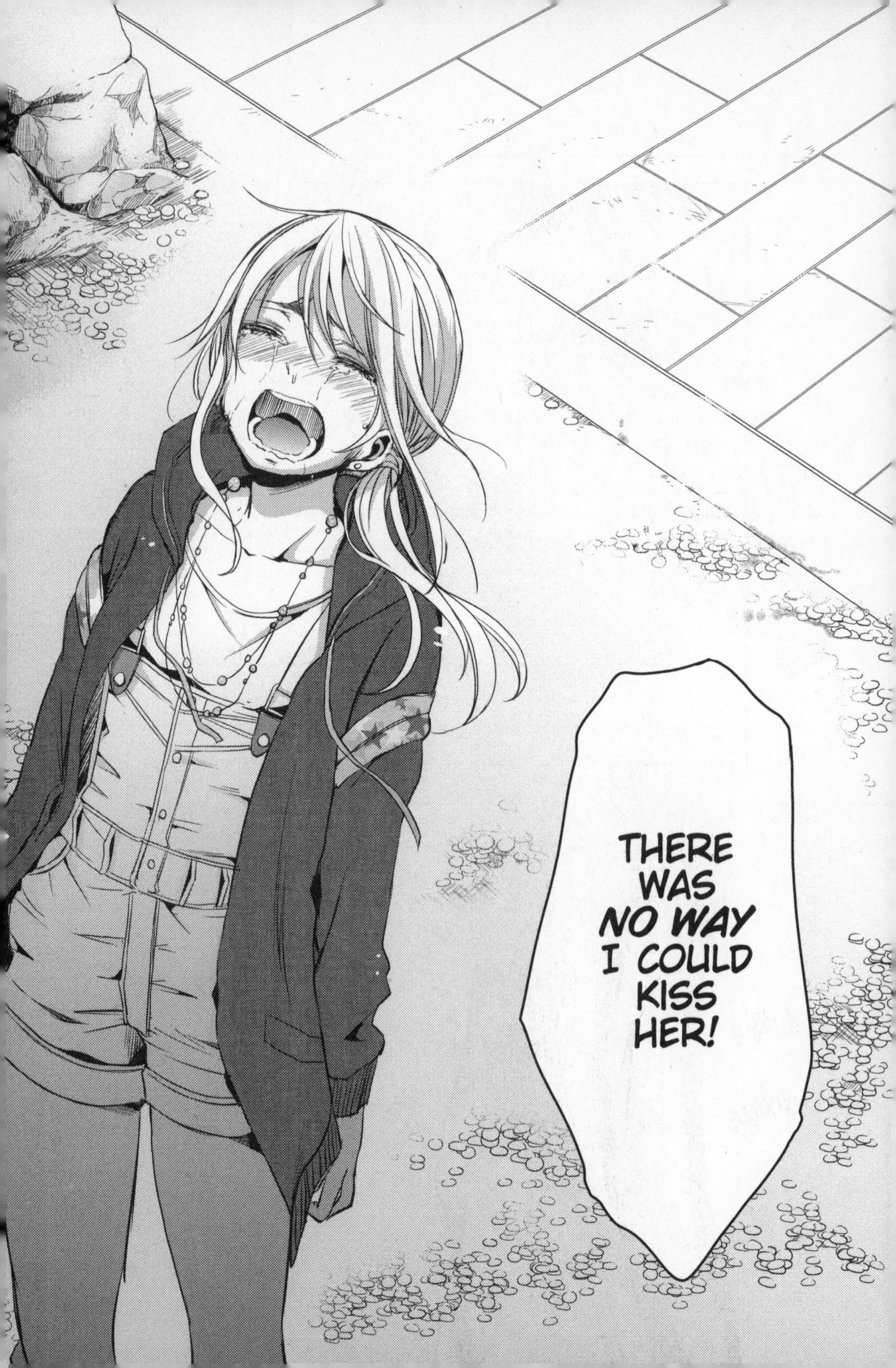
THERE WAS NO WAY I COULD KISS HER!

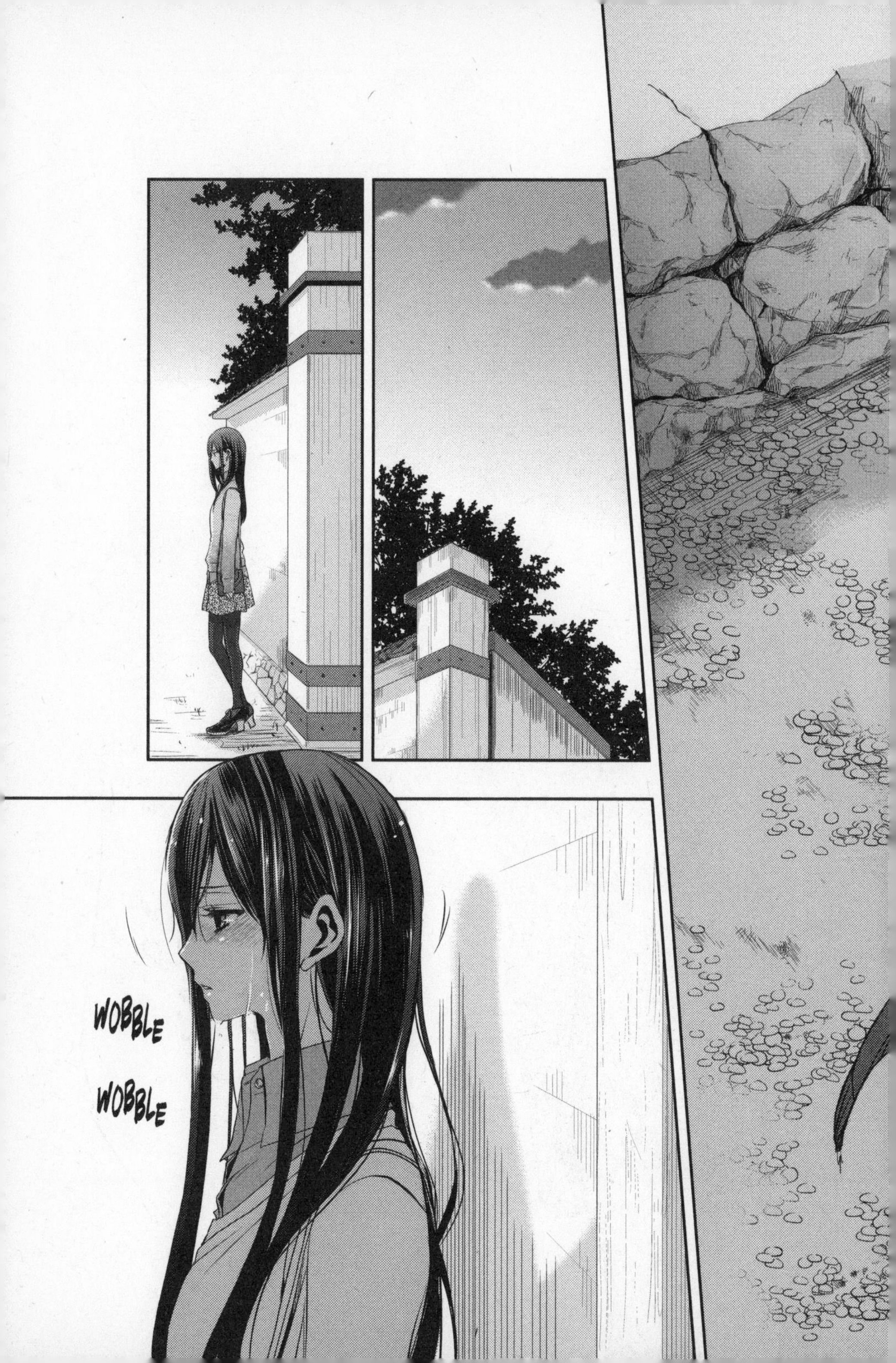
WOBBLE
WOBBLE

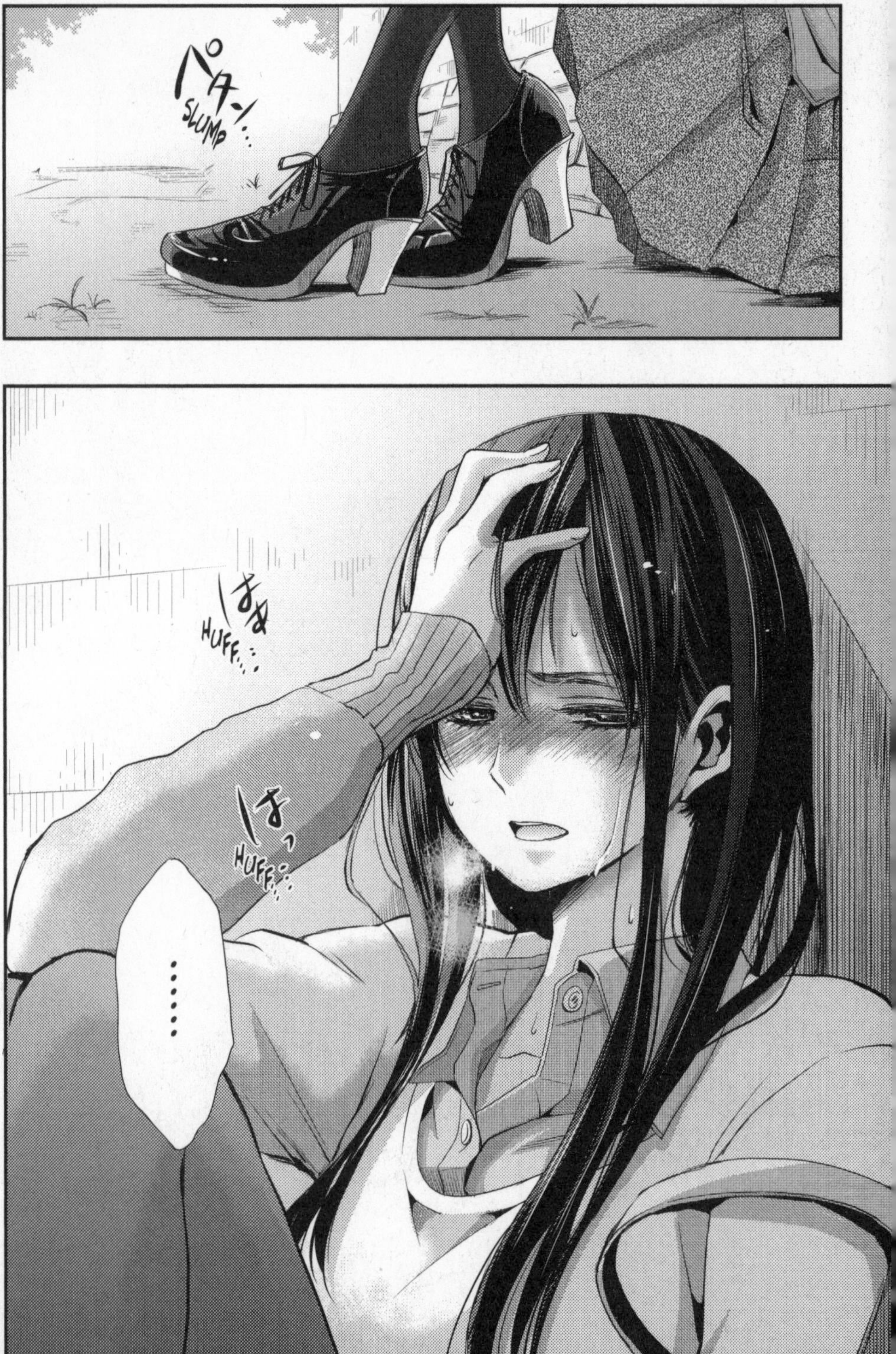
パタン…
SLUMP
はぁ
HUFF…
はっ
HUFF…
……

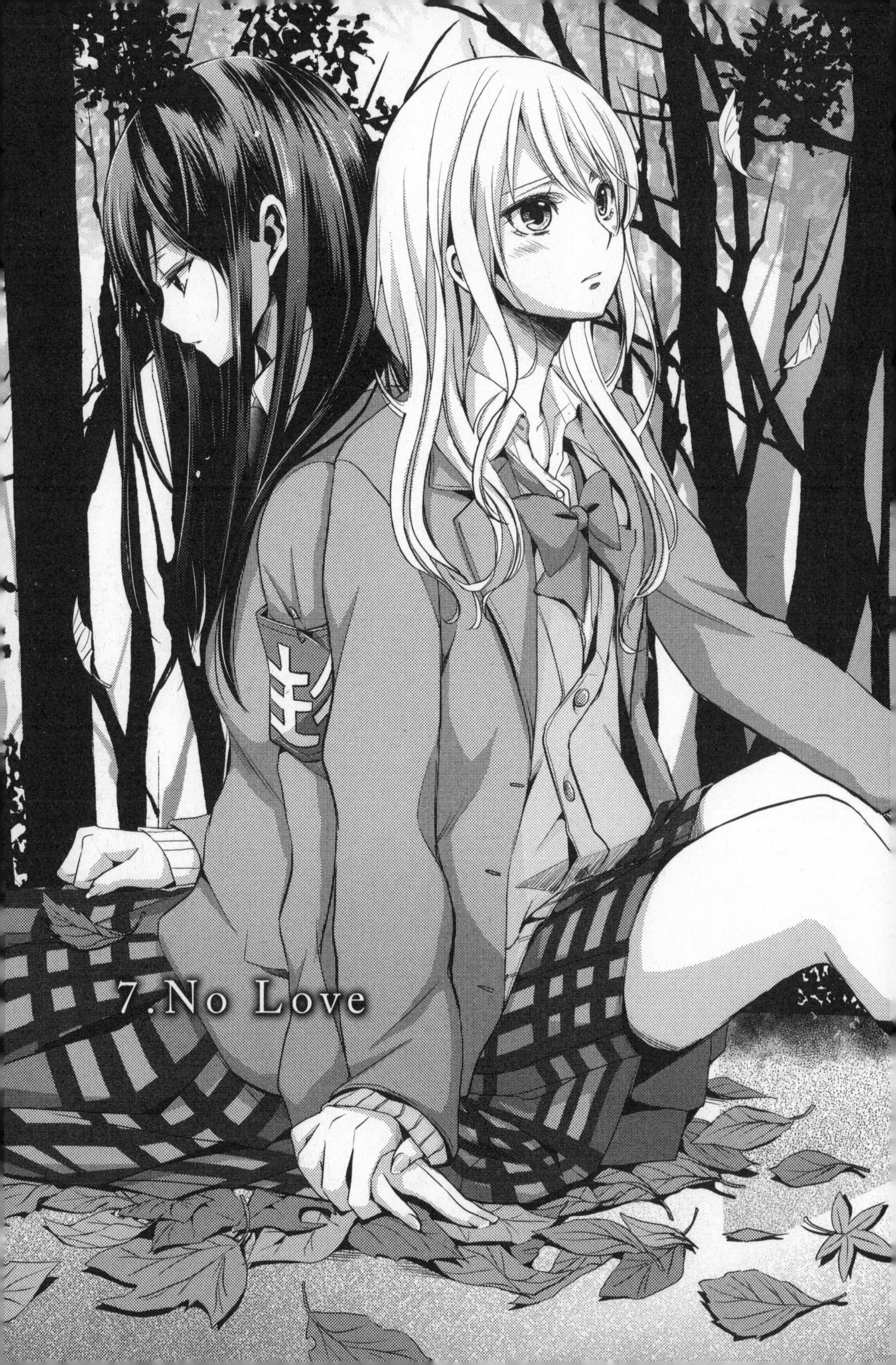
7. No Love

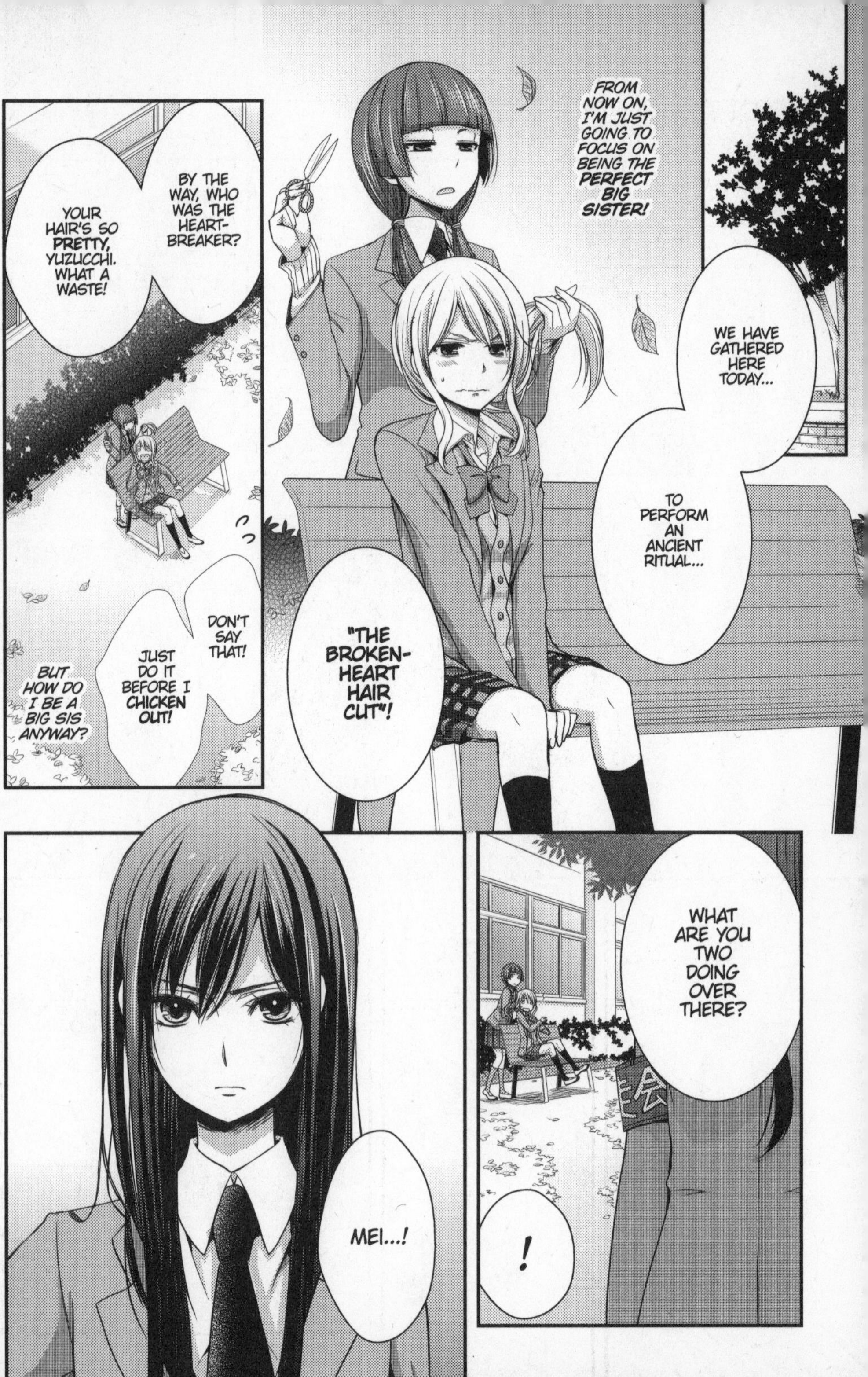
FROM NOW ON, I'M JUST GOING TO FOCUS ON BEING THE PERFECT BIG SISTER!
WE HAVE GATHERED HERE TODAY...
TO PERFORM AN ANCIENT RITUAL...
"THE BROKEN-HEART HAIR CUT"!
BY THE WAY, WHO WAS THE HEART-BREAKER?
YOUR HAIR'S SO PRETTY, YUZUCCHI. WHAT A WASTE!
DON'T SAY THAT!
JUST DO IT BEFORE I CHICKEN OUT!
BUT HOW DO I BE A BIG SIS ANYWAY?
WHAT ARE YOU TWO DOING OVER THERE?
!
MEI...!

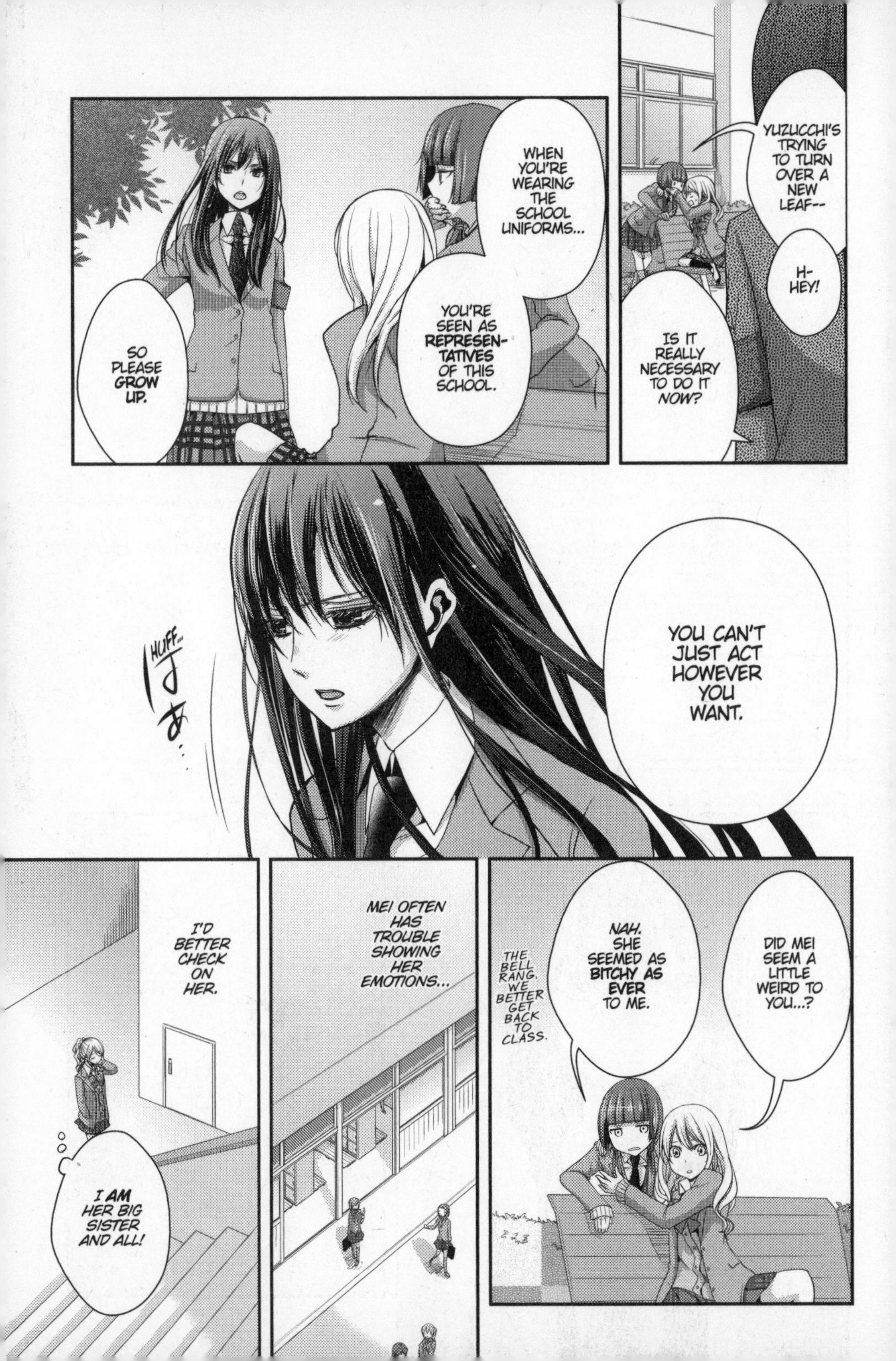
YUZUCCHI'S TRYING TO TURN OVER A NEW LEAF--
H-HEY!
IS IT REALLY NECESSARY TO DO IT NOW?
WHEN YOU'RE WEARING THE SCHOOL UNIFORMS...
YOU'RE SEEN AS REPRESENTATIVES OF THIS SCHOOL.
SO PLEASE GROW UP.
YOU CAN'T JUST ACT HOWEVER YOU WANT.
はぁ…
HUFF...
DID MEI SEEM A LITTLE WEIRD TO YOU...?
NAH. SHE SEEMED AS BITCHY AS EVER TO ME.
THE BELL RANG. WE BETTER GET BACK TO CLASS.
MEI OFTEN HAS TROUBLE SHOWING HER EMOTIONS...
I'D BETTER CHECK ON HER.
I AM HER BIG SISTER AND ALL!

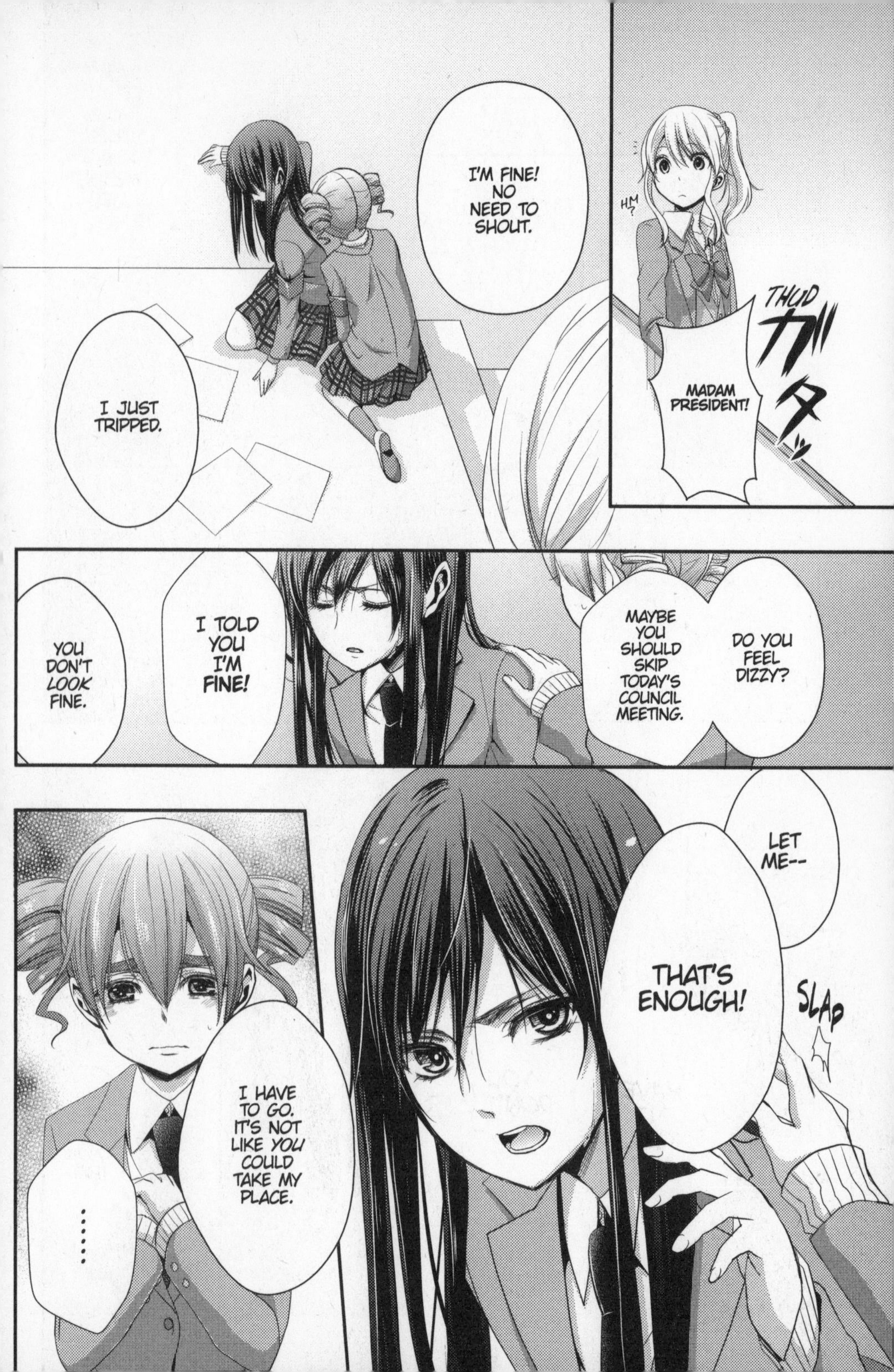

HM?
THUD
ガタッ
MADAM PRESIDENT!
I'M FINE! NO NEED TO SHOUT.
I JUST TRIPPED.
DO YOU FEEL DIZZY?
MAYBE YOU SHOULD SKIP TODAY'S COUNCIL MEETING.
I TOLD YOU I'M FINE!
YOU DON'T *LOOK* FINE.
LET ME--
SLAP
THAT'S ENOUGH!
I HAVE TO GO. IT'S NOT LIKE *YOU* COULD TAKE MY PLACE.
......

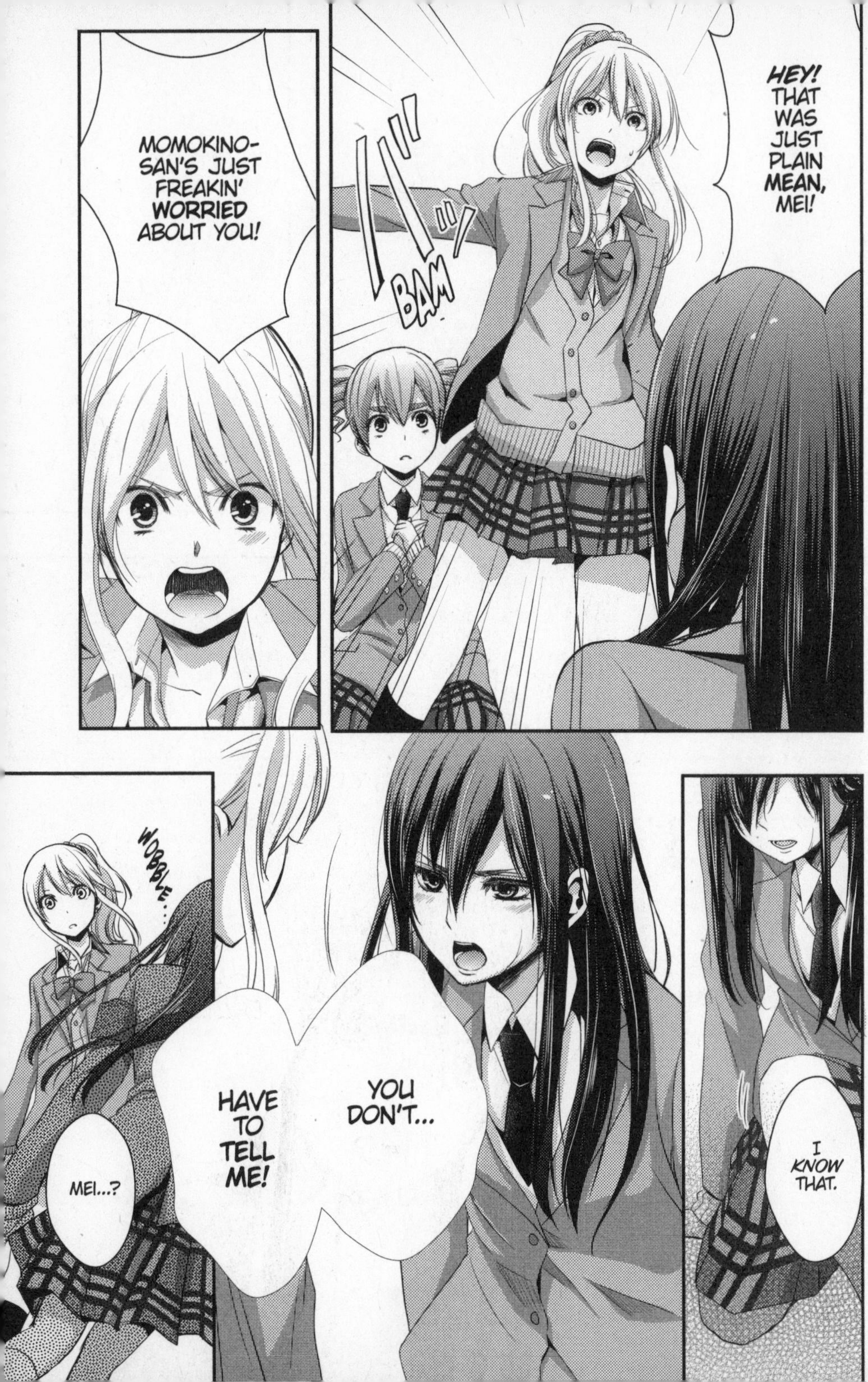
HEY! THAT WAS JUST PLAIN MEAN, MEI!
BAM
MOMOKINO-SAN'S JUST FREAKIN' WORRIED ABOUT YOU!
I KNOW THAT.
YOU DON'T...
HAVE TO TELL ME!
WOBBLE...
MEI...?

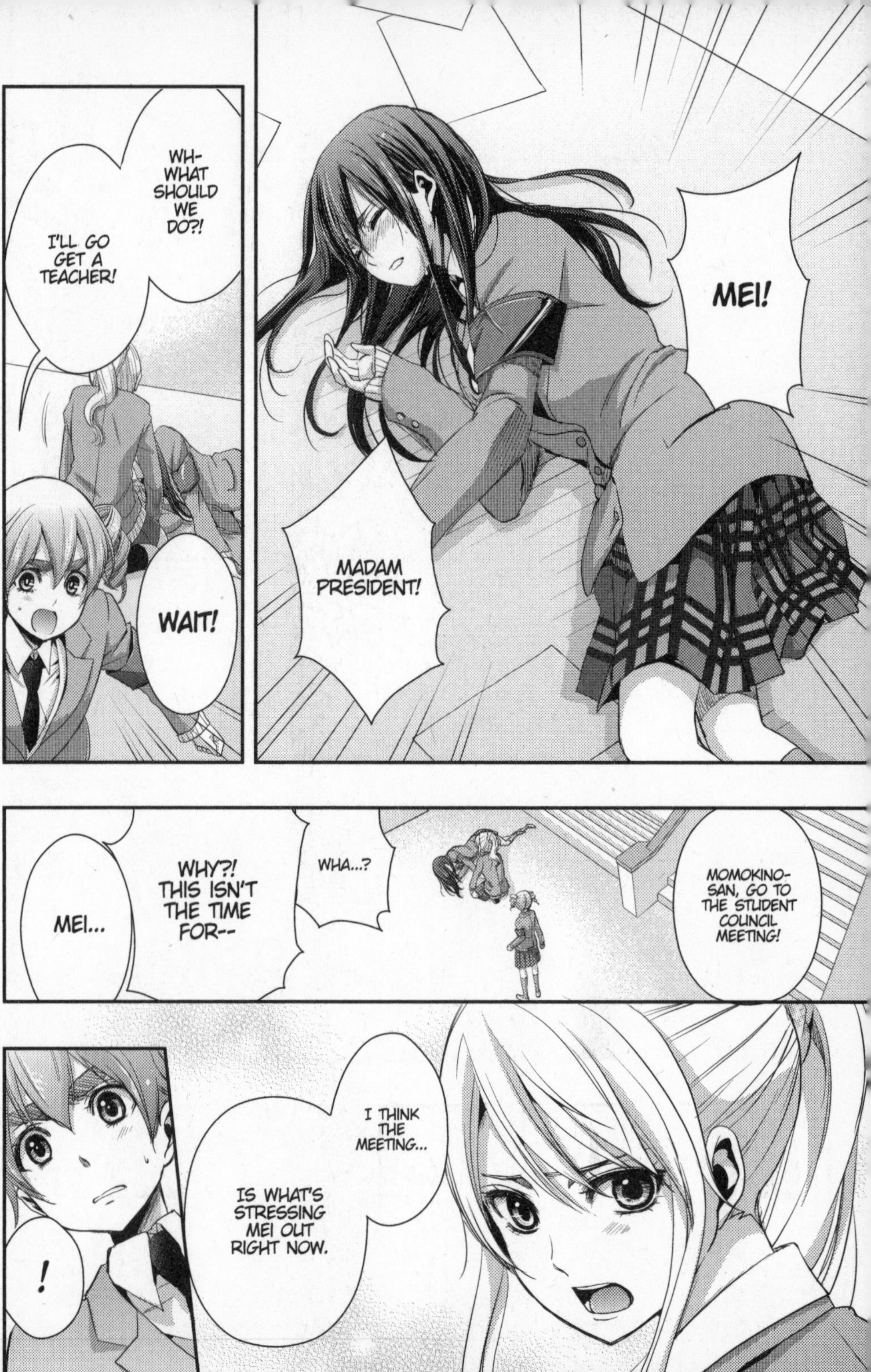
MEI!
MADAM PRESIDENT!
WH- WHAT SHOULD WE DO?!
I'LL GO GET A TEACHER!
WAIT!
MOMOKINO-SAN, GO TO THE STUDENT COUNCIL MEETING!
WHA...?
WHY?! THIS ISN'T THE TIME FOR--
MEI...
I THINK THE MEETING...
IS WHAT'S STRESSING MEI OUT RIGHT NOW.
!

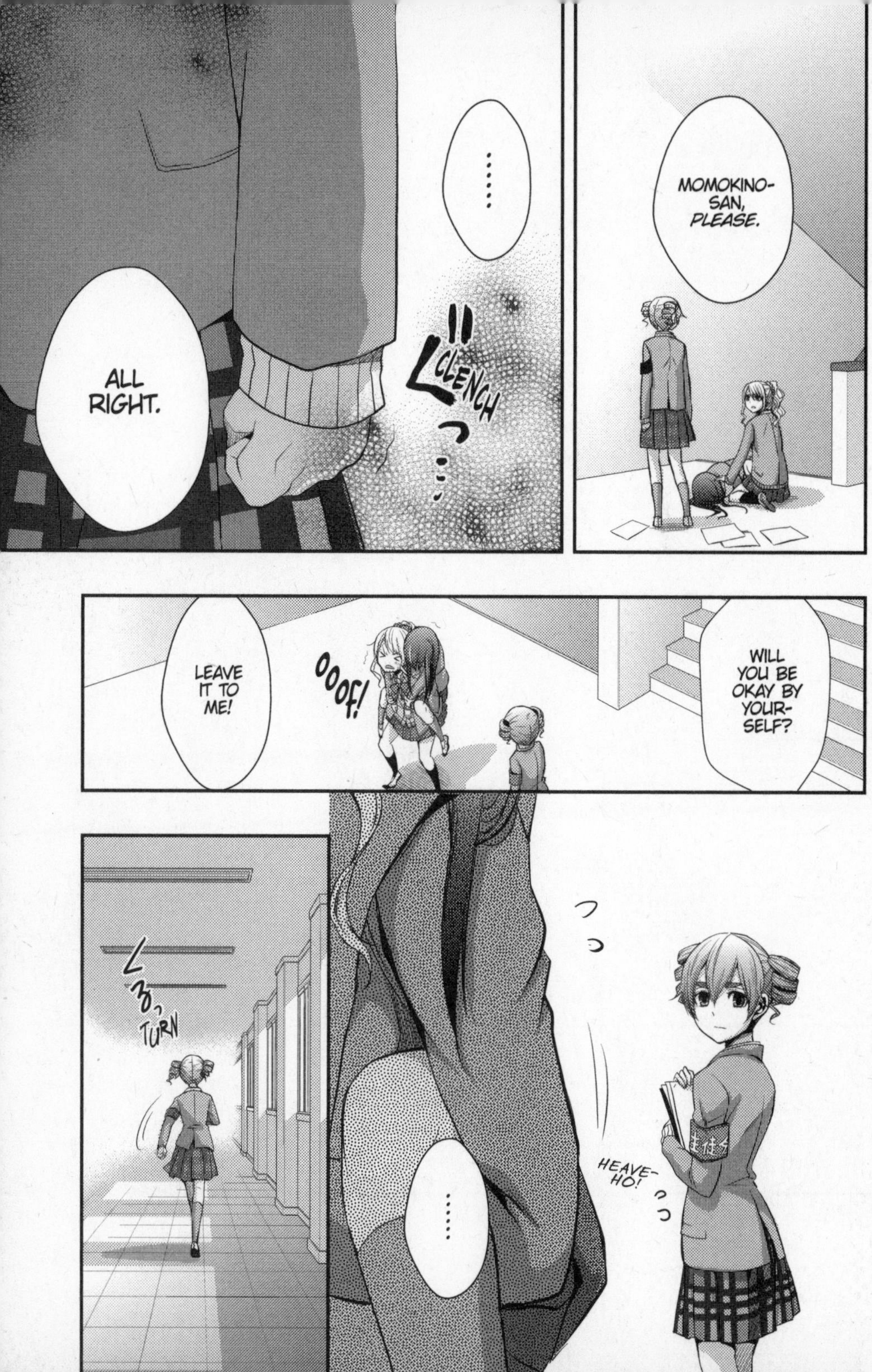
MOMOKINO-SAN, PLEASE.
......
CLENCH
ALL RIGHT.
WILL YOU BE OKAY BY YOUR-SELF?
OOOF!
LEAVE IT TO ME!
HEAVE-HO!
......
TURN

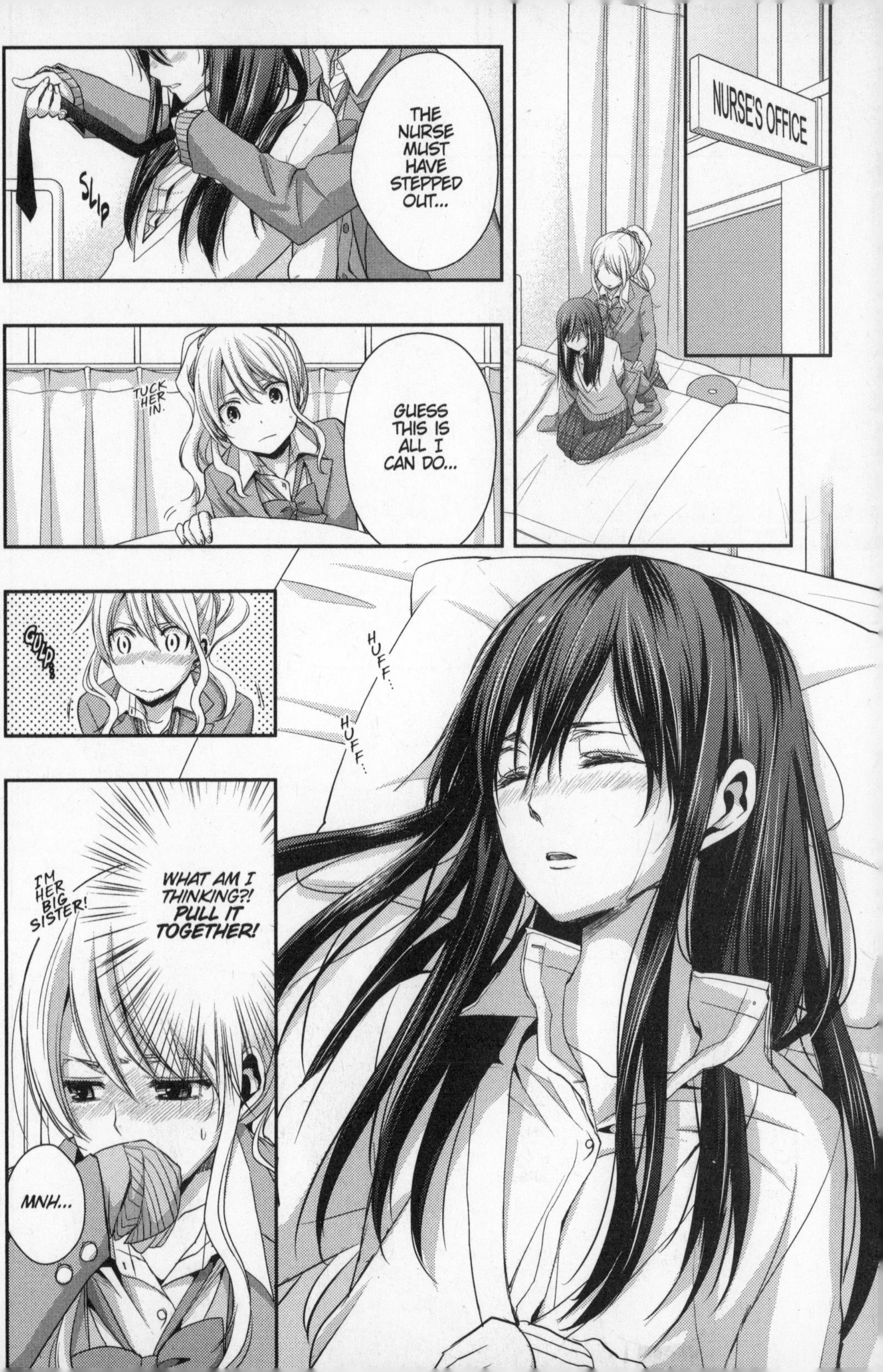
NURSE'S OFFICE
THE NURSE MUST HAVE STEPPED OUT...
SLIP
GUESS THIS IS ALL I CAN DO...
TUCK HER IN.
HUFF...
HUFF...
GULP
WHAT AM I THINKING?! PULL IT TOGETHER!
I'M HER BIG SISTER!
MNH...

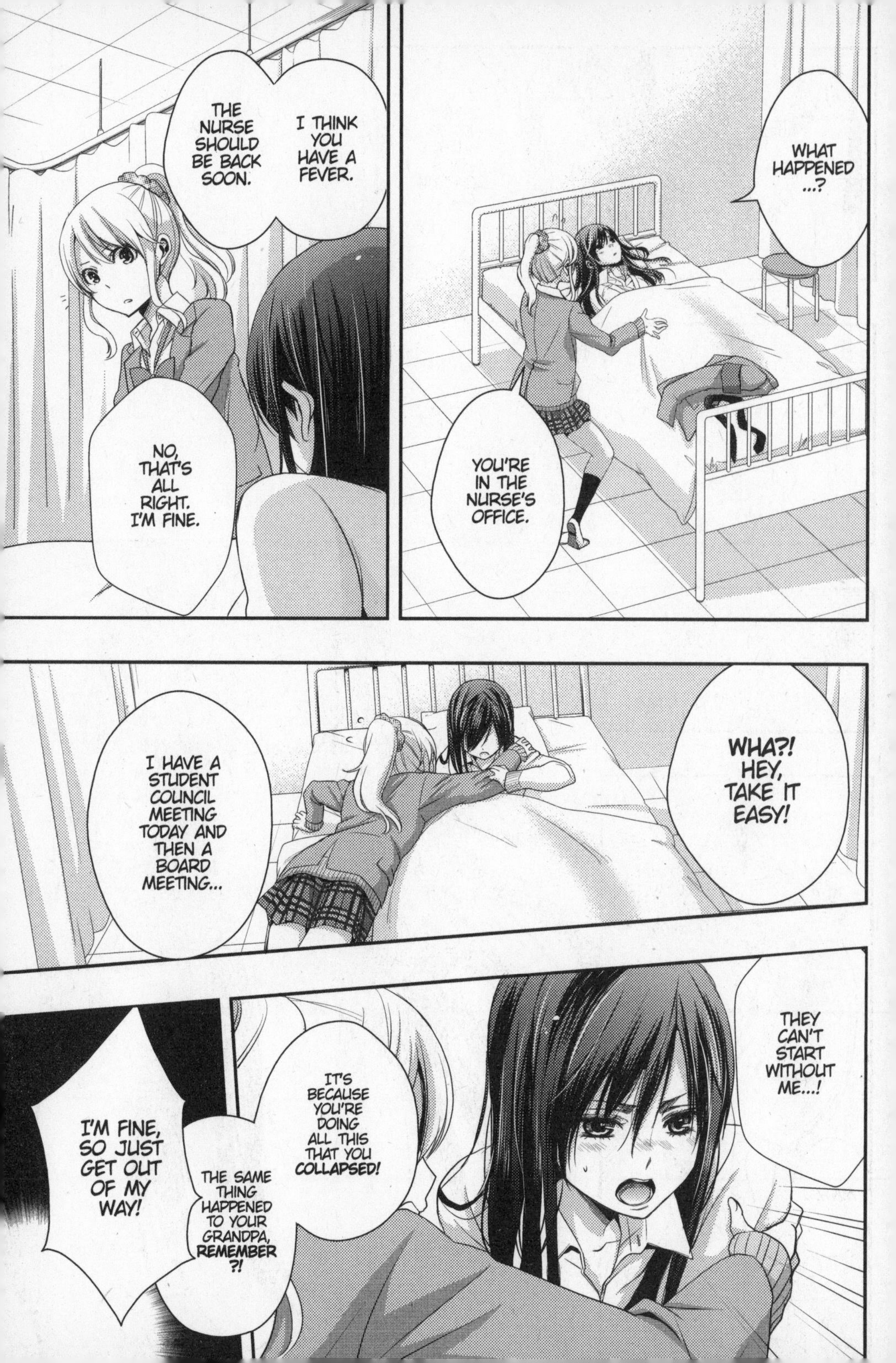
WHAT HAPPENED ...?
YOU'RE IN THE NURSE'S OFFICE.
I THINK YOU HAVE A FEVER.
THE NURSE SHOULD BE BACK SOON.
NO, THAT'S ALL RIGHT. I'M FINE.
WHA?! HEY, TAKE IT EASY!
I HAVE A STUDENT COUNCIL MEETING TODAY AND THEN A BOARD MEETING...
THEY CAN'T START WITHOUT ME...!
IT'S BECAUSE YOU'RE DOING ALL THIS THAT YOU COLLAPSED!
THE SAME THING HAPPENED TO YOUR GRANDPA, REMEMBER?!
I'M FINE, SO JUST GET OUT OF MY WAY!

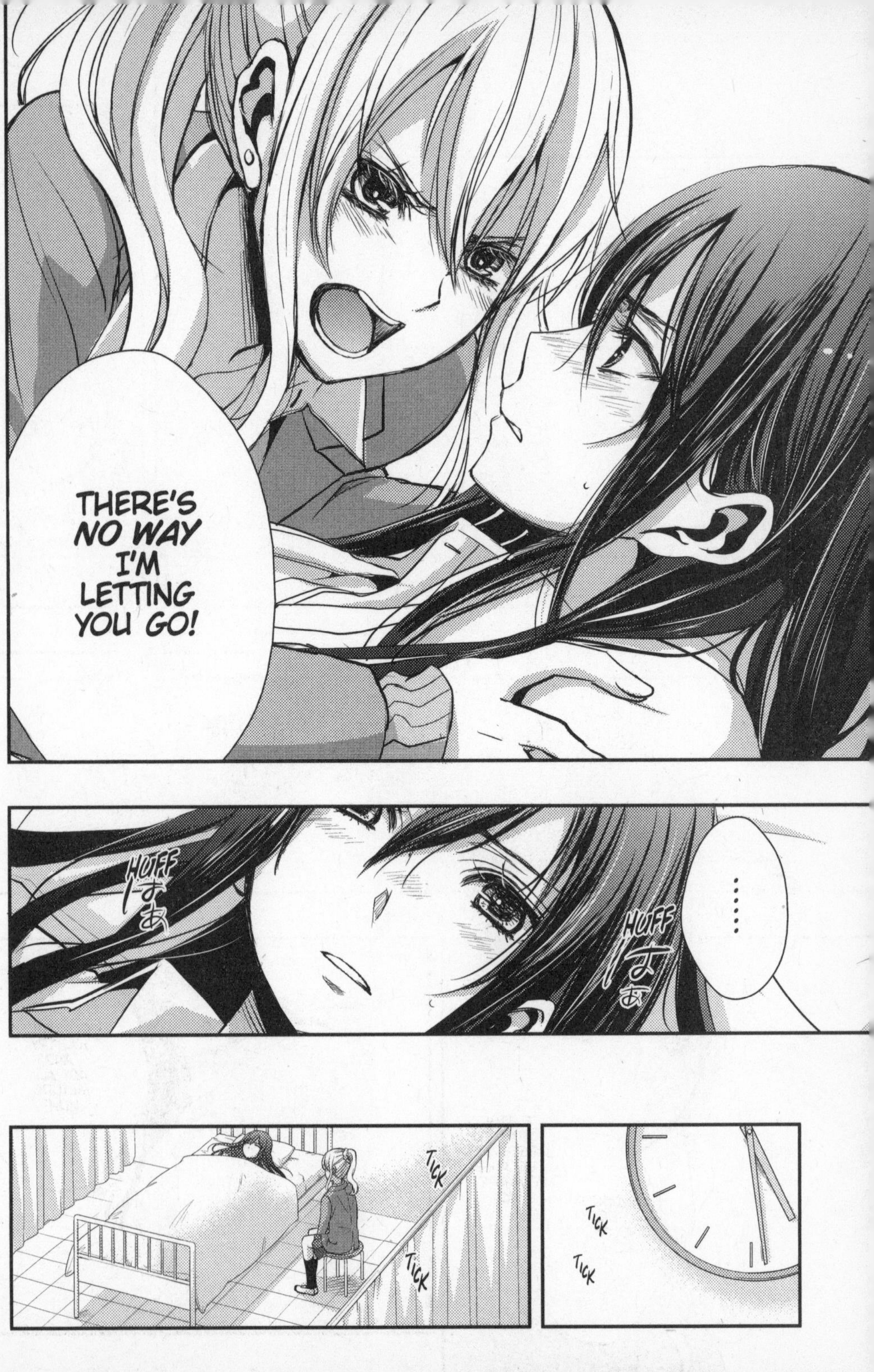
THERE'S NO WAY I'M LETTING YOU GO!
......
HUFF はぁ
HUFF はぁ
TICK
TICK
TICK
TICK

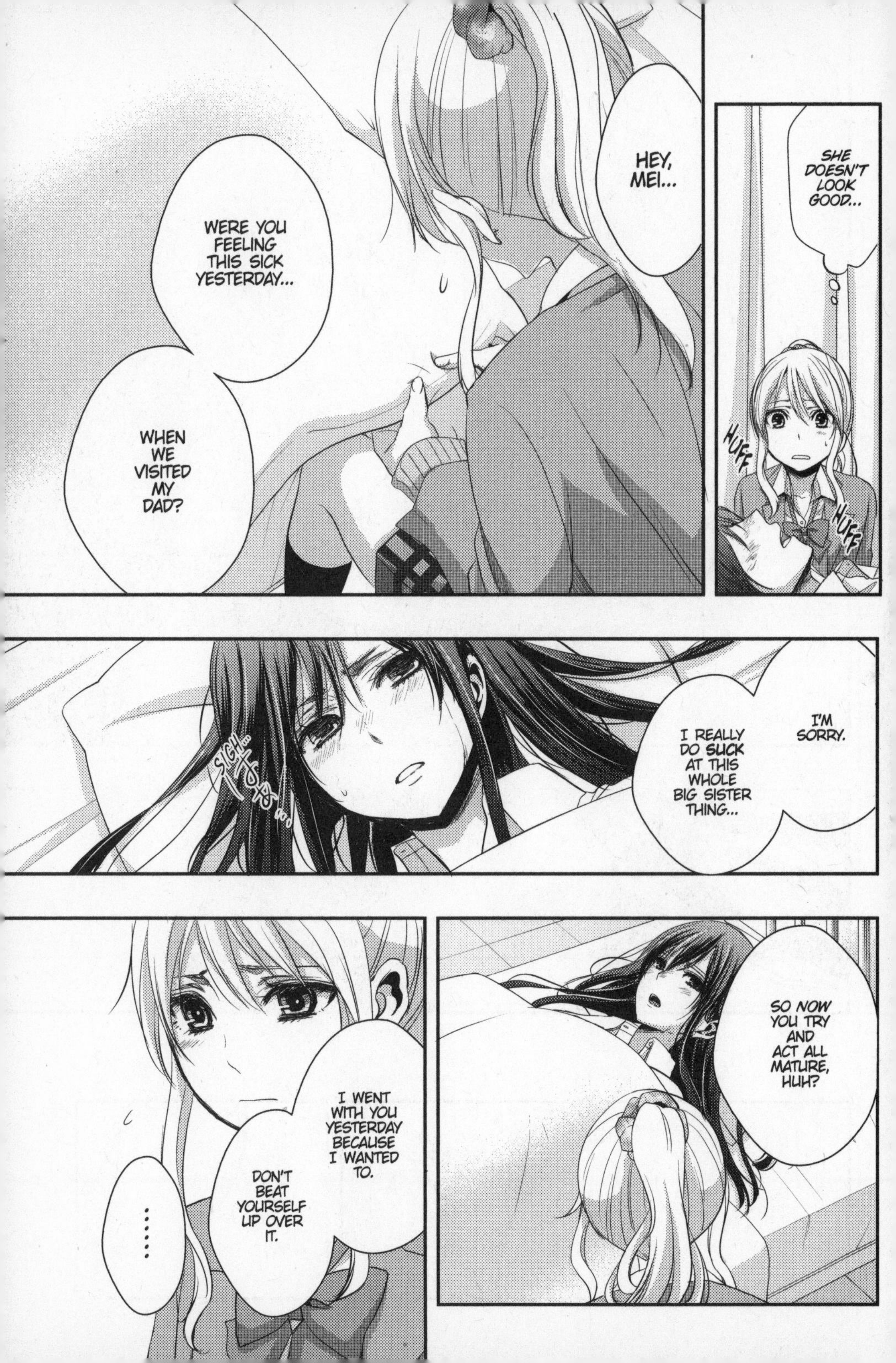
SHE DOESN'T LOOK GOOD...
HUFF
HUFF
HEY, MEI...
WERE YOU FEELING THIS SICK YESTERDAY...
WHEN WE VISITED MY DAD?
I'M SORRY.
I REALLY DO SUCK AT THIS WHOLE BIG SISTER THING...
SO NOW YOU TRY AND ACT ALL MATURE, HUH?
I WENT WITH YOU YESTERDAY BECAUSE I WANTED TO.
DON'T BEAT YOURSELF UP OVER IT.
......

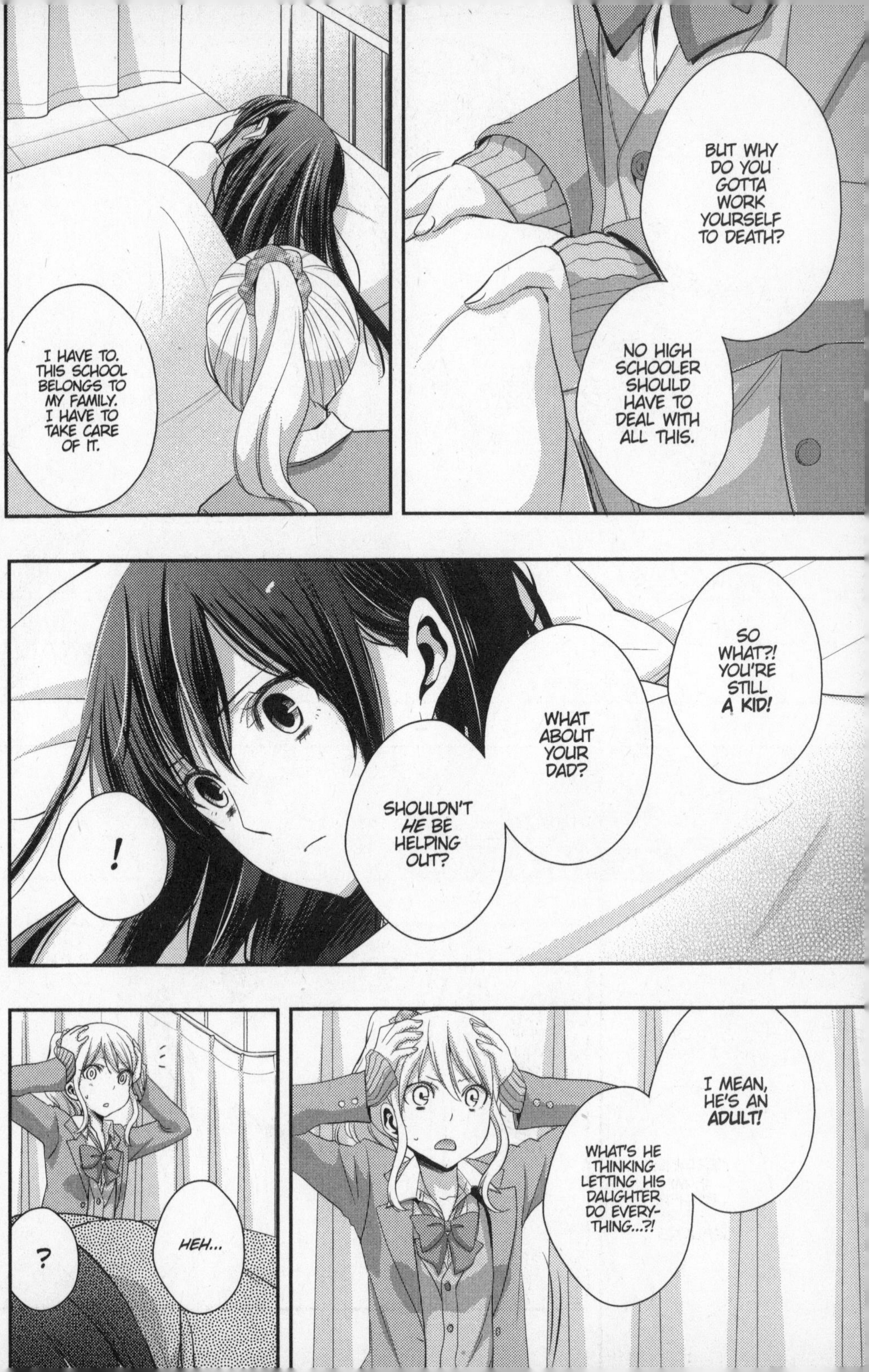
BUT WHY DO YOU GOTTA WORK YOURSELF TO DEATH?
NO HIGH SCHOOLER SHOULD HAVE TO DEAL WITH ALL THIS.
I HAVE TO. THIS SCHOOL BELONGS TO MY FAMILY. I HAVE TO TAKE CARE OF IT.
SO WHAT?! YOU'RE STILL A KID!
WHAT ABOUT YOUR DAD?
SHOULDN'T *HE* BE HELPING OUT?
!
I MEAN, HE'S AN ADULT!
WHAT'S HE THINKING LETTING HIS DAUGHTER DO EVERY-THING...?!
HEH...
?

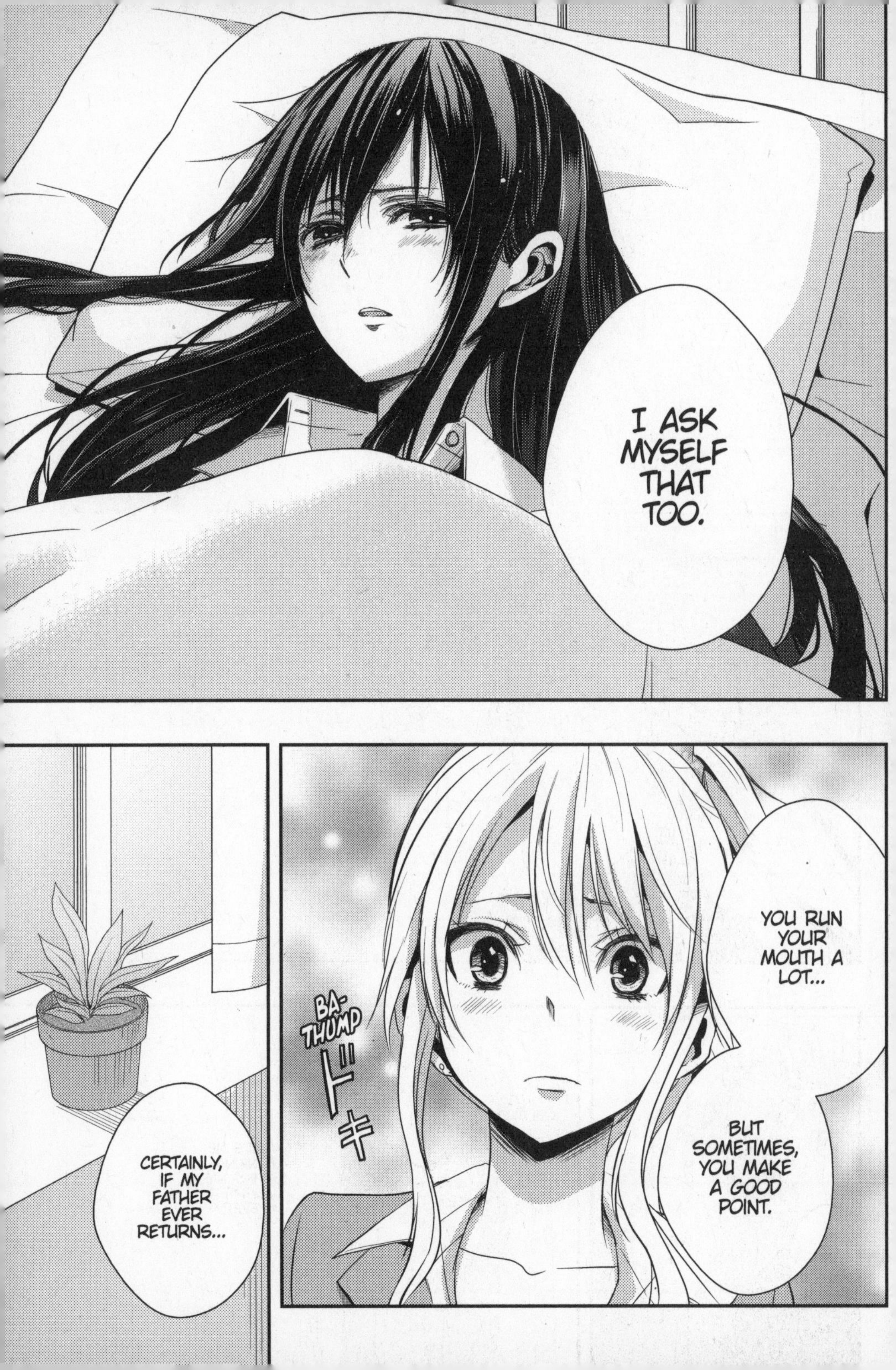
I ASK MYSELF THAT TOO.
YOU RUN YOUR MOUTH A LOT...
BUT SOMETIMES, YOU MAKE A GOOD POINT.
BA-THUMP
ドキ
CERTAINLY, IF MY FATHER EVER RETURNS...

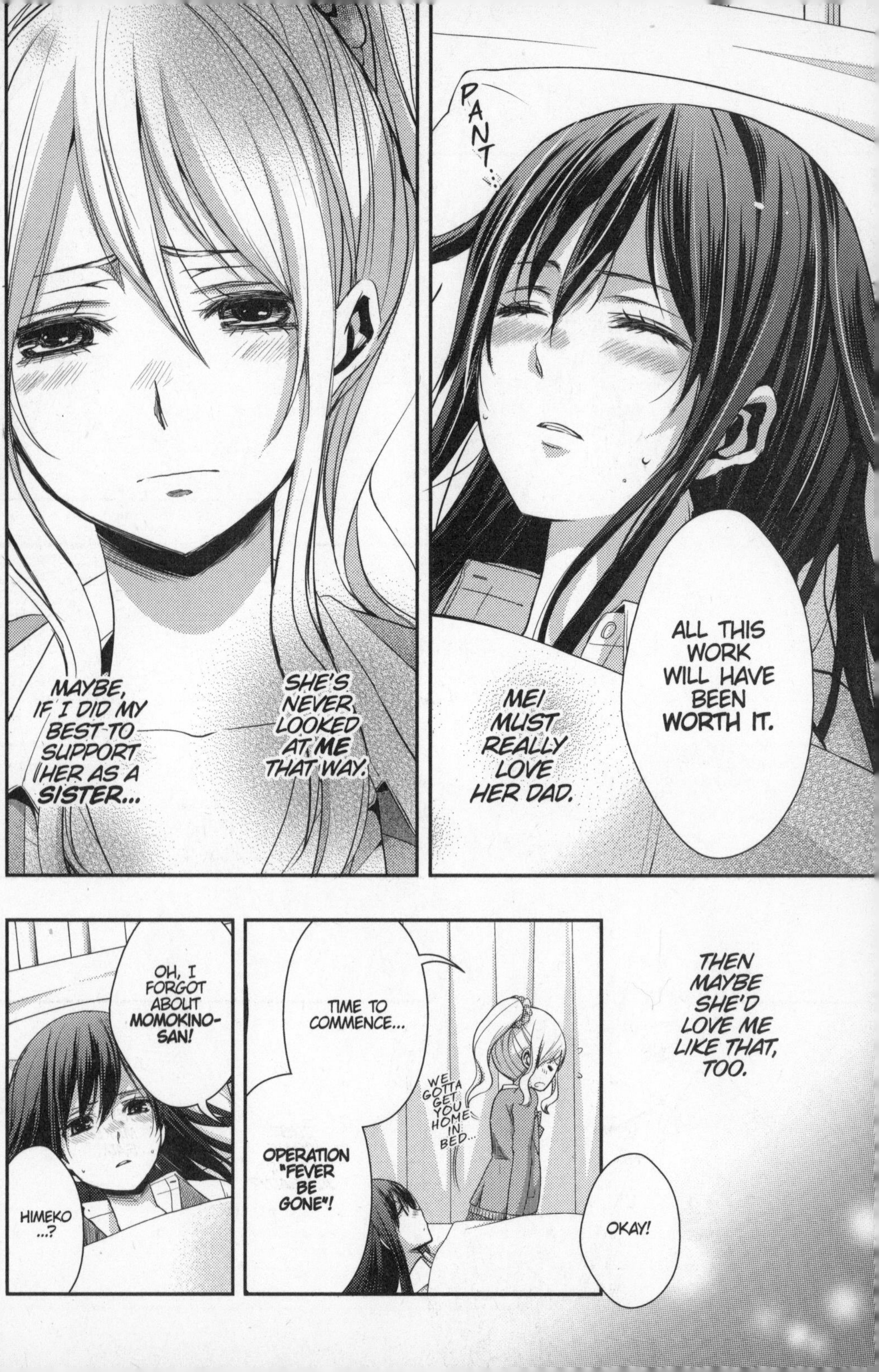
PANT...
ALL THIS WORK WILL HAVE BEEN WORTH IT.
MEI MUST REALLY LOVE HER DAD.
SHE'S NEVER LOOKED AT ME THAT WAY.
MAYBE, IF I DID MY BEST TO SUPPORT HER AS A SISTER...
THEN MAYBE SHE'D LOVE ME LIKE THAT, TOO.
TIME TO COMMENCE...
WE GOTTA GET YOU HOME IN BED...
OPERATION "FEVER BE GONE"!
OKAY!
OH, I FORGOT ABOUT MOMOKINO-SAN!
HIMEKO ...?

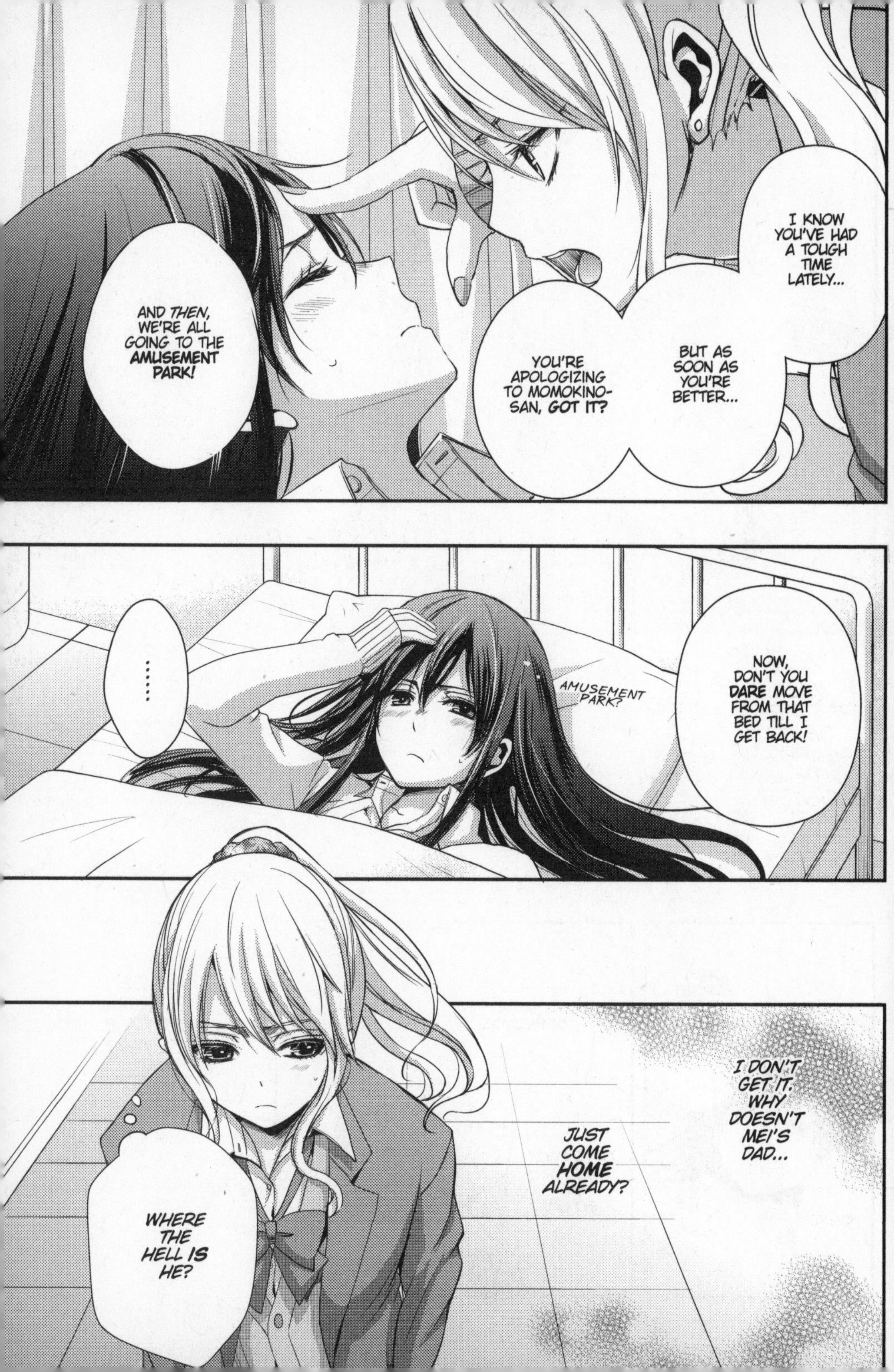

I KNOW YOU'VE HAD A TOUGH TIME LATELY...
BUT AS SOON AS YOU'RE BETTER...
YOU'RE APOLOGIZING TO MOMOKINO-SAN, GOT IT?
AND THEN, WE'RE ALL GOING TO THE AMUSEMENT PARK!
NOW, DON'T YOU DARE MOVE FROM THAT BED TILL I GET BACK!
AMUSEMENT PARK?
......
I DON'T GET IT. WHY DOESN'T MEI'S DAD...
JUST COME HOME ALREADY?
WHERE THE HELL IS HE?

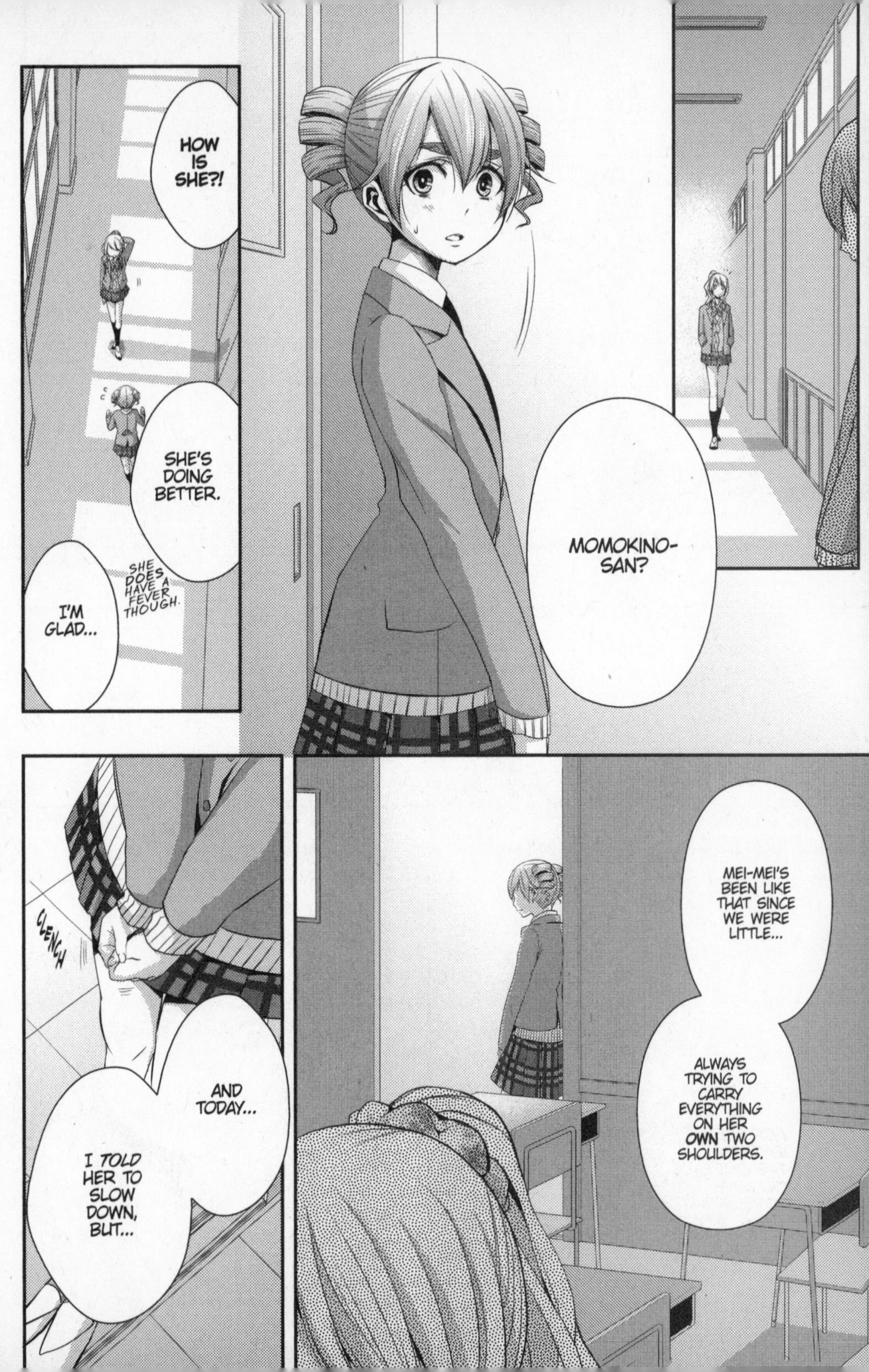
MOMOKINO-SAN?
HOW IS SHE?!
SHE'S DOING BETTER.
SHE DOES HAVE A FEVER THOUGH.
I'M GLAD...
MEI-MEI'S BEEN LIKE THAT SINCE WE WERE LITTLE...
ALWAYS TRYING TO CARRY EVERYTHING ON HER OWN TWO SHOULDERS.
CLENCH
AND TODAY...
I TOLD HER TO SLOW DOWN, BUT...

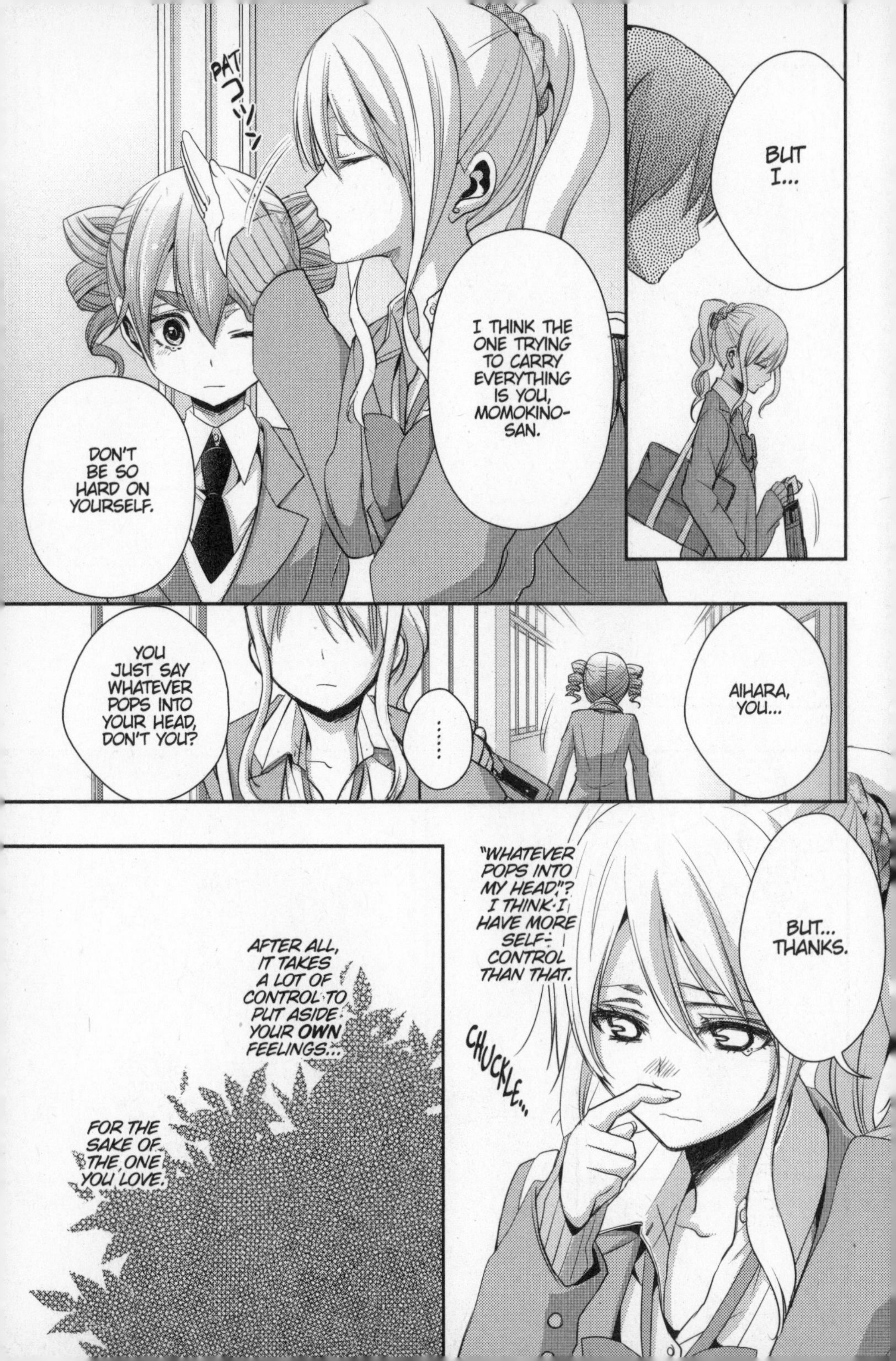
BUT I...
PAT
I THINK THE ONE TRYING TO CARRY EVERYTHING IS YOU, MOMOKINO-SAN.
DON'T BE SO HARD ON YOURSELF.
AIHARA, YOU...
......
YOU JUST SAY WHATEVER POPS INTO YOUR HEAD, DON'T YOU?
BUT... THANKS.
"WHATEVER POPS INTO MY HEAD"? I THINK I HAVE MORE SELF-CONTROL THAN THAT.
CHUCKLE...
AFTER ALL, IT TAKES A LOT OF CONTROL TO PUT ASIDE YOUR OWN FEELINGS...
FOR THE SAKE OF THE ONE YOU LOVE.

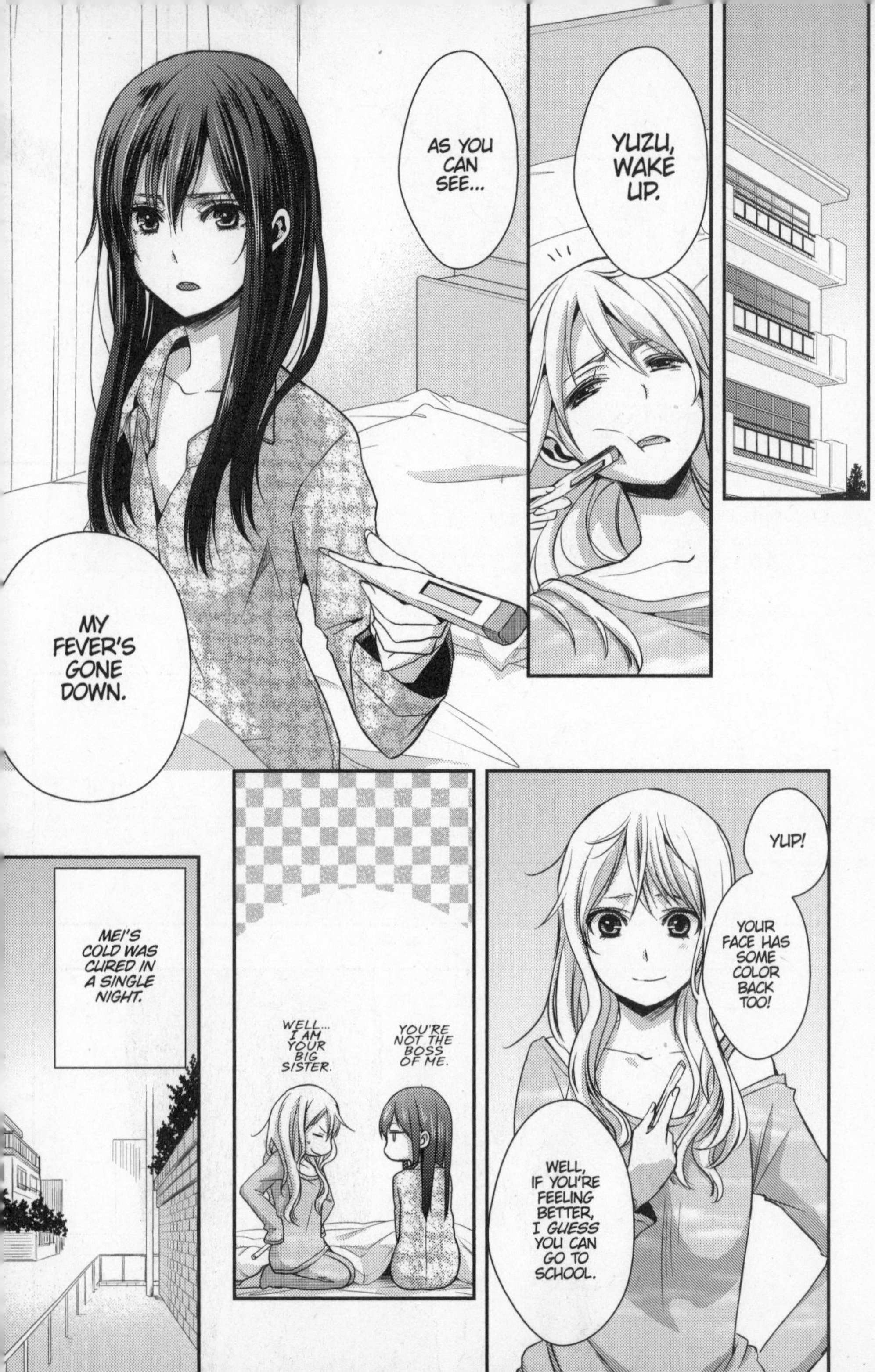
YUZU, WAKE UP.
AS YOU CAN SEE...
MY FEVER'S GONE DOWN.
YUP!
YOUR FACE HAS SOME COLOR BACK TOO!
WELL, IF YOU'RE FEELING BETTER, I GUESS YOU CAN GO TO SCHOOL.
YOU'RE NOT THE BOSS OF ME.
WELL... I AM YOUR BIG SISTER.
MEI'S COLD WAS CURED IN A SINGLE NIGHT.

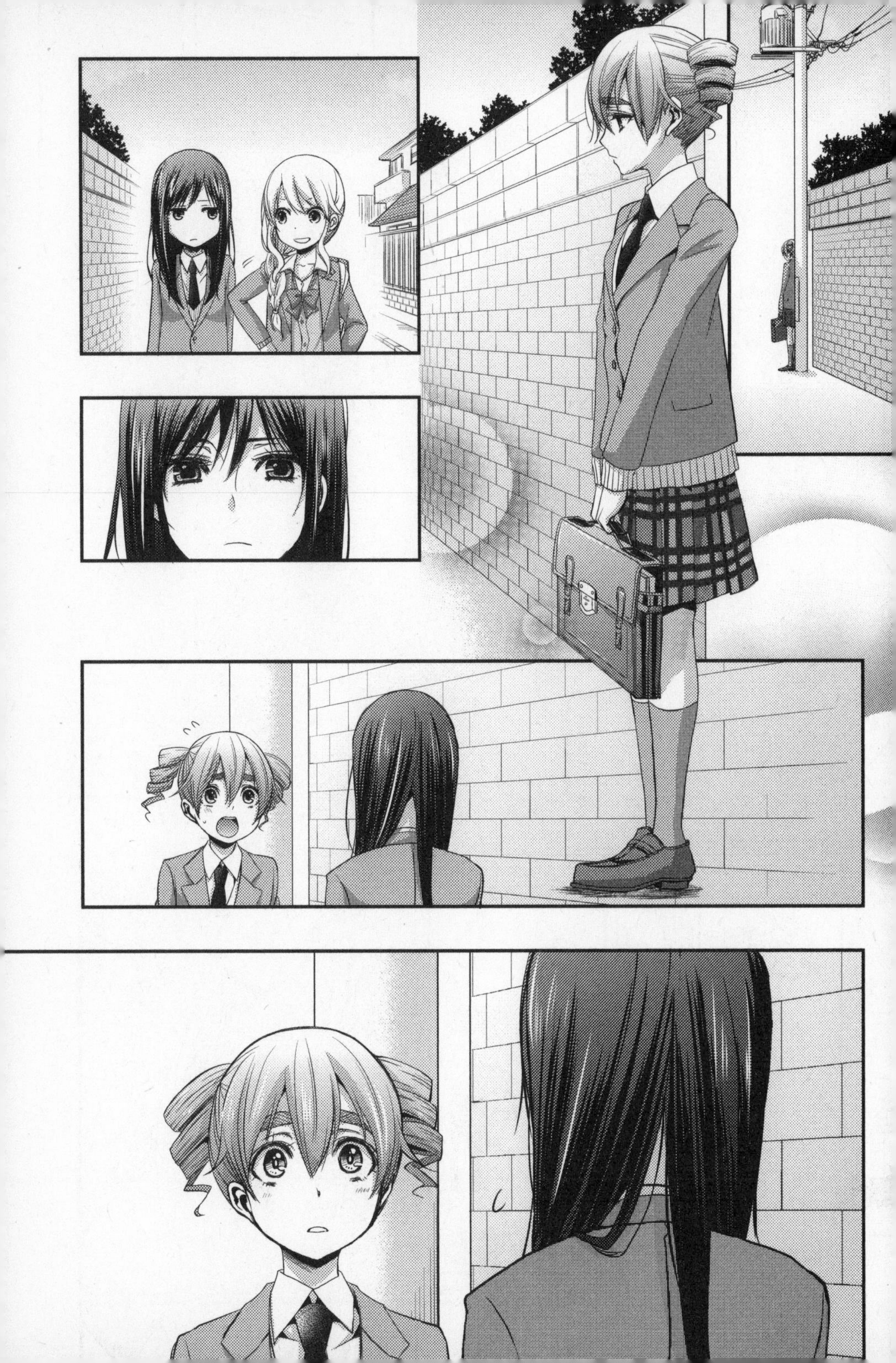

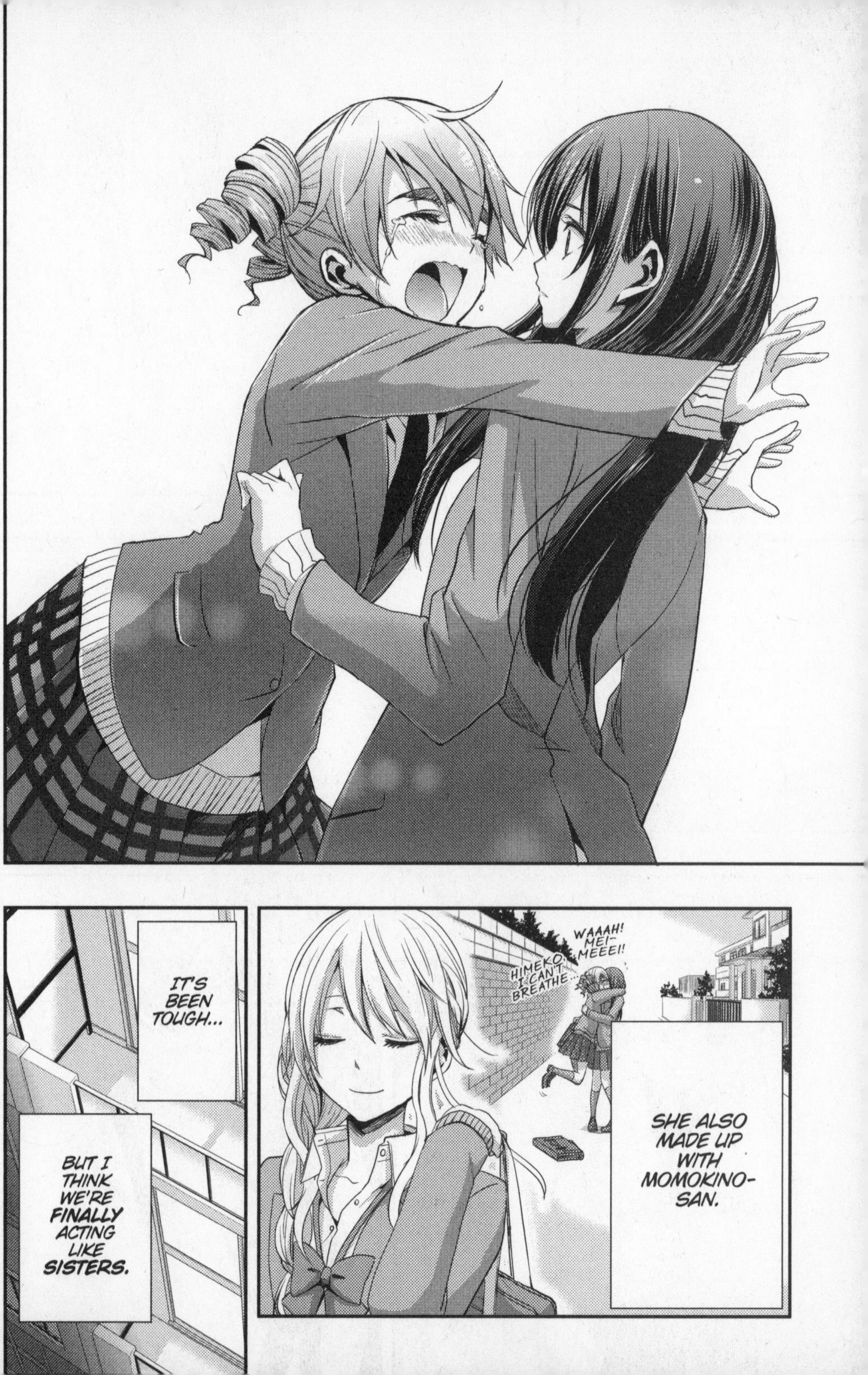
WAAAH! MEI-MEEEI!
HIMEKO, I CAN'T BREATHE...
SHE ALSO MADE UP WITH MOMOKINO-SAN.
IT'S BEEN TOUGH...
BUT I THINK WE'RE FINALLY ACTING LIKE SISTERS.

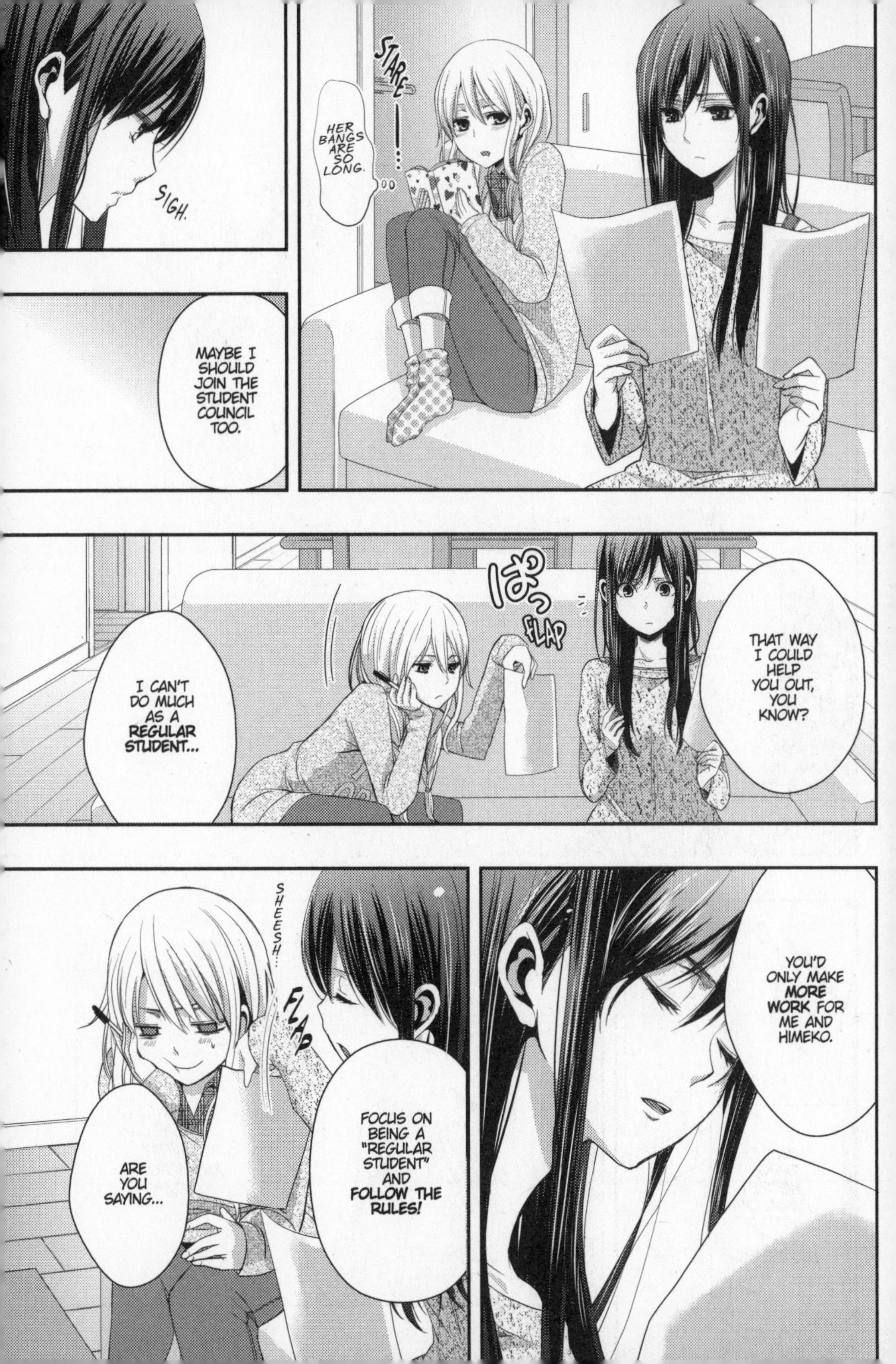
STARE—!!
HER BANGS ARE SO LONG.
SIGH.
MAYBE I SHOULD JOIN THE STUDENT COUNCIL TOO.
THAT WAY I COULD HELP YOU OUT, YOU KNOW?
ぱっ
FLAP
I CAN'T DO MUCH AS A REGULAR STUDENT...
YOU'D ONLY MAKE MORE WORK FOR ME AND HIMEKO.
SHEESH...
FLAP
FOCUS ON BEING A "REGULAR STUDENT" AND FOLLOW THE RULES!
ARE YOU SAYING...

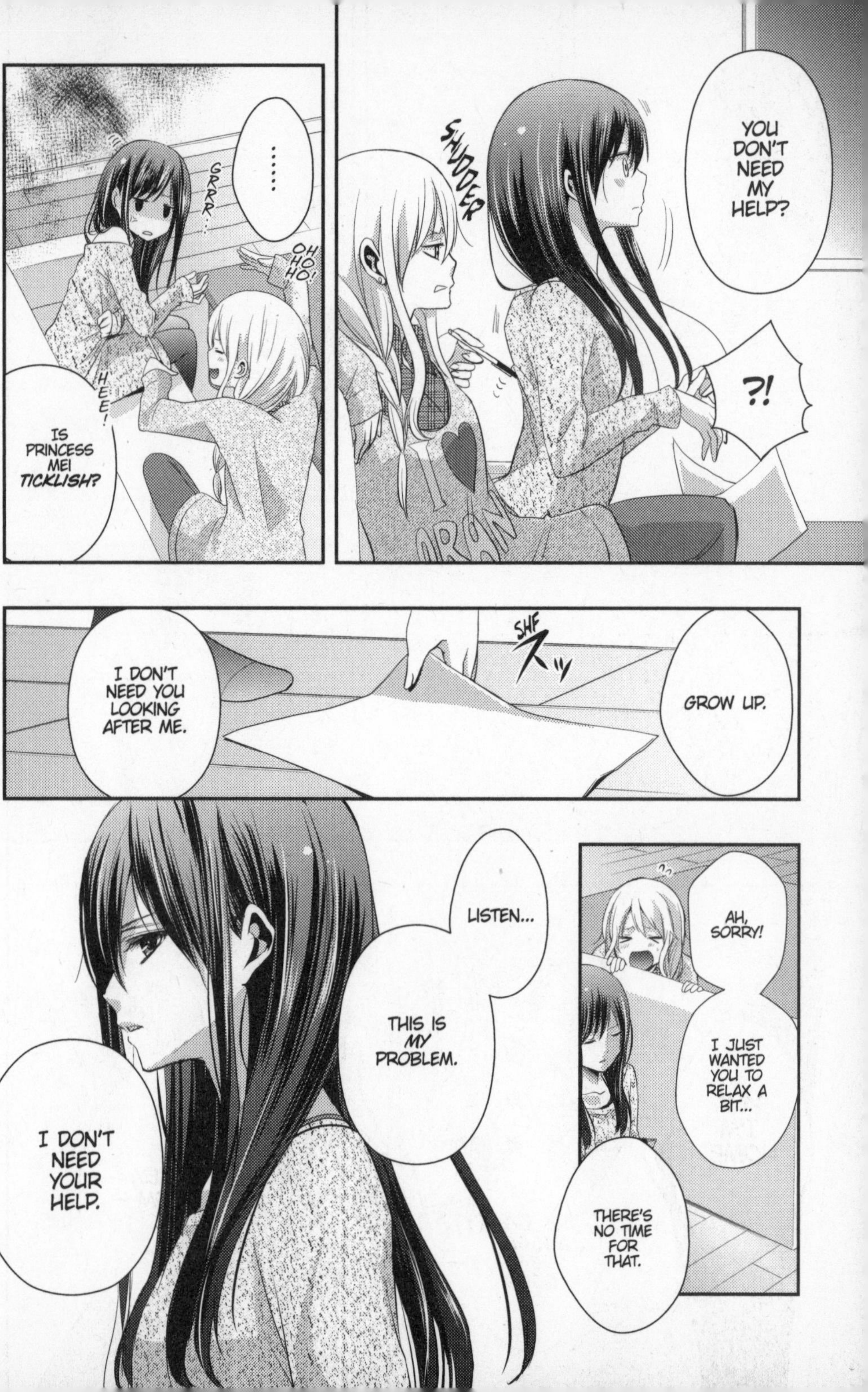
YOU DON'T NEED MY HELP?
SHUDDER
?!
......
GRRR...
OHOHOHO!
HEE!
IS PRINCESS MEI TICKLISH?
GROW UP.
SHF スッ
I DON'T NEED YOU LOOKING AFTER ME.
AH, SORRY!
I JUST WANTED YOU TO RELAX A BIT...
THERE'S NO TIME FOR THAT.
LISTEN...
THIS IS MY PROBLEM.
I DON'T NEED YOUR HELP.

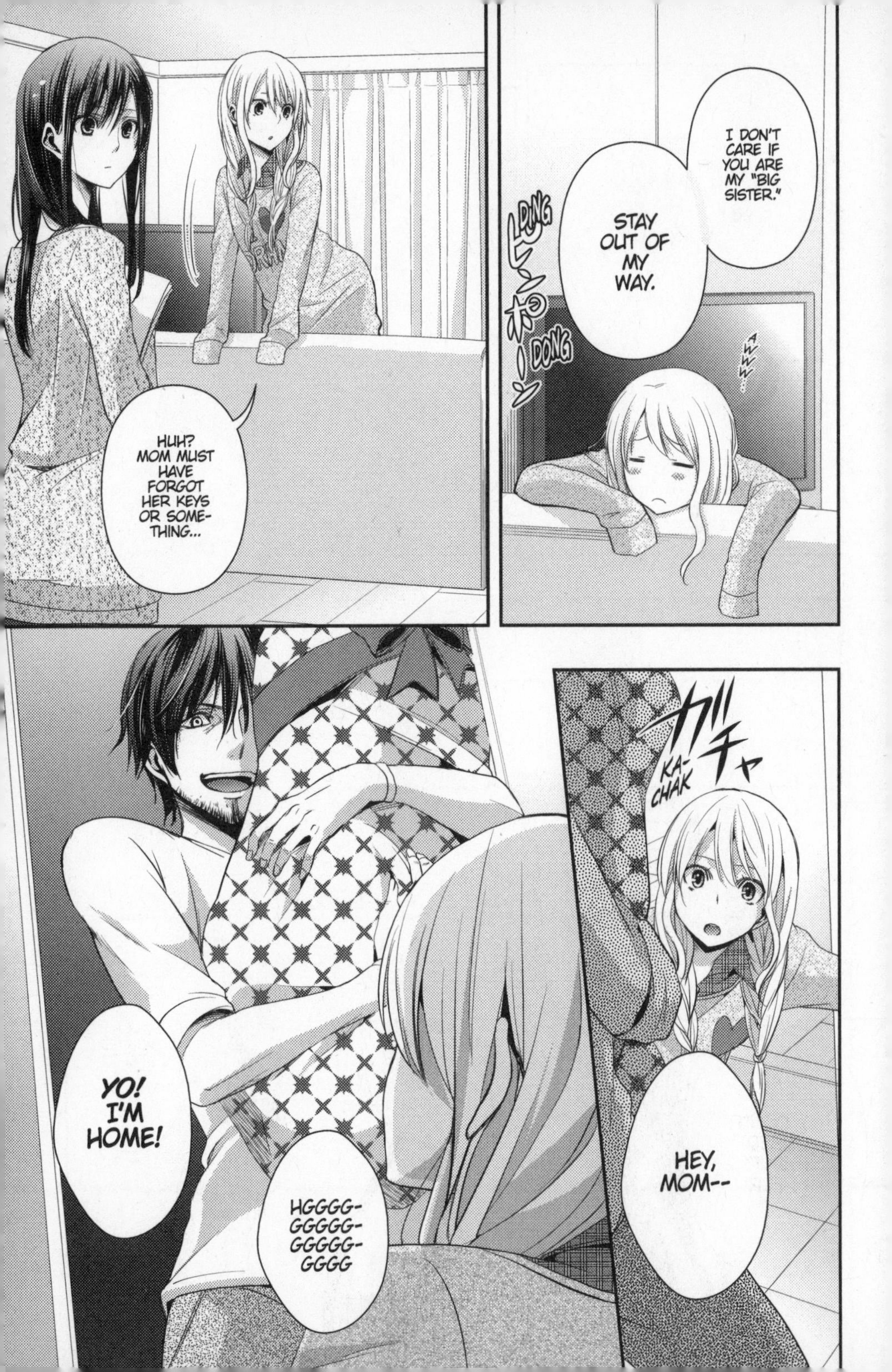
I DON'T CARE IF YOU ARE MY "BIG SISTER."
STAY OUT OF MY WAY.
ピンポーン
DING DONG
AWWW...
HUH? MOM MUST HAVE FORGOT HER KEYS OR SOME-THING...
ガチャ
KA-CHAK
HEY, MOM--
YO! I'M HOME!
HGGGG-GGGGG-GGGGG-GGGG

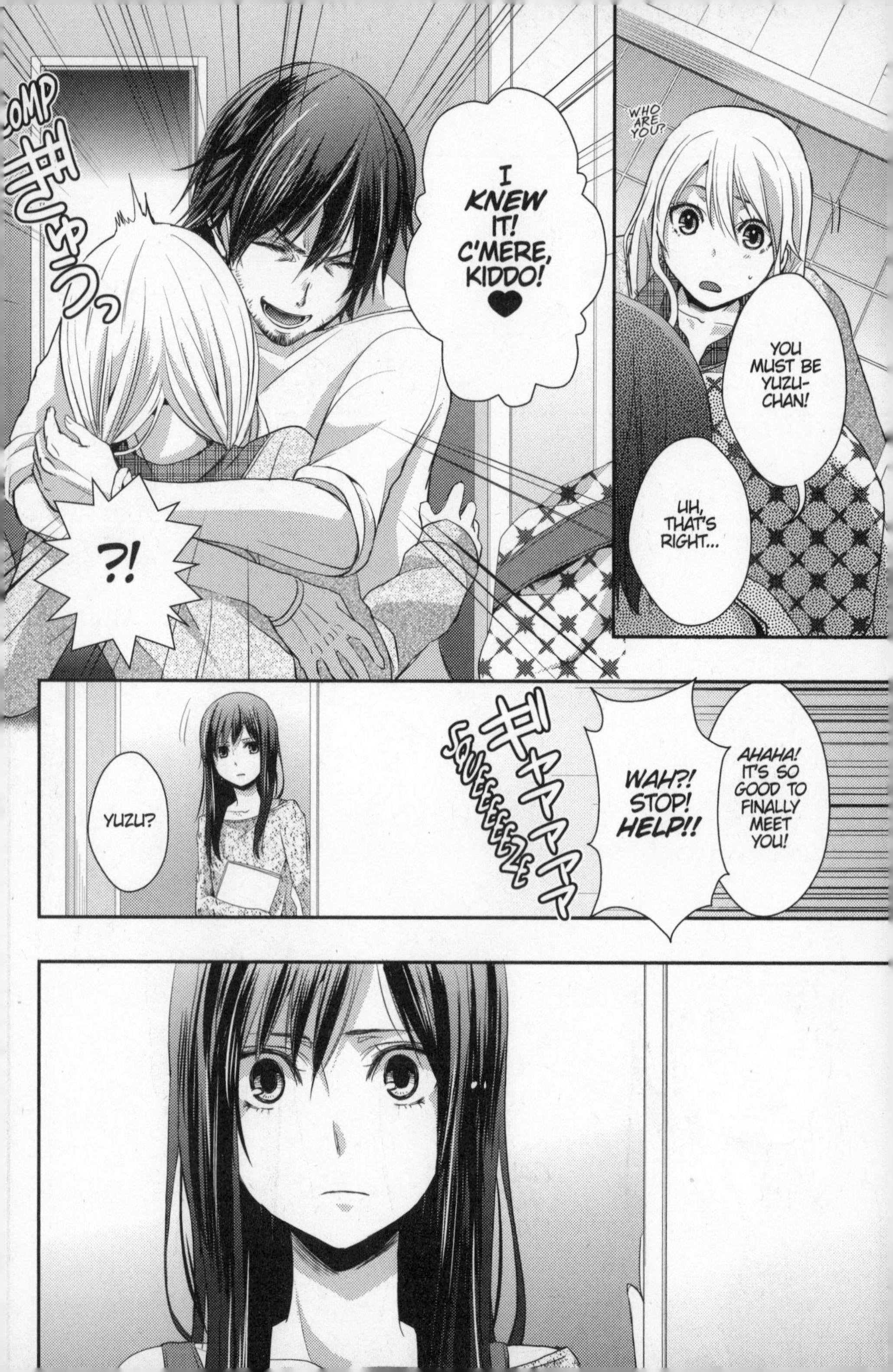
WHO ARE YOU?
YOU MUST BE YUZU-CHAN!
UH, THAT'S RIGHT...
I KNEW IT! C'MERE, KIDDO! ♥
ぎゅうっ
?!
AHAHA! IT'S SO GOOD TO FINALLY MEET YOU!
WAH?! STOP! HELP!!
ギャアアア
SQUEEEEEEZE
YUZU?

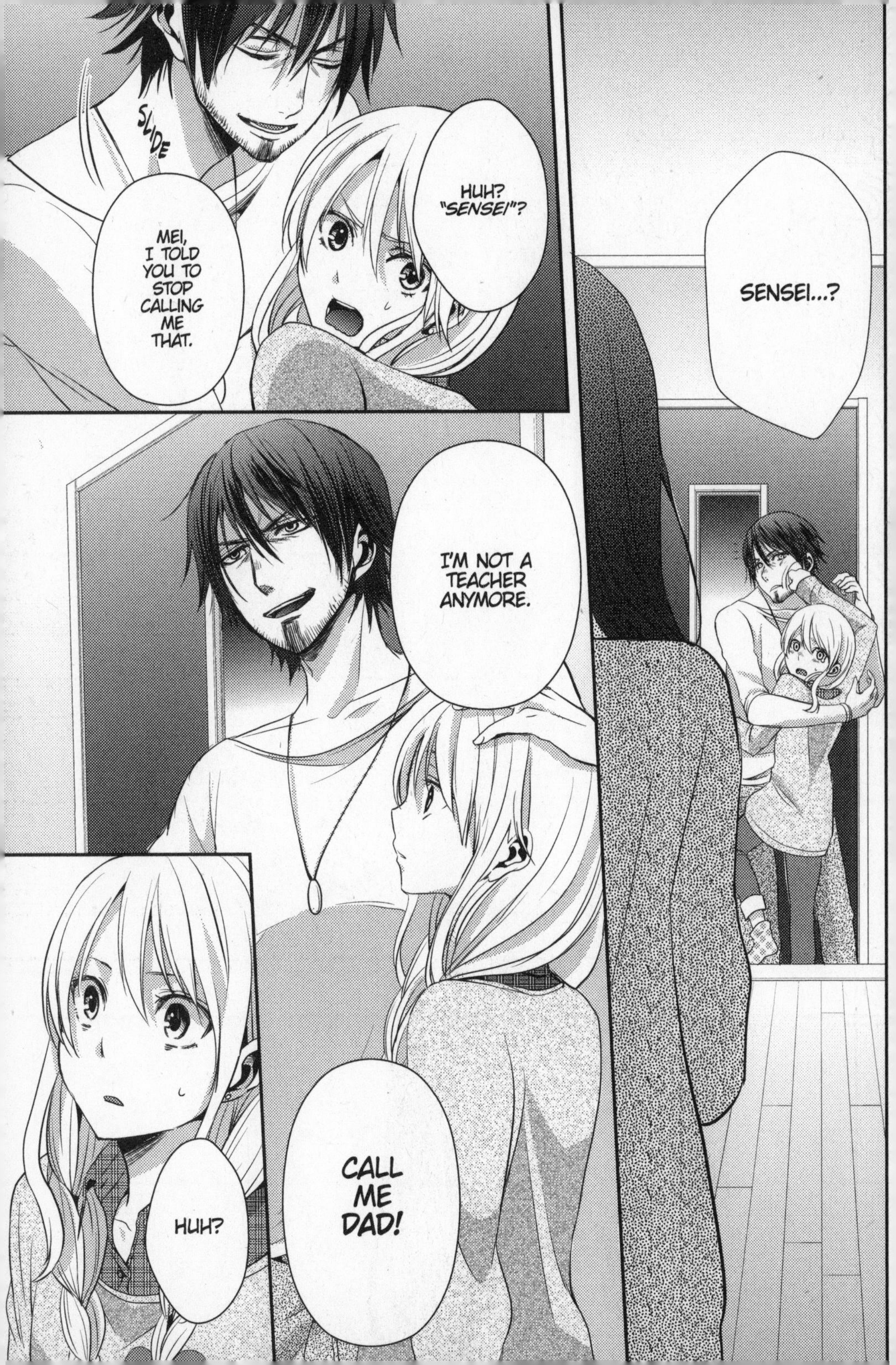
SENSEI...?
HUH? "SENSEI"?
SLIDE
MEI, I TOLD YOU TO STOP CALLING ME THAT.
I'M NOT A TEACHER ANYMORE.
CALL ME DAD!
HUH?

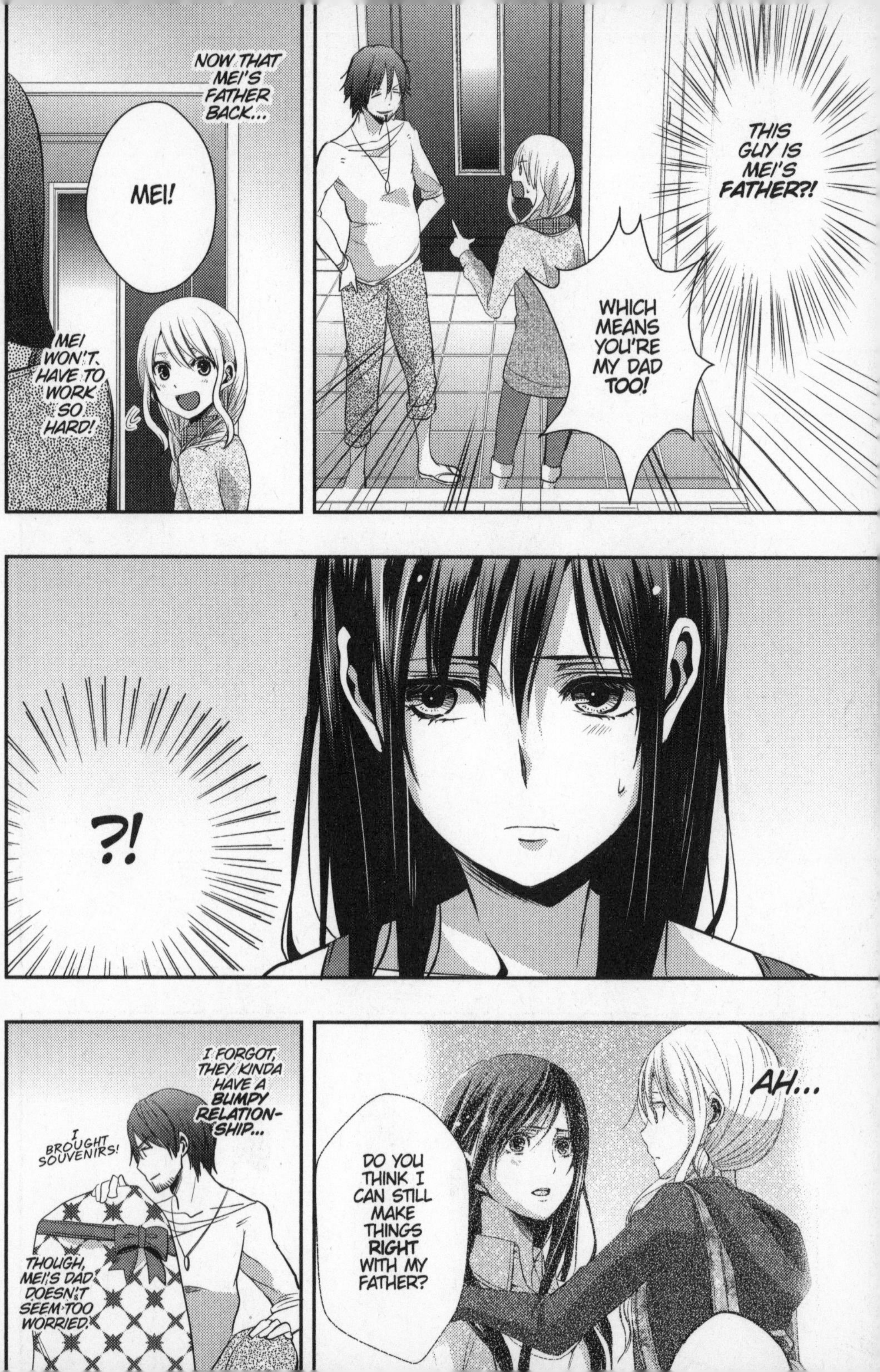
THIS GUY IS MEI'S FATHER?!
WHICH MEANS YOU'RE MY DAD TOO!
NOW THAT MEI'S FATHER BACK...
MEI!
MEI WON'T HAVE TO WORK SO HARD!
?!
AH...
DO YOU THINK I CAN STILL MAKE THINGS RIGHT WITH MY FATHER?
I FORGOT, THEY KINDA HAVE A BUMPY RELATIONSHIP...
I BROUGHT SOUVENIRS!
THOUGH, MEI'S DAD DOESN'T SEEM TOO WORRIED.

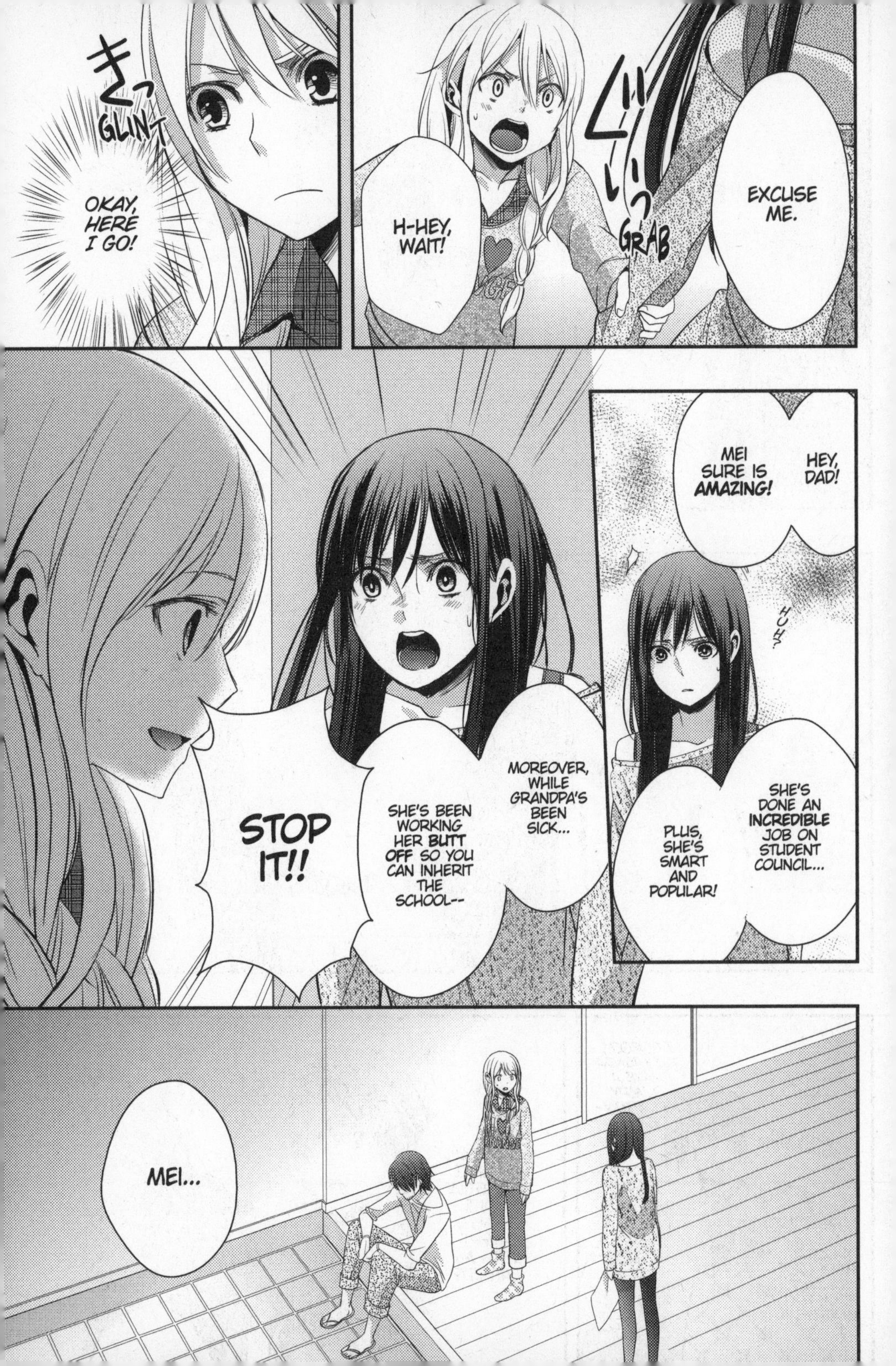
EXCUSE ME.
ぐいっ GRAB
H-HEY, WAIT!
きっ GLINT
OKAY, HERE I GO!
HEY, DAD!
MEI SURE IS AMAZING!
HUH?
SHE'S DONE AN INCREDIBLE JOB ON STUDENT COUNCIL...
PLUS, SHE'S SMART AND POPULAR!
MOREOVER, WHILE GRANDPA'S BEEN SICK...
SHE'S BEEN WORKING HER BUTT OFF SO YOU CAN INHERIT THE SCHOOL--
STOP IT!!
MEI...

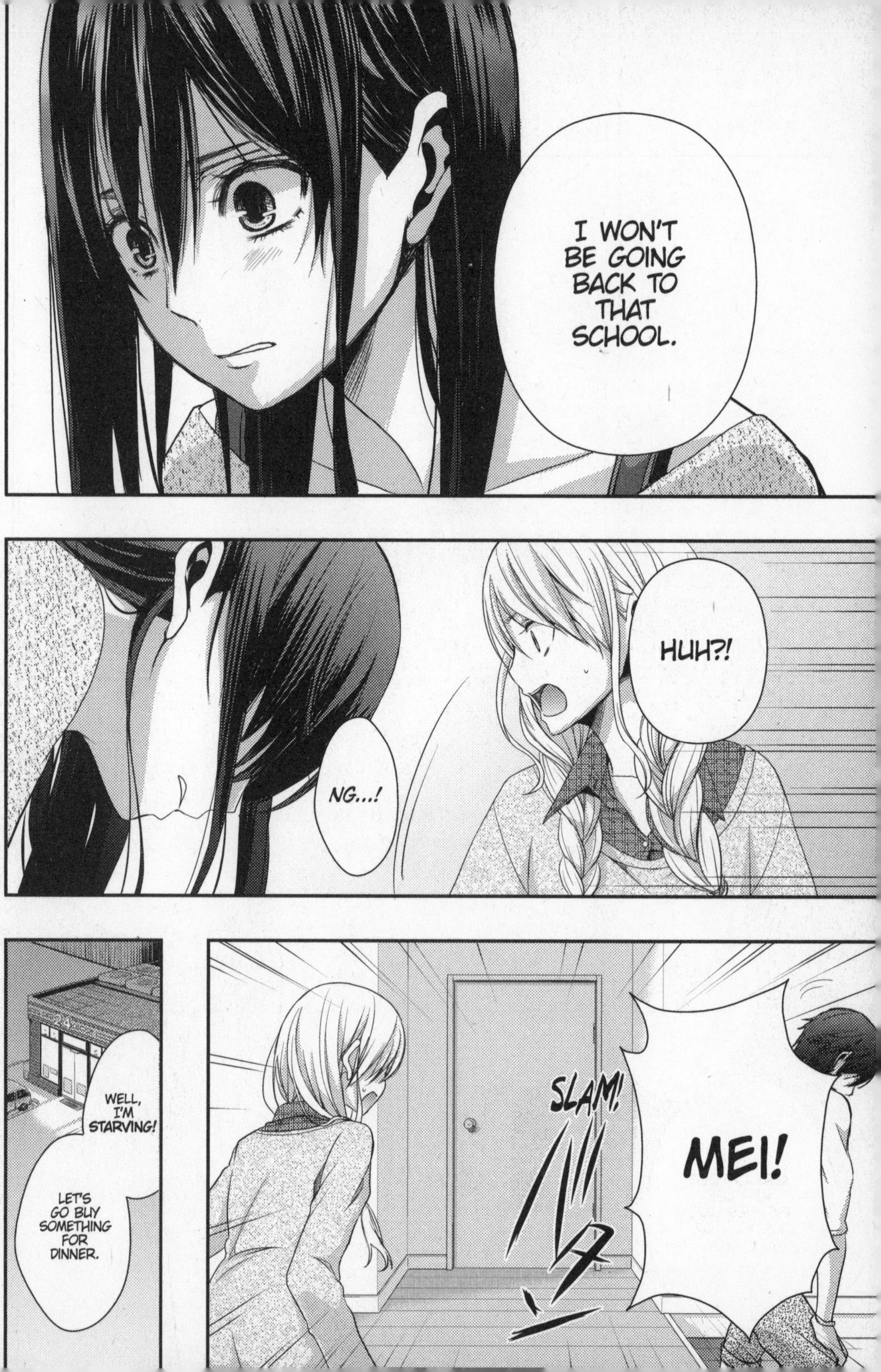
I WON'T BE GOING BACK TO THAT SCHOOL.
HUH?!
NG...!
MEI!
SLAM!
WELL, I'M STARVING!
LET'S GO BUY SOMETHING FOR DINNER.

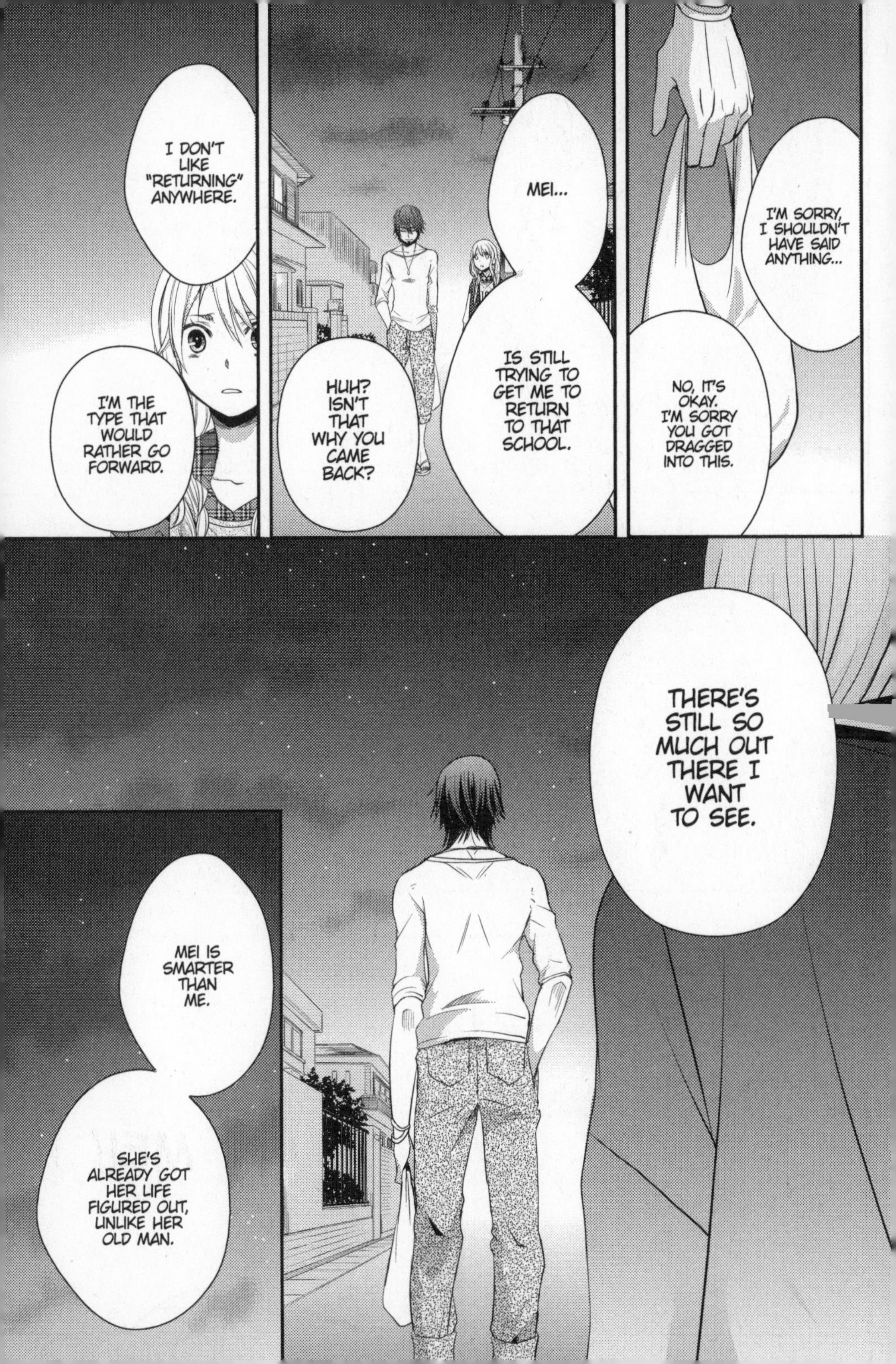

I'M SORRY, I SHOULDN'T HAVE SAID ANYTHING...
NO, IT'S OKAY. I'M SORRY YOU GOT DRAGGED INTO THIS.
MEI...
IS STILL TRYING TO GET ME TO RETURN TO THAT SCHOOL.
HUH? ISN'T THAT WHY YOU CAME BACK?
I DON'T LIKE "RETURNING" ANYWHERE.
I'M THE TYPE THAT WOULD RATHER GO FORWARD.
THERE'S STILL SO MUCH OUT THERE I WANT TO SEE.
MEI IS SMARTER THAN ME.
SHE'S ALREADY GOT HER LIFE FIGURED OUT, UNLIKE HER OLD MAN.

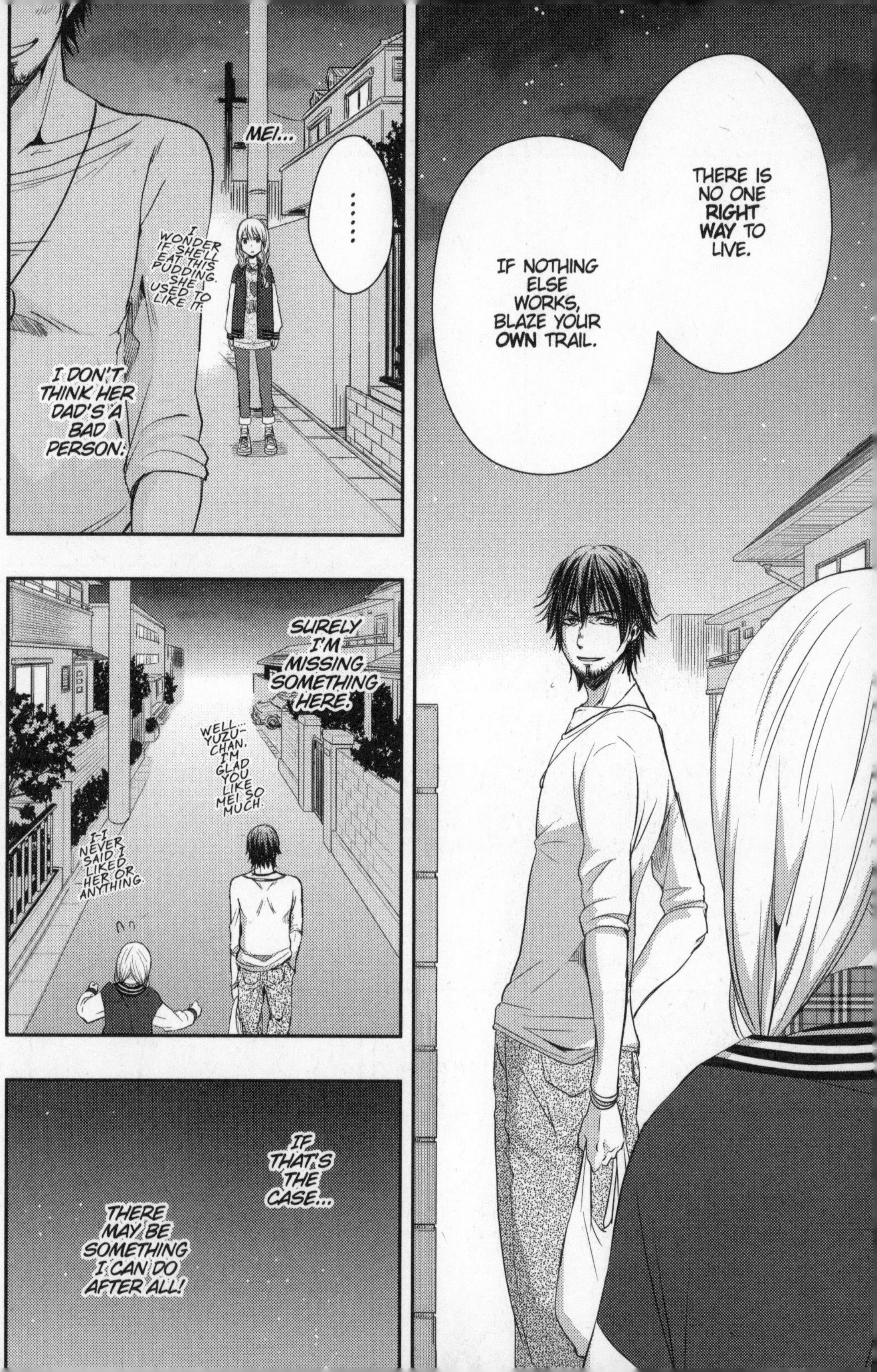

THERE IS NO ONE RIGHT WAY TO LIVE.
IF NOTHING ELSE WORKS, BLAZE YOUR OWN TRAIL.
MEI...
......
I WONDER IF SHE'LL EAT THIS PUDDING. SHE USED TO LIKE IT.
I DON'T THINK HER DAD'S A BAD PERSON.
SURELY I'M MISSING SOMETHING HERE.
WELL... YUZU-CHAN, I'M GLAD YOU LIKE MEI SO MUCH.
I-I NEVER SAID I LIKED HER OR ANYTHING.
IF THAT'S THE CASE...
THERE MAY BE SOMETHING I CAN DO AFTER ALL!

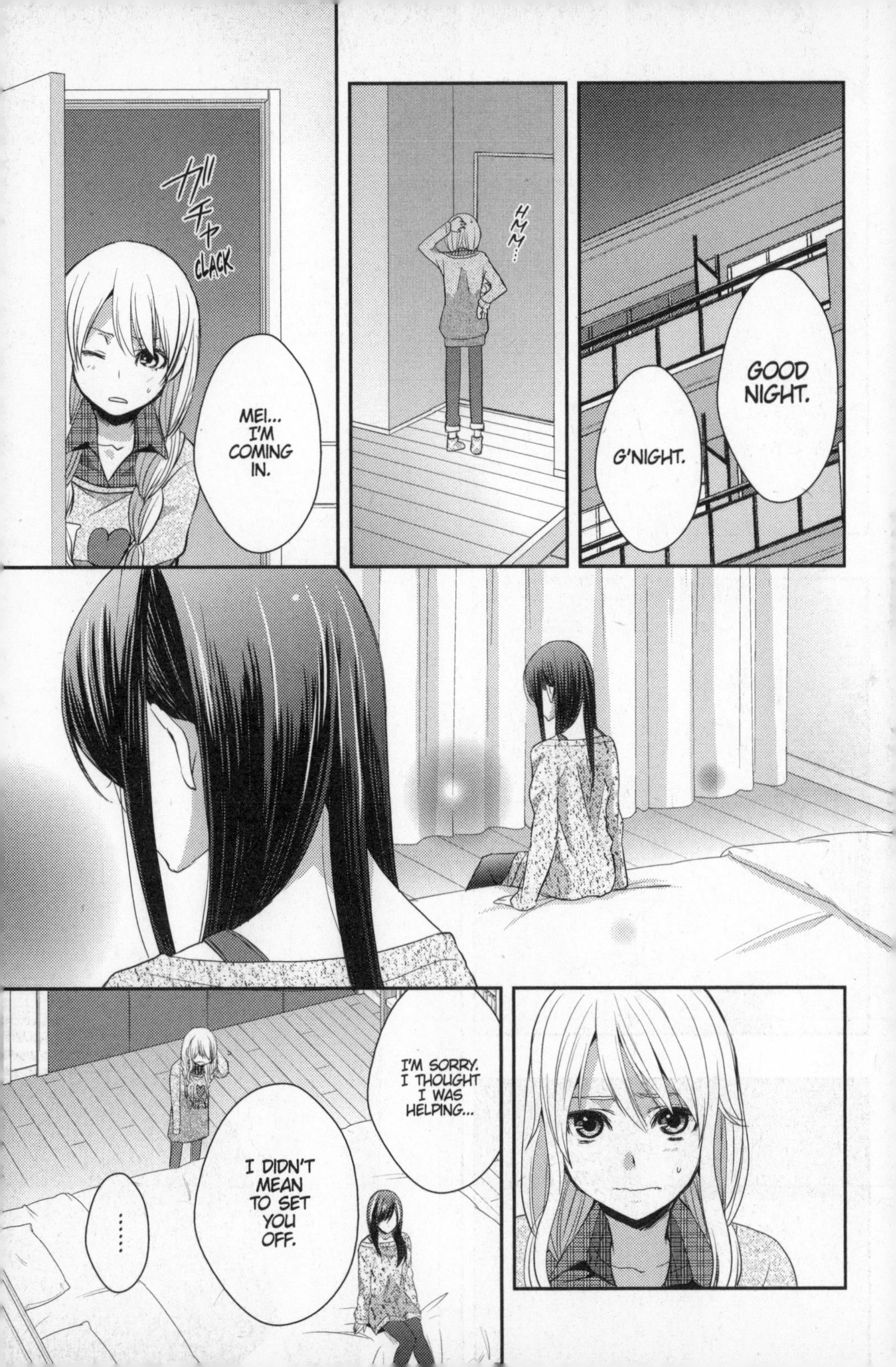
GOOD NIGHT.
G'NIGHT.
HMM...
ガチャ
CLACK
MEI... I'M COMING IN.
I'M SORRY. I THOUGHT I WAS HELPING...
I DIDN'T MEAN TO SET YOU OFF.
......

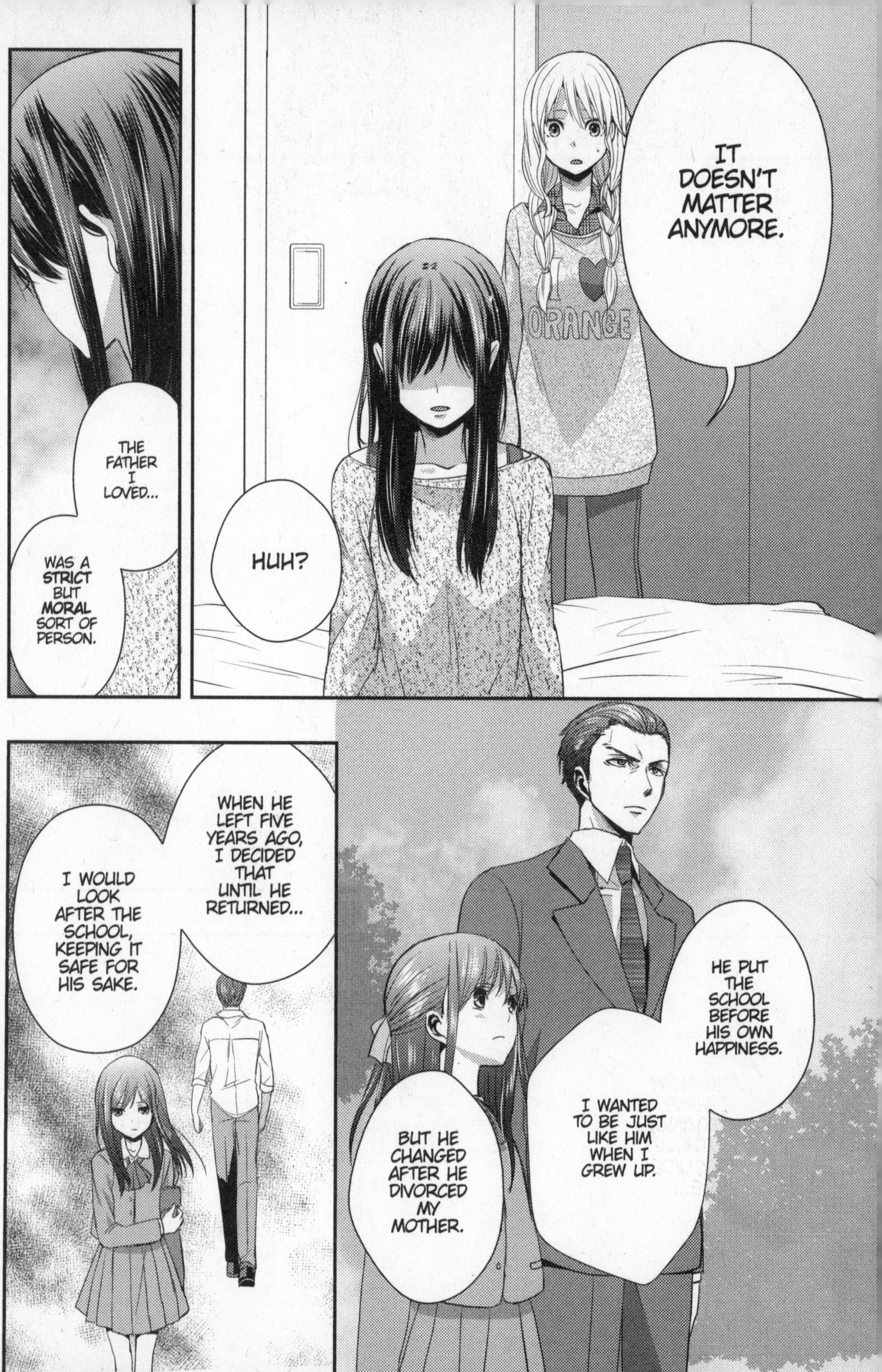
IT DOESN'T MATTER ANYMORE.
HUH?
THE FATHER I LOVED...
WAS A STRICT BUT MORAL SORT OF PERSON.
HE PUT THE SCHOOL BEFORE HIS OWN HAPPINESS.
I WANTED TO BE JUST LIKE HIM WHEN I GREW UP.
BUT HE CHANGED AFTER HE DIVORCED MY MOTHER.
WHEN HE LEFT FIVE YEARS AGO, I DECIDED THAT UNTIL HE RETURNED...
I WOULD LOOK AFTER THE SCHOOL, KEEPING IT SAFE FOR HIS SAKE.

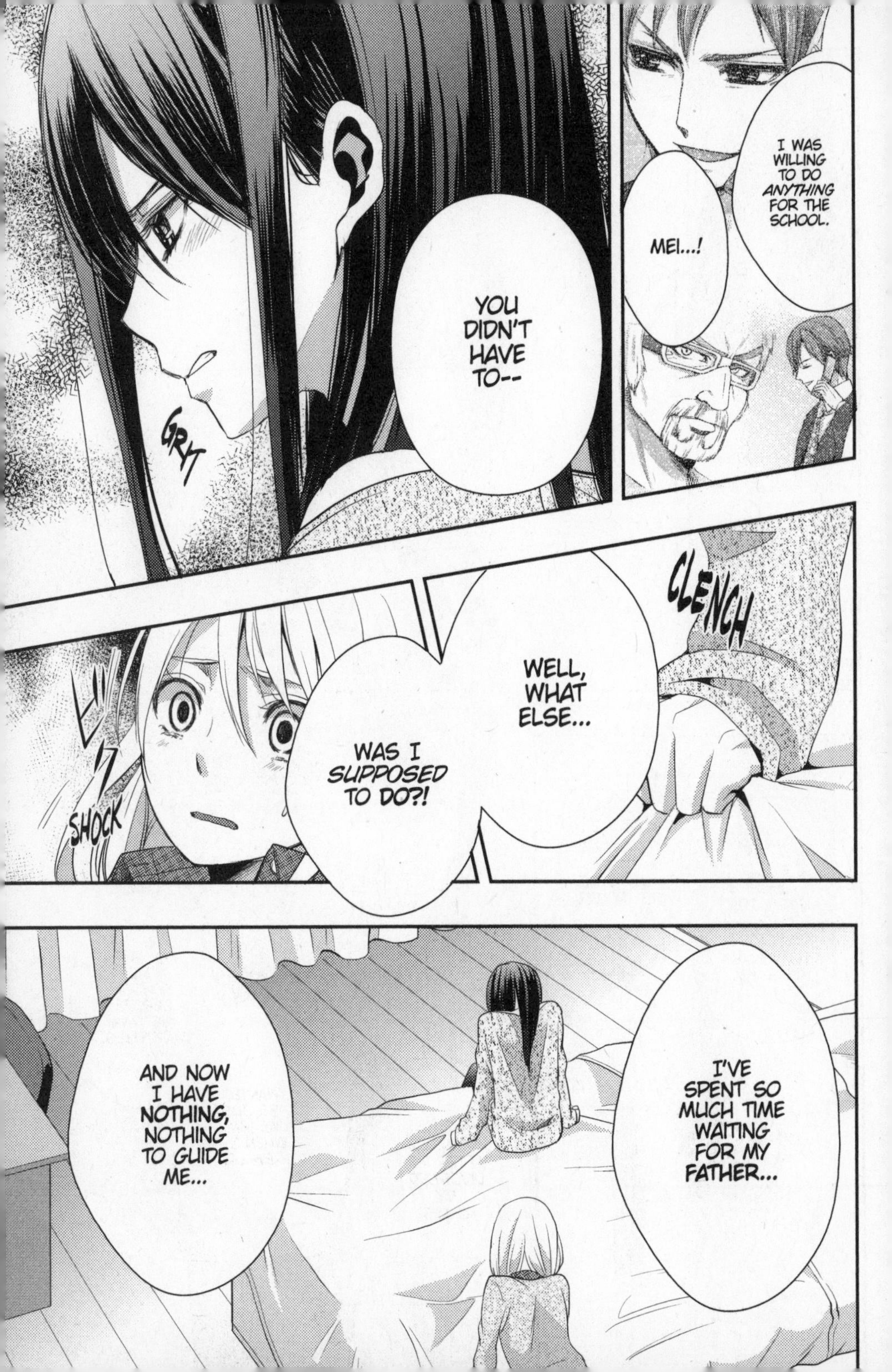
I WAS WILLING TO DO *ANYTHING* FOR THE SCHOOL.
MEI...!
YOU DIDN'T HAVE TO--
GRYT
CLENCH
WELL, WHAT ELSE...
WAS I SUPPOSED TO DO?!
SHOCK
I'VE SPENT SO MUCH TIME WAITING FOR MY FATHER...
AND NOW I HAVE NOTHING, NOTHING TO GUIDE ME...

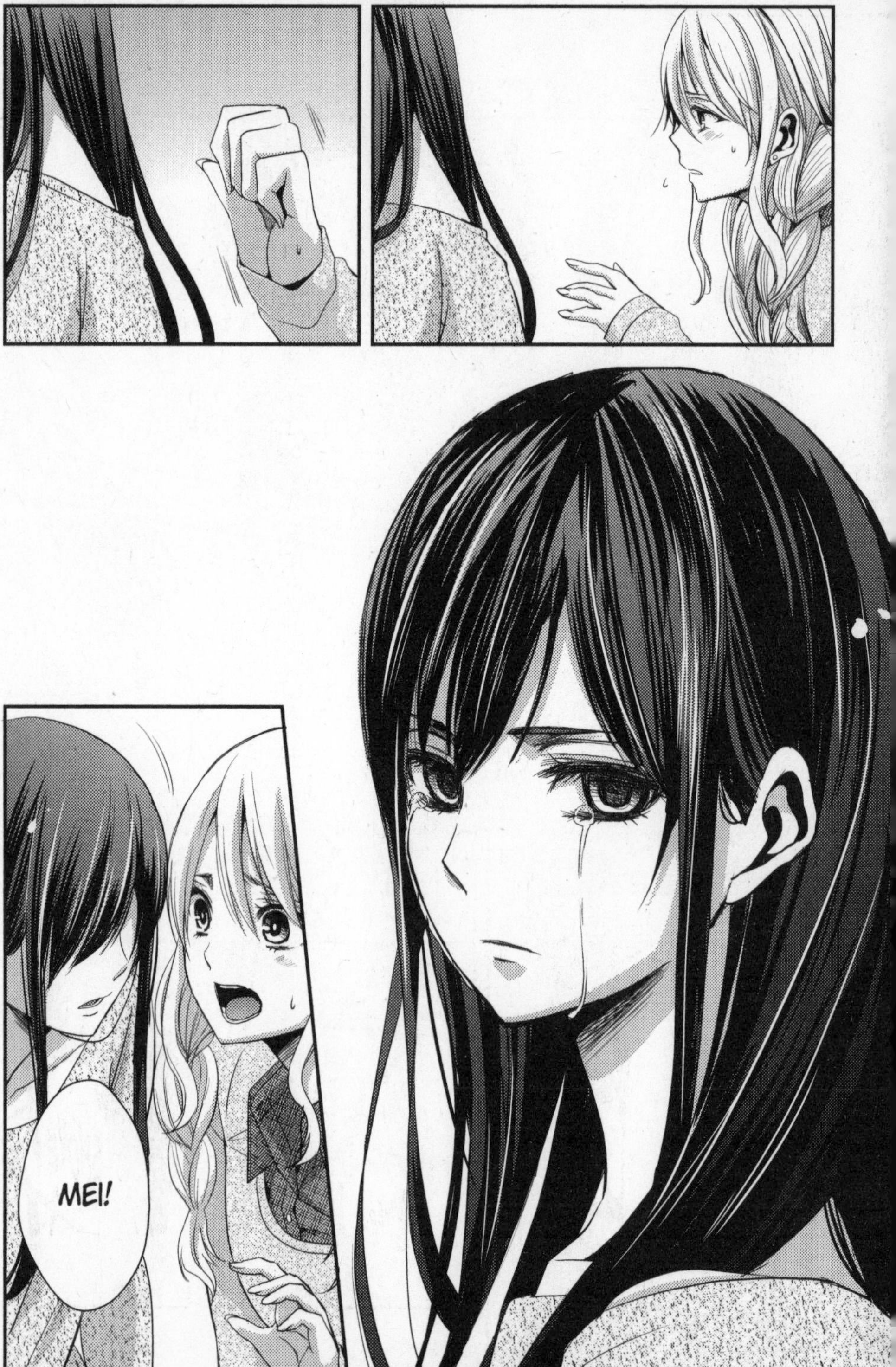
MEI!

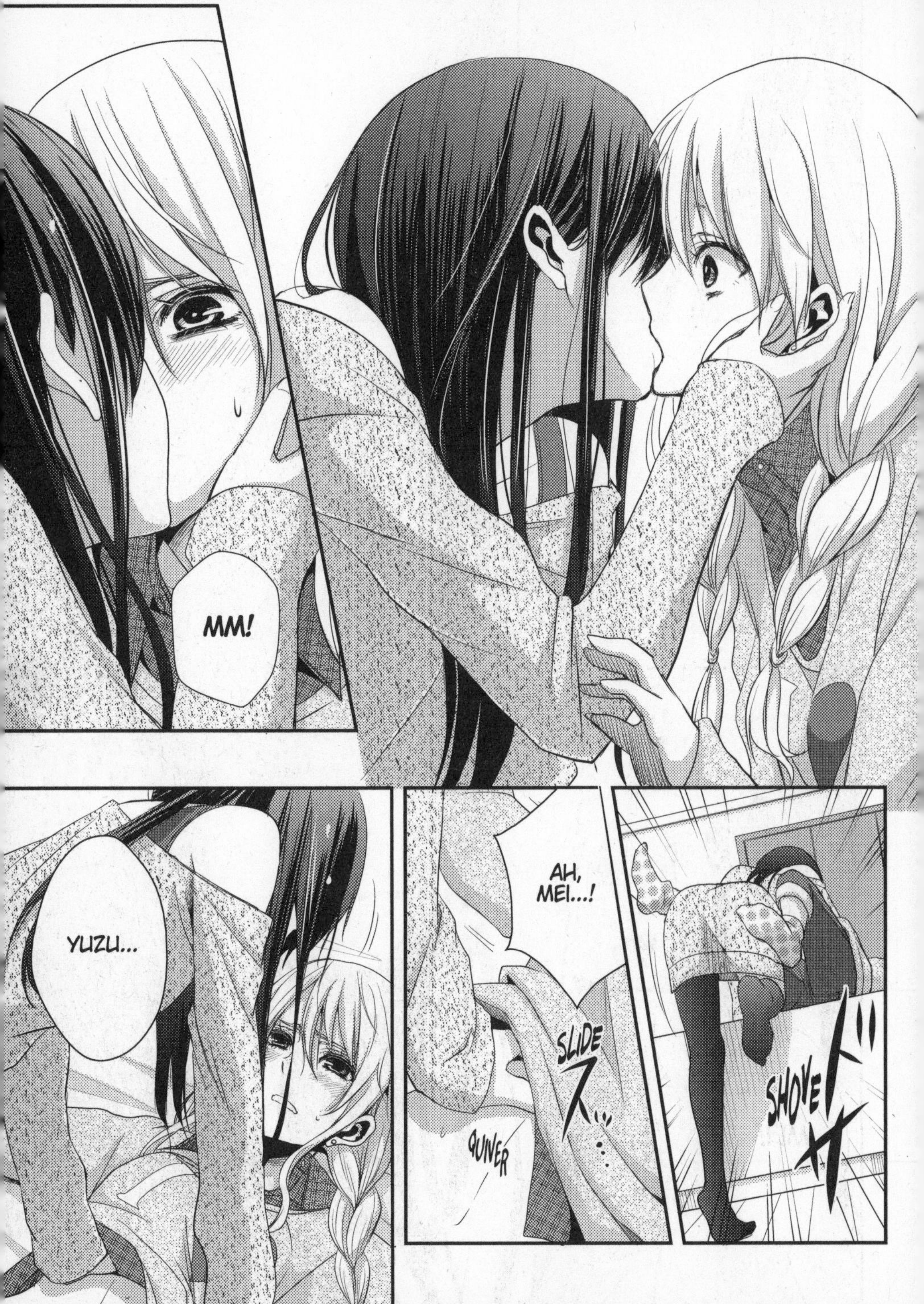
MM!
SHOVE
AH, MEI...!
SLIDE
QUIVER
YUZU...

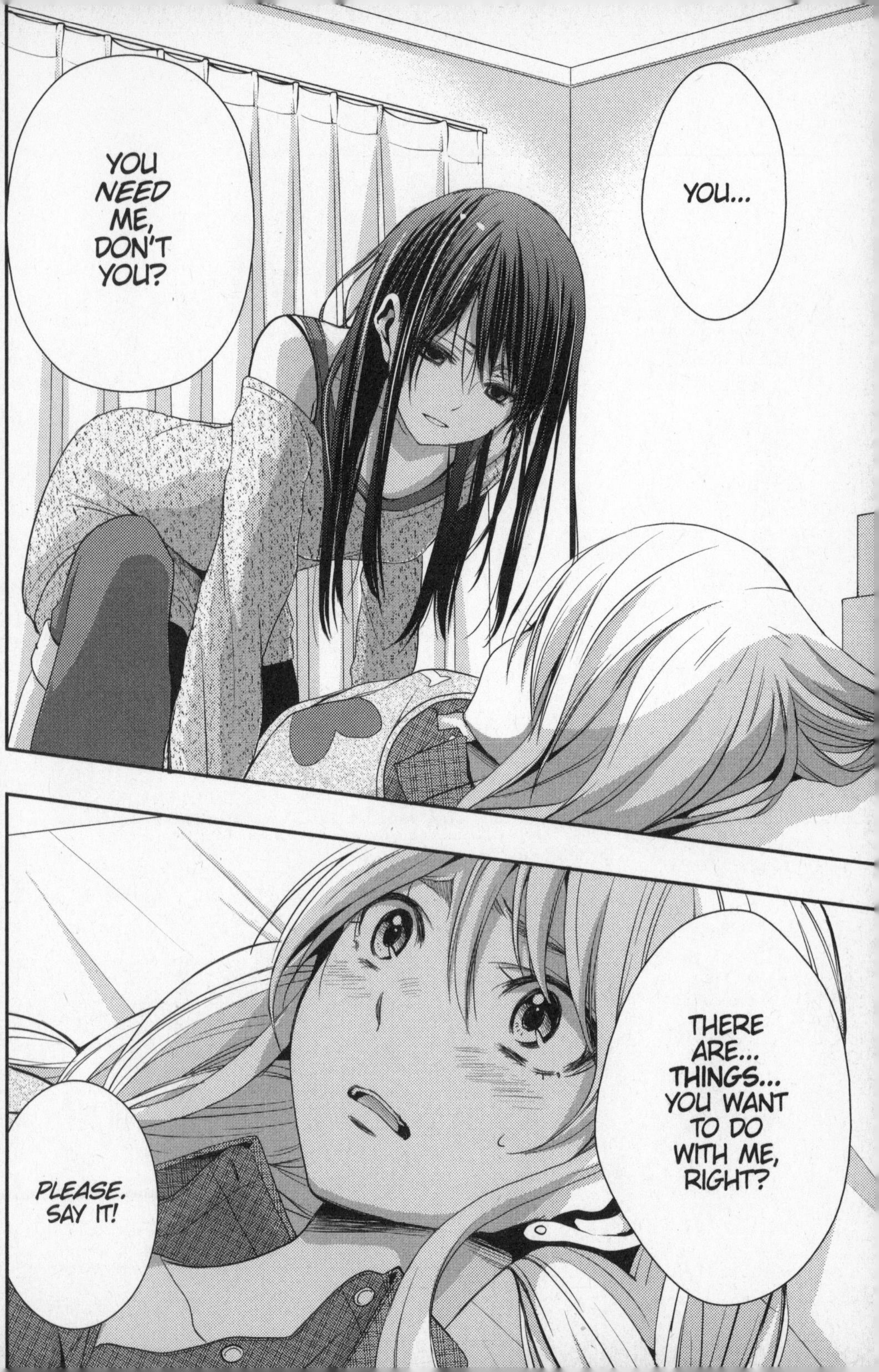
YOU...
YOU NEED ME, DON'T YOU?
THERE ARE... THINGS... YOU WANT TO DO WITH ME, RIGHT?
PLEASE. SAY IT!

citrus

【シトラス】

SECRET LOVE AFFAIR WITH SISTER

citrus

SABUROUTA PRESENTS SECRET LOVE AFFAIR WITH SISTER

2

8.out of love

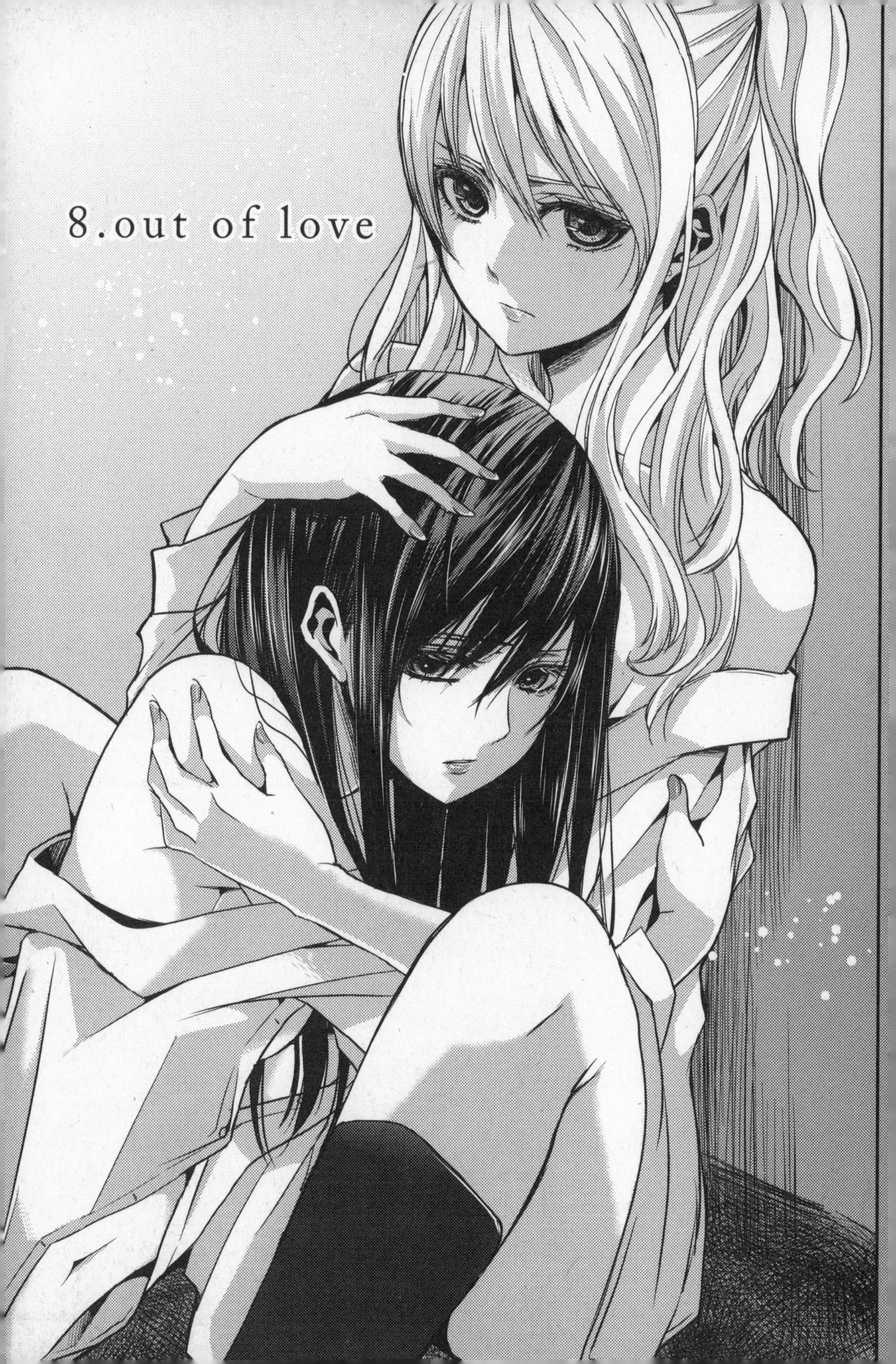

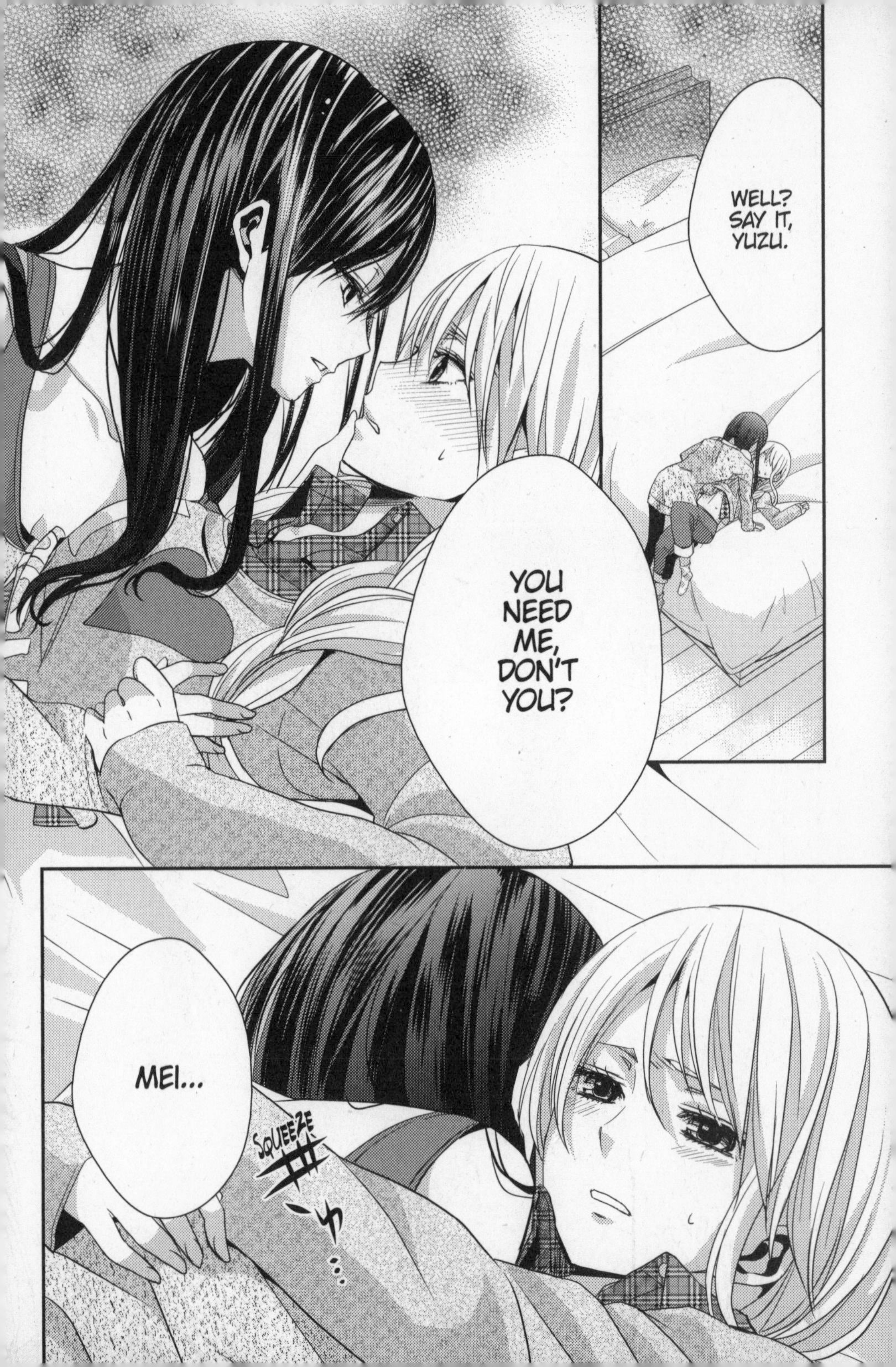
WELL? SAY IT, YUZU.
YOU NEED ME, DON'T YOU?
MEI...
SQUEEZE

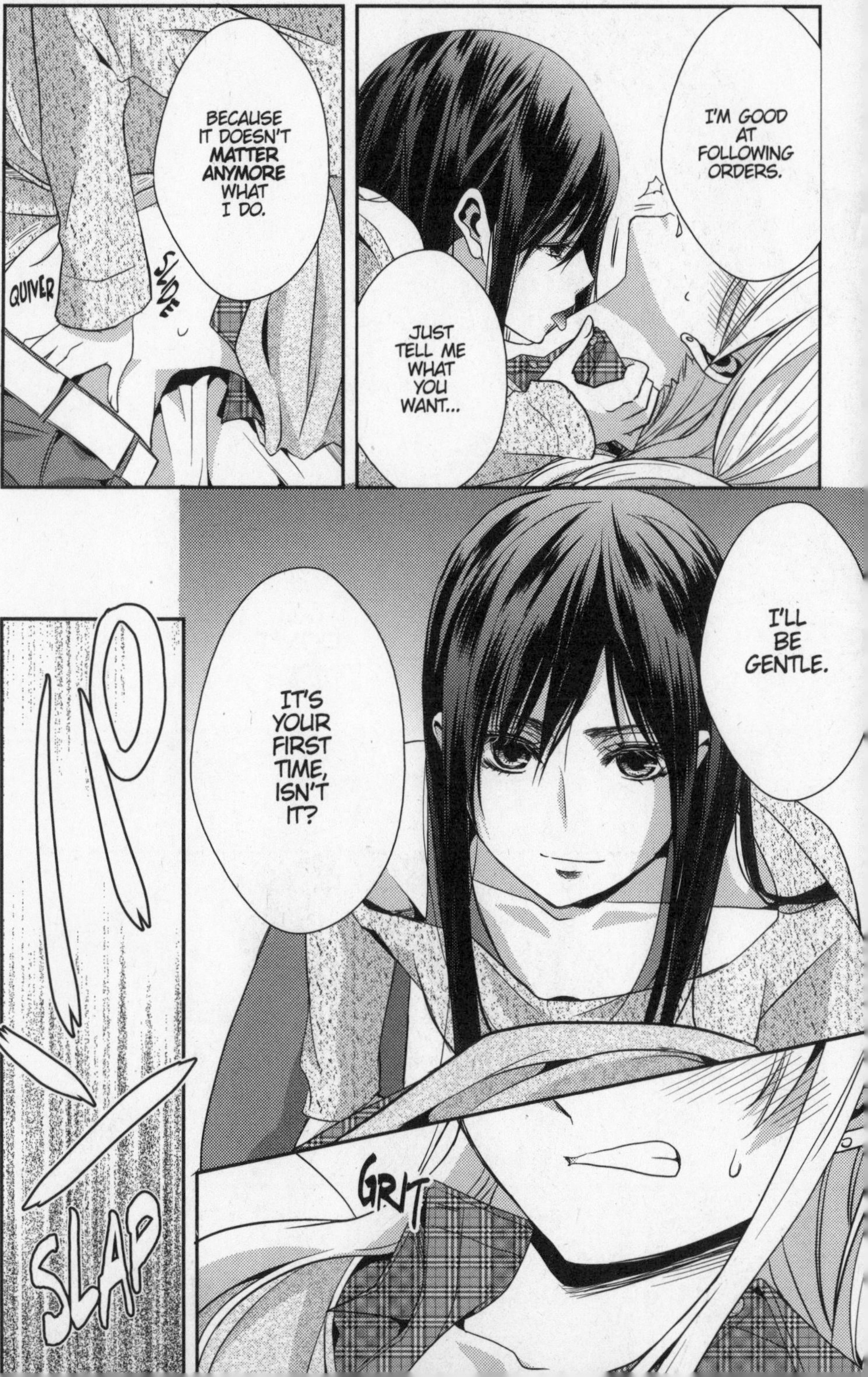
I'M GOOD AT FOLLOWING ORDERS.
JUST TELL ME WHAT YOU WANT...
BECAUSE IT DOESN'T MATTER ANYMORE WHAT I DO.
SLIDE
QUIVER
I'LL BE GENTLE.
IT'S YOUR FIRST TIME, ISN'T IT?
GRIT
SLAP

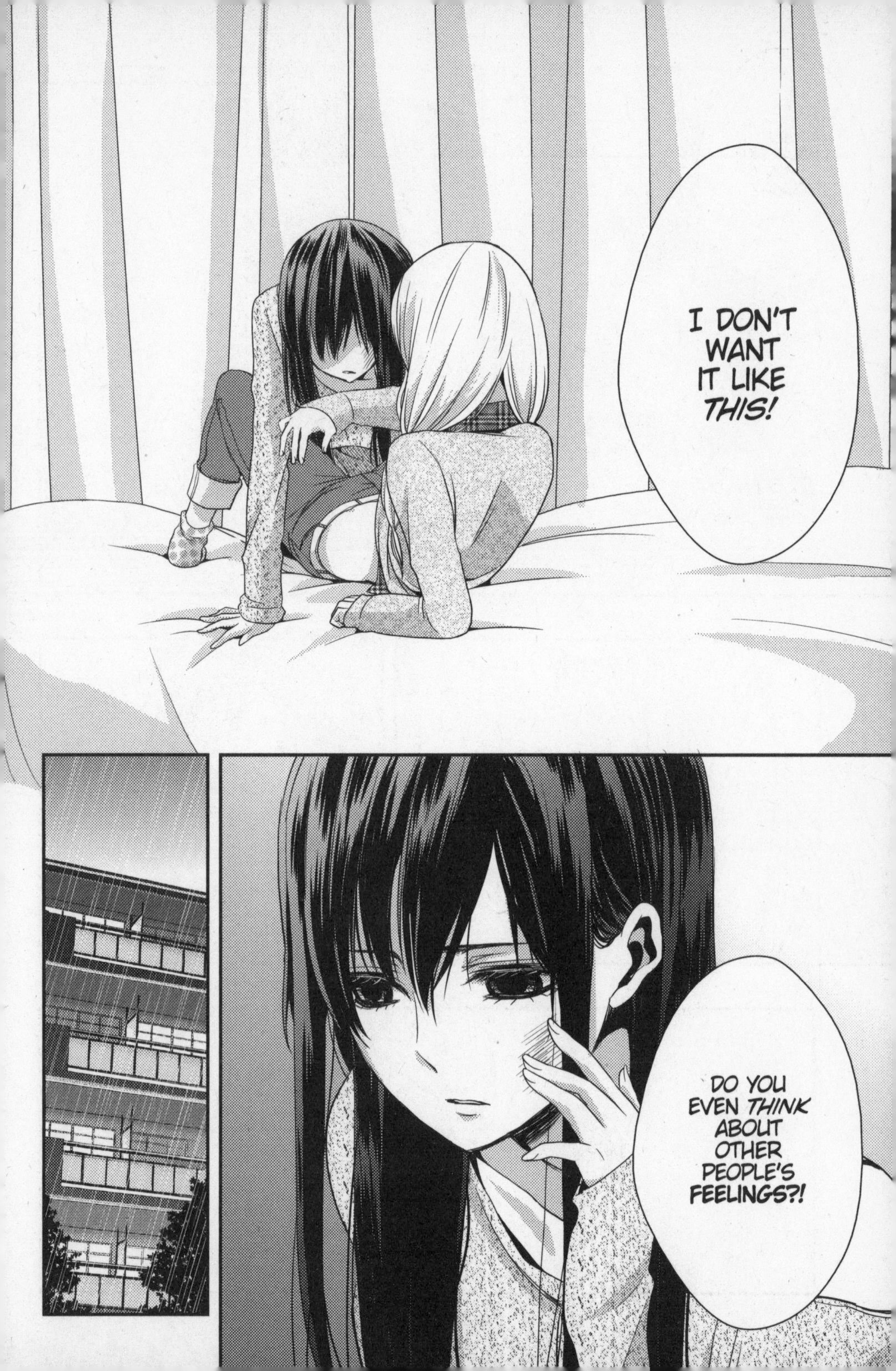
I DON'T WANT IT LIKE *THIS!*
DO YOU EVEN *THINK* ABOUT OTHER PEOPLE'S FEELINGS?!

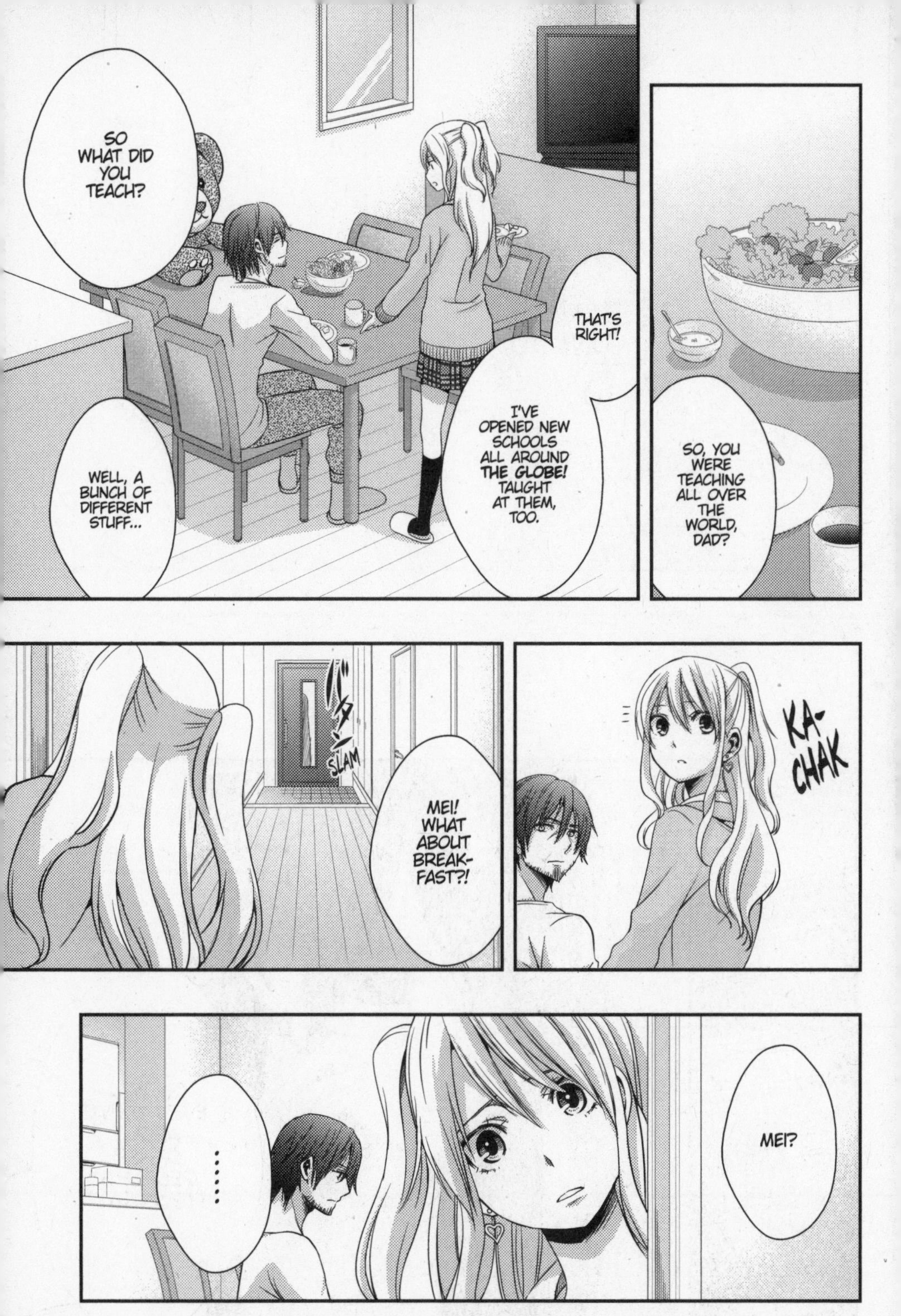
SO, YOU WERE TEACHING ALL OVER THE WORLD, DAD?
THAT'S RIGHT!
I'VE OPENED NEW SCHOOLS ALL AROUND THE GLOBE! TAUGHT AT THEM, TOO.
SO WHAT DID YOU TEACH?
WELL, A BUNCH OF DIFFERENT STUFF...
KA-CHAK
バタン
SLAM
MEI! WHAT ABOUT BREAK-FAST?!
MEI?
......

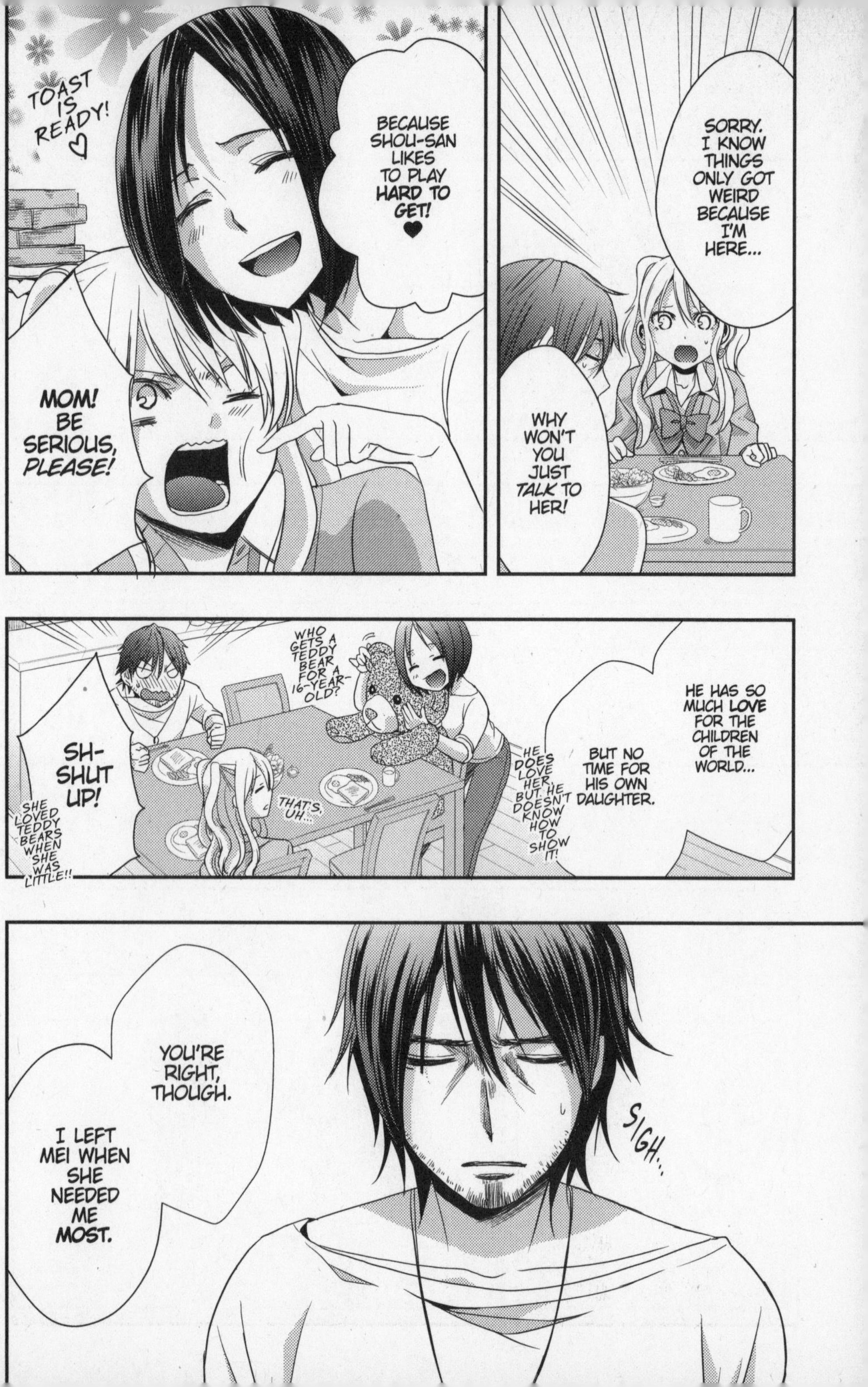
SORRY. I KNOW THINGS ONLY GOT WEIRD BECAUSE I'M HERE...
WHY WON'T YOU JUST TALK TO HER!
BECAUSE SHOU-SAN LIKES TO PLAY HARD TO GET! ♥
TOAST IS READY! ♡
MOM! BE SERIOUS, PLEASE!
HE HAS SO MUCH LOVE FOR THE CHILDREN OF THE WORLD...
BUT NO TIME FOR HIS OWN DAUGHTER.
HE DOES LOVE HER, BUT HE DOESN'T KNOW HOW TO SHOW IT!
WHO GETS A TEDDY BEAR FOR A 16-YEAR-OLD?
THAT'S, UH...
SH-SHUT UP!
SHE LOVED TEDDY BEARS WHEN SHE WAS LITTLE!!
SIGH...
YOU'RE RIGHT, THOUGH.
I LEFT MEI WHEN SHE NEEDED ME MOST.

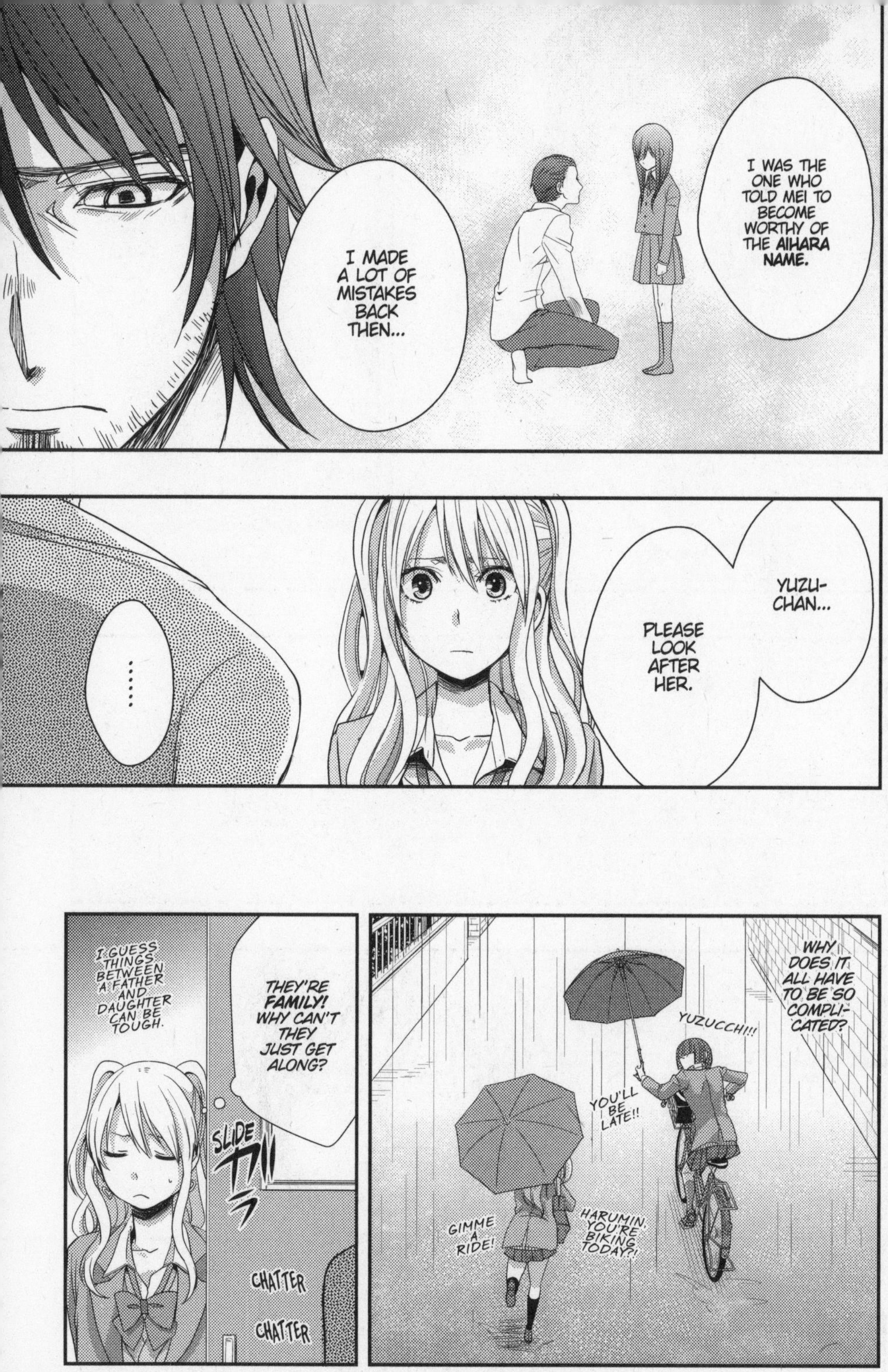
I WAS THE ONE WHO TOLD MEI TO BECOME WORTHY OF THE AIHARA NAME.
I MADE A LOT OF MISTAKES BACK THEN...
YUZU-CHAN...
PLEASE LOOK AFTER HER.
......
WHY DOES IT ALL HAVE TO BE SO COMPLICATED?
YUZUCCHI!!!
YOU'LL BE LATE!!
HARUMIN, YOU'RE BIKING TODAY?!
GIMME A RIDE!
THEY'RE FAMILY! WHY CAN'T THEY JUST GET ALONG?
I GUESS THINGS BETWEEN A FATHER AND DAUGHTER CAN BE TOUGH.
SLIDE
CHATTER
CHATTER

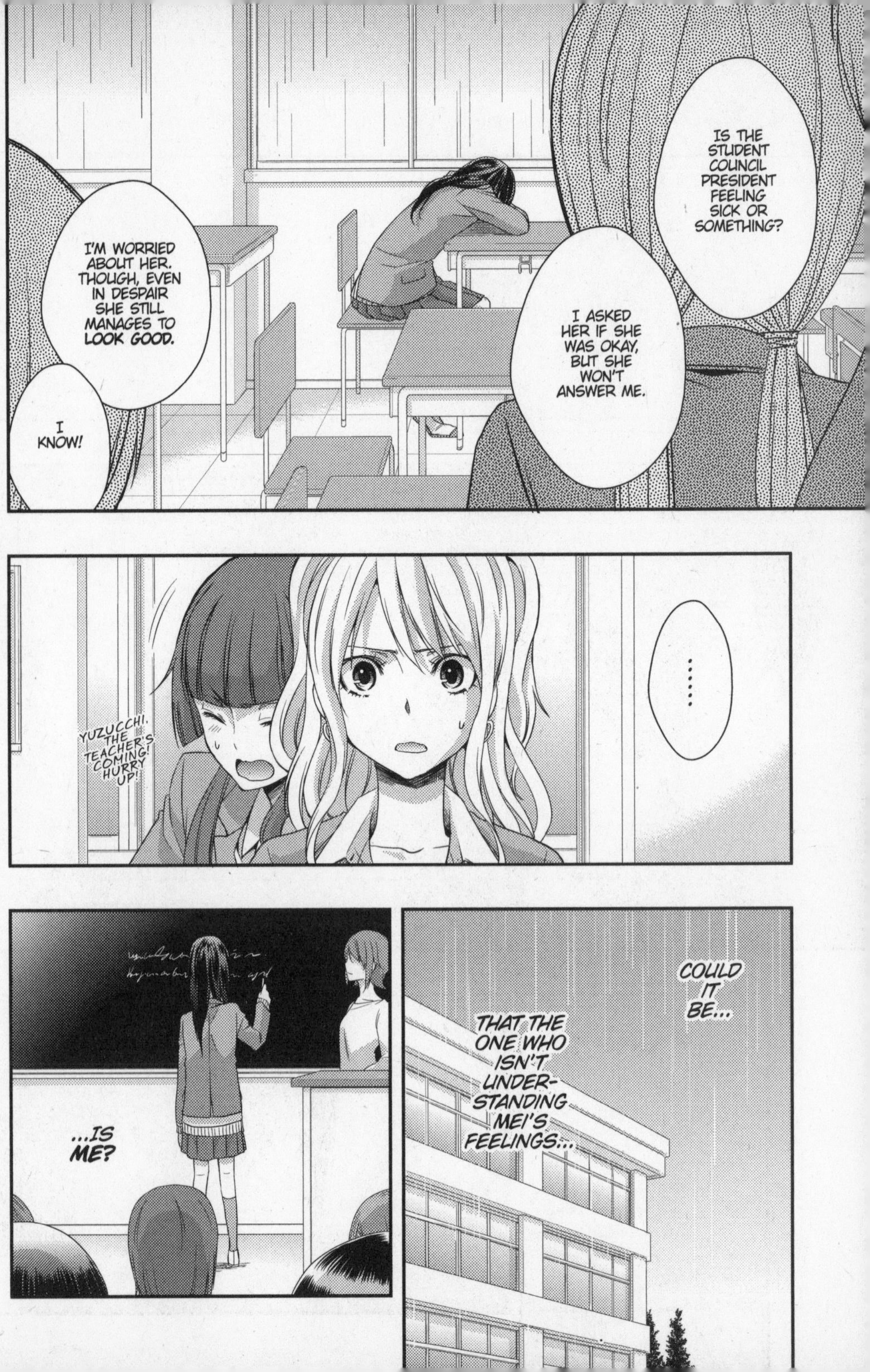
IS THE STUDENT COUNCIL PRESIDENT FEELING SICK OR SOMETHING?
I ASKED HER IF SHE WAS OKAY, BUT SHE WON'T ANSWER ME.
I'M WORRIED ABOUT HER. THOUGH, EVEN IN DESPAIR SHE STILL MANAGES TO LOOK GOOD.
I KNOW!
......
YUZUCCHI, THE TEACHER'S COMING! HURRY UP!
COULD IT BE...
THAT THE ONE WHO ISN'T UNDER-STANDING MEI'S FEELINGS...
...IS ME?

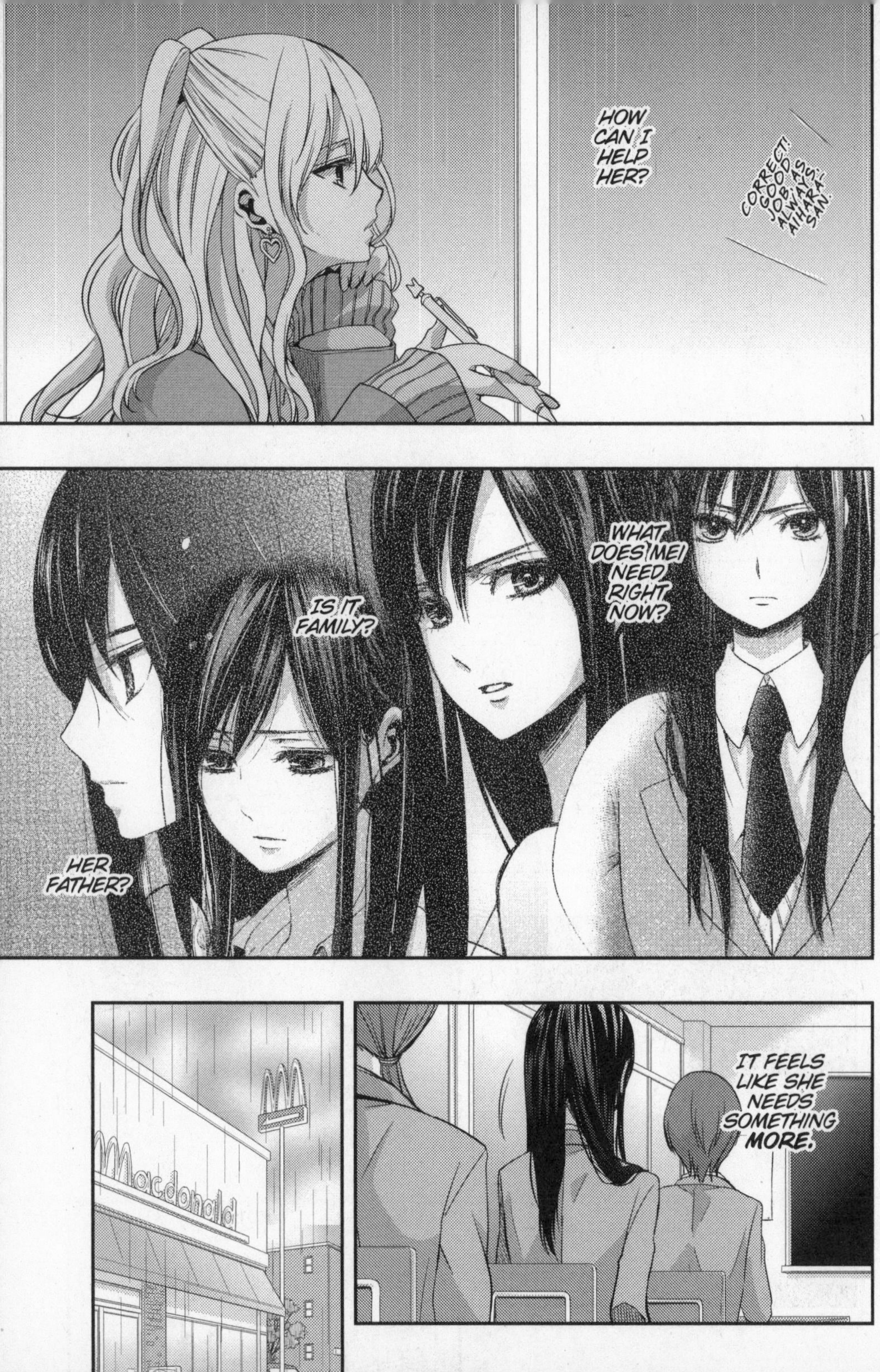
CORRECT! GOOD JOB AS ALWAYS, AIHARA-SAN.
HOW CAN I HELP HER?
WHAT DOES MEI NEED RIGHT NOW?
IS IT FAMILY?
HER FATHER?
IT FEELS LIKE SHE NEEDS SOMETHING MORE.
Macdonald

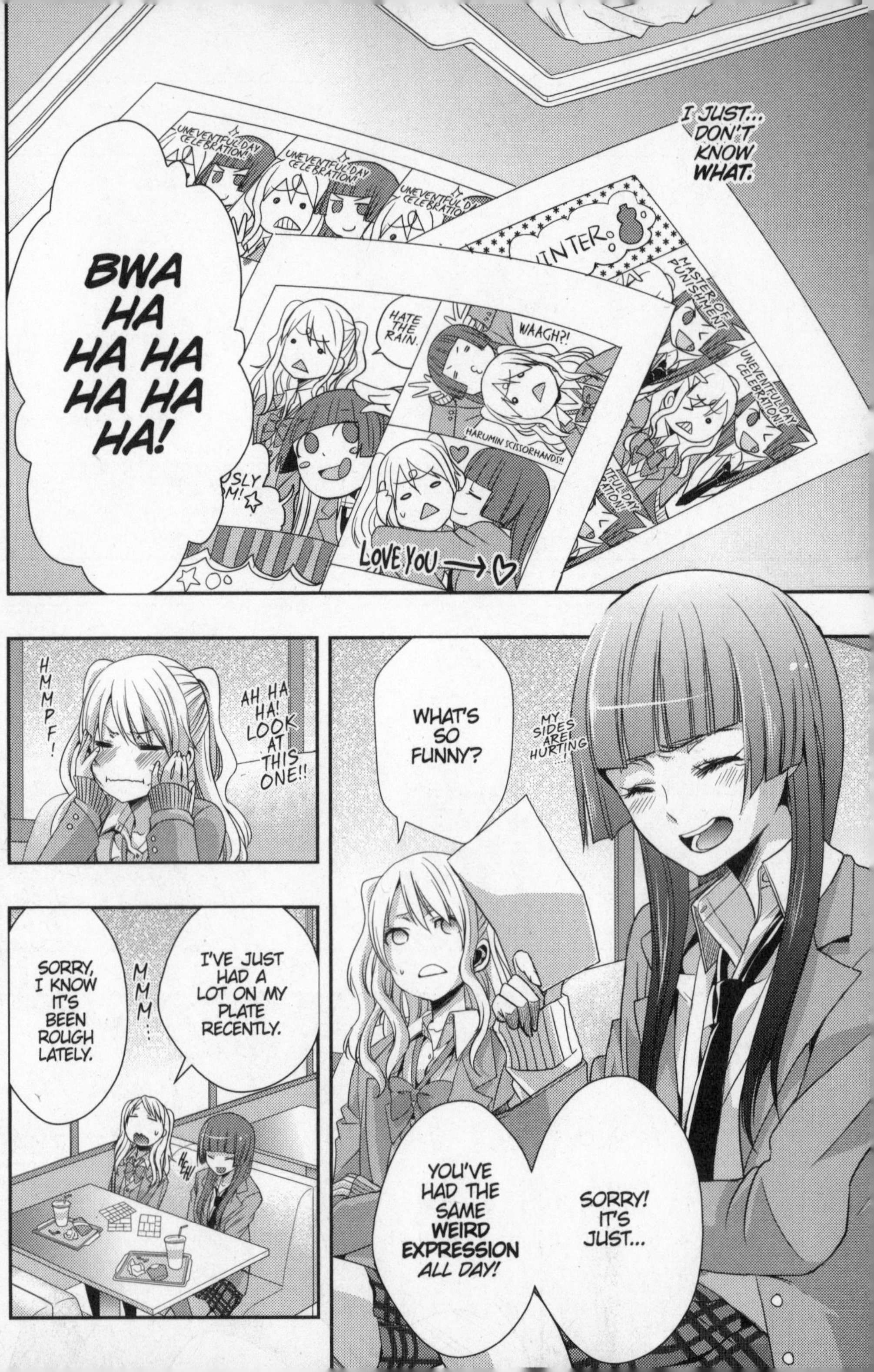
I JUST... DON'T KNOW WHAT.
UNEVENTFUL-DAY CELEBRATION!
UNEVENTFUL-DAY CELEBRATION!
UNEVENTFUL-DAY CELEBRATION!
MASTER OF PUNISHMENT
UNEVENTFUL-DAY CELEBRATION!
WAAGH?!
HARUMIN SCISSORHANDS!!
HATE THE RAIN.
LOVE YOU →
BWA HA HA HA HA HA HA!
MY SIDES ARE! HURTING...
WHAT'S SO FUNNY?
SORRY! IT'S JUST...
YOU'VE HAD THE SAME WEIRD EXPRESSION ALL DAY!
AH HA HA! LOOK AT THIS ONE!!
HMMPF!
I'VE JUST HAD A LOT ON MY PLATE RECENTLY.
MMM...
SORRY, I KNOW IT'S BEEN ROUGH LATELY.
HEH!

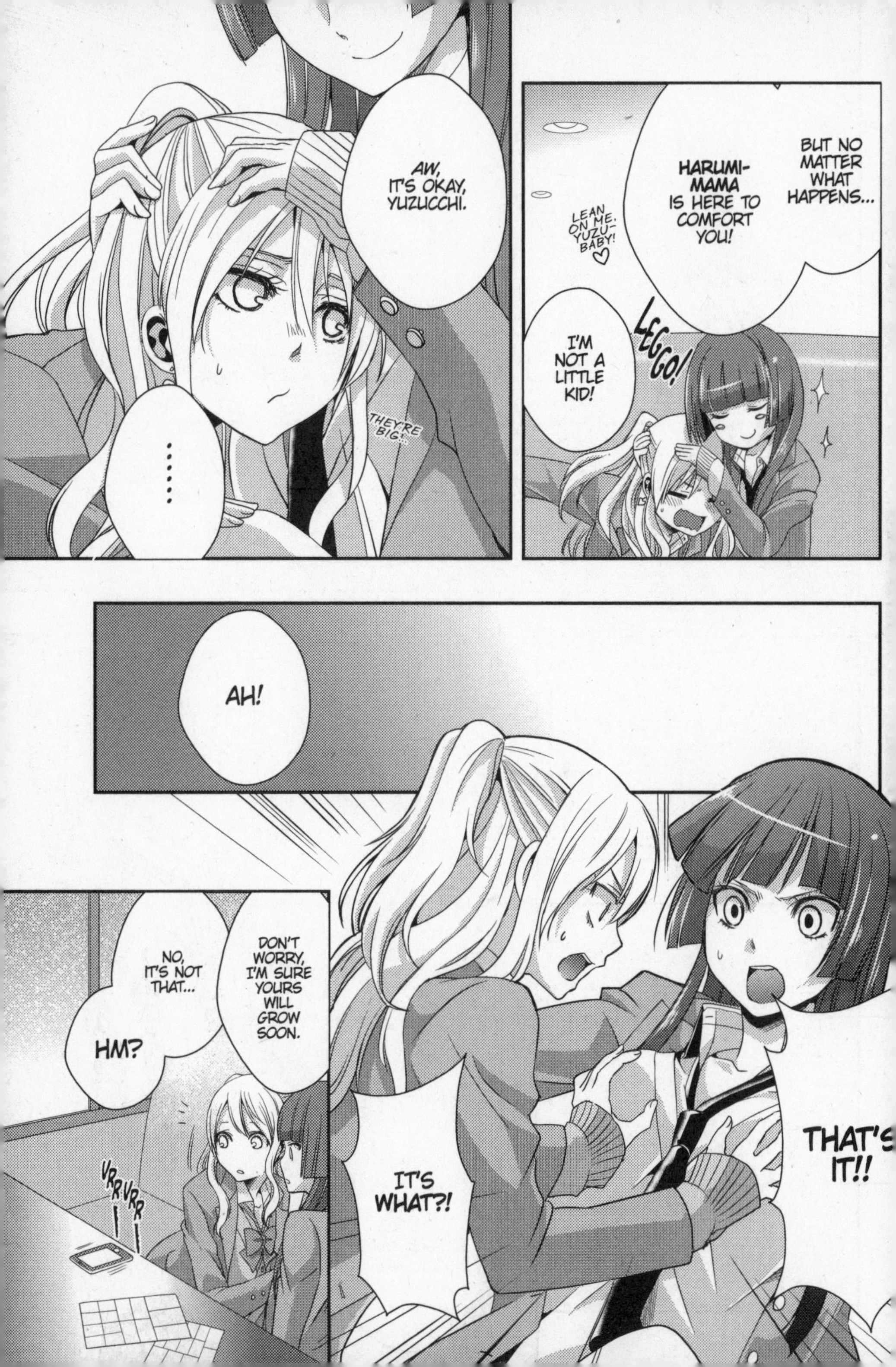
BUT NO MATTER WHAT HAPPENS...
HARUMI-MAMA IS HERE TO COMFORT YOU!
LEAN ON ME, YUZU-BABY! ♥
LEGGO!
I'M NOT A LITTLE KID!
AW, IT'S OKAY, YUZUCCHI.
THEY'RE BIG...
......
AH!
THAT'S IT!!
IT'S WHAT?!
DON'T WORRY, I'M SURE YOURS WILL GROW SOON.
NO, IT'S NOT THAT...
HM?
VRR VRR

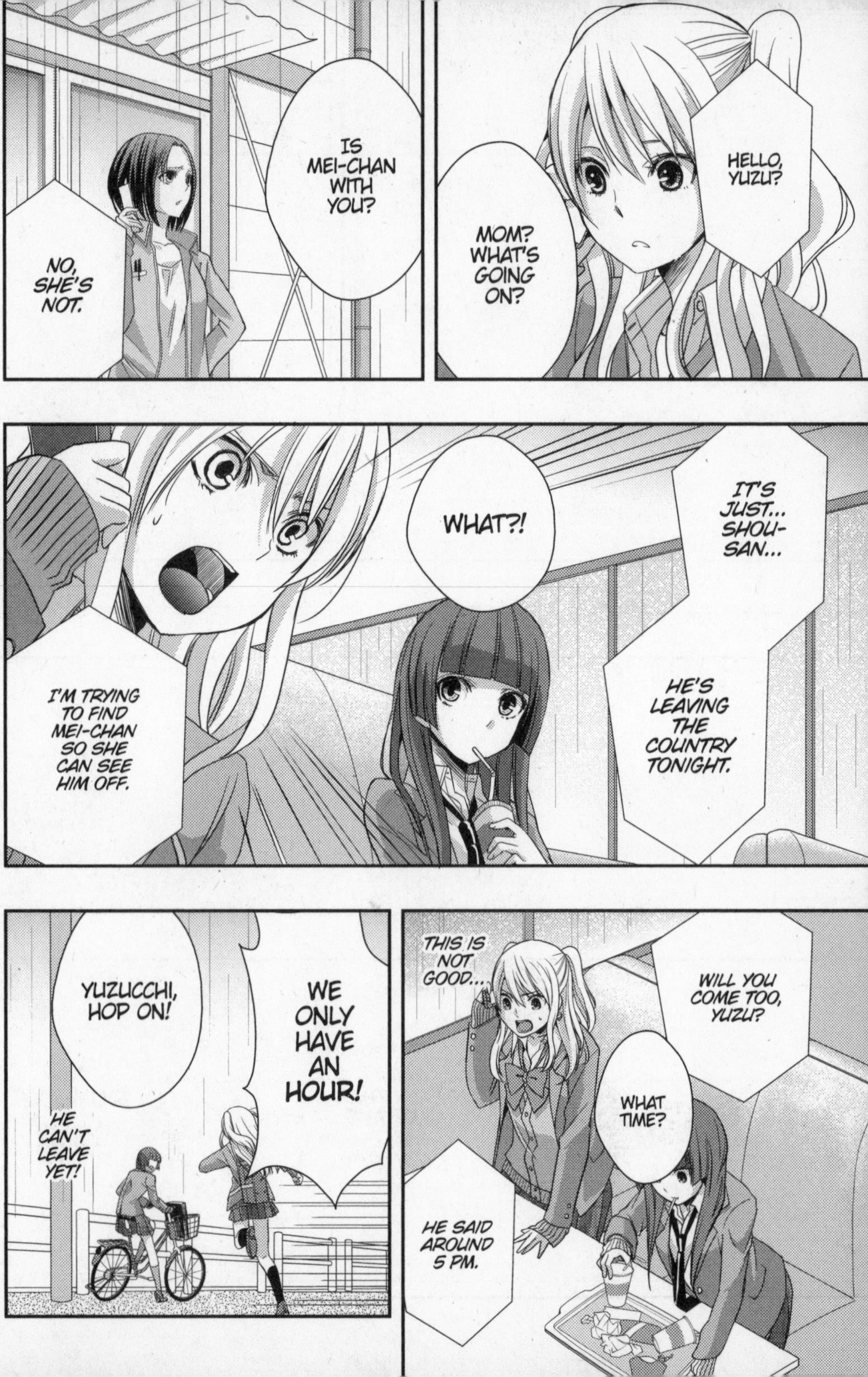
HELLO, YUZU?
MOM? WHAT'S GOING ON?
IS MEI-CHAN WITH YOU?
NO, SHE'S NOT.
IT'S JUST... SHOU-SAN...
HE'S LEAVING THE COUNTRY TONIGHT.
WHAT?!
I'M TRYING TO FIND MEI-CHAN SO SHE CAN SEE HIM OFF.
WILL YOU COME TOO, YUZU?
THIS IS NOT GOOD...
WHAT TIME?
HE SAID AROUND 5 PM.
WE ONLY HAVE AN HOUR!
YUZUCCHI, HOP ON!
HE CAN'T LEAVE YET!

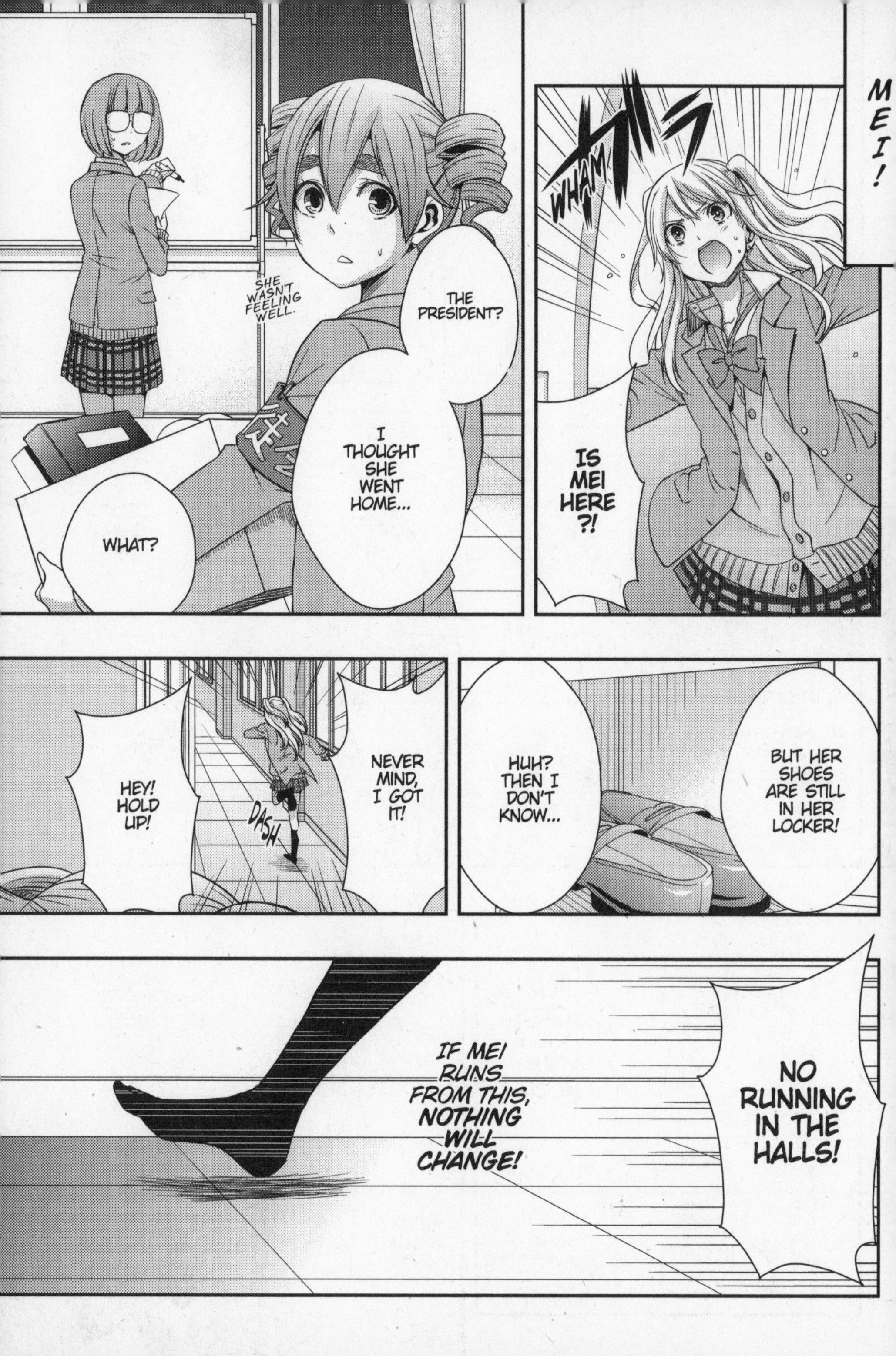
MEI!
WHAM
IS MEI HERE?!
THE PRESIDENT?
SHE WASN'T FEELING WELL.
I THOUGHT SHE WENT HOME...
WHAT?
BUT HER SHOES ARE STILL IN HER LOCKER!
HUH? THEN I DON'T KNOW...
NEVER MIND, I GOT IT!
DASH
HEY! HOLD UP!
NO RUNNING IN THE HALLS!
IF MEI RUNS FROM THIS, NOTHING WILL CHANGE!

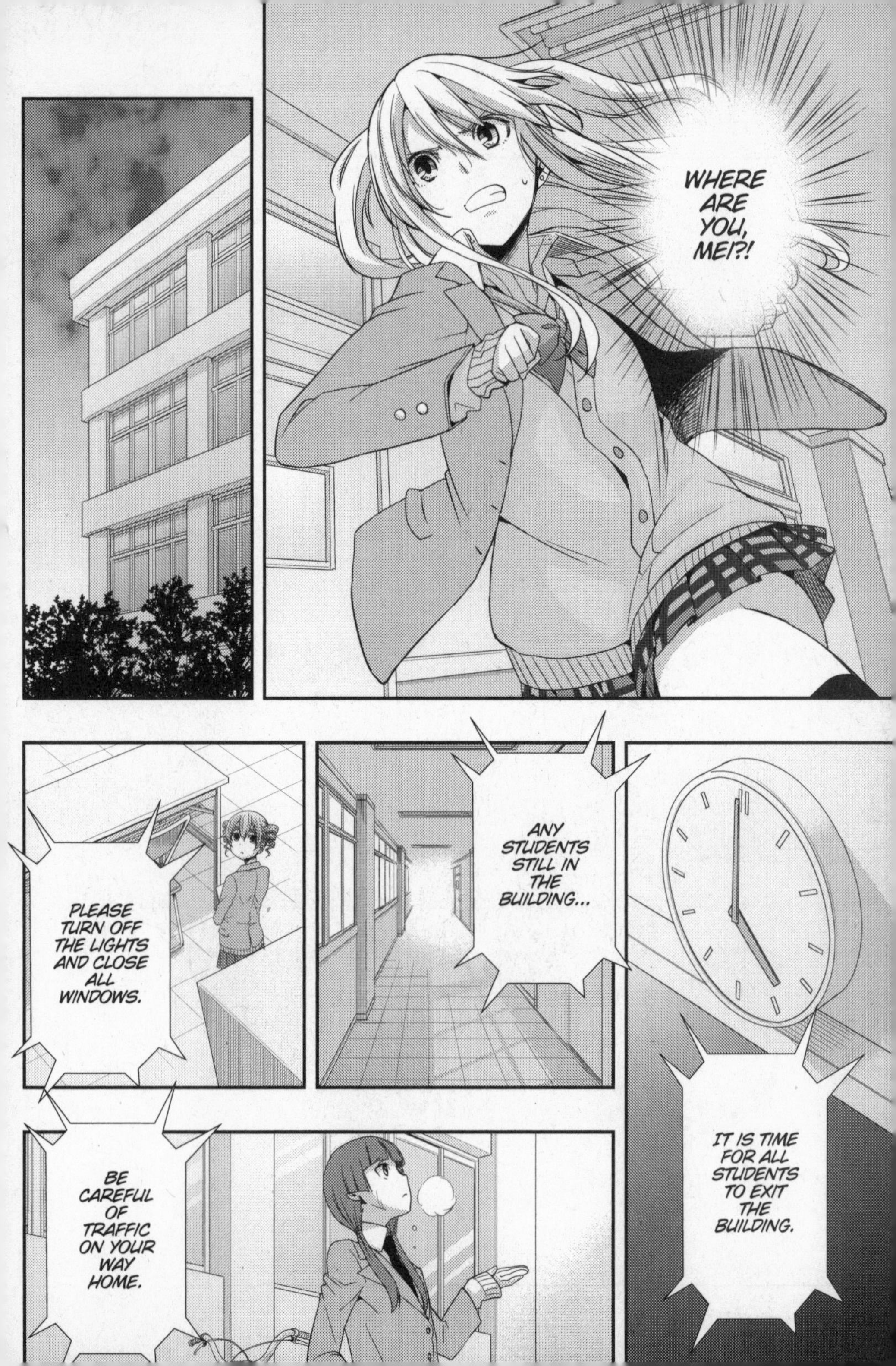
WHERE ARE YOU, MEI?!
IT IS TIME FOR ALL STUDENTS TO EXIT THE BUILDING.
ANY STUDENTS STILL IN THE BUILDING...
PLEASE TURN OFF THE LIGHTS AND CLOSE ALL WINDOWS.
BE CAREFUL OF TRAFFIC ON YOUR WAY HOME.

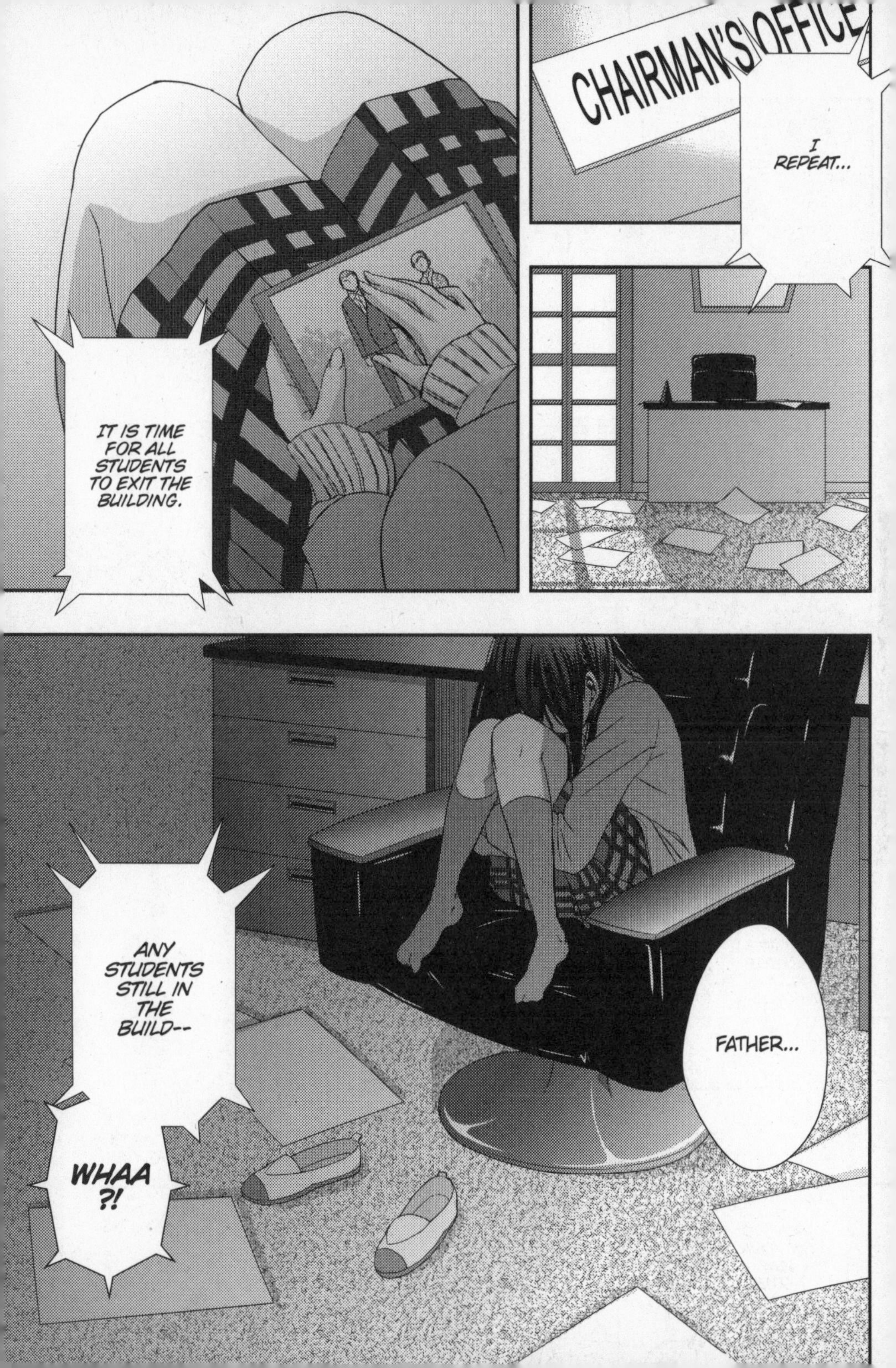
CHAIRMAN'S OFFICE
I REPEAT...
IT IS TIME FOR ALL STUDENTS TO EXIT THE BUILDING.
FATHER...
ANY STUDENTS STILL IN THE BUILD--
WHAA ?!

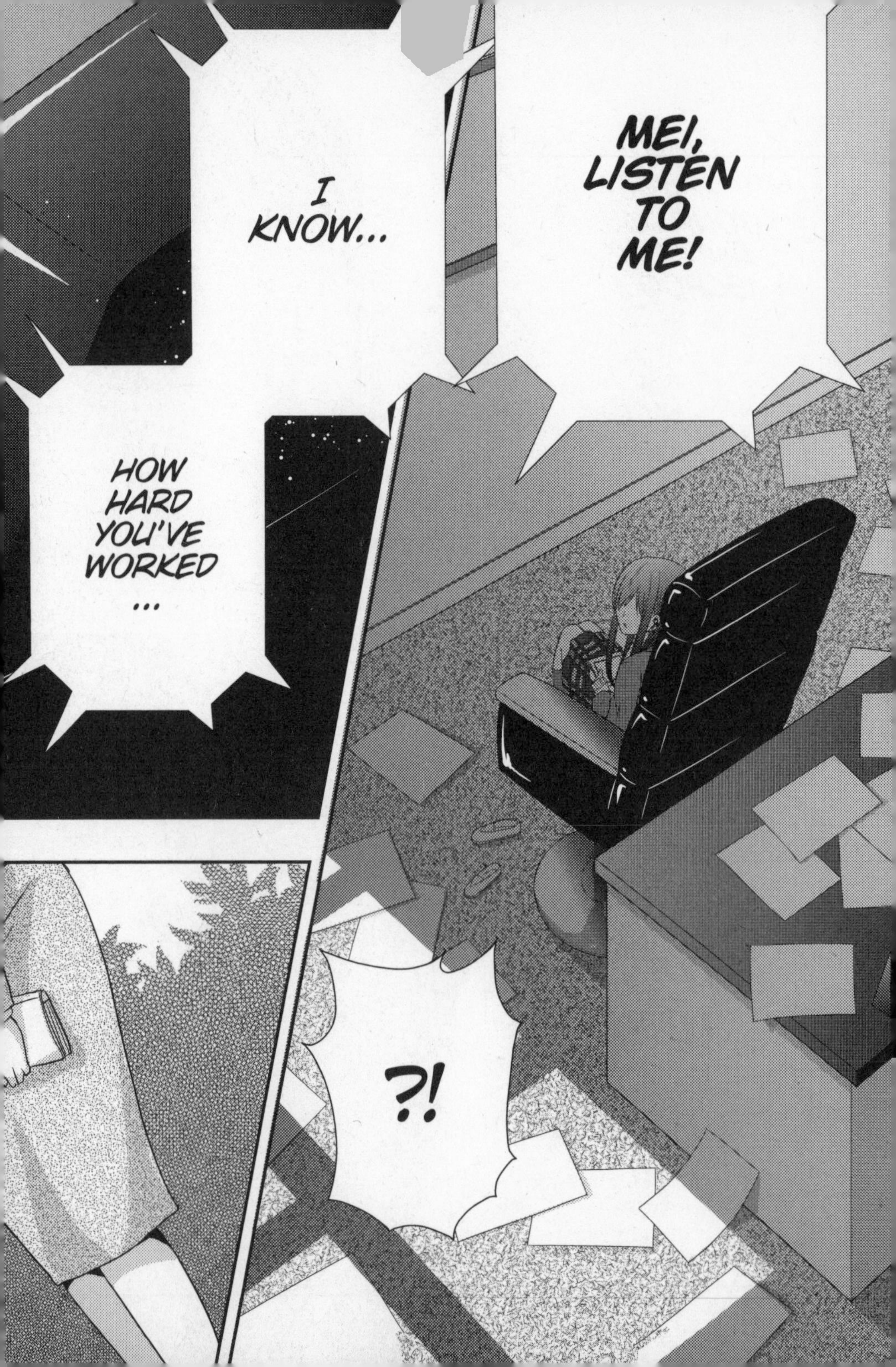
MEI, LISTEN TO ME!
I KNOW...
HOW HARD YOU'VE WORKED ...
?!

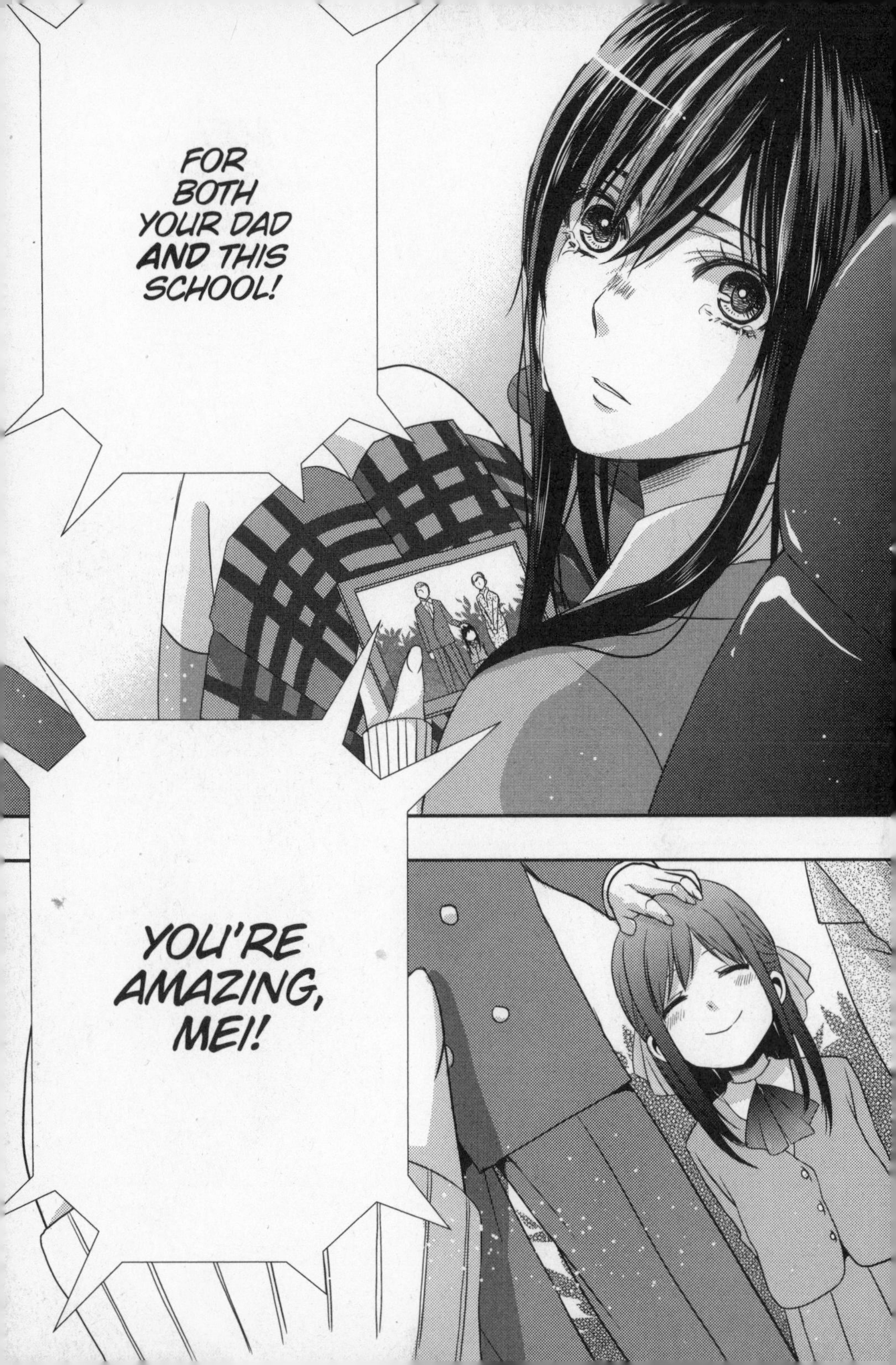
FOR BOTH YOUR DAD AND THIS SCHOOL!
YOU'RE AMAZING, MEI!

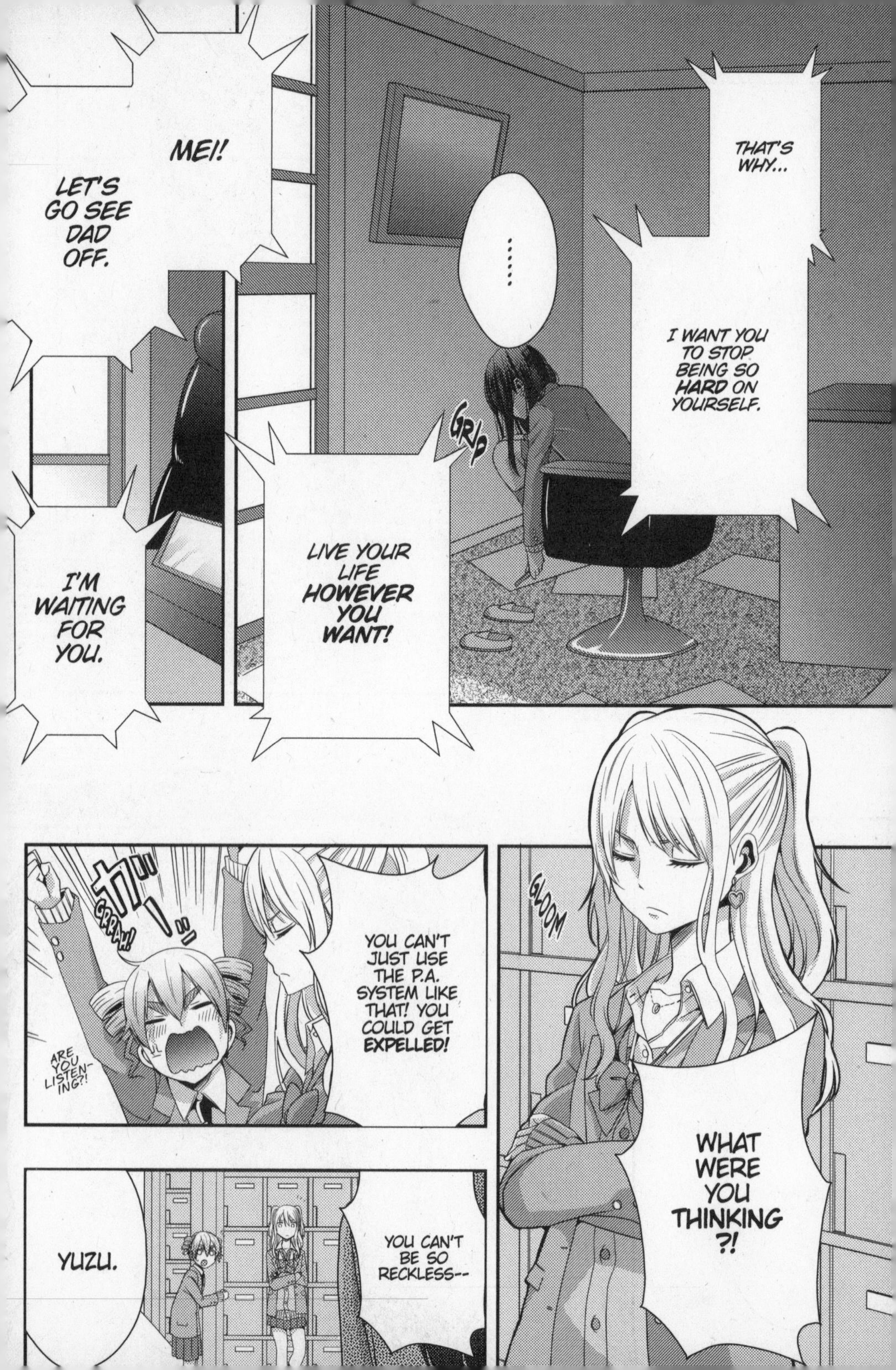
THAT'S WHY...
I WANT YOU TO STOP BEING SO HARD ON YOURSELF.
GRIP
......
LIVE YOUR LIFE HOWEVER YOU WANT!
MEI!
LET'S GO SEE DAD OFF.
I'M WAITING FOR YOU.
GLOOM
WHAT WERE YOU THINKING ?!
YOU CAN'T JUST USE THE P.A. SYSTEM LIKE THAT! YOU COULD GET EXPELLED!
GRRAH!
ARE YOU LISTENING?!
YOU CAN'T BE SO RECKLESS--
YUZU.

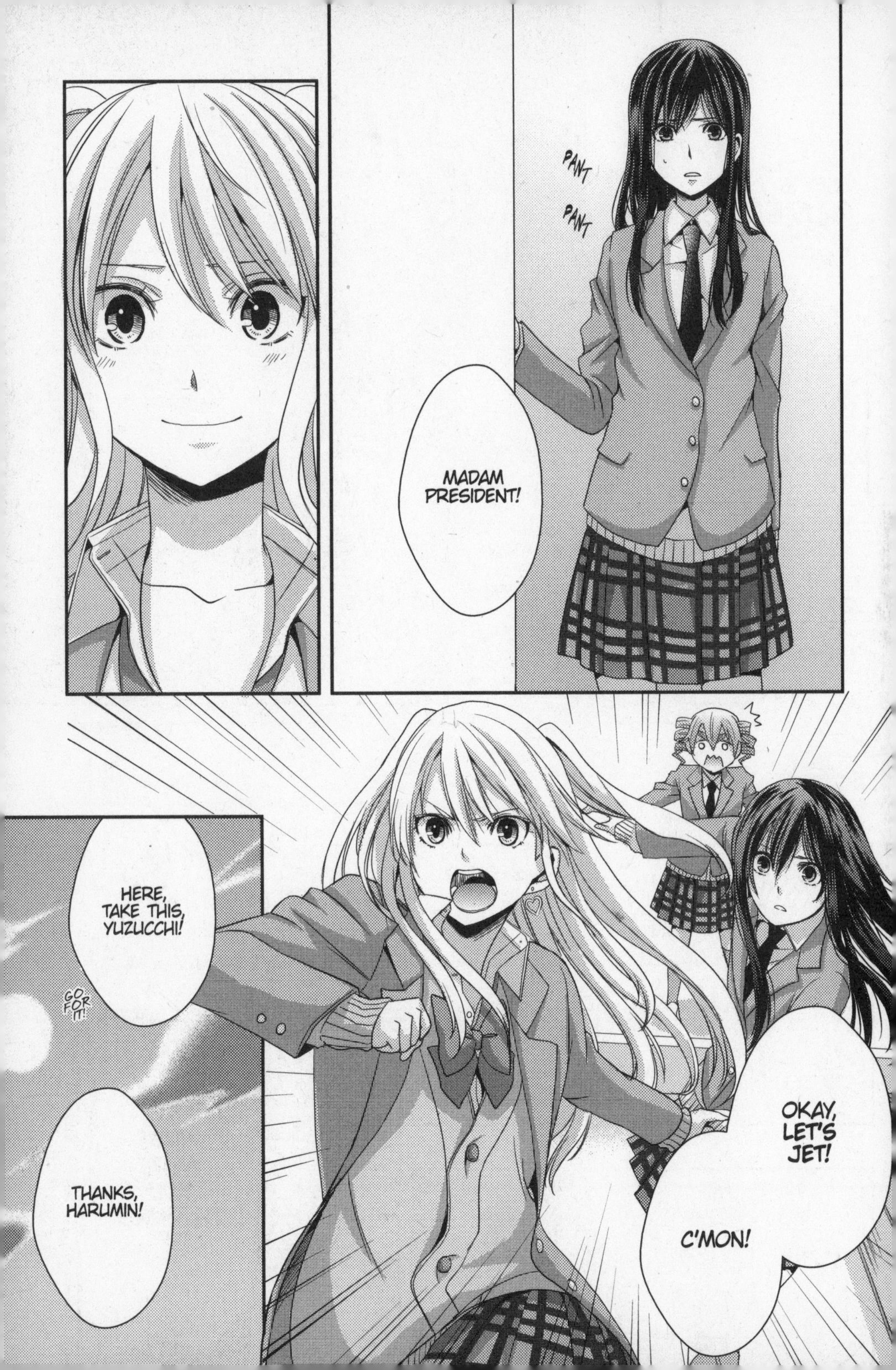
PANT
PANT
MADAM PRESIDENT!
OKAY, LET'S JET!
C'MON!
HERE, TAKE THIS, YUZUCCHI!
GO FOR IT!
THANKS, HARUMIN!

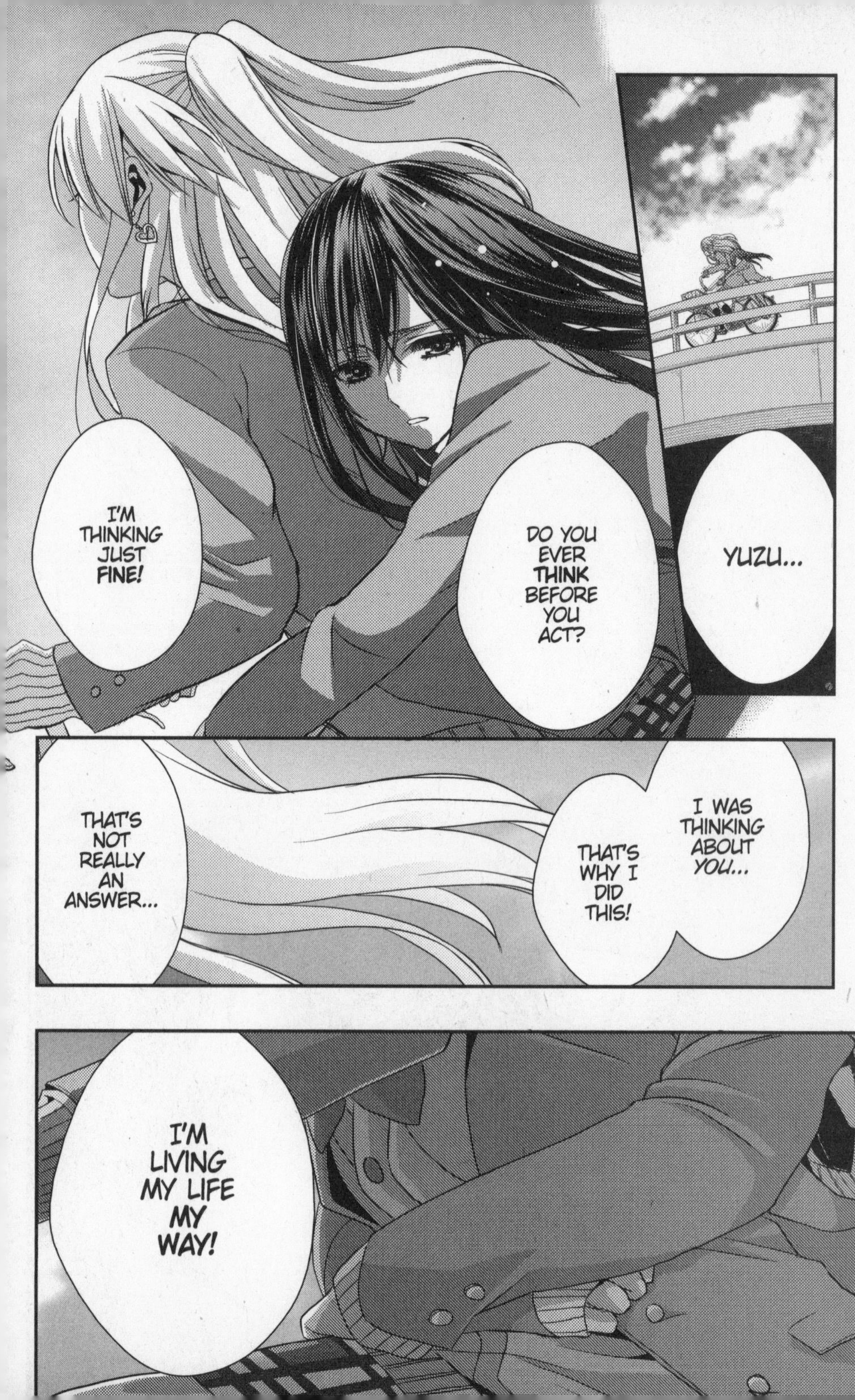
YUZU...
DO YOU EVER THINK BEFORE YOU ACT?
I'M THINKING JUST FINE!
I WAS THINKING ABOUT YOU...
THAT'S WHY I DID THIS!
THAT'S NOT REALLY AN ANSWER...
I'M LIVING MY LIFE MY WAY!

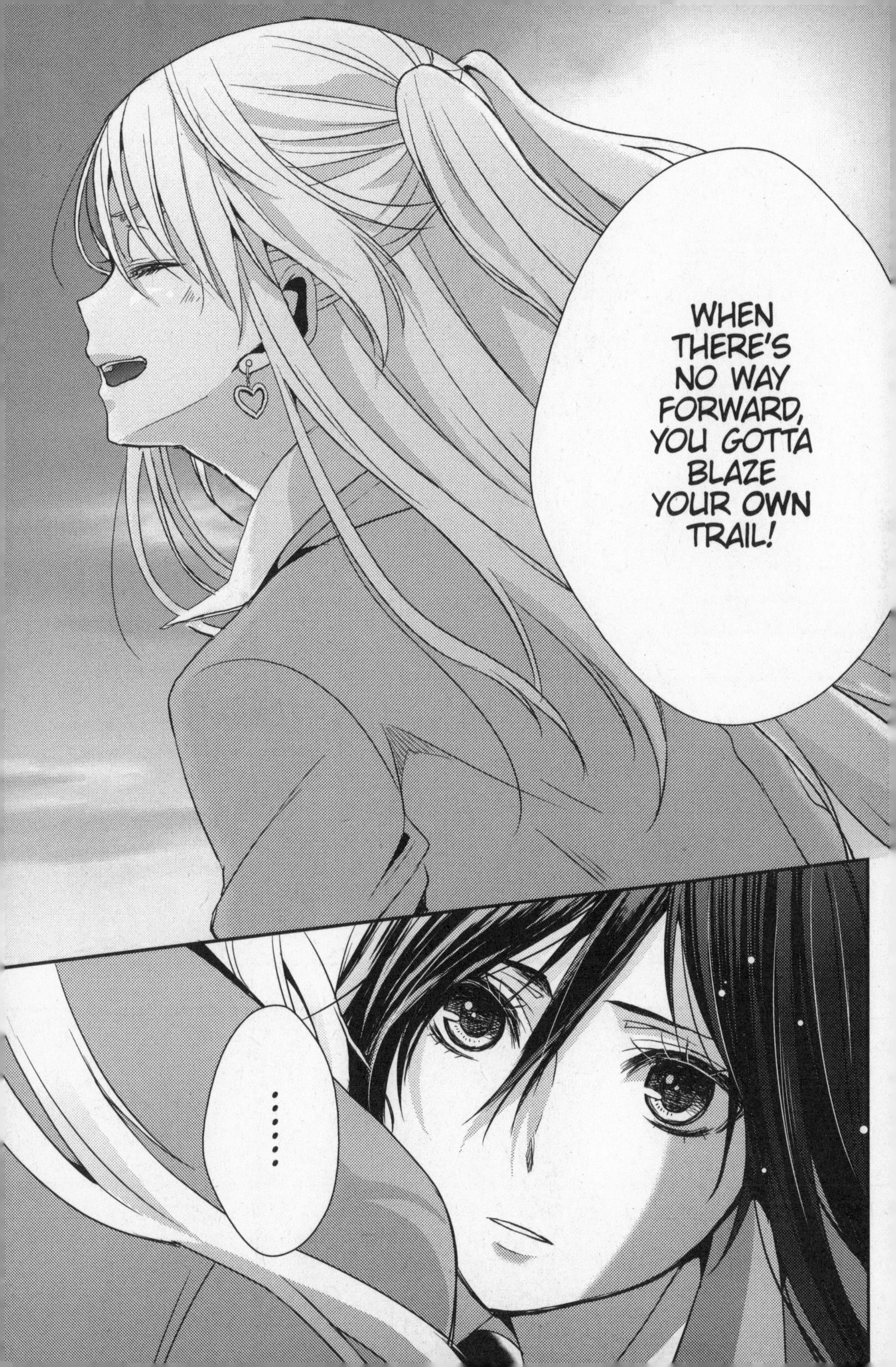
WHEN THERE'S NO WAY FORWARD, YOU GOTTA BLAZE YOUR OWN TRAIL!
......

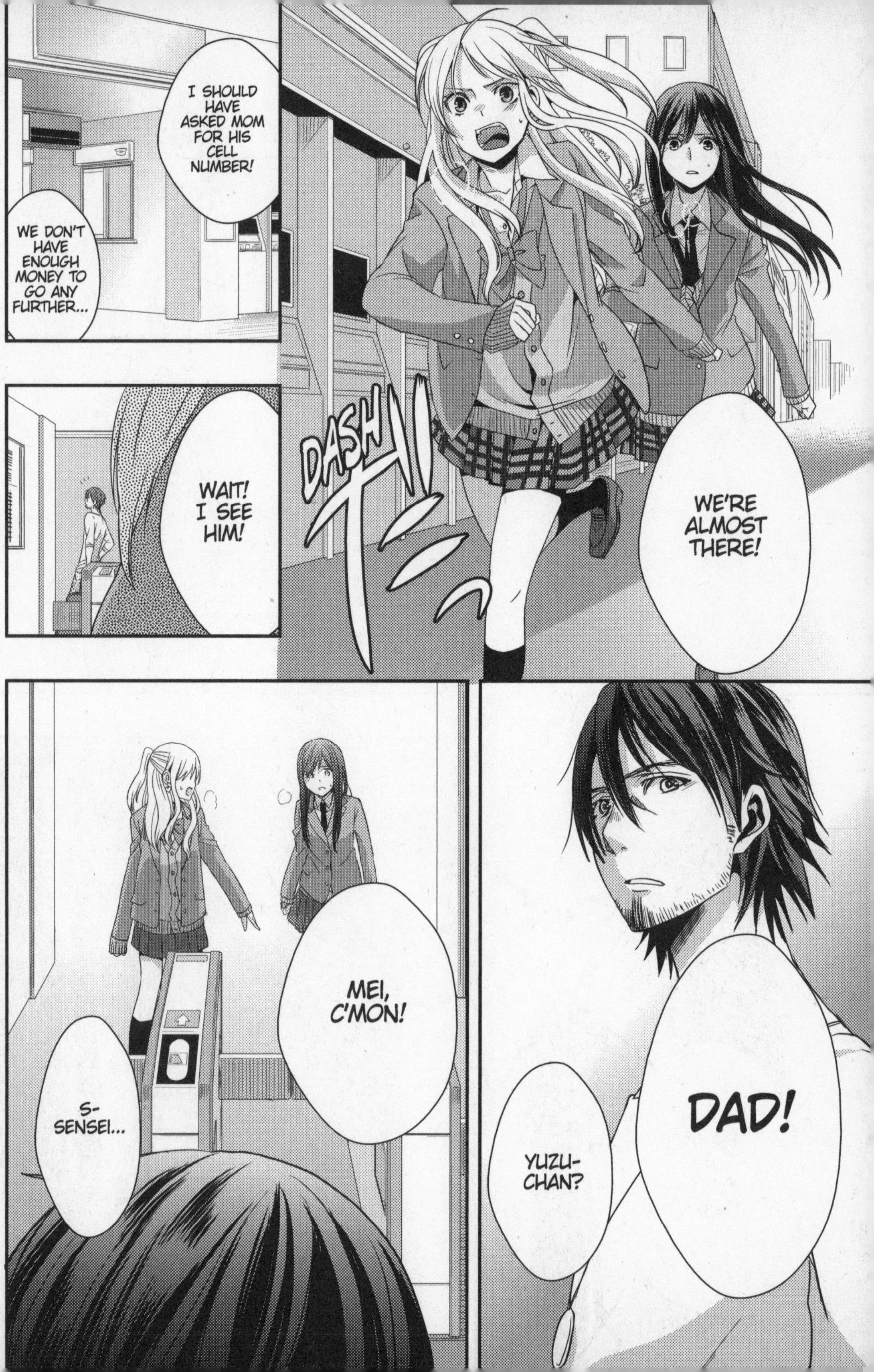
WE'RE ALMOST THERE!
DASH
I SHOULD HAVE ASKED MOM FOR HIS CELL NUMBER!
WE DON'T HAVE ENOUGH MONEY TO GO ANY FURTHER...
WAIT! I SEE HIM!
DAD!
YUZU-CHAN?
MEI, C'MON!
S-SENSEI...

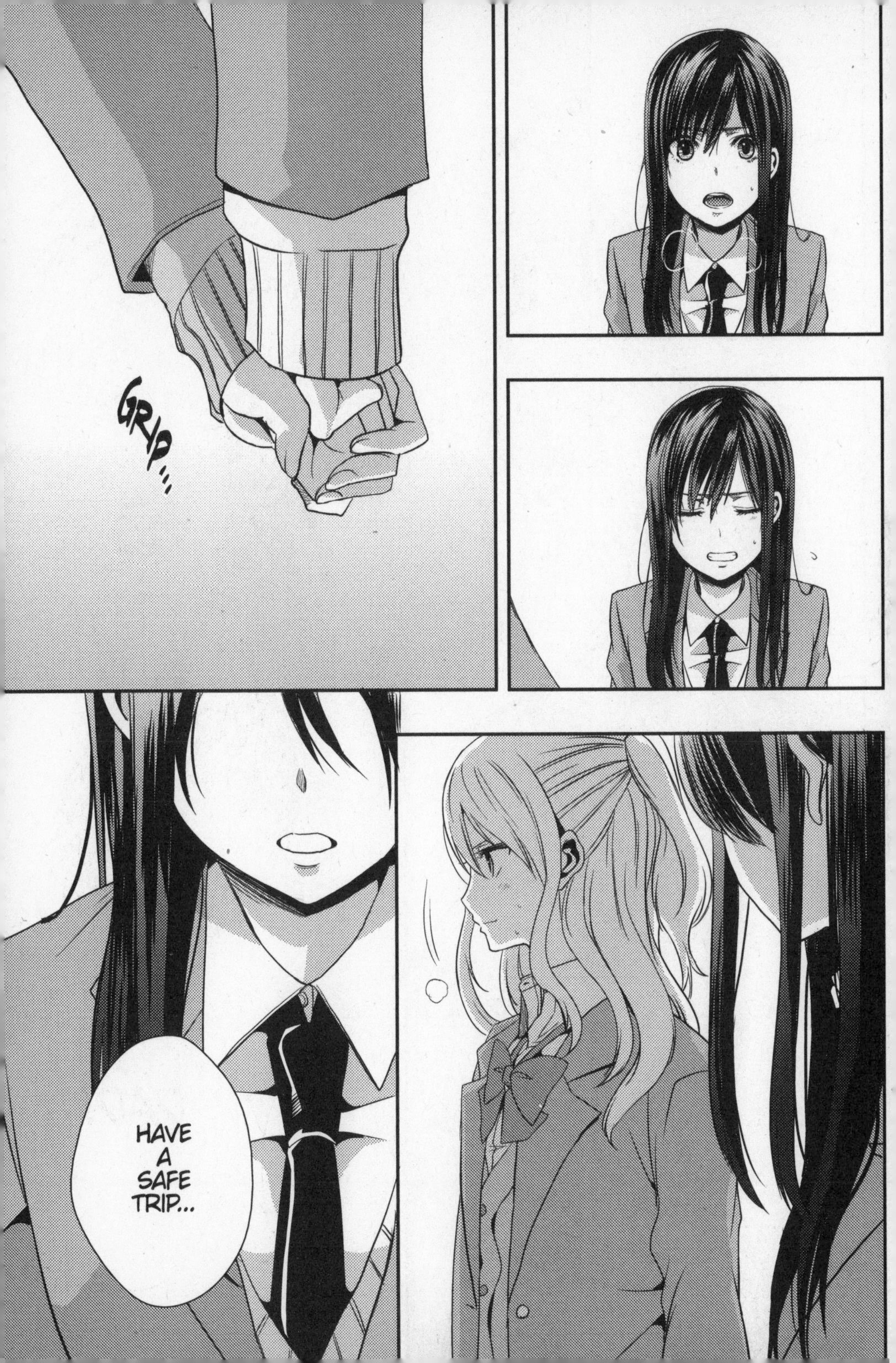
GRIP...
HAVE A SAFE TRIP...

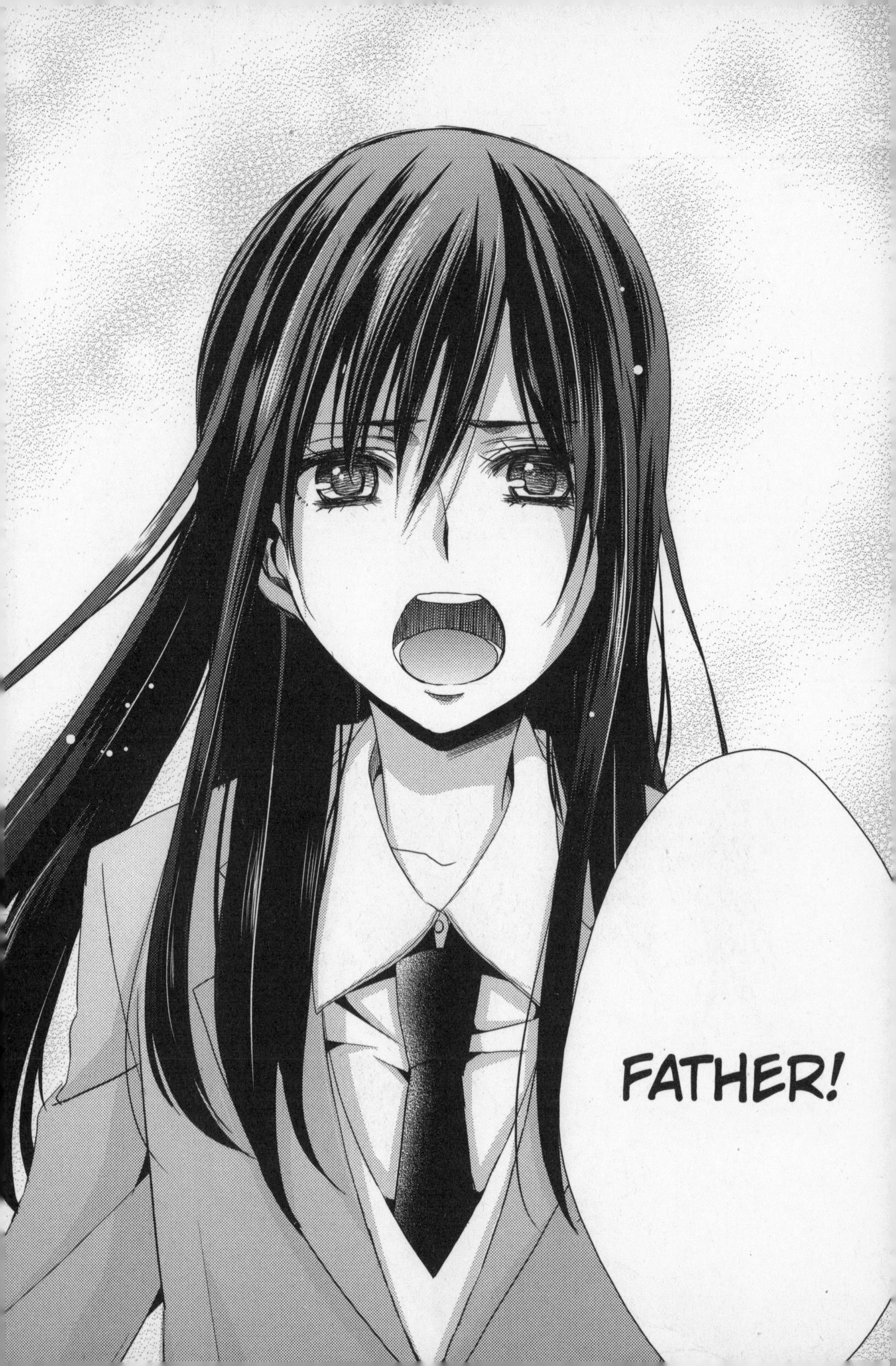
FATHER!

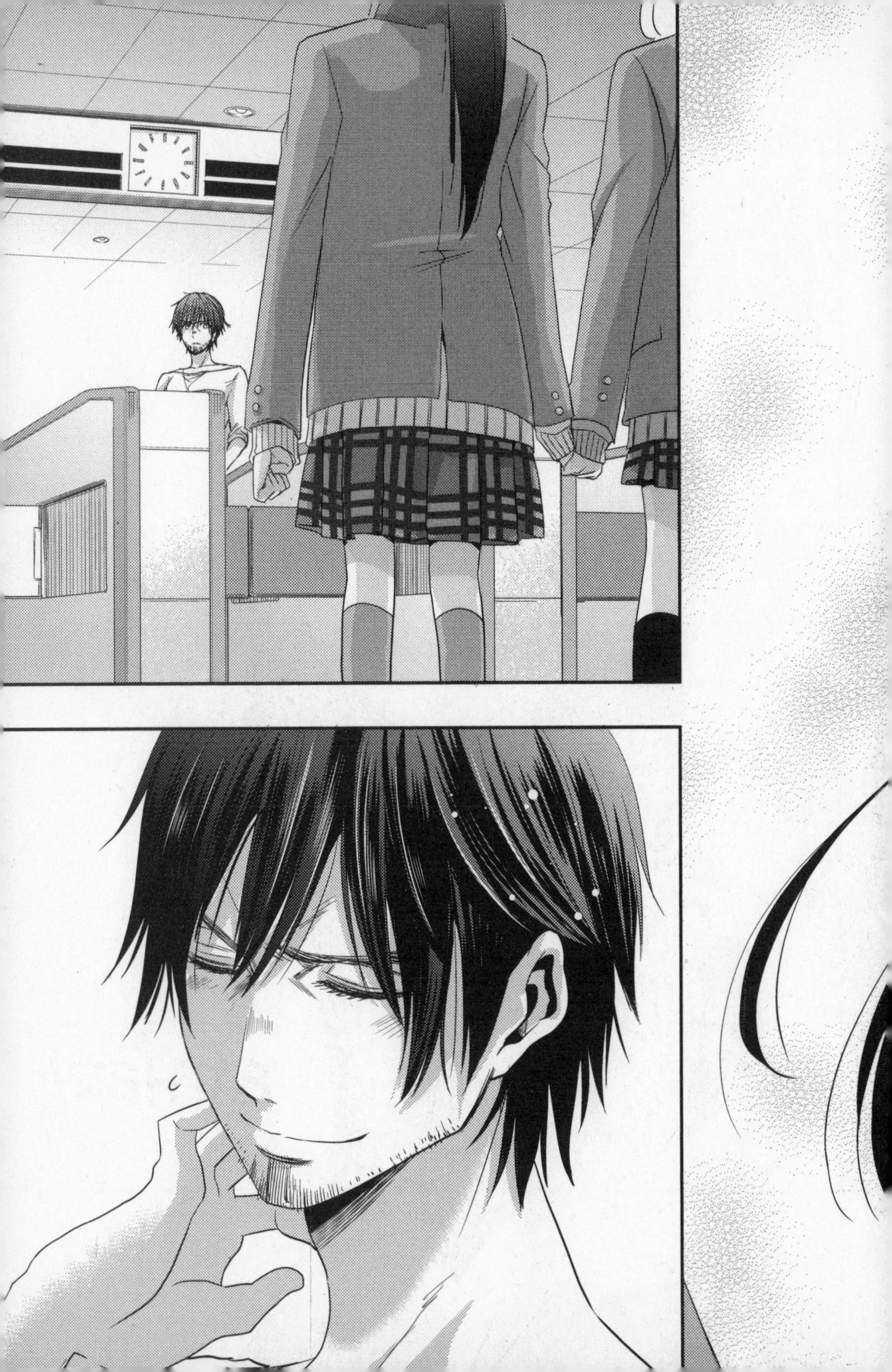

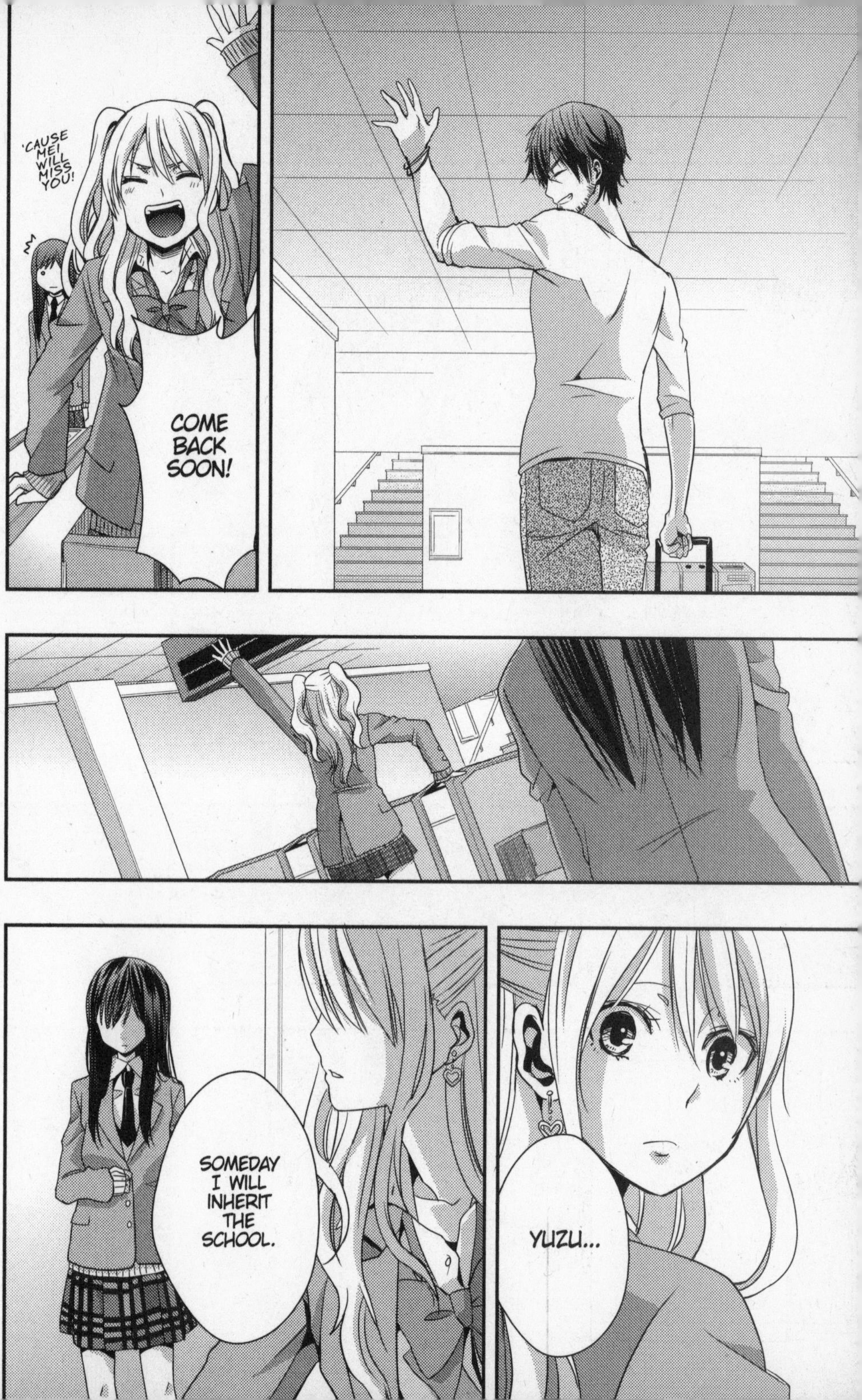
COME BACK SOON!
'CAUSE MEI WILL MISS YOU!
YUZU...
SOMEDAY I WILL INHERIT THE SCHOOL.

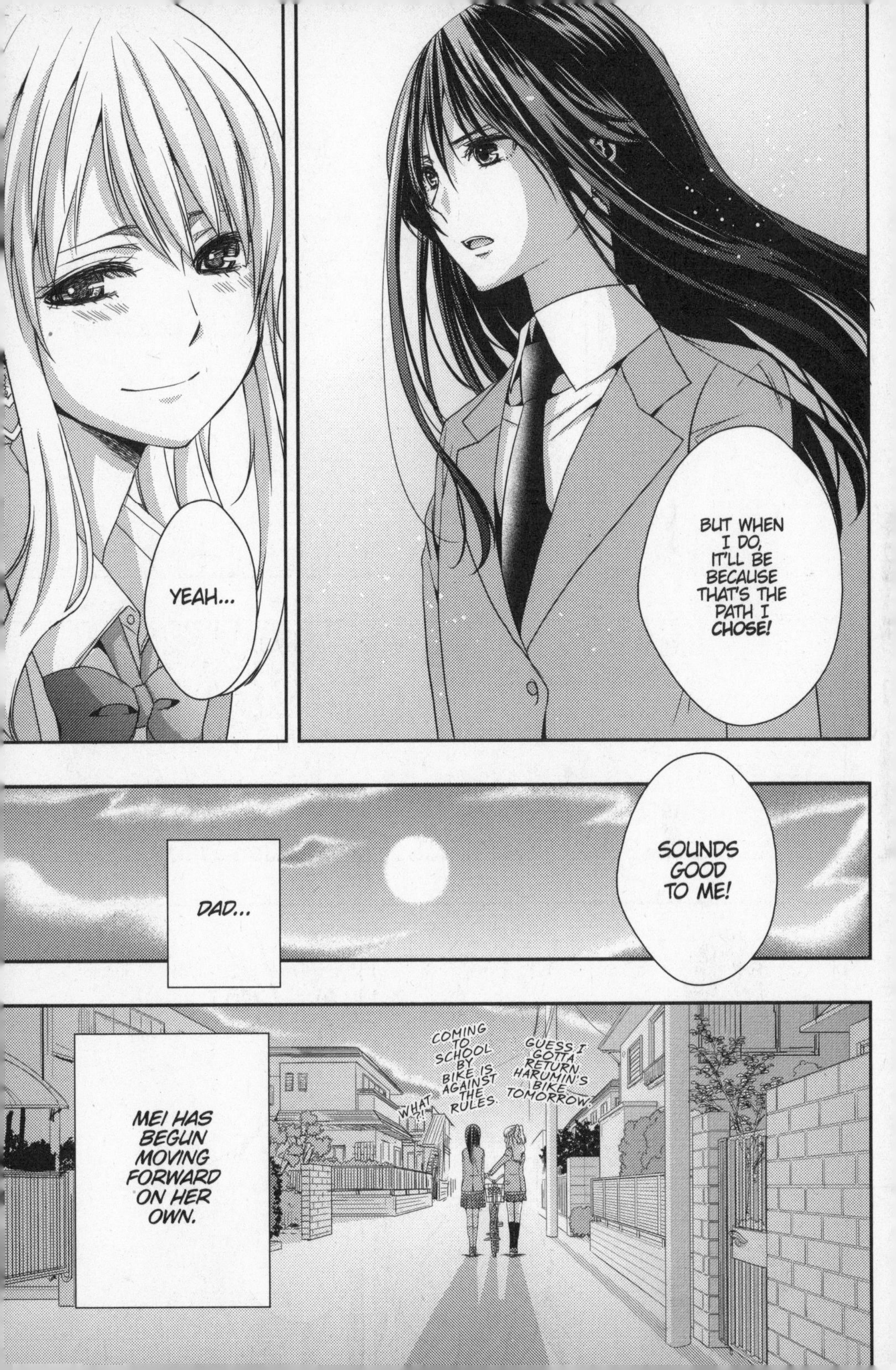
BUT WHEN I DO, IT'LL BE BECAUSE THAT'S THE PATH I CHOSE!
YEAH...
SOUNDS GOOD TO ME!
DAD...
GUESS I GOTTA RETURN HARUMIN'S BIKE TOMORROW.
COMING TO SCHOOL BY BIKE IS AGAINST THE RULES.
WHAT?!
MEI HAS BEGUN MOVING FORWARD ON HER OWN.

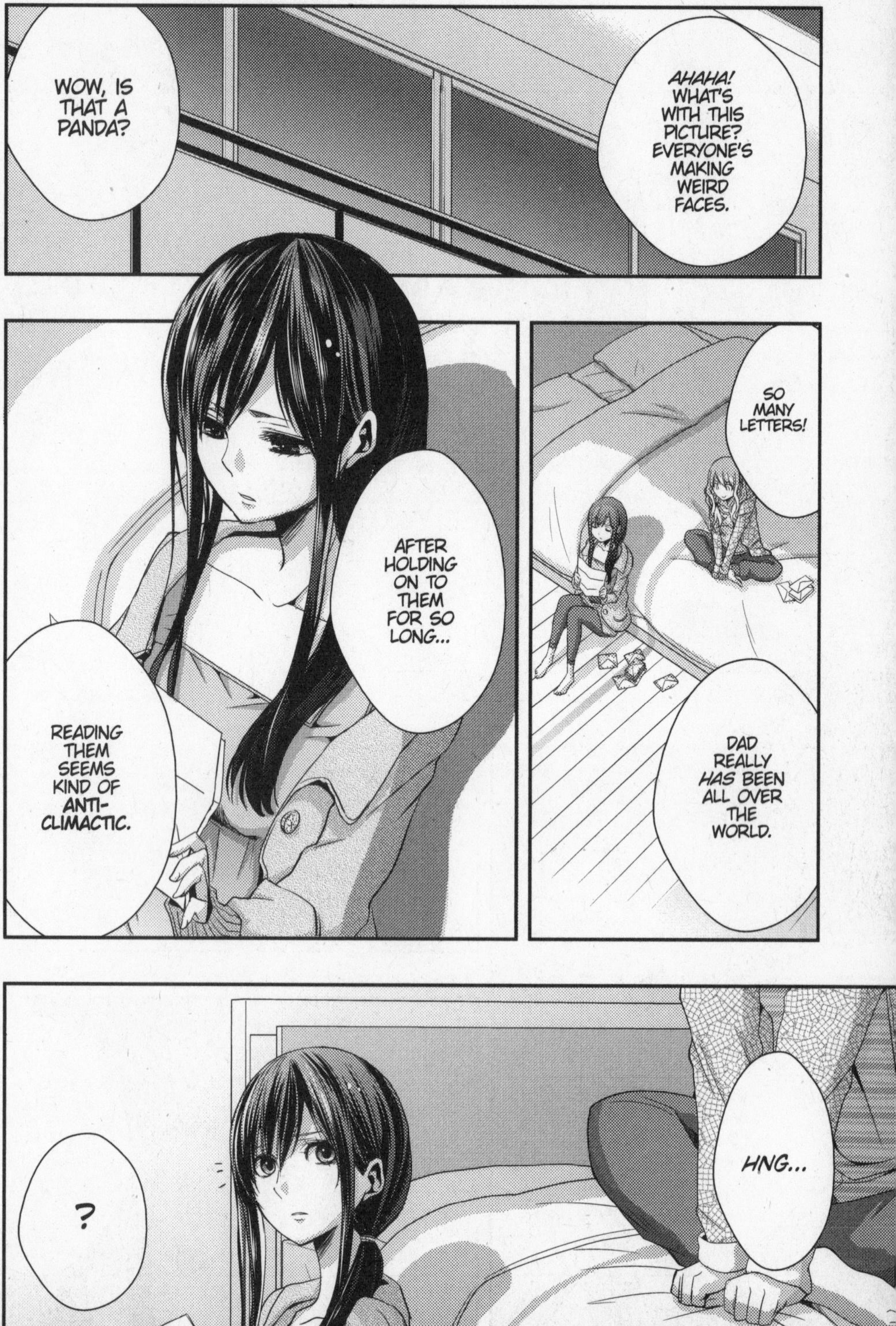

AHAHA! WHAT'S WITH THIS PICTURE? EVERYONE'S MAKING WEIRD FACES.
WOW, IS THAT A PANDA?
SO MANY LETTERS!
DAD REALLY *HAS* BEEN ALL OVER THE WORLD.
AFTER HOLDING ON TO THEM FOR SO LONG...
READING THEM SEEMS KIND OF ANTI-CLIMACTIC.
HNG...
?

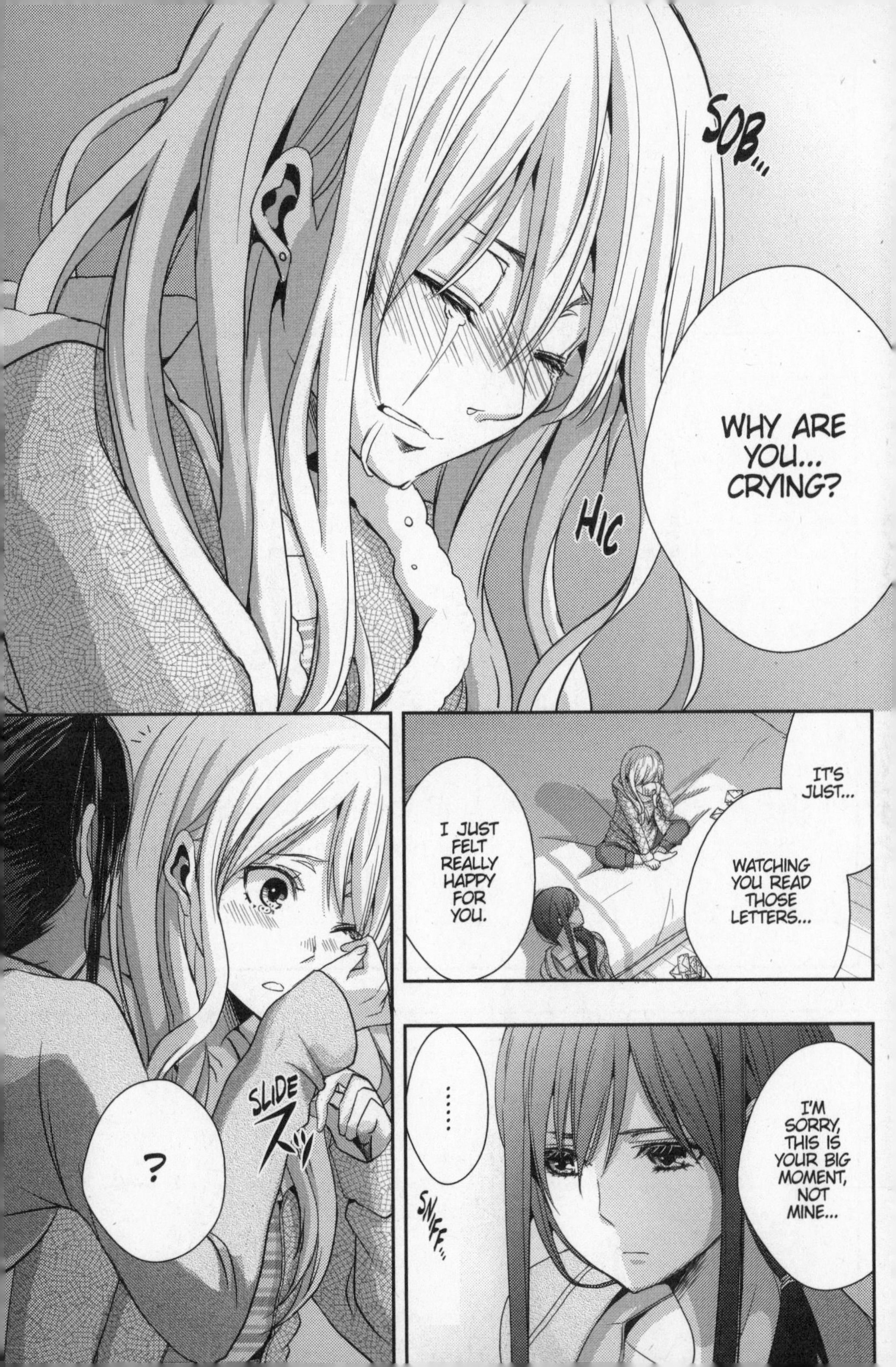
SOB...
WHY ARE YOU... CRYING?
HIC
IT'S JUST...
WATCHING YOU READ THOSE LETTERS...
I JUST FELT REALLY HAPPY FOR YOU.
I'M SORRY, THIS IS YOUR BIG MOMENT, NOT MINE...
......
SNIFF...
SLIDE
?

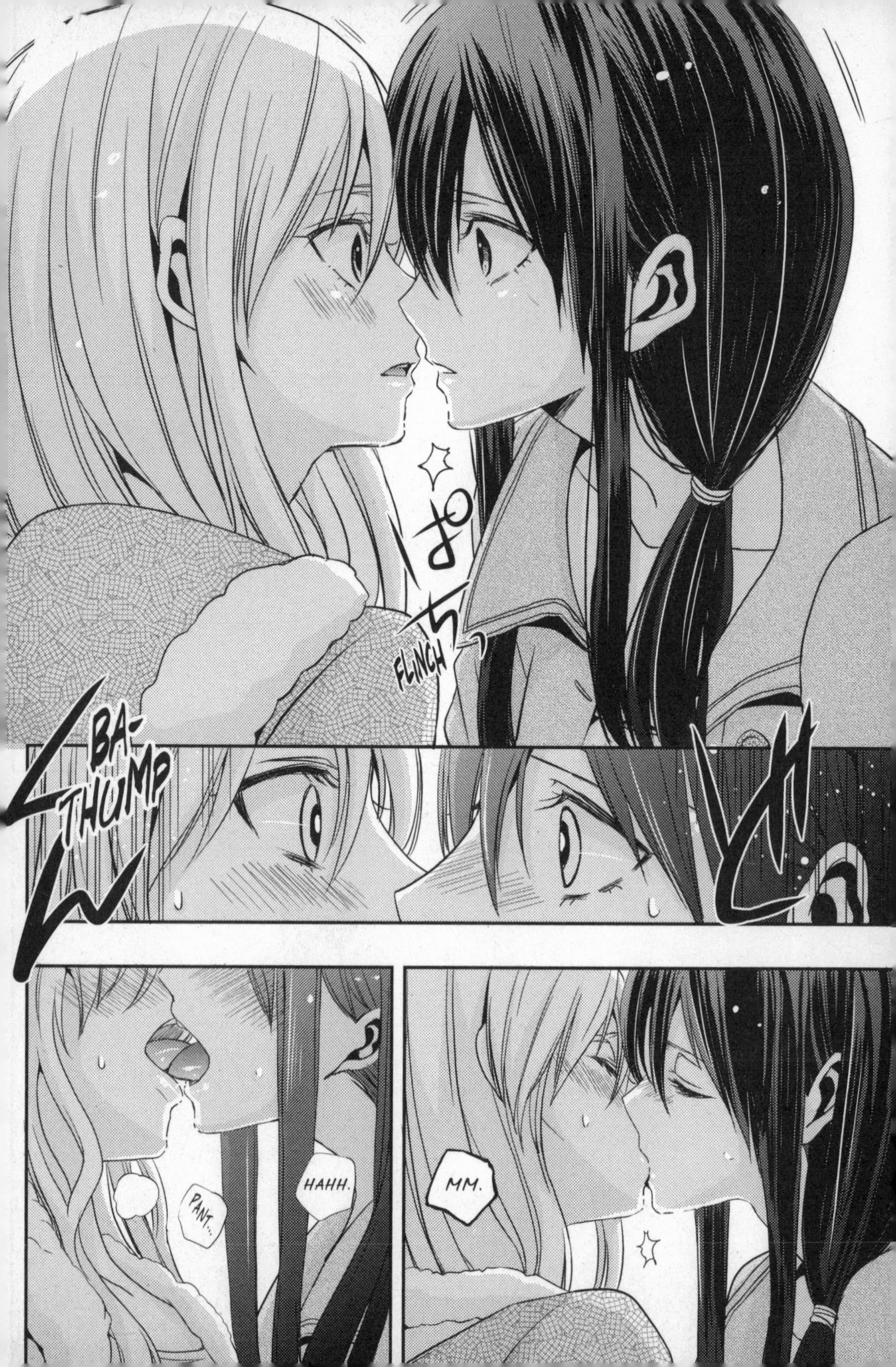
FLINCH
BA-THUMP
MM.
HAHH.
PANT..

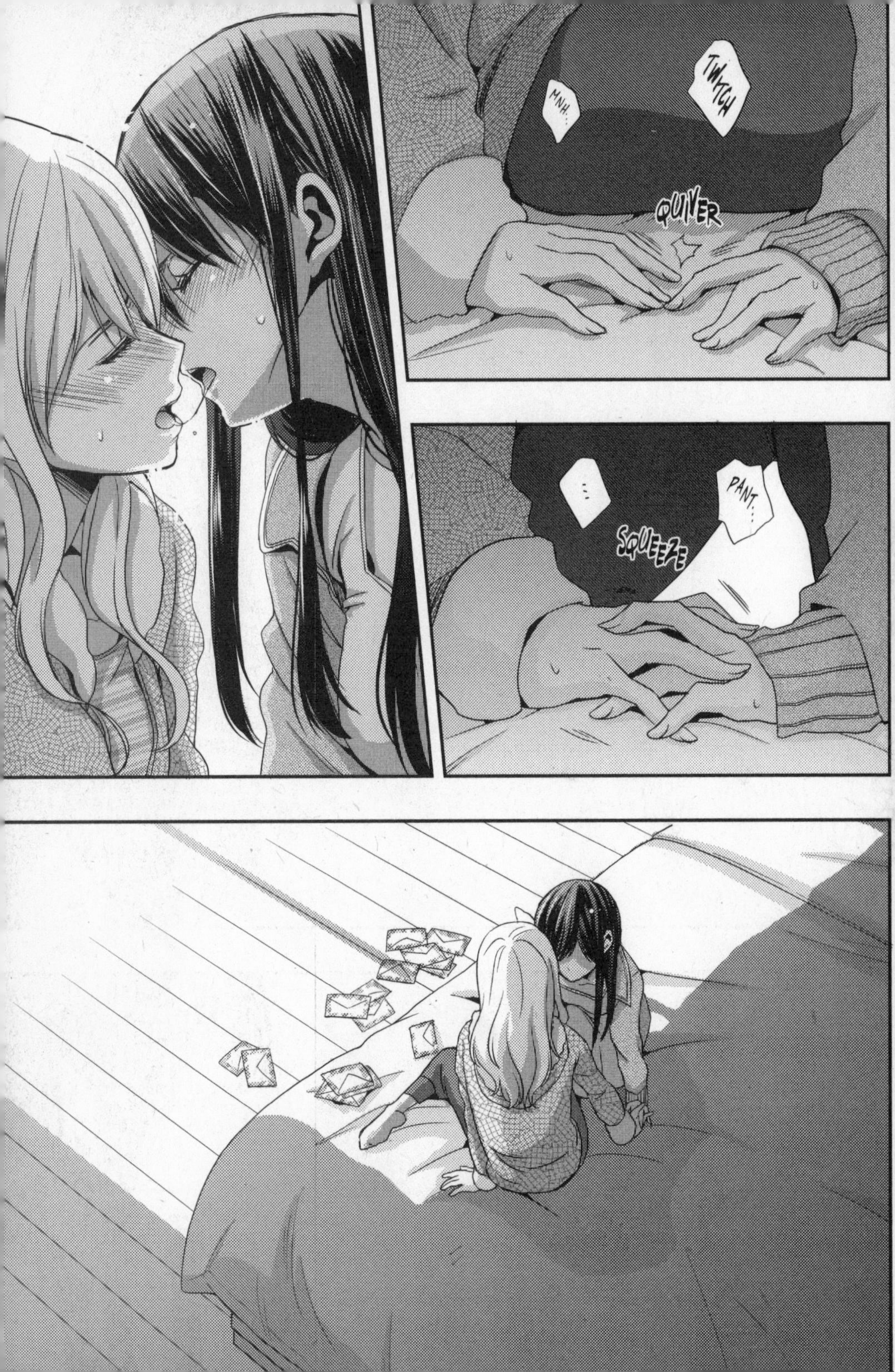
TWITCH
MNH...
QUIVER
PANT...
...
SQUEEZE

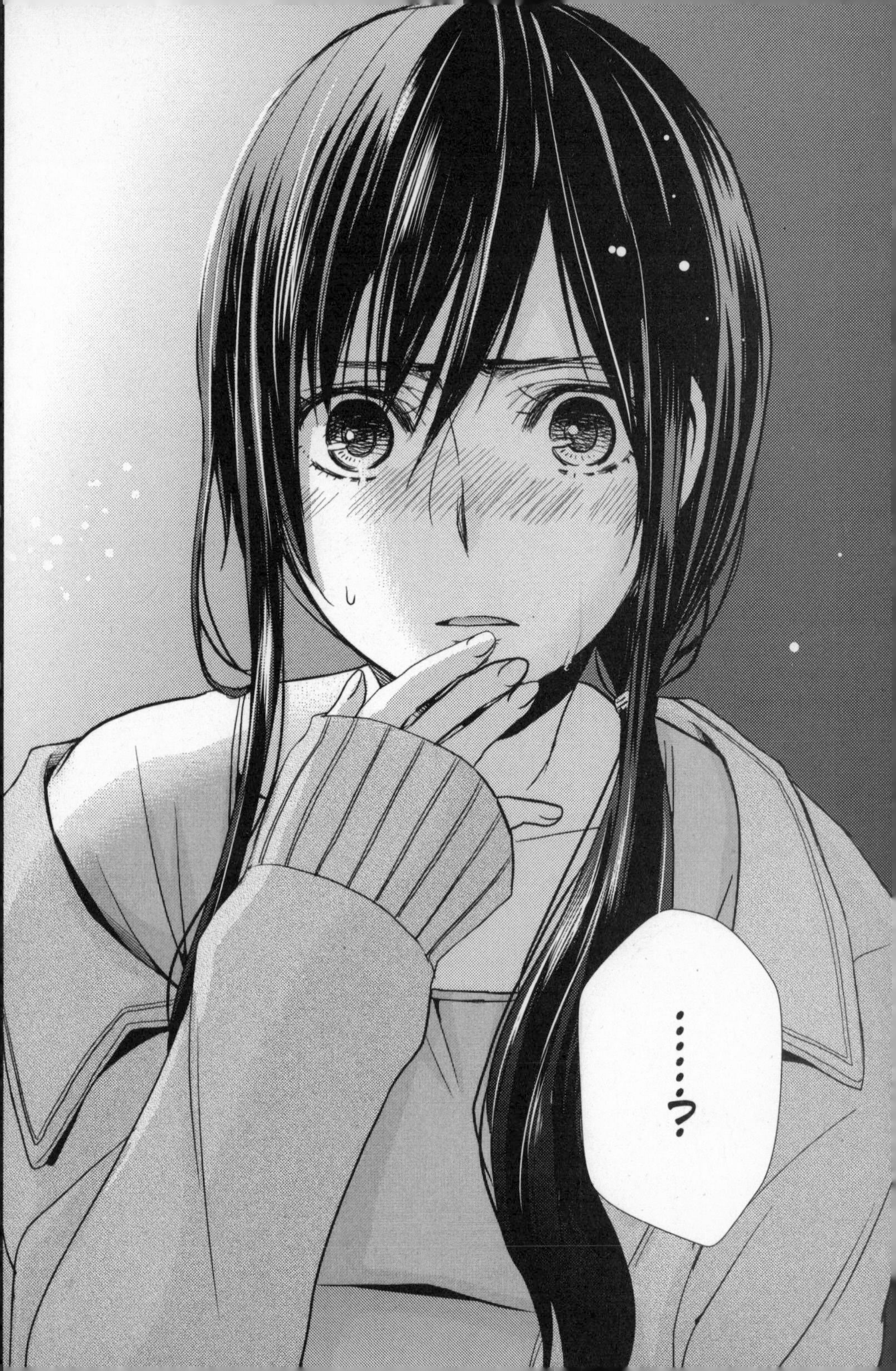
……っ

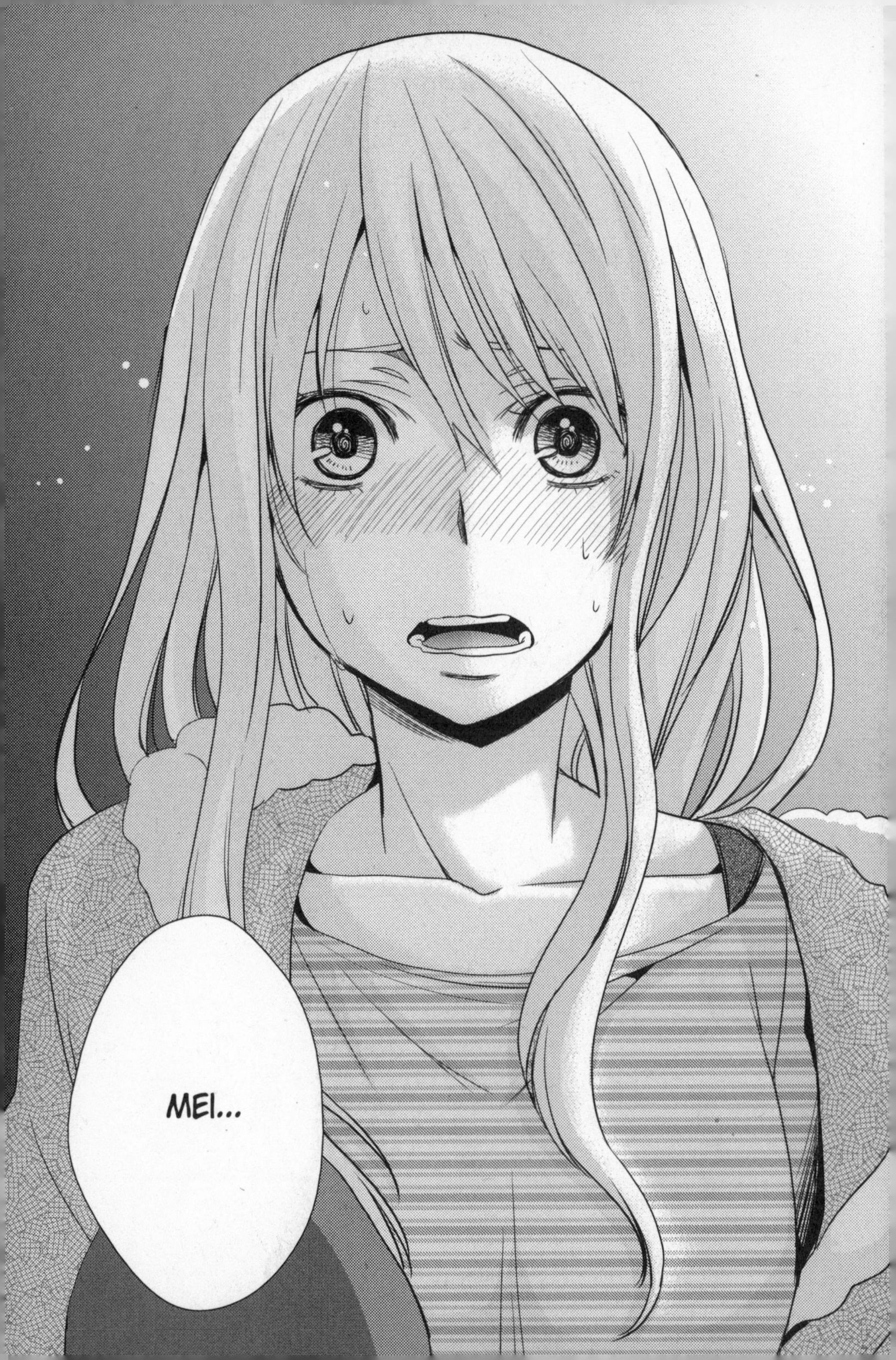
MEI...

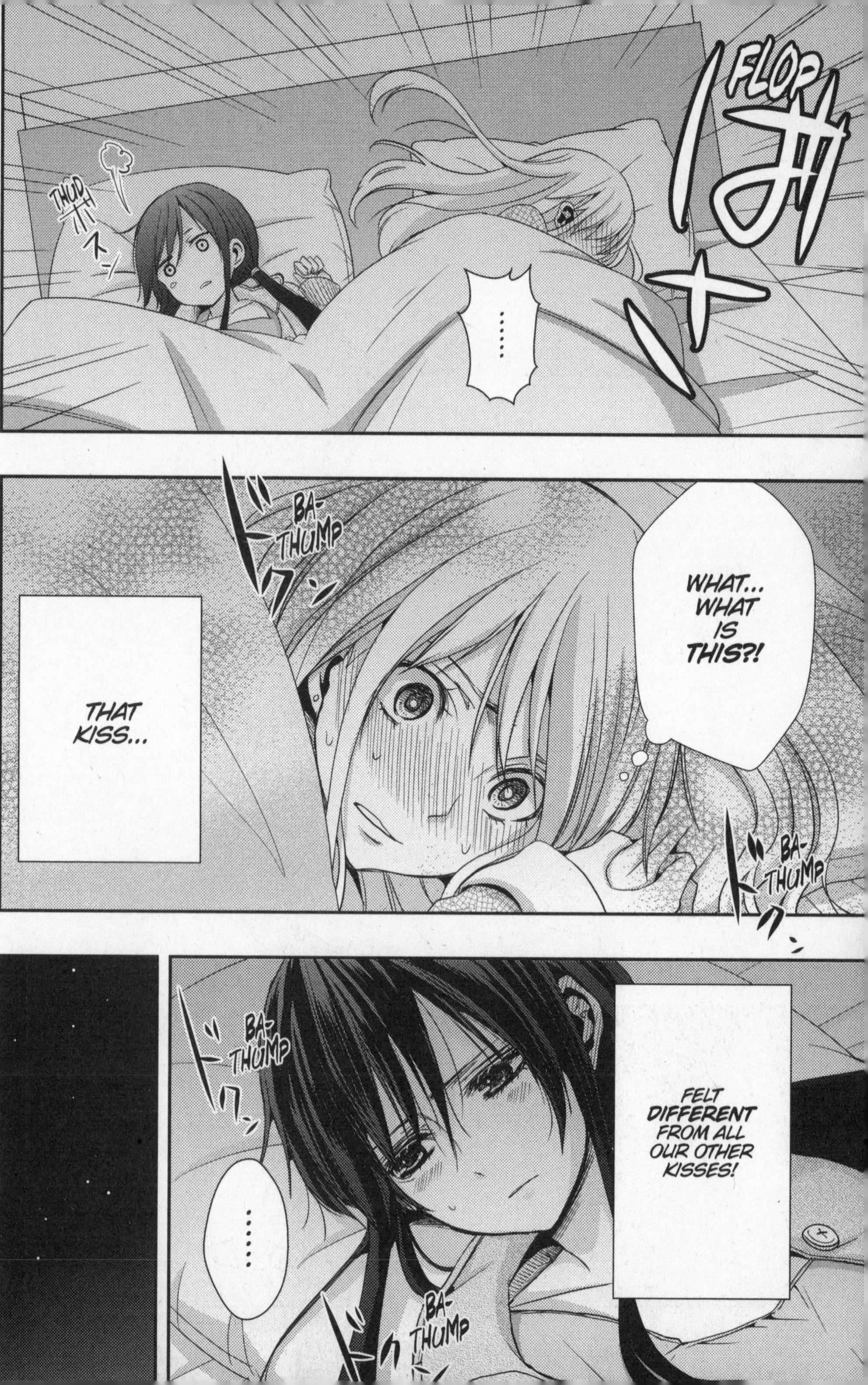
FLOP
......
THUD
WHAT... WHAT IS THIS?!
BA-THUMP
BA-THUMP
THAT KISS...
FELT DIFFERENT FROM ALL OUR OTHER KISSES!
BA-THUMP
......
BA-THUMP

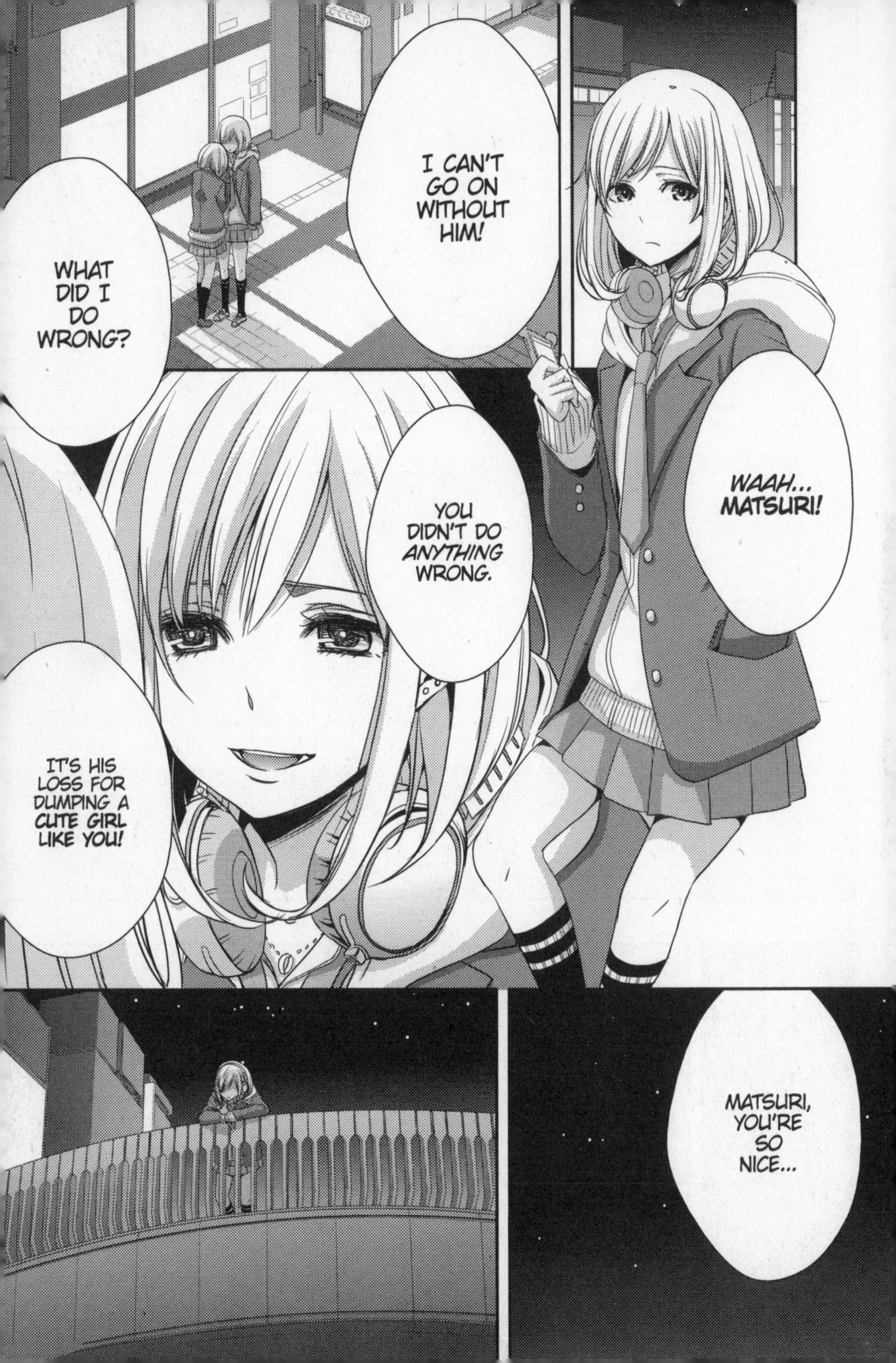
I CAN'T GO ON WITHOUT HIM!
WHAT DID I DO WRONG?
WAAH... MATSURI!
YOU DIDN'T DO ANYTHING WRONG.
IT'S HIS LOSS FOR DUMPING A CUTE GIRL LIKE YOU!
MATSURI, YOU'RE SO NICE...

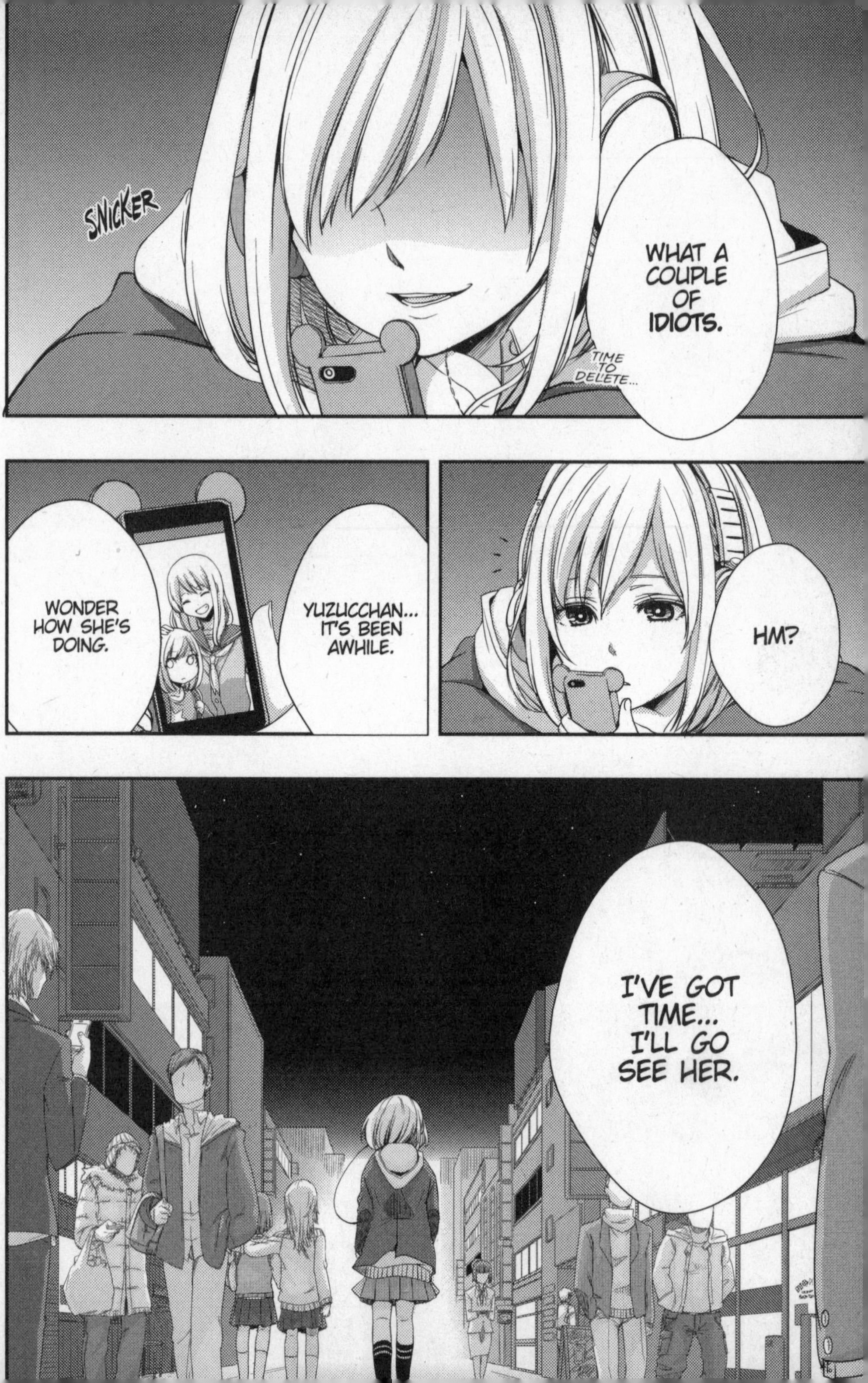
WHAT A COUPLE OF IDIOTS.
SNICKER
TIME TO DELETE...
HM?
YUZUCCHAN... IT'S BEEN AWHILE.
WONDER HOW SHE'S DOING.
I'VE GOT TIME... I'LL GO SEE HER.

To be continued...

citrus

SABUROUTA PRESENTS SECRET LOVE AFFAIR WITH SISTER

2

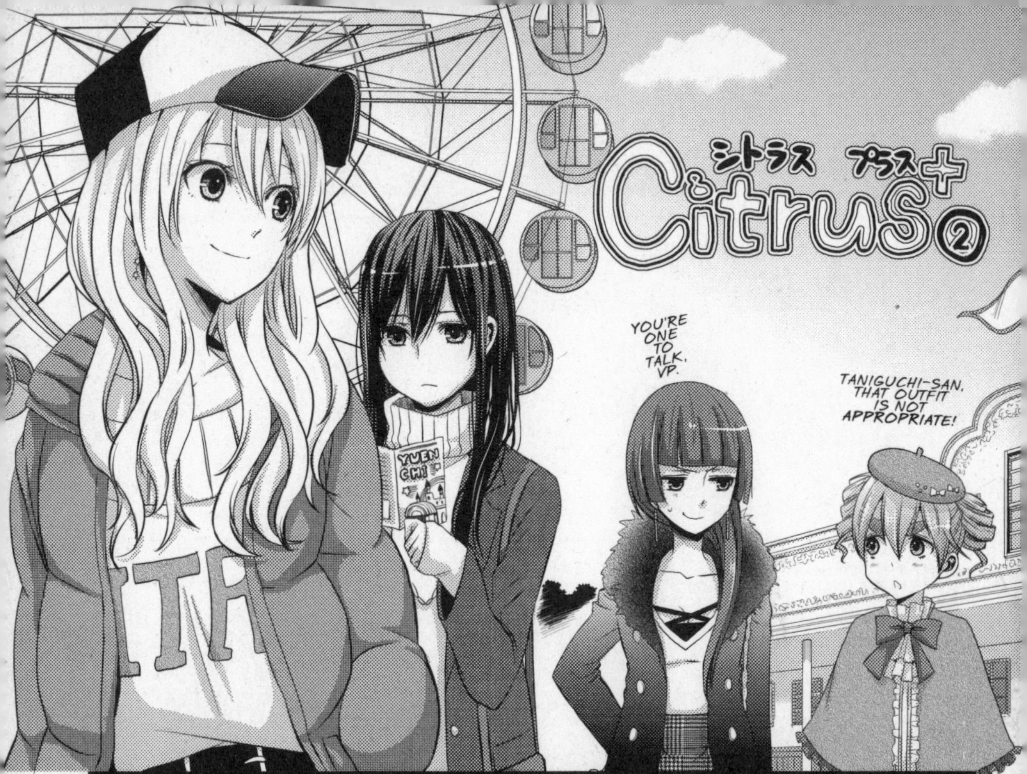
シトラス プラス
Citrus+ 2
TANIGUCHI-SAN, THAT OUTFIT IS NOT APPROPRIATE!
YOU'RE ONE TO TALK, VP.
YUEN CHI

THERE'S A BEAR HERE, TOO

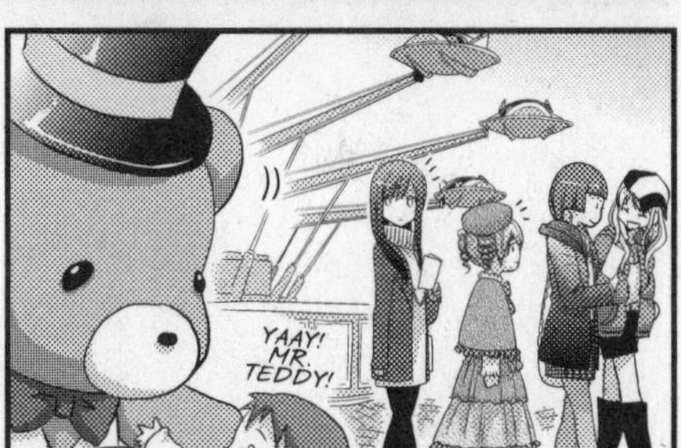
YAAY! MR. TEDDY!

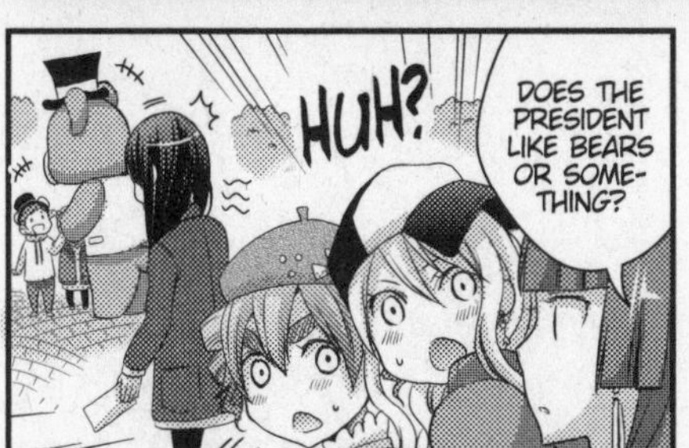
DOES THE PRESIDENT LIKE BEARS OR SOMETHING?
HUH?

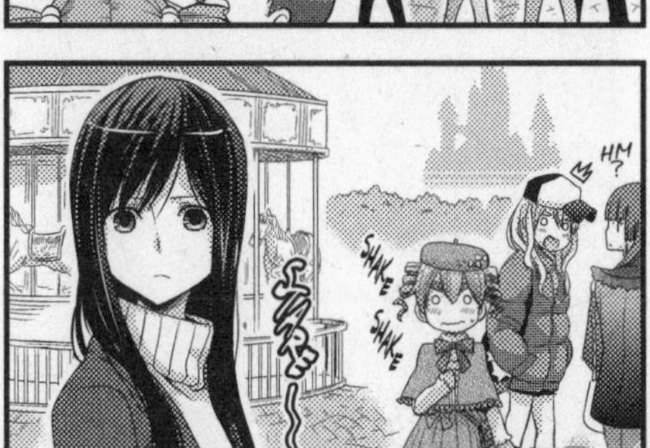
HM?
SHAKE
SHAKE

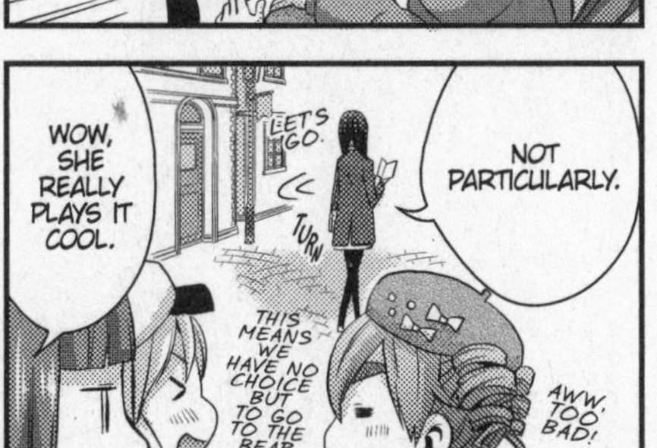
NOT PARTICULARLY.
LET'S GO.
TURN
WOW, SHE REALLY PLAYS IT COOL.
THIS MEANS WE HAVE NO CHOICE BUT TO GO TO THE BEAR HOUSE, HUH?
AWW, TOO BAD!

It Was an Accident!

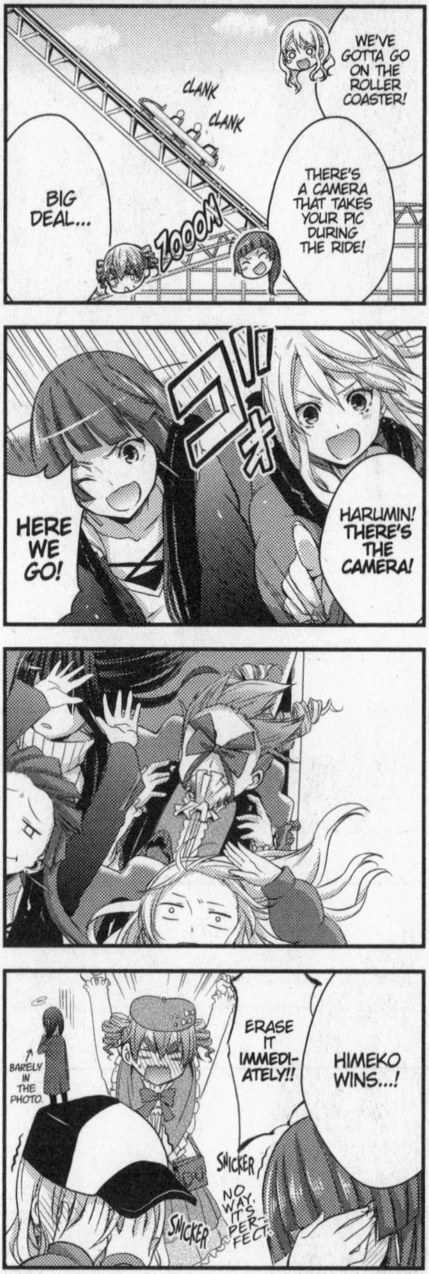
WE'VE GOTTA GO ON THE ROLLER COASTER!
CLANK
CLANK
THERE'S A CAMERA THAT TAKES YOUR PIC DURING THE RIDE!
BIG DEAL...
ZOOOM
HARUMIN! THERE'S THE CAMERA!
HERE WE GO!
HIMEKO WINS...!
ERASE IT IMMEDIATELY!!
SNICKER
NO WAY. IT'S PERFECT.
SNICKER
BARELY IN THE PHOTO.

Aren't They the Same?

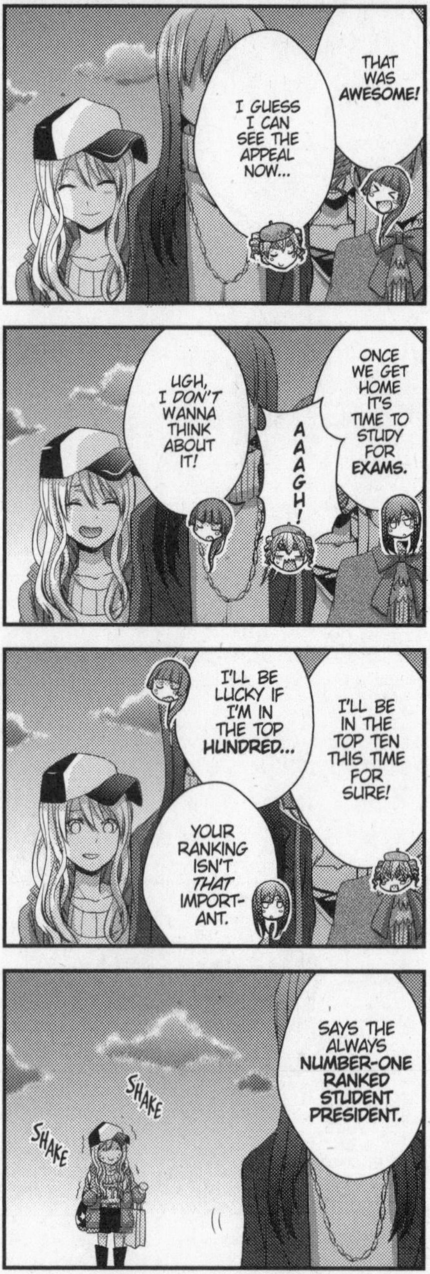
THAT WAS AWESOME!
I GUESS I CAN SEE THE APPEAL NOW...
ONCE WE GET HOME IT'S TIME TO STUDY FOR EXAMS.
AAAAGH!
UGH, I *DON'T* WANNA THINK ABOUT IT!
I'LL BE IN THE TOP TEN THIS TIME FOR SURE!
I'LL BE LUCKY IF I'M IN THE TOP HUNDRED...
YOUR RANKING ISN'T *THAT* IMPORTANT.
SAYS THE ALWAYS NUMBER-ONE RANKED STUDENT PRESIDENT.
SHAKE
SHAKE

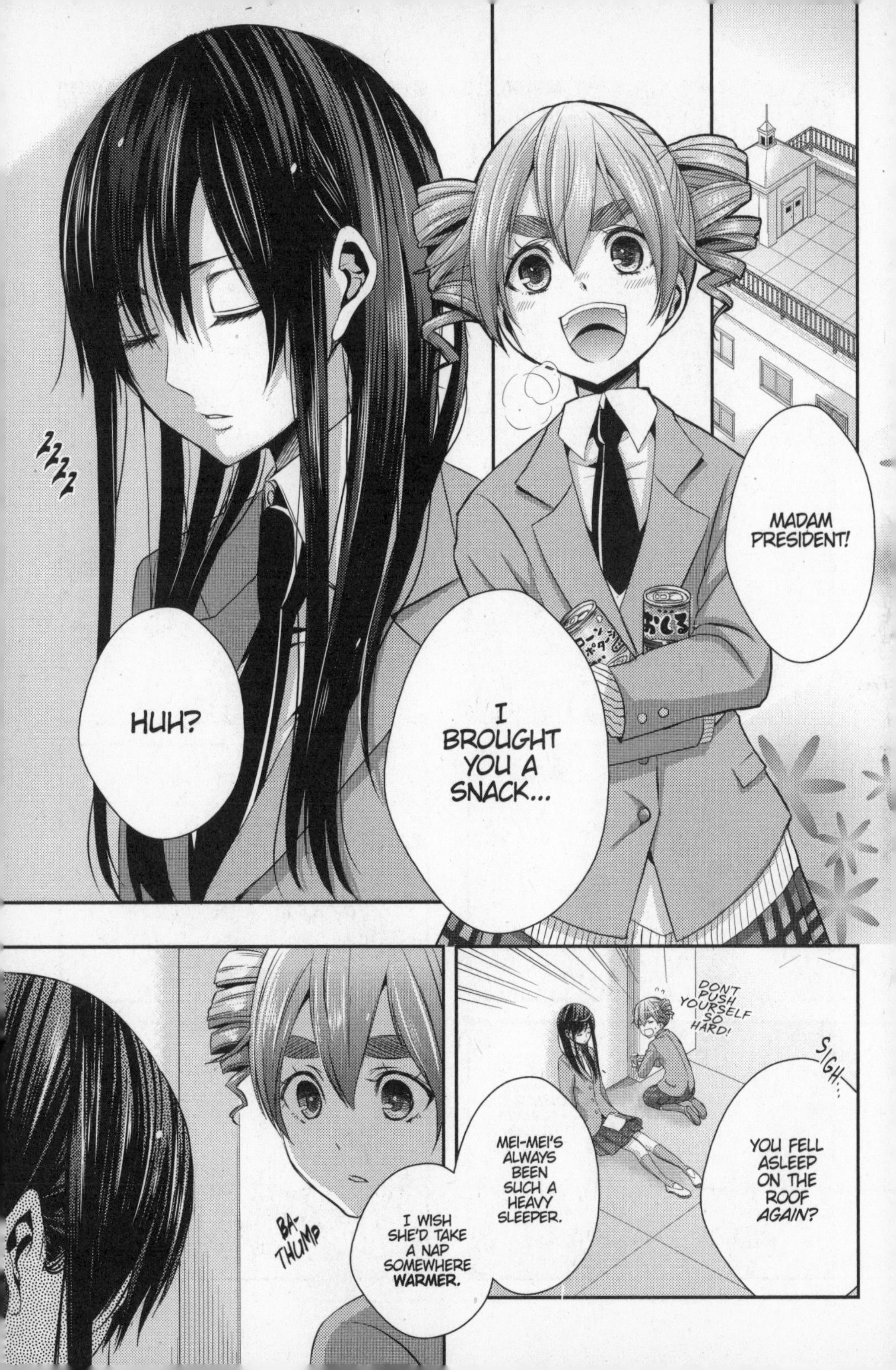
MADAM PRESIDENT!
I BROUGHT YOU A SNACK...
HUH?
ZZZZ
SIGH...
DON'T PUSH YOURSELF SO HARD!
YOU FELL ASLEEP ON THE ROOF AGAIN?
MEI-MEI'S ALWAYS BEEN SUCH A HEAVY SLEEPER.
I WISH SHE'D TAKE A NAP SOMEWHERE WARMER.
BA-THUMP

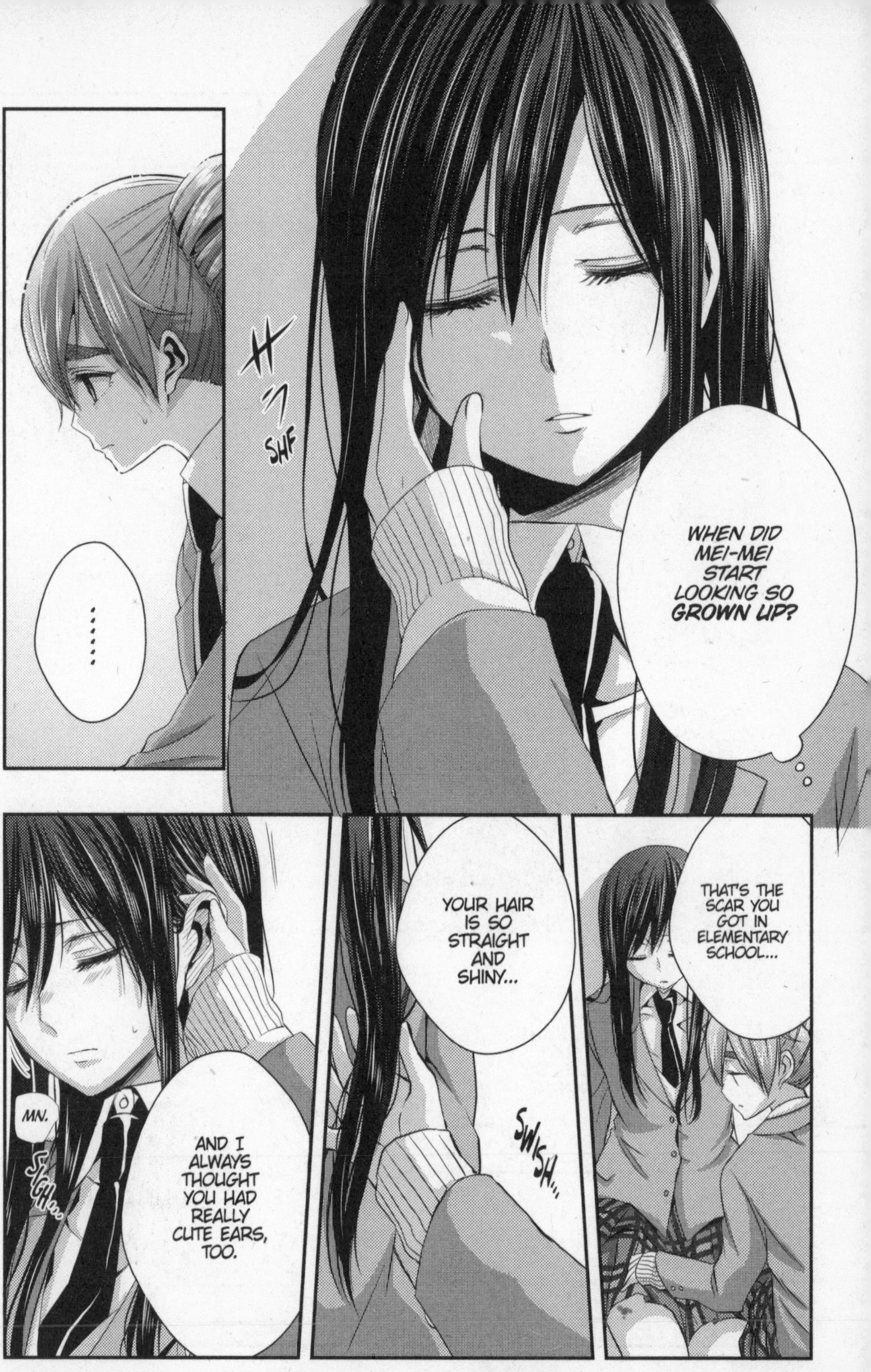
SHF
WHEN DID MEI-MEI START LOOKING SO GROWN UP?
......
THAT'S THE SCAR YOU GOT IN ELEMENTARY SCHOOL...
YOUR HAIR IS SO STRAIGHT AND SHINY...
SWISH...
AND I ALWAYS THOUGHT YOU HAD REALLY CUTE EARS, TOO.
MN.
SIGH...

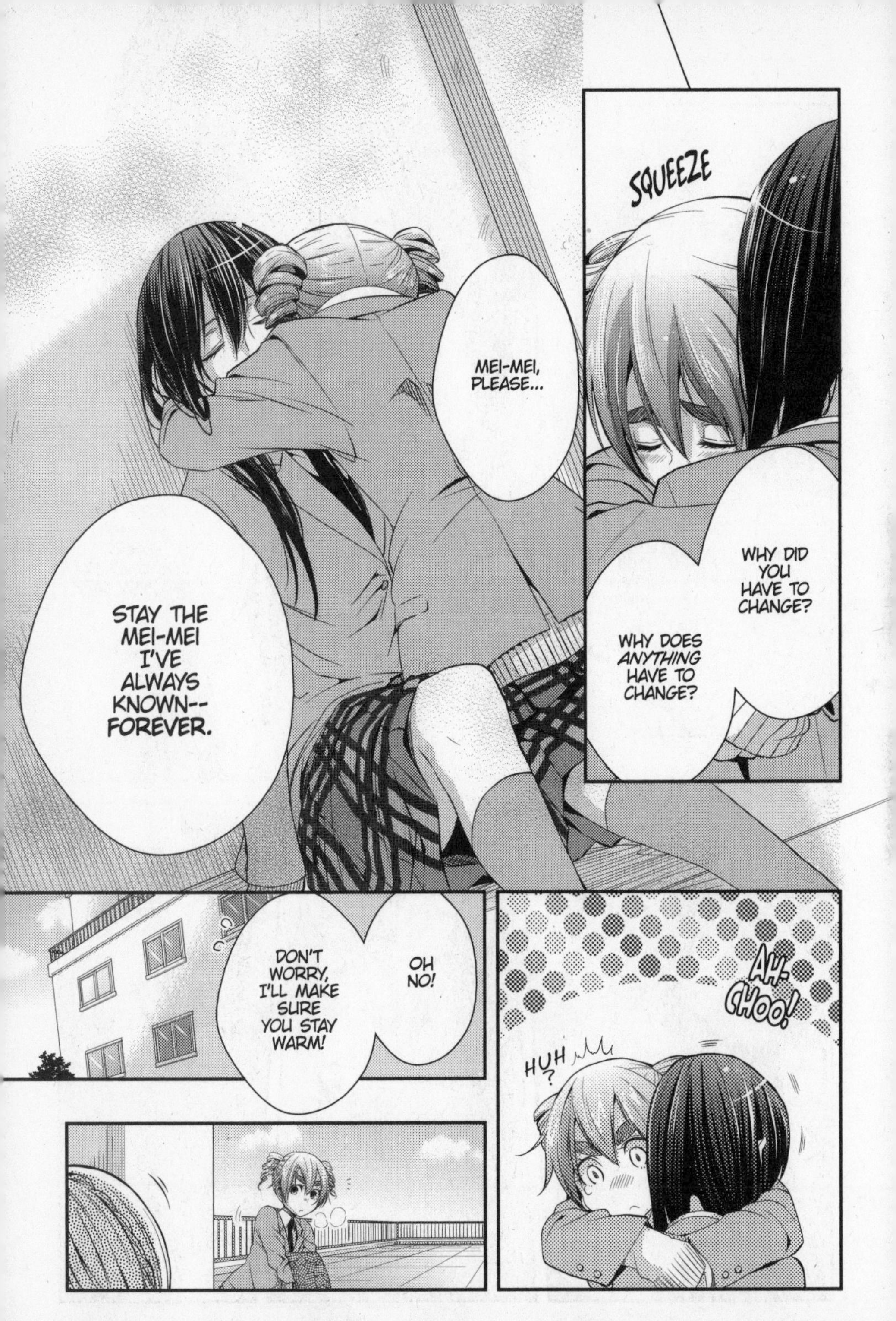
MEI-MEI, PLEASE...
STAY THE MEI-MEI I'VE ALWAYS KNOWN--FOREVER.
SQUEEZE
WHY DID YOU HAVE TO CHANGE?
WHY DOES *ANYTHING* HAVE TO CHANGE?
AH-CHOO!
HUH?
OH NO!
DON'T WORRY, I'LL MAKE SURE YOU STAY WARM!

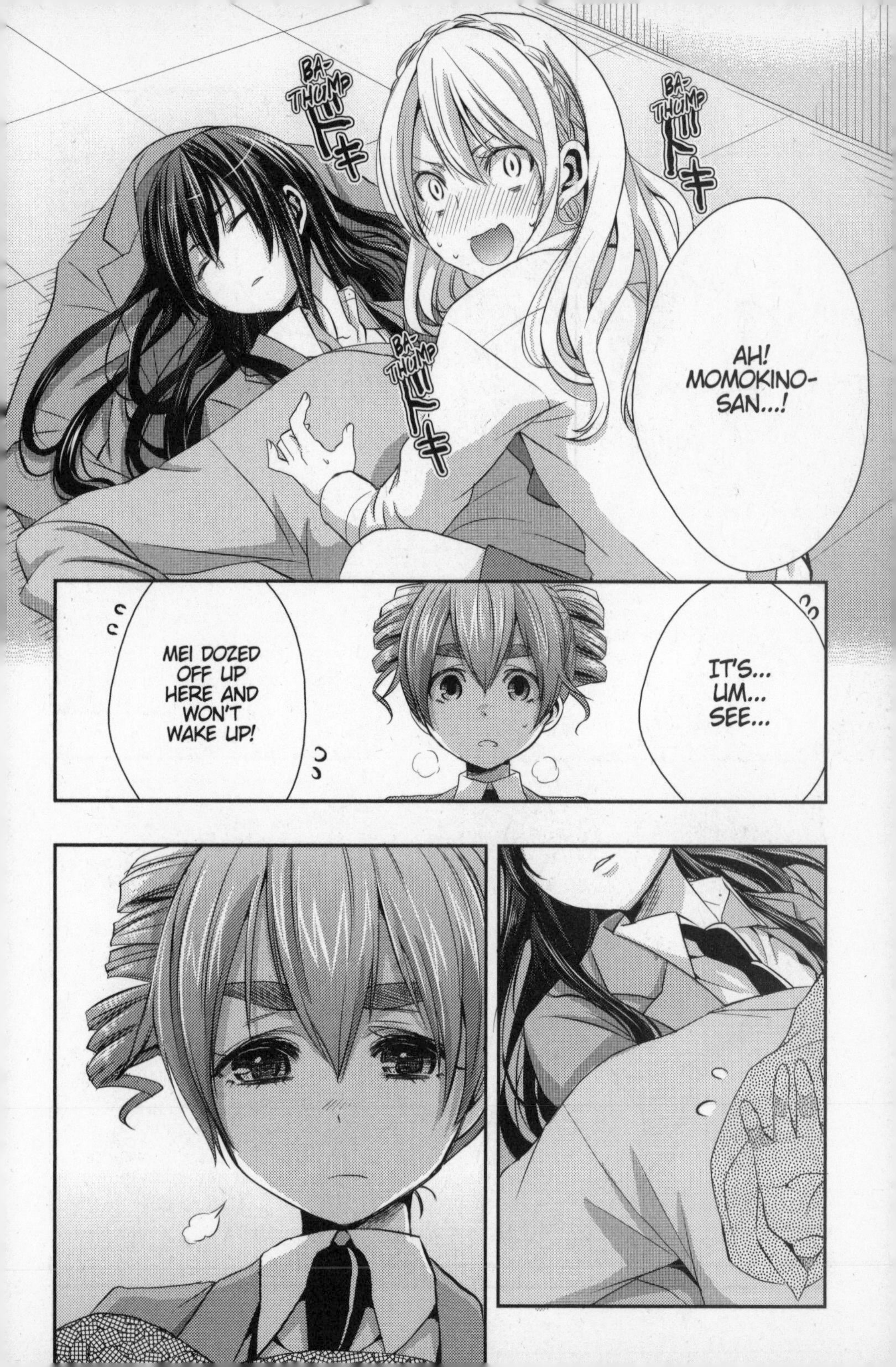
BA-THUMP ドキ
AH! MOMOKINO-SAN...!
BA-THUMP ドキ
BA-THUMP ドキ
IT'S... UM... SEE...
MEI DOZED OFF UP HERE AND WON'T WAKE UP!

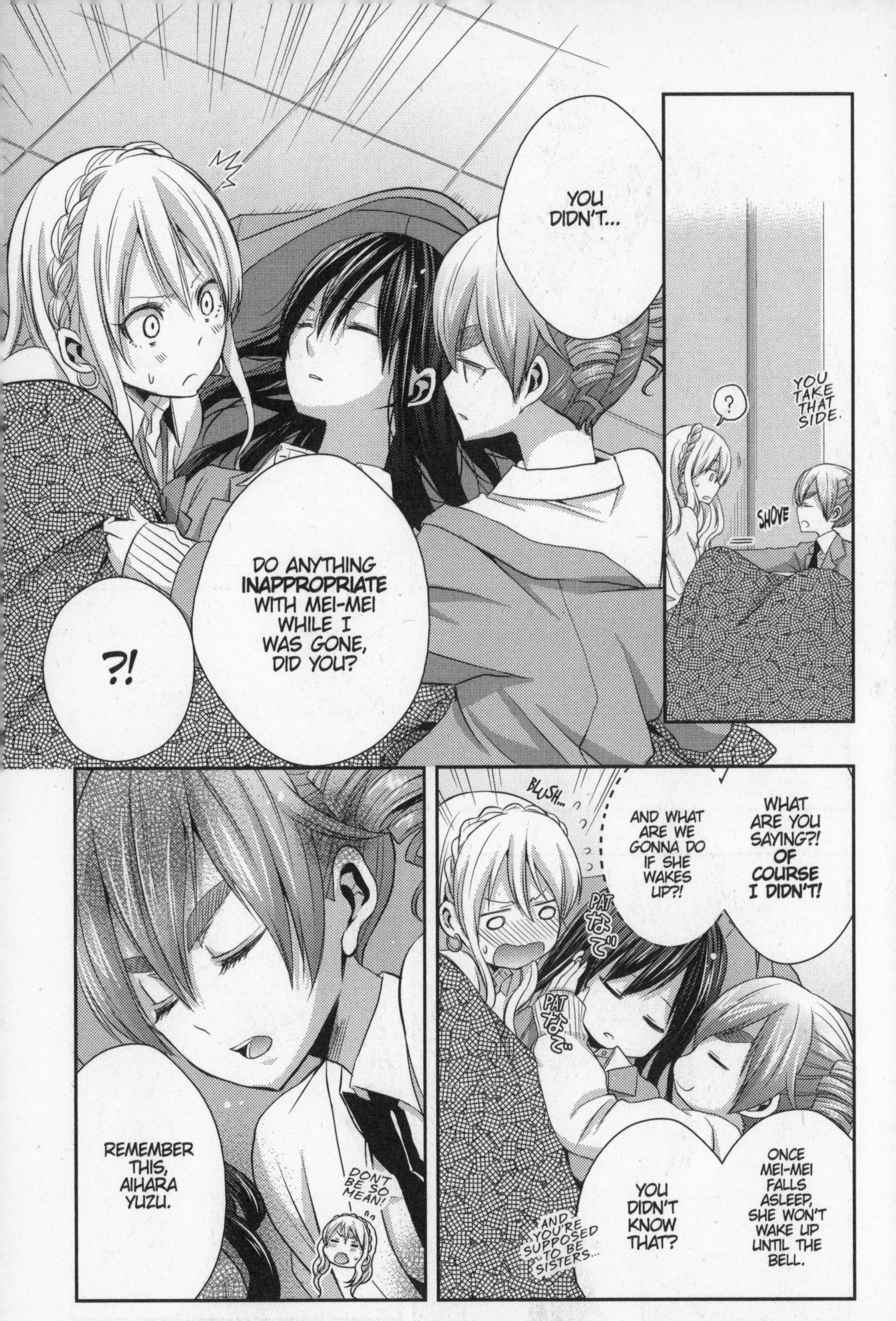
?
YOU TAKE THAT SIDE.
SHOVE
YOU DIDN'T...
DO ANYTHING INAPPROPRIATE WITH MEI-MEI WHILE I WAS GONE, DID YOU?
?!
WHAT ARE YOU SAYING?! OF COURSE I DIDN'T!
AND WHAT ARE WE GONNA DO IF SHE WAKES UP?!
BLUSH...
PAT なで
PAT なで
ONCE MEI-MEI FALLS ASLEEP, SHE WON'T WAKE UP UNTIL THE BELL.
YOU DIDN'T KNOW THAT?
AND YOU'RE SUPPOSED TO BE SISTERS...
REMEMBER THIS, AIHARA YUZU.
DON'T BE SO MEAN!

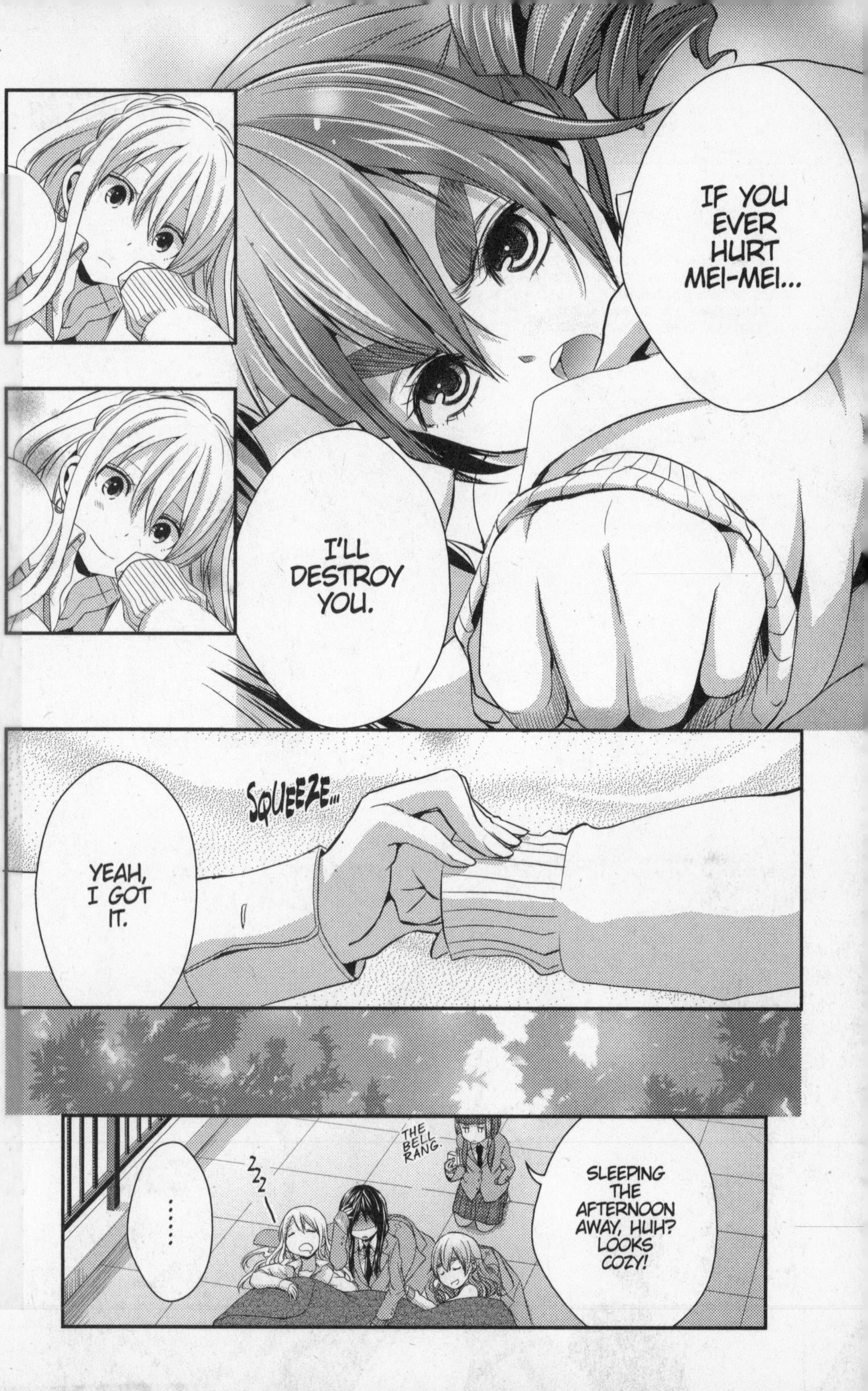
IF YOU EVER HURT MEI-MEI...
I'LL DESTROY YOU.
SQUEEZE...
YEAH, I GOT IT.
SLEEPING THE AFTERNOON AWAY, HUH? LOOKS COZY!
THE BELL RANG.
ZZZ
......